W9-BDN-919

INDIAN BLOOD
FINDING YOUR NATIVE AMERICAN ANCESTOR

VOLUME 1

INDIAN BLOOD

Finding Your Native American Ancestor

Richard L. Pangburn

Butler Books
Louisville, Kentucky

ISBN 1-884532-05-5

On the Cover:

There is no known painting made of Tecumseh during his lifetime, and whatever the inaccuracies of Kihn's portrait, he presented Tecumseh as he was described by those who knew him:

Tecumseh was "light-complexioned, more of an olive-tan than red shade, whites thought...The nose and mouth were both straight and prominent...In easy circumstances, he had a pleasant warm, smile. Some thought the eyes were the most striking facial feature. They were hazel in color, deep-set, and a bit hooded by his brows, giving him a habitual—from what whites saw—intense, brooding expression."

This description is from *God Gave Us This Country: Tekamthi and the First American Civil War*, by Bil Gilbert, to whom we are indebted. If you are yet unfamiliar with Shawnee history, I recommend that you buy a copy of Gilbert's masterful work before all others. I also heartily recommend *A Sorrow in the Heart: The Life of Tecumseh*, by Allen W. Eckert, who has no peer.

INDIAN BLOOD

Is there a tradition in your family that you have Indian blood? If so, it is probably founded in truth. But the truth is often hard to find. You might have your family tree traced by Mrs. Proper or some other competent genealogist and find only solid English, Scottish, Irish, French, or German names. From whence, then, does the Indian blood tradition originate?

I will show you.

But first, let's get our definitions straight. Mrs. Proper, our local librarian and genealogist, is always pointing out to me that what we call Indian should actually be called American and what we call American should actually be called European. We're not going to worry about that at this stage of the game. And it stands to reason that when people use the term "Indian blood" they actually mean Indian genealogy, the Native Americans sharing the same blood types with the rest of humanity.

The term is also accurately descriptive of the results of the Indian wars, since so much Indian blood was spilled across the landscape. But what I mean by "Indian blood" in this work is "direct descent from a member of an American Indian tribe, either born into the tribe or adopted into it."

Now let's take that family-tree chart that Mrs. Proper gave you and see if we can find the origin of your Indian blood tradition.

Mrs. Proper is a typically competent genealogist, and her methods are proven. You tell her what you know of your family history, including traditions, and she takes it from there. She works from the present backward, one step at a time. She goes back through the census, through the birth, marriage, and death records, through the wills, through the deed books. Some of your lines connect with people already in the DAR lineage books, and Mrs. Proper can easily follow the beaten path back to the Revolution on those.

Unfortunately, many of the established DAR lineages are dead wrong, which is why, if you are interested in finding the truth, you need to look for yourself.

If you told Mrs. Proper of your Indian blood tradition, she probably gave you one of her looks. Mrs. Proper has heard it before. She hears it all the time. She thinks that it is usually just some silly story people tell their grandchildren, and it never pans out.

Mrs. Proper is wrong, of course, but she's set in her ways and she'll be a long time coming around to another point of view. Never mind. Just bring your family-tree chart over here and tell me your Indian blood tradition, exactly as it has been handed down in your family.

People sometimes are reluctant. They stammer over the re-telling of the tradition, because the way they originally heard it sounds incredibly hokey, like some fairy tale. That's alright with me, tell me anyway. Don't leave anything out.

Some people have no concrete story to tell, just a vague tradition of Indian blood in the family, the details having been lost over the years. We can find it eventually, but the more clues we have, the faster we solve the mystery.

Stop me if you've heard this one. Your white ancestor is captured and brought before the chief and tribal council. The sentence is that he be forced to run the gauntlet and then put to death. The stone axe is raised, but before he can be executed, the chief's daughter (or some other Indian princess) intercedes and pleads for his life to be spared. The chief relents, and adopts the newcomer as his son or son-in-law. In some versions of this story, the white man marries the chief's daughter.

Pretty silly, huh? Mrs. Proper thinks so. She has heard that particular fairy tale several times. The sheer abundance of such romantic stories is additional proof to her of the fictitious nature of such traditions. But Mrs. Proper is being blind to what is right in front of her. The multitude of times she hears this story is not an indication that the story is false, but rather, an indication that something is going on here.

The story is true, of course, and it has happened hundreds of times. The details differ each time, but the basic format is the same. It is the adoption ritual as practiced by the Algonquin nations (and many others as well). The scenario was this:

A captive would be threatened, told that he was dead meat, scowled at. One of his captors suggests that he be burned at the stake; another wants to bury him up to his neck in an anthill. Recollections of the tortures inflicted upon other captives are bandied about. One of them wants to tear his eyes out of his sockets and eat them, as the eyes of the last captive tasted especially sweet. One of them can hardly wait for the captive to run the gauntlet, and the others howl in fiendish glee at the mention of it, shaking their tomahawks. Such talk, in English or translated to the captive, is a part of the initiation play, a part of the adoptive process.

The Algonquins were masters of psychology, and their methods were similar to those in use in recent times by the U. S. Marine boot camp. First they tear you down, then they build you up. They paint you black and tell you your life is over, but then you are saved, born again, and become blessed.

Just in the nick of time you are saved, and you are grateful toward your savior. There were instances when they sensed too much terror in their captive, and they would ease off or let them in on the joke, assuring them that it was all in fun. There were times, especially with woman and young children, when this procedure was omitted entirely and a substitute ritual, such as a symbolic washing in the river, was done. After the gauntlet ritual, the captive is "built up," given compliments on his speed if he ran, on his agility if he evaded the blows, on his courage if he was defiant.

Bil Gilbert, who has written the best biography of Tecumseh, commented on this ritual washing, "the symbolic intent of which was to remove foreign taints. Other prisoners, generally grown men, were required to run between two lines of their captors...commonly this was a rough form of initiation in which the captors tried to determine what kind of person, brave or cowardly, they had. James Smith, who became the foster grandson of Tecaughretanego, endured a gauntlet and, when he finished it, asked a warrior why he had been so roughly treated. The man, amused, told him not to take it personally, it was a kind of red greeting, 'like how do you do.'"

Examples are everywhere. Robert Orr, captured by Joseph Brant at Lochry's Defeat, wrote of the ease of running the gauntlet, even during a time of bitter war: "All prisoners when brought into the Indian towns have to run what they call the gauntlet unless they are wounded; they are then excused. Two lines are formed composed of old men, squaws, and boys...each one with a stick or staff to strike the prisoner with as he passes along through the line...They are instructed and dare not strike the prisoner on the front part of the body. They must strike him, if they get a stroke at all, behind; and when a right active man that passes smartly runs fast, they cannot many of them get much of a stroke on him to hurt him."

Orr says that the women and old men act angry

and put up a fuss when their blows miss, "but the warriors in looking on are pleased with the fun, and the less a prisoner is whipped in passing through the better it pleases them, and they will laugh very hearty at it...."

Sometimes, if no one has yet come forward to adopt the captive, he is threatened with the stake. But always, in the nick of time, some red citizen comes forward and the captive is adopted to replace a relative who was lost. The Shawnees were a happier people than the whites, and they knew it. They knew it because almost all white captives, once they got to know what it was like to be Shawnee, never wanted to return to the whites again. Adopted captives made good Shawnees, generally.

By the end of Pontiac's War in 1764, there were hundreds of white people living red. General Henry Bouquet demanded as a condition of the peace that all whites living among the tribes be turned over, forcibly if necessary. Some would only come in if they were bound, and vowed to run back to the woods at the first opportunity. Women begged to be allowed to return to their red families. Some were turned over with their children, and some of the children were half-breeds. Many, of course, went right back to the Indian towns at the first opportunity.

Some stayed on the edge of the frontier and served as interpreters, guides, scouts, but the usual employment for former captives was in the Indian trade. Many of the traders married white women who were former captives among the Indians. And many of the Indian traders found it advantageous and natural for them to have red wives. Trader John Hart talked this over with James Kenny at Ft. Pitt in 1762 and it was his opinion that they were the only two traders at the place "clear of lying with the squaws."

As with Ft. Pitt, so it was across the entire frontier, wherever it went. George Croghan visited the Ouittan settlement (in present Indiana) in 1765 and noted in his journal: "...they are a mixture of all nations. The principal inhabitants are French intermarried with Indians, and pay little regard to religion or law..."

Most of the women available to the traders and military men on the early Pennsylvania and Virginia frontiers were Indians or the half-breed daughters of white traders. It was that way all across the continent as the frontier moved west. It was that way at Ft. Jefferson in Kentucky; it was later that way at Ft. Jefferson in Ohio. James Lockwood visited Prairie Du Chien in 1816, and found that the white men were all married to women of at least part-Indian blood. At Green Bay, he noted that of all of the women there, only one "pretended to be white." Some of these red/white unions were celebrated by a marriage ceremony, some were not. Most of the half-blood children of Indian traders adopted their father's surname. Some of these half-reds lived white and their descendants melded into the general population.

For a large number of us, genealogical research will reveal some red ancestry. Intrigued by what we find, we will sometimes turn to the works of ethnologists to discover the customs by which our red ancestors directed their lives. This ethnology should not be taken too strictly when studying specific individuals.

Some ethnologists generalize, form stereotypes, make blanket pronouncements. Some make conclusions about the free-hunter nomadic Shawnees based upon their study of fifth-generation reservation Cherokee/Shawnees. Although the theories of these ethnologists and social scientists have their value, they also have their limitations. Whenever there is a clash between between ethnological theory and specific historic facts, please give me the facts. Every time.

Unfortunately, the mistakes of ethnologists influence television, the movies, historical novelists, and prevailing opinions. For instance, at the re-enactment of a battle of the War of 1812, you can find a reconstructed pioneer village (circa 1812) alongside a Shawnee village (circa 1620). It is not unusual to hear boasts of authenticity about such an incongruent Shawnee village, consisting entirely of wigwams. The truth is, however, that cabins were to be found alongside the wigwams in Shawnee villages as soon as whites were living among them and taught them how to build them, as early as the 1750s. These historic Shawnee villages always had their blacksmiths and gunsmiths such as Thomas Burney, Moses Henry, and Caesar.

When the Rev. David Jones visited the Shawnees and Delawares in the early 1770s, he remarked on the fine quality of some of their cabins, and did not think them unusual. When Daniel Boone and the saltmakers were taken prisoner in 1778, they were led to the Indian town of Chillicothe where they saw over a hundred Shawnee homes, most of them cabins. It was a town "built in the form of a Kentucky station," but "considerably larger and more impressive" than any of the contemporary white Kentucky settlements (see Faragher, p. 163).

This was also true of other villages as Kentuckians found out when they repeatedly burned them. When General Scott destroyed the Wea town in 1791, he wrote that the village "consisted of about seventy houses, many of them well-furnished." Most of the inhabitants had fled before his advancing army but he surmised that most of them must have been French as they "lived in a state of civilization."

Shawnees such as Bluejacket, Blackhoof, and the Big Snake lived comfortably in cabins, and some of their "wealthy plantations" were described in contemporary journals. These journals are ignored by some writers of historical fiction as well as some ethnologists, who have come to the conclusion, in spite of the historical evidence, that the "real Indians" disdained material wealth. It is the prevailing opinion that the accumulation of wealth is "the white man's disease," then as now. I often hear it at pow-wows. As recently as October, 1993, a speaker at one of the red-revivalist pow wows announced to the public that it was white values, "the white man's disease," that led the red nations down the road to white decadence, complete with an unnatural love of material things, predatory capitalism, and trophy wives.

The truth, of course, is that the historical Shawnees were natural capitalists and gamblers, and the argument might be made that some of them did have trophy wives. Early on, wealth was measured by the number of wives and horses a man could afford. Later, by 1790, the Shawnees became generally monogamous, perhaps influenced by the large number of adopted whites and missionaries among them.

How many whites were there among the Shawnees? An increasingly large percentage dating from the first Shawnee contact with runaway servants and white traders. In 1745, there were maybe five percent whites among a Shawnee population that numbered about three or four hundred scattered in small villages in what is now Maryland, Pennsylvania, Ohio, Indiana, and Kentucky.

What? Is that all? The popular imagination sees hordes of Shawnees but in fact the vast forest was largely vacant of humans of any tribe. The Shawnees moved around to where the game was plentiful. There were semi-permanent villages, hunting camps, and wintering grounds. There were not many humans in the area even when all tribes were counted. The woods were largely empty.

In September, 1748, the deputies of all the Ohio

tribes met with Tanacharisson at a Logstown council. He requested of them the numbers of warriors — men able to fight — in each tribe. Conrad Weiser tabulated the results that were returned to the Half King in council: 163 Senecas, 162 Shawnees, 100 Wyandots, 40 Turcarawas, 74 Mohawks, 15 Mohicans, 35 Onondagas, 20 Cayugas, 15 Oneidas, and 165 Delawares.

Later historians have found this hard to believe, and the numbers of Shawnees alive at any one time has been greatly inflated. The Shawnees had a superior culture, and they knew it, but their numbers were small compared to the whites and they knew that too. Under the sage leadership of the Pheasant and continuing under such leaders as Hard Striker, Cornstalk, and the Hard Man, they recruited warriors to take the place of those who had fallen. In doing so, they grew to become the most powerful force in the Ohio Valley, except for the whites.

Some of the Shawnee recruits were from other tribes — Creeks, Cherokees, the disenchanted Iroquois, the fleeing remnants of the small tribes such as the Conestoga, Conoys, and Powhatans. But the main source of recruits were the whites who were captured, adopted, and assimilated. This was especially true during the French and Indian War, the Beaver Wars, and Pontiac's War. In 1764, an officer reported the capture of "prisoners who included the wife of John Davis and one child, two of John Mitchell's children and a son of Adam Simms, all of whom...may be preserved to enlarge the savage tribes...."

General Henry Bouquet demanded as a provision of the peace that all of the whites and blacks among the tribes be delivered up whether they wanted to come back to the whites or not. The reds then bound some of these whites and took them to Ft. Pitt, but as soon as they were unbound, almost all of them ran back into the woods toward the Indian towns. Some were white women with mixed-blood children who kissed their red husbands goodbye, weeping as they turned away and came into the fort, bringing their children with them. One red husband risked his life by accompanying his wife in her journey back to her white relations, bringing her presents along the way, making sure that her every need was met. Some of these "captives" returned to the whites for a brief time and then ran off. It was a common story.

Again, how many whites were living among the Shawnees? In 1765, I'd say that there were ten percent whites, ten percent halfbreeds, counting women and children. The percentage was slightly larger when David Jones visited the Shawnee in 1772 and 1773. He remarked on the white people among them, including Kishanosity's wife, but it became more difficult to distinguish between a regular half-blood Shawnee and an adopted Shawnee as the generations turned.

Still, the Shawnees were increasingly outnumbered. Cornstalk could only muster 700 warriors in his entire red force in 1774, a number which included some recruits from the Cherokees, Wyandots, Ottawas, Mingoes, and Delawares. At the Battle of Point Pleasant, the red and part-red force — which included Cornstalk, Black Hoof, Black Fish, Wryneck, Hard Striker, Blue Jacket, and Logan's Mingo band — beat back a white force of roughly 1000, killing 222, and losing over 100 of their own. The loss affected the Shawnee more than the whites. For this was their entire population at war, not just a few of their adventurous young men. Their nation was on the verge of annihilation, and Cornstalk knew it. He quite adeptly negotiated an immediate peace and saved his nation. This was more complicated than I give it here, but it is explained in depth in Bil Gilbert's excellent biography of Tecumseh.

It seems to me that, not counting expatriates in Texas, Missouri, Alabama and elsewhere, there were less than 1200 Shawnees left, counting women and children. The population consisted of about 60 adopted whites, about 120 half-breeds, about 240 quarter-breeds, and less than 800 fullbloods, many of whom were married to whites or part-whites. There were some more women and children captured during Dunmore's War (to replace fallen Shawnees), and not all returned to the whites.

This pattern continued through the 1770s and 1780s. In 1782, Jean de Crevecoeur estimated that there were thousands of whites living red, none of whom had "the least desire to return to their white life." Well, there were thousands of whites among the Eastern tribes, but there were not thousands of whites among the Eastern Shawnees, because there were just not that many of them. Young men from other tribes and from the whites were adopted to replace fallen Shawnees, white children were captured and raised Shawnee, and still the Shawnee population remained relatively low. And the Shawnees became lighter and lighter.

How badly were they outnumbered? By 1785, there were 45,000 Kentuckians, and by 1790, there were over 73,000 and many thousands more north of the Ohio River. The population of Kentucky exceeded 220,000 by 1800; it exceeded 406,000 by 1810.

Early on, despite being so outnumbered, the Shawnees (with allied tribes) won some major military victories through stealth and superior tactics. Notable was St. Clair's defeat which, as Gilbert points out, was a greater red victory than Custer's Last Stand. But Shawnees died in these engagements also, and the Shawnees did not have men to spare. I believe that, were it not for the Shawnee long standing policy of adopting whites, the Ohio Shawnee would have completely disappeared by the year 1819 when there were only 800 of them left (see Howard, p. 32).

Indian agent John Johnston then broke the population down as 197 Shawnee men at Piqua, 15 at Hog Creek, and 53 at Lewistown. With women and children, their numbers approached 800, but I submit that there were maybe four times this number of part-Shawnees then living among the whites and blacks in the general population where the life for them was relatively attractive compared to the squalor of the Indian reserve — especially if they could pass for white and speak English, as many of them could.

Through the 1780s and early 1790s, the Shawnee population grew slowly until Bluejacket's defeat at Fallen Timbers in 1794. Thereafter, a large number of whites and part-whites deserted them, adapting to white-styled civilization as best they could. The Ohio tribes wallowed in a mood of despair and decadence. It was out of this decadence that the Prophet and Tecumseh arose. Contrary to popular belief, they attracted more Potawatomis than they did Shawnees, most of whom stayed neutral, although watching the turn of events closely in case Tecumseh pulled off some miracle. But the total red forces were so outnumbered that it would have made no difference in the play of historical events if you had doubled or tripled the red population.

In January, 1812, Indian agent John Johnston estimated the numbers of Indians in all of Ohio as 500 Ottawa, 300 Wyandot, 250 Seneca, 200 Delaware, and 700 Shawnee (see Thornbrough, p. 183n). No more than 200 of these Shawnees and Delawares left Johnston's agency to join Tecumseh. The majority of Shawnees stayed neutral with the traditional Shawnee chief, Blackhoof, and twenty or thirty of these Shawnees fought on the side of the United States against Tecumseh's forces, and most if not all of these were at least part-white.

What percentage of Shawnees had some white

blood by 1812? *Almost all of them.* Johnston told Draper that the Shawnees had the lightest skin of any Indian tribe, and by the time the Shawnees were forced to sell their Ohio lands and move to Kansas, many could pass for white.

The Shawnees were even whiter than the Wyandots, another tribe which readily adopted whites. After the Wyandots moved from Ohio to Kansas in 1843, a newspaper reported that "the civilized Wyandots, more white than Indian through intermarriage with captives adopted into their tribe, brought a code of laws, a Methodist church, a Masonic lodge; set up their school and their own trading store. It is said that when the Nation (then numbering about 700) came to Kansas, no Wyandot was more than one-quarter Indian...."

One of the Wyandots, William Walker, became the Provisional Governor of Nebraska Territory. Like the Shawnees, these "civilized" Wyandots spread the Indian blood tradition across the country, entering every walk of life, doing exactly what white citizens did. In the records, the names of Shawnees and Wyandots became indistinguishable from white people.

Before the Treaty of Greenville, the tribes were slowly increasing in population. But from the time of that treaty on, there was a change, and a gradual reverse migration. The main appeal of the red way of life was freedom, and that freedom was fast disappearing. The way of living was gone, and the means of living — the economic system by which the red cultures survived — was replaced by a welfare system which encouraged the industrious reds to leave the reservation while encouraging those who remained to become indolent and alcoholic. That is, the remnant Indians were cooped up on a reservation and given annuities on which to live. But the annuities dulled imagination and stifled self-respect. If you were a "reservation Indian," you were likely to develop a dependence upon both alcohol and government handouts.

Many of the industrious part-Shawnees adjusted to white-style capitalism and established commercial enterprises and prosperous farms. Some became preachers, some rode further west to be free hunters, some became outlaws or lawmen, some became professional soldiers for the United States Army, and several became politicians. Tinker, tailor, soldier, thief, doctor, lawyer, Indian chief — it's the American way. When Whipple came through Kansas, he found himself attracted to the beautiful, almost-white young Shawnee women. When Lewis Garrard came through Kansas in 1847, he spent the night at the comfortable house "a nephew of the renown Indian chief, Logan....Bidding farewell to our kind entertainers in the morning, who would accept no remuneration, we rode through fields of waving corn and pasture, whose fences and careful culture denoted the whiteman's civilizing hand. This was the domain of the Shawnees and Delawares who farm extensively and are prosperous."

But as in most tribes there were always some— mostly dark-skinned traditionalists — who willingly sacrificed their own best interests to stay on the reservation in order to maintain the old ways, to keep the culture going, to keep the tribe together. It is true that, were it not for them, many more tribes might have completely disappeared by now as recognized government entities. But the number of people having, say, Shawnee blood would remain the same whether the BIA officially recognized the Shawnee Nation or not. There's no reason for a subculture to disappear just because it gets no government handout. Look at the Amish, for example.

Most Shawnees who left the reservation entered a mainstream population life that, while not as free as their old lifestyle, was still pretty good. Once off the reservation, their names in the records appeared just the same as non-Indians. Tracing back to them, you can't find where the Indian tradition originates, because all the names in your genealogy are the standard names.

That's where my books can help you, to steer you in the right direction, to scout out the clues that will help you find your own way. They will enable you to know what names in your genealogy will warrant a closer look.

This book is designed for people who already know how to do research. If you are just starting out, my advice is to see Mrs. Proper or any other competent genealogical librarian who will normally point you in the right direction for free. Start with the present and follow the trail back.

If you have an Indian-blood tie and would like to have your work considered for publication in a future volume of Indian Blood, please send it to me.

In the crazy politics of the nation today, there is a tendency on the part of some to read a racist motive into everything. This book is motivated by a love of history. There is no motive here to prove one race superior to another, and I personally do not believe that there is one "race" of the human race genetically superior to another. Moreover, as a point of history, the Indians generally fared much better under the leadership of fullbloods than halfbloods or whites. For instance, fullbloods like Sitting Bull and Little Turtle were much better war chiefs than Tecumseh or Blue Jacket. But not because they were fullbloods.

The little-known truth is, most of the descendants of historical Indians like Tecumseh or Blackhoof are now in the general population, not on the reservations. It is to their descendants that this book is dedicated. These people tracing their Indian heritage have no desire to "go back to the reservation," for goodness sakes; they want no handouts from government, no redress of ancient wrongs.

They just want to know their own history.

History and genealogy are games like any other. Anyone can play. One need not be related to kings or princes, passengers on the Mayflower or those who met the boat. The game's object is not what the general public believes it to be — it is not the glory gleaned from proving descent from this or that illustrious ancestor. It matters little if one's ancestors owned slaves or were slaves, lived by the Good Book or cheated at cards. To win is to find out, to discover light amid the historical darkness. It doesn't come easy. Unfortunately, much has been lost over the years through neglect, and much has been deliberately concealed — the proverbial skeleton in the closet. But the historian works at it — a clue here, a piece of the puzzle there — and gradually the stories of the past fit together and the people of the past take form.

As historian Howard Leckey pointed out, genealogy is usually an older person's game. This is true not because older people have more free time, but because it takes most people several decades to develop a sense of history. Maybe in order to develop a sense of history, you need to either have studied it in detail or have lived through enough of it yourself to be mellowed by it. This seems to be true in such cultures as the traditional Shawnees, who revered the wisdom of the old stories told by their elders.

Studying history helps us to put our own lives in an intelligent context in the continual turning of events. We see clearly how people in the past have been torn by the same forces that have touched us. This knowledge helps to sophisticate us and to mellow our outlook. Eventually we develop such a philosophical frame of mind that we are insulated against what lies ahead. Whatever happens, we have seen it before—there, in the past.

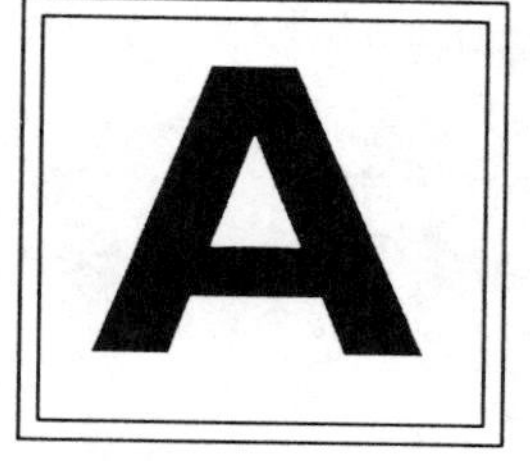

ABBOTT or ABBET – a Shawnee/ Delaware/Miami name.

Rachel Abbott, a young white woman from the Conegocheague settlement in Pennsylvania, was captured by French and Indians about 1755. She was taken to Ohio where she was "kindly treated and adopted, and some years afterwards was married to a Delaware chief of respectability, by whom she had several children..." See Heckewelder, pp. 341-342. The Reverend Heckewelder said that her children later resided among the Christian Indians in Canada.

A James Abbott was a white man with an Indian (or part-Indian) wife. He traded at the Glaize in 1790, consorting with the Miamis, Delawares, and Shawnees. He is mentioned in Hay's Journal: "Got infernally drunk last night with Mr. Abbott and Mr. Kinzie. Mr. A. gave me his daughter Betsy over the bottle. Damnation sick this morning in consequence of last night debashe..."

Quaife identifies this man as James Abbott, born in Dublin in 1725. He settled in Albany then moved to Detroit about 1763. He engaged in the fur trade at several frontier outposts, and his children included James, Robert, Samuel, and Elizabeth (Betsy) Abbott. The family stayed in the Indian trade and sometimes engaged in government service amongst the various tribes.

James Abbott, jr., married Sarah Whistler. Betsy Abbott married James Baby and thus became the sister-in-law of both William Caldwell and Bluejacket. A Hiram Abbott was one of Issac McCoys "well-armed" assistants in ascertaining the southern boundary of Shawnee land in 1843. See Barry, p. 243. A James Abbott was an Indian agent in Kansas. Some of the Abbotts associated with the Miami, and there is a

Miami tradition among part of the Abbott family in Indiana today. See Anson, p. 81, 145.

Lucy and Thomas Abbet were among the Shawnees on the 1880 Cherokee Nation Census. See JAIFR, vol X, #1, p. 40.

ADAM or ADAMS – a name associated with Indian blood traditions.

James Adams was an interpreter for the Powhatan Indians. Adams was a surname among the Powhatans in the 1800s, and in modern times several members of the family have led the Upper Mattaponi branch of the Powhatan Nation — including Jasper Lewis Adams, chief until 1971, Andrew Adams, chief during the years 1971-1984, and Raymond S. Adams who was a chief in 1988. See Rountree, pp. 154, 158, 160-161, 250, 255, 265, 266.

Thomas Adams (Peekeetelemund), a Delaware chief, maintained a village in Indiana on the White River in the early 1800s. See Netterville, p. 50.

John Adams appears on the muster roll of the company of Shawnees that Joseph Parks led from the eastern reservation lands to Kansas in 1832. His family of three consisted of one male over 25 and under 50, one female over 10 and under 25, and one male over 10 and under 25. See Roy, pp. 38-43.

Among the Shawnees who settled on the lands of the Cherokee nation by 1869 were Samuel, Jane, and Alpheus Adams. See JAIFR, vol. IV, #2, pp. 100-111.

Sam Adams, age 45, appears among the Shawnees on the 1880 Cherokee Nation Census. See JAIFR, vol X, #1, p. 40. Also on the census were the Delawares Abner G., Clinton L., Horrace M., Louisa, Nathan F., Richard C. and William Adams.

ALECK, ELLICK, ETLICK, etc. – a Shawnee name.

The 1832 muster roll of the Shawnees brought

from the Ohio Hog Creek and Wapakonetta bands included the Etlick (or Alick) family of four, consisting of one male over between 25 and 50, one female between 10 and 25, and two boys under 10. See Roy, p. 42.

Among the Shawnees who went with Capt. Joseph Parks and served in the Florida War was Bill Ellick.

Among the Shawnees who settled on the lands of the Cherokee nation by 1869 were Henry, Elizabeth, Julia, and Penola Ellick. See JAIFR, vol. IV, #2, pp. 100-111.

Among the Shawnees living in the Delaware District of the Cherokee Nation in 1880 were Henry Aleck, 43, and Phebe Aleck, 23, along with the Cherokee Aleck family which included James (age 27), Thomas (25), Nelly (23), Allsey (23), Chsee-sa (1), and Nannie (4 months). JAIFR, vol. XIII, #1, p. 42.

ALBERT – a Delaware/Shawnee name.

Among the Munsee Delawares on the 1881 Ontario Census was George Albert, age 34, born in Ontario and a member of the Church of England, listed with his family which included Sarah, 34, George, 9, William Dodge, 16, Charles Dodge, 14, John Dodge, 12, and George Kamman, 8. Also listed is the household of several members of the Alliert families, and one of several spellings may represent the same family. See Prevost, p. 96.

In Kansas, the Rev. Joab Spencer performed the marriage of the part-Shawnee Thomas Blackhoof to Alice T. Albert, March 29th, 1859. See the Johnson County (Kansas) Genealogist, vol. I, #1, p. 16.

ALDER – an Ottawa/Shawnee name.

Jonathan Alder was an adopted Shawnee. He fought on the red side at Harmer's Defeat and St. Clair's Defeat. According to *The Story of Logan County,*

p. 173, Jonathan Alder was found "living with an Indian wife and their family of half-breed children." The narrative which Alder dictated to a white son by his second marriage says nothing about children by his first wife, but that is not surprising.

Although he says almost nothing about his own red family, Alder has a lot to say about the family in which he was raised. His adopted Shawnee mother was Winecheoh whose husband was the Mingo, Succopanas. His mother loved him, and would do everything she could to make him comfortable.

"About the first words that my parents taught me was to call them father and mother. I did not call them by anything else as long as I remained with the Indians...My father and mother being of different tribes, each spoke a different language, although each could speak the others' language and understand it. Yet such was their partiality for their tribe that when Succopanas spoke to Winecheoh, he spoke in Mingo, and when Winecheoh spoke to him she spoke in the Shawnee tongue, and when either of them spoke to me, it was in their native tongue, and in that way I learned both the Mingo and the Shawnee languages, replying and speaking to each in their native language.

"My adopted father was determined that I should be a Mingo and my mother was equally determined that I should be a Shawnee, and in their desire to accomplish their purpose, there were frequently family jars, but no serious quarrels. My mother would not continue in their disputes. I do think that she was one of the most splendid and beautiful women that I ever saw — at least, she appeared that way to me after I had become fully acquainted with her.

"My sisters were kind to me, especially Mary. She would take as much care of me as if I was the most tender infant and would have protected me, I verily believe, with her life." His adopted sister, Sally, sometimes teased him, and then his other two sisters, Mary and Hannah, would take his part.

Alder grew up healthy and happy, a typical story among those raised among the Shawnee. According to the Alder narrative, after the Treaty of Greenville, he and his Shawnee wife built a cabin on Darby Creek and settled down. A white man named Daniel Taylor claimed the land, and Alder had to give up his cabin to him, moving his wife temporarily to a bark hut.

Shortly thereafter, in 1805, Alder separated from his wife, dividing up his money and horses with her. His wife returned to the Shawnee villages unwillingly, threatening to kill his wife should he ever marry again. Alder took the threat seriously and, when he did marry again, he would not permit his new wife to remain alone in their cabin. If he went to the fields to work, he took his wife with him.

"On their return from a trading expedition to a neighboring town, they found the tinware bent and cut, the ironware broken by an axe, and Mrs. Alder's dresses slashed and cut in shreads." Although his first wife was not seen, "the mischief was attributed to her hands.

"...Alder's long life with the red men had bred in him Indian traits and manners, which clung to him through life. Though he possessed good business talent, he disliked hard work and confined his farm labors principally to stock-raising. He was dark hued and bore some resemblance to the Indian race. He was a large, tall man and could move about almost noiselessly."

Jonathan Alder's prowess as a hunter was unquestioned. But he is quoted as telling this story on himself, which occurred while camping on Darby Creek, in Union County, Ohio: "One day about noon I saw a large bear in the top of a big, white oak tree, picking off and eating acorns. I sat down on the ground about one hundred yards off to watch...I did not wish to kill it, as bears were not yet fat, and fur was not yet good, or rather not of full growth. I sat there amusing myself [watching] for some time. It was really funny to see it get about in the top branches while the whole tree shook with its enormous weight at every motion.

"All at once it ceased to gather in the branches and slid down and commenced picking up the acorns that had fallen on the ground. In a few moments, without the least warning, it started in the direction I was as rapidly as it could pace. I had my gun resting in my lap and saw it would run right over me. I had no time to get up and get out of its way, so I raised my gun and fired as soon as possible when it was within a few yards of me. I shot it through the brain and it fell right across my lap. I was badly scared, for I did not know that I had killed it. I kicked and struggled to get from beneath it, but it was so heavy that it took some time before I could get out. I had shot it so dead that it never kicked, but laid like a log upon me, all of which, had I not been so frightened, I might have observed. When I finally got out, I was so much exhausted from the fright and effort I could hardly stand."

Jonathan Alder was elected Captain of a company raised at Plain City, Ohio in 1811 or 1812. See OA&HSP, p. 264-268.

ALLEN – a name with common Indian blood traditions.

"James Allen was a North Carolinian, well-educated and of a family in easy circumstances. He came to Nashville, intending to settle there as a lawyer but from some disgust entered the Chickasaw nation, where he soon conciliated the favor of General Colbert, a half-breed chief of large fortune. Allen married their daughter Susie Colbert. Their daughter, Peggy, was very beautiful and received numerous proposals from traders returning from New Orleans to Tennessee, and from sons of the other Chickasaw chiefs.

"The United States agent in charge of the Chickasaws, Samuel Mitchell, became deeply in love with her, but she did not return it. He applied to her grandmother, and she considering it a very desirable match,...[butPeggy]...persistently refused Mitchell... there turned up a handsome young fellow, Simon Burney, from the neighborhood of Natchez, who loved her very deeply, and...fearing interference from Mitchell and his friends, they married and immediately left the Nation." Reminiscences of John L. Swaney, in the Gallatin Tennessee *Examiner*, quoted in Claiborne's *Mississippi*, p. 182.

Claiborne notes that David Burney was an early resident of Natchez and one of the first breeders of throughbreds and a patron of the turf. He says that "one of the granddaughters of this James Allen, educated at Elliot mission school, married a Mr. McAuley, a Scotch trader in that vicinity, and having the blood of the Chickasaws, Choctaws, and whites, was the most beautiful woman in Mississippi."

Among the Choctaws who were killed fighting for America in World War II was Bob Allen, who was killed in the Solomons. See JAIFR, vol XI, #1, p. 24

Mary Allen was a registered Delaware in 1867, when she was fifty years old. She was listed on the Delaware register as Mary Journeycake but had married Dr. R. M. Allen, a non-Indian. See Prevost, p. 30.

Sarah Allen was born in 1849 in Kansas. Her father, a white man, was born in Kentucky. Her mother, a Shawnee, was born in Ohio. See Prevost, p. 67.

Among the Shawnees who settled on the lands of the Cherokee nation by 1869 were Francis, Rachel, and Jane Allen. See JAIFR, vol. IV, #2, pp. 100-111. Annie and Hiram Allen were Shawnees who were allotted Cherokee lands in 1900.

ALLINGTON, ALLONTON, ELLINGTON – a Shawnee/Cherokee name.

Clarinda Allington was captured at Morgan's Station in Kentucky in the 1780s. See Draper 13CC78.

"A notice regarding Linde Allonton, daughter of Jacob Allonton, who was taken prisoner by the Shawanee Indians from Arrinton's Station in Kentucky about 15 years ago. She was born on the Holston River and was about 12 years old when taken. She had brothers Jacob, Jonathan, and John and sisters Sarah, Rebeccah, and Nancy. Apply to Joel Scott near Georgetown." The notice was dated April 5th, 1803, and it is reprinted in Karen Mauer Green's *The Kentucky Gazette* 1801-1820, p. 27.

Clarinda Allington was captured by Shawnees and adopted. She married a Cherokee chief named Tuscorigo who lived among the Shawnees and they had three children. She separated from her Cherokee husband, and she asked the Kentucky legislature to give her a divorce. This was granted December 15th, 1804.

In the interview with W. Boyd in Draper's papers, he says that "when she came back she married a Newcomb and moved to Ohio." Boyd said that Clarinda was about twelve-years-old when captured, that her children by the Indian chief were named John, Sally, and William. "These children came to me after their mother came back. I was teaching school. William was very wolfish." What became of them? Boyd said that "Sally and William are up in Floyds. John went south..." See Draper 12CC57-58; also see Kentucky Divorce Records 1792-1849, Clarinda Allington vs. Cherokee chief, 3 Littel, p. 193.

Was Boyd referring to Floyd County in Kentucky, Indiana, or Ohio, or did he mean Floyd's Fork in

Kentucky? Does anyone have the additional genealogy of this family?

A Clarinda Ellington married James Newsome or Newcomb on November 7th, 1806 in Greenup County, Kentucky — almost certainly the same lady. A William Allington married Francis Bennett in Franklin County, Indiana in 1820.

In the late 1960s, a researcher from Memphis, Missouri ran a query in an Ohio genealogical periodical: "Want info on James Newcom who m. Clarinda Allington in 1808, probably in Madison County, Ohio as this is where her 2nd marriage is recorded and also the last child by Newcomb in 1812. No record of death or divorce. Probably died in the War of 1812."

I found this recently while looking through back issues. I got her phone number by calling information, but when I called, a man answered who told me that she had been dead for years; and that, yes, she had been quite enthusiastic about this genealogy stuff, but he could not tell me anything about it and he did not know who could. So it goes. Perhaps I will be able to present more of Clarinda Allington's story in a future volume of Indian Blood.

ANDERSON – a Delaware name.

Anderson's Cabin was about four miles below the Shawnee Upper Old Town in 1746. This was the trading post of Charles Anderson who would keep moving his trade west, always on the edge of the frontier. See Marye, pp. 326-332.

From Nicholas Cresswell's journal: "August 18th, 1775...Mr. John Anderson ...offered to find me a horse and go with me into Indian Country, serving as an Interpreter and guide. This gentleman is an Indian trader and has business at their towns...August 31, 1775...Mr. Anderson tells me that the Indians are not well pleased at anyone going into their country dressed in a hunting shirt...One of the Indian squaws invited me to sleep with her..."

Cresswell noted that John Anderson also slept with an Indian woman. This was "Honest John" Anderson, a Quaker, who long traded among them and was a noted man among the Shawnees and Delawares. He served a major role in red politics in the 1770s (see Schaaf, index) and the Rev. John Bacon saw him still among them in Ohio in the early 1800s.

There may have been several half-breed children of the Indian traders named Anderson, but the most famous of these was William Anderson who became chief of the Delawares. In 1767, the Delaware chief, Newcomer, sent a message to the Governor of Virginia to set up a conference. John Walker delivered the message and it was signed by the Delawares John Armstrong, William Anderson, Capt. John (Willopothee), Cakanas, Fine Day (Wallachesqua), Flower (Lukos), Andrew Trump, and Coole. She SWJ Papers 1764-1774, p. 666; index.

This was either the half-breed William Anderson, Kik-tha-we-nund, or a close relation. The William Anderson who later became chief of the Delawares lived on the site of what is now Anderson, Indiana, named in his honor. His father was the Quaker trader, honest John Anderson, and his mother was a sister of Killbuck. Chief William Anderson was an agreeable man, and put up with the whites in Indiana. But he stated that he did not like the two things which the whites brought to him — the whiskey and the missionaries. Anderson kept his Delawares officially neutral during the War of 1812, although some of the young warriors ran off to join Tecumseh, and about thirty Delaware scouts fought on the side of the United States, including James Swannuck and Machingwe Pooshies.

Chief Anderson moved to Missouri with the

main Delaware emigration. The Delawares adjusted to the west — first Missouri, then Kansas — quite well, with only occasional conflicts with the Osages, Pawnees, and other neighboring tribes. Rather than taking to the mule and plow, many Delawares ranged across the west, hiring out as guides and free hunters. They were accepted as equals by the white mountain men, and were regarded as white men by most western tribes.

Chief Anderson's sons included Se-so-cum, James Swannuck, Machingwe Pooshies (the Big Cat) Anderson, James Secondine, and Anderson Sarcoxie. Weslager suggests that most of these may have been adopted. Chief Anderson referred to Se-co-cum as "my only one boy" after the Osages killed him in 1824. After that event, the Delawares saw Se-co-cum's horse among the Osage horse herd, and there was then a running war between the two tribes. Killbuck (possibly a great grandson of William Henry Killbuck) lead a retaliatory war party against the Osages.

The sporadic violence continued for years. In February and March of 1826, the Osage killed George Bullet, George White Eyes, and some other Delaware hunters. A month later, a hunting party of ten Delawares and ten Kickapoos killed some Osage warriors. Peace was eventually made, but shortly thereafter, Delawares left the area and became the neighbors of their old allies, the Shawnees, in Kansas.

About this time, 1831, Chief William Anderson died. The following year, one of his sons, Machingwe Pooshies Anderson, was killed in a fight with the Pawnees. The Pawnees probably resented yet another tribe of strangers invading the area. James Swannuck then led a retaliatory raid against the Pawnees. Swannuck's forty warriors found an Osage village almost abandoned as the tribe was off on their summer hunt. The Delawares left it "a heap of ashes" to avenge the death of Machingwe Pooshies.

Machingwe Pooshies was a "risen up" name, and possibly this son of William Anderson was named after his uncle. Among the children of Machingwe Pooshies Anderson was William Henry Anderson (Win-set-tund), born in 1830. William Henry Anderson married Wen-da-a-la-qua and their children included Oliver, James, John, Sam, and George Thomas Anderson.

John Anderson married Nellie Beaver and their sons included Raymond and Fred Anderson.

Sam Anderson married Josie Bullett and their children included Anna Anderson. Anna Anderson married a white man named Conrad O. Davis and their children included William (m. Faye Mesneck), Annette (m. James Reeve), Sam (m. Charlotte ---), Conrad Jr. (m. Leonra Brookshire), Bernard (m. Barbara Haugh), Loren and Margaret.

George Thomas Anderson married Ollie Beaver and their children included Andred, Lillian, Irene, George, Jodi, and Mildred. One of these, Jodi Thomas Anderson, left at least three children in Oklahoma when he was killed in 1949. Ruby Cranor says that there are descendants of Mechingwe Pooshies Anderson in the same area today. See Cranor, Weslager, and Barry for additional information and sources.

Among the Delawares appearing on the 1880 Cherokee Nation Census were Alenor, C.J., Daniel George, J.A., J.M., James, Jane, John, Josh, Kittie (age 24), Mary (age 40), Matilda, Rachel, Sam, and Willie Bob Anderson. See JAIFR, vol. X, #1, p. 40.

Attending the Ft. Leavenworth Shawnee School in Kansas in 1848 were Peter and John Anderson, both Potawatomis.

ARMS – a Wyandot name.

The John Arms Family was on the 1843 Muster

Roll of Wyandots from Sandusky, Ohio. The family then consisted of one male and one female 10 to 25, and two males and two females under 10. Also see BIGARMS.

ARMSTRONG – a Delaware/Wyandot/Seneca/ Shawnee name.

There were members of the Armstrong family among the Indians at an early date.

In the 1760s, John Armstrong and his Indian wife were among the Indians dealing with Pennsylvania Indian trader James Kenney. Kenny noted their conversation in his journal. Why did the white people want back those that had been captured and adopted, Armstrong wanted to know, "seeing they were satisfied to live with ye Indians." Kenny replied that "their fathers and mothers and friends longed to see them and was not satisfied without seeing them." See Kenny, vol. 37, p. 12-13.

John Brickell, who had been adopted by Delawares, saw several white men who lived with the Indians including William Wells, William May, Christopher Miller, Jeremiah and Robert Armstrong, and Mahaffy.

The 1817 Treaty of the Miami Rapids said that Robert Armstrong "in recognition of his services as interpreter and guide to United States officers," was to be given 640 acres of land. Robert Armstrong had been captured in Pennsylvania when young and adopted by the Wyandots. He married a half-breed Cayuga woman and lived on his land, "one of the most beautiful spots in the state." He died in Ohio in 1825.

James Armstrong (Zeshauau) and Silas Armstrong (Sa-Nou-Do-Yea-Squaw), chiefs of the Delaware Indians living on the waters of the Sandusky, were also given land in accordance to the treaty passed by Congress on March 3, 1817. Later, in 1829, James

Armstrong, Silas Armstrong, John Armstrong (Mahantoo), and the Widow Armstrong (Tishatahomms) were provided for when the Delawares, Wyandots, Senecas, and Shawnees were considering a move west. Some went, some did not, but all moved off their land. Some who went later came back to Ohio, and they were white enough to pass for white, melting into the general population.

The Armstrong families listed on the 1843 Muster Roll of Wyandots from Sandusky were:

1. John M. Armstrong's family, consisting of one male 25 to 55, one female 10 to 25, and two males under 10.
2. George Armstrong's family, consisting of one male and one female over 25, four females between 10 and 25, and three children under 10, two of them boys.
3. Silas Armstrong's family, consisting of one male 25 to 55, three females 10 to 25, and three males under 10.

But the Armstrongs were prolific and they intermarried with whites, blacks, and other tribes.

Among the Wyandot guardian cases reviewed by the commissioner of Indian Affairs in 1871 was the case of Silas Armstrong, who was then deceased. His widow was living in Wyandotte, Kansas. A. B. Bartlett and Silas Armstrong, jr. were administrators of his estate. His Wards were John Bland, Eliza Bland (formerly Armstrong), Mary Faber (formerly Armstrong), Eliza Punch, Margaret Punch, Zack Longhouse, Mary Punch (said to be the wife of Zack Longhouse), John Zane (said to have gone to California), Mary Coonhawk, John Warpole (adm. by Bryon Judd), and George Coke (adm. by John Hicks). James Armstrong was the guardian for Starr Young. See JAIFR, vol. VIII, #2, p. 18, 21.

Arthur, Johnny, Charles H., Mary, Mary E., Maria

L., Caroline, Lillie Ann, Katy Alice, and Solomon, Joseph, Nancy, Sophia, Emma, Henry, Lucy Jane, Albert, Julius, and Penanders Armstrong appear on the 1867 Delaware roll appearing in the JAIFR, vol. IV, #1, 1985, pp. 31-52.

Attending the Ft. Leavenworth Methodist Shawnee School in 1850 was Robert Armstrong, age 14, listed as a Wyandot. Among the students attending the Baptist Mission School in 1858 were Arthur Armstong, age 14, and Edson Armstrong, age 10, both listed as Delawares.

Among the Shawnees who settled on the lands of the Cherokee nation by 1869 were James, Susan, Eliza, and Monday Armstrong. See JAIFR, vol. IV, #2, pp. 100-111.

Eliza, Jo, Katy, Louis, Old Susie (age 56), and William (age 45) Armstrong were among the Shawnees on the 1880 Cherokee Nation Census. See JAIFR, vol X, #1, p. 40.

ARCHER – a Seneca/Shawnee/Delaware name.

Several members of the Archer family have told me of their Indian-blood traditions and some of their research is given here.

The family includes John Archer who, in 1767, was living in Ridley Township in Chester County, Pennsylvania. His sons George, Thomas, and Joseph, along with a daughter, were taken prisoner by Indians at Conecocheague in Cumberland County, Pennsylvania on the 4th of November, 1757.

The children were divided between the tribes. The Indians reluctantly turned Joseph over to Gen. Henry Bouquet in 1764, but George and Thomas Archer remained with the Indians. Joseph described his brother George, with whom he had been separated, as "18 years old, fair complexion, with dark eyes. Was well-grown when taken." Of his brother Thomas, he said that "he was a hearty well set lad with dark eyes," and that he left him behind "in the Mingo nation."

James Archer was an ensign in Capt. David Owens' Company of frontier rangers recruited at Ft. Jackson on Ten Mile Creek in western Pennsylvania. And when David Owens removed to Kentucky, James Archer assumed command. Among the soldiers in this company were Lt. Thomas Brashears, James Pribble, Samuel Meranda, John Wiley, Richard Jackson, and David Owens, possibly the son of John Owens, Jr. Most of this company later removed to Bracken County, Kentucky.

William Harrod,Jr., said that "about 1783, Indians fell upon the families of Robert McClelland and James Archer, who were related and whose families resided in the same cabin about three-fourths of a mile from Ft. Jackson. They came on a foggy morning..." Many were supposed to be killed but a few escaped. Some of those reported killed may have been captured to be adopted.

Among those related to the family was Joshua Archer, a member of Capt. George Owens' Company at Ft. Jefferson, many of whom were said to have had Indian wives. He was probably in the same family as James Archer who claimed land on the South Fork of Ten Mile Creek near John Owens old trading post and David Owens' claim in 1772. Joshua Archer's name was often abbreviated in the court records as "Jos." so that he and Joseph Archer are sometimes indistinguishable. See "Virginia Land Grants in Pennsylvania" which is reprinted in The Pennsylvania Genealogist, vol. II, 1967, pp. 126-127.

James Archer's family included his father, Patrick, his brothers, John, Joseph, Michael, Simon, and possibly Stephen, Zachariah, and Joshua. The Archers were supposed to have been the first Roman Catholic family in the Ten Mile Creek, Pennsylvania area. Historian Howard Leckey described them as "a family of roving hunters." For several adventures and genealogical sketches of this family, see Leckey's *The Ten Mile Country*, deluxe edition, pp. 344-345.

Descendants of Joshua Archer tell of an Indian blood tradition in the family, and it could be that he was a former adopted captive or that his wife, a daughter of Joseph Hunter, was part-red. Joshua Archer was with a party of explorers and surveyors "from the back part of Pennsylvania" including John Finley at Upper Blue Licks in 1773. See Fleming County Land Book B, p. 2594, deposition of James F. Moore, taken at Bush's tavern in Frankfort, Ky, 1804.

In Kentucky with David and George Owens, Joshua Archer claimed the land "lying on the south side of Salt River about three miles from Bullitt's Lick at the Buffalo Crossings to include his improvement about three or four hundred yards from the river." Like David Owens, he had abandoned his land claims at Hannastown, Pennsylvania and their land was sold at a sheriff's sale in 1785. See WPHQ, vol. 59, #2, p. 158.

After Ft. Jefferson was abandoned, Joshua Archer returned to Louisville with his father-in-law, Joseph Hunter. The name Joshua Archer appears often in the court records of Jefferson County, Kentucky — often abbreviated as "Jos." In the original drawing of lots in Louisville, Joshua Hunter drew lot #26 on the old plan. In 1784, he was sued by his brother-in-law, John Donne, for assault and battery. Also in that year, Joshua Archer and his wife were involved in a scandal with Richard Clark, a brother of Gen. George Rogers Clark.

Joshua had married his wife, Jane Hunter, at Ft. Jefferson and they had at least one child, Mary Posey Hunter, and perhaps more. Joshua Archer was captain of the Jefferson County Militia in 1787. He seems to have left the area by 1796, and his name thereafter appears in the early records of Brown County, Ohio, associated with Joseph Hunter. Jane Archer remarried Jeffersonville tavern-keeper George Jones, who administered Joshua Archer's Kentucky estate. Some members of both the Hunter and Archer families have an Indian blood tradition.

Among the Cherokees living in the Saline District of the Cherokee Nation in 1880 was the family of M. F. Archer, 55. Her family included Ada, 22, Cora, 17, and Carrie, 13.

ASH – a Shawnee name.

John Ash was a member of Robert George's Company at Ft. Jefferson (Kentucky). Early in the Revolution, he had served on James Willing's boat. He accompanied Willing, Robert George, Simon Burney, George Girty, and others in the raids on the lower Mississippi.

At the battle at Ft. Jefferson, John Ash jr., who was called Jack Ash, was sent on a dangerous mission. The second night after the attack, he slipped out of the fort with one of the Kaskakia Indians and they either rode or ran to the Illinois settlements for help. Running is not out of the question, but if so, then John Ash must have been one of the fastest men at the fort. The fastest man there at the time, according to first-hand accounts in the Draper mss., was the Kaskakia Baptist Ducoign, who would always get the best of Clark's men in foot races. The two swiftest men in the fort may have been chosen to slip out of the fort unnoticed and run for it.

The necessary help arrived in time and the fort was not taken, but the crops were burned and winter was coming on, and so Ft. Jefferson was virtually abandoned. John and Jack Ash returned to the Louisville area and were for a while two of the regular scouts at Ft. Nelson.

John Ash Sr. claimed 1000 acres, settled in 1776, "on the waters of the town fork of Salt River about two miles from Josh Cox's land." Adjacent to this claim, John Ash Jr. had 1000 acres, settled 1776, "lying on the westerly fork of Ash Creek, with 'JA' cut on a beech tree near the improvement." John Ash Jr. was called Jack, and the westerly fork of Ash's Creek became known as Jack's Creek.

Part of the Ash family lived near Kinchloe's and Polk's Station on Simpson Creek flowing through what is now Spencer and Nelson Counties. In 1782, this station was attacked and some of the family — including young Benjamin Ash — were captured, and the younger John Ash was mortally wounded. Thirty-seven people were taken prisoner there.

In the Bardstown Gazette in 1841, there appeared a narrative of the event, and several articles have been written on the attack and a few of the known survivors. The men were taken to Detroit and sold to the British, while the children and some of the woman were detained to be later adopted into the tribes. See "Memoir of the Burnt Station," KYHQ, vol. 32, p. 172; see the letter in the Calendar of Virginia State Papers, August 31st, 1782, p. 282.

John Ash jr., in his will of October 29th, 1782, mentions wife Elizabeth, "child she is going with," his estate and part of his father's, "and my desire is that my brother who is here shall have his equal part with me, and if any of my brothers that are now in captivity should return, my desire is that they should have equal part in my father's estate."

Among his brothers still living among the Indians were Sylvester Ash who later became a noted interpreter among the Wyandots; Abraham Ash, who later became a Shawnee interpreter and was one of Anthony Shane's band of scouts in the War of 1812;

and George Ash, who had previously been captured by Shawnees in the spring of 1780 and then adopted.

Also captured — in March, 1781, on Simpson's Creek — was Reuben Ash whose age was 17 as given on the British prisoner list. He seems to have returned with his grandfather, 60-year-old John Ash. See McHenry, p. 69.

Draper 13CC37 contains an interesting, first-hand account of George Ash (or Mash or Nash as it was often given). "He had been taken prisoner when ten years of age, had light hair....The Indians had been peaceable and we had seen none of them 'til the first snow fell on the ground, when the Indians came.... they came down the hill, riding fast, this Mash and Blackfish in the lead. Some of the men prepared to shoot at them when Mash yelled not to shoot. Could talk English as well as anybody. They had come to trade. About 20 Indians, Shawnees and Wyandots, 10 squaws — some with paposes — came and traded...at first would not let them in the cabins...but they were proved friendly...had a good trade all winter...."

Thomas Ridout, who was captured in 1788, saw "Nash" and Blackfish at the Indian towns. This was George Ash, probably, who reassured Ridout and took him to the home of Major Snake who, in turn, treated him with kindness and helped to insure his release. See Ridout, pp. 10, 27.

A pioneer living in Carrolton, Kentucky, told Draper that "One Ash got the first piece of land on the Indian side of the river. Ash had been taken prisoner, in Kentucky somewhere, when a boy, and carried off west. Was with them so long, he became very much like them. Something was said about his having killed some persons — and he even said that he had done so. When the treaty with the Indians was made, he tried to get Congress to recognize a gift of land made by the Indians to him...they refused to let him have it that way and he had to pay for it..." See Draper Mss. 15CC42.

This man was George Ash, who built a two-story brick house on his land near the present city of Vevey, Indiana. According to an article in the September 20th, 1970, Indianapolis Star, the Ash family was originally from North Carolina. When George Ash was about ten years old he was captured and adopted by the Shawnee chief Blackfish.

George Ash fought on the Shawnee side in most battles of the period. Once, he left the Shawnees and tried to return to his father in Nelson County, Kentucky, but his father's second wife would have nothing to do with him. So, George Ash returned to his adopted people. He first married a Shawnee woman named She Bear, then married a woman named Combs from Carrolton, Kentucky (opposite Vevey, Indiana), and his people have held the brick house continuously since then. As with the descendants of Jonathan Alder, Stephen Ruddle, and many others, the immediate heirs of George Ash did not mention the existence of any half-red heirs.

The will of John Ash Sr., probated October 4th, 1799, in Nelson County, mentions his wife, Arrabella, daughter Elizabeth, sons Sylvester, Abraham, George, Joseph, John (by his second wife), Henry, and Issac. He gave his son Issac "3 lbs. or a cow if ever he is found." He gave his son Reuben but one dollar "for I have poshoned him of when he was mared."

I am not yet certain whom Reuben Ash "mared," but he seems to have become an Indian trader in Floyd County, Indiana where his will was filed.

Abraham Ash became an interpreter at the Ft. Wayne Agency in Indiana and married a Shawnee woman of Capt. John Lewis' band. See Thornbrough, index, Letter Book of the Indian Agency at Fort Wayne 1809-1815, Strickney to Harrison, May 8th, 1812.

One of the Lewistown Shawnee/Seneca band

named Ash signed the 1816 treaty in Ohio. A Shawnee named Big Ash signed the treaty with the Lewistown, Ohio band in 1831. See Prevost, p. 2; Watson, pt. 2, p. 67.

For the captivity of John Ash, see Draper 13CC115-120. For George Ash and Blackfish, see Draper 13CC57-59. For a plat showing the location of the Kinchloe's Burnt Station on Simpson's Creek, see Nelson County Records Book B, p. 21, James Davis vs. Wm. Day; and the plat on page 165, Hammond vs. Fitch devises.

ASHBY, ASHBAUGH – a Shawnee/Delaware name.

Stephen Ashby, from Virginia, was coming down the river to Nelson County, Kentucky in 1789. The family was attacked by Indians and the eldest son, then nineteen, killed after a heroic and fearless defense. The Indians cut the brave man's heart out, broiled it over a fire, and ate of it. This was sometimes done, for some tribes believed that this would imbue the Indian with the bravery of the slain.

On the trip, Stephen Ashby and one of his older sons managed to escape on a raft and floated down to Louisville. Mrs. Ashby and the remaining six children were taken to the Indian towns. The children were then divided up and adopted into different tribes.

Meanwhile, Mr. Ashby sold his land to obtain funds with which to search for his family. He searched through the frontier outposts, including the headquarters of General Anthony Wayne. In one of his searches he found the Indian who had cut his son's heart out, but he did not see any of his family again until the Treaty of Greenville many years later.

Soon after, some of the family went to what is now Spencer County, Kentucky and became two of the constituting members of the Little Mount Baptist Church in 1801. Later, some of them moved to Indiana. See "The Capture of Stephan Ashby and His Family," by Logan Essrey in the Indiana Magazine of History, vol. 9, p. 109-112.

Who were the members of the family who came back to the whites after the treaty? Did the women who came back, after seven years, have children with them? Did some of them return to the Indians?

I do not yet know. But an Indian blood tradition exists among some of the descendants of the Spencer / Nelson county Ashby / Ashbaugh families that has not yet been explained. In 1811, in Nelson County, an Andrew Ashbaugh married Nancy Shields, a daughter of John Shields, apparently the John Shields of the Lewis and Clark expedition. Samuel Morton signed the bond. In 1814, an Andrew Ashbaugh married Isabell Shields, and James Langley signed the bond. In 1816, Sophia Ashbaugh married Samuel Hahn. Where is the Indian connection?

ASKIN – a Shawnee name.

Indian trader John Askin had a son, John Askin Jr., by a Shawnee woman. See Knoft. Some of the family appears to have settled in Ohio after the Treaty of Greenville, but some remained with the Shawnees in Canada.

On the 1883 Ontario Census, which included the Munsee Delaware Reserve, was listed Henry Askin, 45, Jane Askin, 32, and Mary Yawwan, 13, all born in Ontario. See Prevost, p. 96.

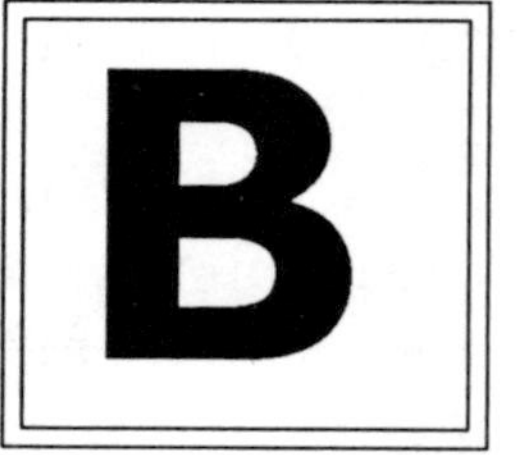

BAILEY or BAILY – a Shawnee name.

John Bailey and his wife, born in Indiana, had a family which included:

1. Josephine, born 1845 at Indianapolis, who married Thomas Bluejacket; both are buried at Vinita, Oklahoma.
2. Frank, who married Sallie Bluejacket, daughter of John and Mary Bluejacket.
3. Robert Bailey.
4. William Bailey.
5. Rebecca Jane, who married John Francis, likely the Shawnee of that name.
6. Matilda Ann.

The children of Thomas and Josephine Bailey Bluejacket included:

1. Stephen A. who married Jennie Burris.
2. William Thomas, b. 1866 in Kansas, married Nellie Curle.
3. Sarah, b. 1868 in Kansas, m. 1st Nate Wilbur.

See SOCC, vol. I, p. 256. Virginia Bluejacket Slack says that Matilda Ann Bailey was possibly the one who married Joseph Daugherty in Johnson County, Kansas on March 15, 1866. That would be my bet.

Among the Shawnees who settled on the lands of the Cherokee nation by 1869 was the family of John H., George, and Samuel H. Baily; another Shawnee family included William, Mary, Ida, and Jane Bailey. See JAIFR, vol. IV, #2, pp. 100-111; Prevost, p. 55.

Among the Shawnees living in the Delaware District of the Cherokee Nation in 1880 were G. F. Bailey, 19, and Samuel Bailey, 14. JAIFR, vol. XIII, #1, p. 44.

BAKER – a Shawnee name.

A Bolin Baker was a descendant of Powhatan.

John Baker, one of Indian trader George Croghan's assistants, was captured by Delawares near Ft. Shirley in January, 1756. He escaped in March and, in September, it was John Baker who guided Col. John Armstrong back to the Delaware town of Kittanning. Armstrong destroyed the town and killed many of the warriors. See *The Delaware Westward Migration* by C. Weslager, p. 6.

Susanna Baker was captured in Kentucky, spent over two years among the Shawnees and Delawares, and was delivered up in 1795. See Knoft, p. 67.

A Baker was also supposed to have been a Revolutionary soldier, and at one time a renegade white man who married the Shawnee woman named Aracoma, a daughter of Cornstalk. This tradition is mentioned in The History of Clay County, Kentucky, ed. by Kelly Morgan.

Among the Shawnees given tracts of land in Ohio by the 1817 Treaty of the Miami of Lake Erie was Davy Baker (Peetah). See Harvey, p. 167.

John Baker is listed as a 24-year-old white man living among the Shawnees and Delawares in the Cooweecoowee District of the Cherokee Nation. He apparently had a 24-year-old Cherokee wife, Lizzie, a 4-year-old daughter M. J., and a 5-month-old daughter S. E. Baker on the 1880 Cherokee Census. See JAIFR, vol. X, #1, p. 42.

BALDWIN – an Ottawa name.

Several members of the family were captured by Indians during Pontiac's War. Among those given up to Henry Bouquet was ten-year-old Abraham Baldwin. His deposition appears in SWJ Papers 1763-1777. He said that the Delawares treated him badly but that the Senecas treated him well; that the Delawares were for war, the Senecas for peace. "That [James] Sherlock is a bad man and goes around painted [for war] and threatens to kill the English for whipping him..."

One of the family, John Baldwin, later became an Indian trader and was associated with the Potawatomi and Ottawa tribes for many years. The 1832 Treaty with the Potawatomis gave him $1000 for claims he had against the Potawatamis of the Wabash. See Watson, pt. 10, p. 12.

The Baldwin name, for one reason or another, became an Ottawa surname. Appearing on the 1939 roll of Ottawas are Delphena Baldwin, age 36, and her family which included sons Henry (19), William (14), Fred (12), George (8), John (2), and daughters May (10), Della (4), Ella (4), as well as an infant Baldwin daughter. See JAIFR, vol. VI, #3, p. 19.

BALL – a Mingo name.

Henry Ball and Polly Meadows were among those spared at St. Clair's Defeat. They were "brought to the Shawnee village on the Auglaize River. There they became acquainted with Oliver Spencer, another American boy who after being captured on the Ohio River, had spent a few grand years living red. Later Spencer returned to the whites and, as did many ex-captives, wrote a memoir about his experiences. In it he mentioned Ball and Meadows, who spoke of themselves as husband and wife. By the summer of 1792 the couple was well established among the Indians and prospering. Ball operated a flatboat, the management of which was not congenial work for the Shawnee, and was hauling freight up the river from British suppliers near what is now Toledo..." See Gilbert, p. 152.

Listed on the 1894 Seneca Census of the Quapaw Agency was Thomas Ball, 44; his wife Lucinda, 44; his son Andrew, 8; and his daughters Lizzie Shilo, 15,

Rachael R., 14, Lida, 5, and Ollie Ball, 2.

BALLOU, BELLIEU, etc. – a Cherokee/Osage name.

Jeff Ballou (who sometimes went by the name of Jack Foster) was given the Cherokee name of Cun-dee-sta-chih, the Wasp. See Cherokee Roll #10730, deposition of Francis Fritz, Vinita, Okla., March 10, 1909.

Jeff Ballou married a daughter of Bob Guess (Gist), a Cherokee, and had a daughter named Nancy Nolen. "Mrs. Nolen has seven children living and every one of them are married including Janie Ballou who married Lon Colvin. All these children are the children of my wife by Jeff Ballou, her former husband." See the deposition of Peter Woodall, Vinita, Okla., March 10, 1909.

The children of Jeff Ballou were Jennie Ballou who married John Hickery, Carrie Ballou who married Lon Colvin, and Susie Ballou who married W. F. Hall. See Cherokee roll #2143.

Nathan Ballow and Jane his part-red wife, formerly Jane Martin, tried to sell their land in Indiana to William Polke in 1832, but as this was a part of the Indian reserve, the sale was disallowed. See Tipton Papers, p. 656.

On the Osage roll of 1908 is listed Thomas A. Bellieu, born 1882, 5/16th blood. Walter S. Bellieu, an Osage, died in 1910 leaving daughters Stella Bellieu Morris and Anna Bellieu Caughron, and sons Emmet, Leo F., Stephen H. Bellieu. All of the children are listed as being 1/4 blood Osage. See JAIFR, vol. X, #2, p. 45.

BAPTISTE, BATTISE, etc. – a Wyandot/Shawnee name.

Baptiste (Battise, Baptist) was a brother of Roundhead, Tecumseh's second in command during the War of 1812. Baptiste may have been there when Roundhead was killed and perhaps it was then that his nose was broken. Nearly everyone who knew him in later years commented on his big "jelly-nose," which would bounce when he walked.

According to those who knew him, Baptiste's wife was a white woman. See Draper 17S274.

According to Brelsford, Martha Beck lived on the Indian trail that led from Thorntown (Indiana) to Cornstalk Creek. The Indians frequently came to her home to trade. Two of the women among them looked like white women to Martha Beck, and she asked them their names. They gave their names as Nancy and Sallie Battiste. See Brelsford.

The 1842 Muster Roll of Wyandots from Sandusky, Ohio, included the Widow Battise's household, consisting of one female 25 to 55, one male 10 to 25, and one female under 10.

The muster roll of the Shawnees brought from the Ohio Hog Creek and Wapakonetta bands included the Baptist family of five, consisting of one male over 50, two males between 25 and 50, and two children under 10, one boy, one girl. See Roy, p. 42.

Among the Shawnees who settled on the lands of the Cherokee nation by 1869 were James and Charles Baptiste. See JAIFR, vol. IV, #2, pp. 100-111.

BARBEE – a Shawnee name.

Spybuck was a Shawnee and looked and acted like a white man, people said. John Johnston told Draper that Spybuck married "the daughter of Col. Barbee of Kentucky, a fine looking woman." See Draper 11YY2.

Well, this is a mystery.

There were as many colonels in the Barbee family as there were generals in the Clark family. He might have meant Col. Joshua Barbee who was the jail keeper at Danville and who, along with John Crow, might have overseen the Shawnee women who were held captive there in the mid-1780s. Also, Joshua Barbee claimed membership in the Political Club of Danville which met to discuss such controversial topics as Peyton Short's theory that "the Indian problem" should be solved by intermarriage with them. It was even proposed to Congress that a mixed red/white married couple should be exempted from taxes or even given a bonus as an additional incentive.

Col. Joshua Barbee (one source says Col. Thomas Barbee) wintered at the Indian town of St. Mary's in 1812. And we know that Indian blood traditions often have a common source leading to officers stationed in remote frontier outposts.

But more likely, Col. William Barbee, Sr. is meant. One of the Barbees — the senior William, I think — was at Piqua when it was burnt by the whites in 1782. It rose up from the ashes, however. The Shawnee blood in the family may originate with Mary Smith who married William Barbee, sr., probably in the 1770s or 1780s. Margaret Marshall (Indian trader William Marshall's sister-in-law?) married William Barbee, jr., in 1809. William Tullis married Sally Barbee in 1812. Nancy Barbee married James Brown in 1814. David R. Tullis married Susana Barbee in 1815. Aaron Tullis, sr. married Mary Barbee in 1816. Lucy Barbee married Dr. John Tilford at Troy, Ohio, in 1816. Melinda Barbee married Findley Telford in 1833. Where's the source of the Indian blood tradition?

According to one source in the Barbee family files, about 1804 William Barbee and his wife Margaret (Marshall) Barbee joined up with the Rev. Tullis and his wife and went to Ohio around 1804 to minister to the Indians there. Margaret Barbee and the Rev. Tullis both died, and William Barbee married the widow Tullis. Did she have Shawnee blood?

Both families wound up with the Indian blood tradition, and you cannot sort one out without getting tangled up in the other.

According to the History of Miami County, Ohio (Beers, 1880, pp. 221-223), William Barbee settled in Concord Township, but was an officer at Piqua during the War of 1812, where he was struck down by a fatal illness. Quoting a John Tullis, William Barbee was described as a "philosopher" and an "ultra abolitionist." One of the Tullises became the sole proprietor of Bluejacket's plantation after the old chief moved to Wappakonetta.

This family — like the Dawson, Mann, Marshall, Armstrong, Blue, Rankin, Gardner, and other families — had more hidden Indian blood than the standard family historians have suspected. The family chart of a descendant is in the Barbee family file at the Kentucky Historical Society. They can't figure it out; the birth dates don't correspond to the marriages. Must be a mistake here, they write. Well, sure there is. Which William Barbee moved to Missouri and then to Kansas with the Shawnees? Who started the Tullis (Tula, Tooley, Tulley) name among the Shawnees? How many of these mixed-bloods stayed in Ohio? How many who left later returned?

This can be sorted out. Someone just needs to be interested enough to look in the local records, go through the deed books, search the circuit court suits, examine the guardianship accounts. The answers are there, and when someone gets the straight story on this (or if you already know the story), why not send it to me so I can publish it in a future volume of *Indian Blood*?

In Miami County, Ohio, a William Barbee, Jr. married a Miss Tullis at Troy, Ohio in 1850, by whom he had two children, William III and Mary.

A William Barbee came from Ohio to Missouri, then moved to Kansas where he died in 1856. He was involved in white/Shawnee political affairs. See KHC, vol. 3, pp. 247, 266, 272; vol. 4, pp. 420, 628; vol. 5, p.

204; vol. 12, p. 476; vol. 13, p. 308.

Among the Shawnees allotted land in Kansas were William Barbee (head of family) and Mary Eliza Barbee. See KHC, vol. 15, p. 175. A Shawnee named Sarah Barbee is mentioned in the same volume, pp. 108, 130.

Among the Shawnees living in the Delaware District of the Cherokee Nation in 1880 were Billy Barbee, 48, Anna Barbee, 18, and John Barbee, 14. See JAIFR, vol. XIII, #1, p. 45.

A part-Shawnee named John Westley Barbee married Mamie Mann, and their children included John Westley Barbee II, born in Afton, Oklahoma, in 1920. The younger John Barbee served in the United States Navy in World War II. He married Edith Hull in 1940, and their children included John Westley Barbee III who married Madge Grisham. Children of the latter couple included: Darla Renee, born 1964; John Wesley Barbee IV, born 1966; Marsha Tyrene Barbee, born 1967; and Luke Westley Barbee, born 1976. See SOCC, vol. II, pp. 106-107.

BARLOW – a Shawnee name.

Among the Shawnees allotted land in Kansas were John M. Barlow (as head of family), Ann Eliza Barlow, and Mary Barlow. See KHC, vol. 15, p. 174.

Among the Shawnees who settled on the lands of the Cherokee nation by 1869 were Phoebe, Lydia, Nancy, Martha, Julius, Julia, and John M. Barlow. See JAIFR, vol. IV, #2, pp. 100-111.

BARNET, BARNETT – a Shawnee/Wyandot name.

The name has long been common among the Shawnees, and whites by that name appear to have been adopted very early in colonial times.

A James Barnett settled in western Pennsylvania on Ten Mile Creek, along with other Indian traders such as John Owens, Robert McClellan, Samuel Meranda, and William Harrod. See "Virginia Land Grants In Pennsylvania." in *The Pennsylvania Genealogist*, vol. II, 1967, pp. 126-127.

According to Draper Mss. 23CC98-99: "Sometime after Braddock's defeat...two girl sisters by the name of Barnett, the youngest six years old and the other some years older, were taken prisoner by the Indians. The oldest became reconciled to stay with them. The youngest, although but six years old [when captured] never forgot her white name or where she was taken. After having been a prisoner twelve years, she came back to the whites of her own accord, married Thomas Cummins and lived about fourteen miles from Ft. Pitt..." Susanna Cummins' sister was "given up" after Dunmore's War in 1774 but ran off again to rejoin the Indians.

There is the story of Joseph Barnett, who erected a blockhouse on the Manada, who fought Indians under Gen. Braddock and Gen. Bouquet, whose son William Barnett was captured and adopted by Indians circa 1757. When found, the boy did not want to leave his Indian family behind. See *The Indian Forts of the Blue Mountains*, pp. 43-45.

There were Barnetts among the whites and blacks delivered up by the Shawnees and Delawares to Gen. Henry Bouquet in 1764.

A James Barnett served with Capt. Andrew Lewis during Dunmore's War; came to Kentucky with James Harrod; went to Harrodsburg, then to Boonesboro. A James Barnett was one of the forty-four members of Capt. George Owens' Company at Ft. Jefferson during 1780, where many of the men there were said to have Indian wives.

Joseph Barnett came to Kentucky with his brothers Alexander Barnett and Robert Barnett and established Barnett's Station in what became Ohio

County. The station was attacked by Indians and some of the residents, including some of this family, were captured near the fort. Some of those captured there were known to have been later adopted. Accounts of the attack exist in Draper Mss. and elsewhere. See American State Papers, Indian Affairs, deposition of Joseph Barnet, June 8th, 1790.

Joseph Barnett appears on the muster roll of the company of Shawnees led by Joseph Parks from the eastern reservation lands in Ohio to Kansas in 1832. His family of ten consisted of two females over 50, one male between 25 and 50, one female between 25 and 50, two males between 10 and 25, and four children under 10, two boys, two girls. See Roy, p. 40.

In the summer of 1833, the missionary William D. Smith visited Kansas in search of a site for a new mission. He made his headquarters at the home of Joseph Barnett, "a well-educated, part-Shawnee," on the Shawnee reserve. See Barry, p. 236.

Listed on the 1843 Muster Roll of Wyandots from Sandusky was Matthew Barnett's family, consisting of one male 25 to 55, one female 10 to 25, and one female under 10. Matthew and Margaret Barnett were allotted Wyandot land in Kansas in 1855.

Among the Wyandot and Shawnee cases heard in 1871 by Ely Parker, Commissioner of Indian Affairs, were the cases of James, Joseph, and Matthew Barnett, then deceased. Joseph Barnett had been the guardian of Catherine Young, Milton Karryhoo, James Monture, and Abraham Williams. Matthew Barnett, who died in 1856, had been the guardian for Josiah Scott Coon. Joseph Barnett had died leaving two daughters, Mary and Louisa. Joseph's brother, Cassius Barnett, was then living on Grand River in Indian Territory. See JAIFR, vol. VIII, #2, p. 18, 19, 28.

BARRETT – a Shawnee name.

Among the Shawnees who settled on the lands of the Cherokee nation by 1869 were Amanda, Hattie, Emma, and Return Barrett. See JAIFR, vol. IV, #2, pp. 100-111.

BARTH – a Shawnee name.

Among the marriages performed by Methodist Minister Joeb Spencer was that of Charles Barth to Emily Blue Jacket, June 24th, 1859. See The Johnson County (Kansas) Genealogist, vol. I, #1, p. 16.

BARTLE – a Shawnee/Delaware name.

Among the Shawnees who settled on the lands of the Cherokee nation by 1869 were William, Mary, Susan, John, and Anna Bartle. See JAIFR, vol. IV, #2, pp. 100-111.

J. H. Bartles (age 39 and listed as a white man) resided with Joseph, jr., and N. M. Bartles, both Delawares and appearing among the Delawares, Cherokees, and Shawnees in the Cooweescoowee District on the 1880 Cherokee Nation Census. See JAIFR, vol X, #1, p. 43.

BAUBEE, BAWBEE, BABEE, or BABY – a Shawnee name.

Duperon Baby was an Indian trader of Detroit. He had great influence with the Indians. He married Susanne Reaume, and one of their daughters married the Shawnee chief, Blue Jacket. Another married William Caldwell. His son, James Baby, married Betsy Abbott, and was active in the British interest in the War of 1812. After that war, the family resided in Ontario. See Thwaites, Revolution on the Upper Ohio, p. 44n, 54, 62, 126. See also BEAUBIEN.

BAYLES – a Shawnee name.

The Bayles family has a tradition that one of their family who was captured and adopted by Shawnees became the mother of Tecumseh. The tradition says that she came back to the family with her infant, that the child stayed with her during the young, formative years of his life, then went back to his father's people. The tradition asserts that Mary Bayles never said a word against her adopted people, and that she gave up her son to Paxinosa willingly, though by that time she was married to Andrew Ice and had white children by him.

Most historians reject the tradition on the grounds of insufficient evidence. Many experts — like, say, Allan Eckert — uphold the more plausible account of Tecumseh being a part of a set of triplets born to full-blooded Shawnees on a night that a meteor flashed across the sky. I do not believe the Tecumseh/triplet story and think that this was a corrupted version of the parable from which the names Tecumseh and Tecumpease originate.

Tecumseh was a concept name. The original Tecumseh was the main player in a parable which involved a crouching panther ready to pounce and a shooting star. The original story may have been told to Tecumseh, but it was lost on any interpreters who had not grown up Shawnee during Paxinosa's time. The interpreters could translate the words, but not the concepts, because they did not understand the concepts themselves.

I'm not saying that the entire Bayles's tradition is absolute fact either. What I am saying is that it cannot be trashed out-of-hand. We know that Mary Bayles and Andrew Ice did live on the frontier and there were adopted Shawnees in the family. We know that there were women who returned from the Indians with half-breed infants.

Tecumseh was a famous name, a concept name, a "risen up" name. In 1738, when George Miranda and Peter Chartier wrote up the petition demanding that the Pennsylvania authorities stop the liquor trade, Oppessa's son, the Pride, was the leading chief whose name was transcribed on the petition. The Pride was Tecumseh's grandfather. A leading man named Tecomtuk was the first warrior on the list after the chiefs. Tecumseh may have been named after this man, but the concept name was probably "risen up" again and again back through time to the origin of the parable.

Tecumseh could certainly not speak of a white genealogy during his own time and, even though Shane and Ruddle thought he could speak English, he made it a point to speak only in Shawnee in a traditional way for obvious political reasons.

It is possible that the tradition of Mary Bayles's Indian son, Tecumseh, is based on truth.

See G. H. Bayles, "Tecumseh and the Bayles Family Tradition," KYHC, vol. 46, p. 647-655.

BEAR – a Shawnee name.

Jacob (age 26), Amanda (age 19), and William Bear (apparently their six-year-old son) appear among the Shawnees on the 1880 Cherokee Nation Census. See JAIFR, vol X, #1, p. 44.

BEARSKIN – a Wyandot name.

Which trader did the Mingoes call Bearskin?

Logan, the celebrated Mingo, told George Morgan in 1776 that Bearskin, "a trader from Pennsylvania," told him that a reward was offered there for anyone who would entice him to Pittsburgh where he was to be hanged. See Schaaf, pp. 147-148. Bearskin was said to have been caught up in the witchcraft hysteria in 1804.

Bearskin may have been one of Sam Ranken's Wyandot band during the War of 1812. He must have been a lead warrior, a prominent man. He signed the treaty. Later, when the Wyandots were given money for the improvements that they had made upon their Ohio lands, Bearskin was allotted more money than any other Wyandot. He was given $542.22, an enormous amount when compared with that of such notable Wyandots as Alexander Clark ($127), Matthew Grey Eyes ($90), and John Solomon ($223). See Watson, vol. V, pt. 3., p. 19.

The 1843 Muster Roll of Wyandots from Sandusky included:

1. Bear Skin's family, consisting of one male over 55 and one male under 10.
2. John L. Bearskin's family, consisting of one male and one female, both over 55, one female 25 to 55, one male and one female 10 to 25, and three children under 10, two of them male.

In 1855, land was allotted to the Wyandots Peter, John S., Sarah, William, Francis, Oliver, Lucinda, George, Margaret, and Elizabeth, Mary, and Joseph Peacock Bearskin. See KHC, vol. 15, p. 126.

Among the Wyandot cases heard in 1871 by Ely Parker, Commissioner of Indian Affairs, was the case of John Bearskin who had died in 1858 as the guardian of five children. See JAIFR, vol. VIII, #2, p. 18.

In 1870, the heirs of James and Eliza Bearskin were Catherine, George and Joseph Bearskin. See KHC, vol. 15, p. 160.

Among the Wyandots listed on the 1900 Federal Census of Indian Territory were Sara Bearskin, a widow born in 1834, and her sons John and Wesley Bearskin. John Bearskin and his wife Mrytle, listed as a white woman. His parents were born in Ohio and hers in Illinois. He was born in 1874.

Sarah Bearskin lived with her other son, Wesley Bearskin. He was born in 1876 and his wife was born in

1868. Their parents were all born in Ohio. See Prevost, p. 80.

Wyandots Leland (Silver Eagle) and Leaford (Flying Eagle) Bearskin, twins aptly named, joined the United States Air Force out of high school and both had successful careers. During World War II, Leaford Bearskin was sent to New Guinea as an Aircraft Commander on a B-24 Liberator Bomber. He flew 46 combat missions in heavy bombers. Later, in 1948, he was a Squadron Commander during the Berlin Airlift.

Leland Bearskin was sent to Antarctica where he was involved in two phases of a project known as Operation Deepfreeze. Once, a storm forced him to make an emergency landing with his C-124. He got plane, passengers, and crew down safely on the edge of the Antarctic. During World War II, he flew C-47 "Gooney Birds" on missions in Europe and North Africa. Although the brothers flew separate ways, they won a similar array of medals. Leaford married Peggy Vernon of Pilcher, Oklahoma, and his children included Nancy and Ronald Bearskin. For pictures and further details concerning the lives of these gallant gentlemen, see Gridley, pp. 67-68.

BEASLEY – a Shawnee name.

The Shawnees captured a Mr. Beasley and adopted him. He "married a squaw by whom he had two or three children." He later brought his wife and children back to live among the whites. See the interview with J. Rankins in Draper mss. 11CC81. Some of the other members of this frontier family were also captured, including Charles Beasley, but they seem to have either been killed or escaped. Does anyone have the genealogy of this part-Shawnee family?

Alexander McGillivray, a quarter-breed son of a Scotch trader and a French/Creek woman "renown for her beauty," led the Creek Nation through the Revolutionary War period, playing the British, Spanish, and United States off one another, keeping his nation neutral and free. He died in 1793, leaving, among others, his half-brother, Charles Weatherford,who had two sons, John and William. John Weatherford "passed for white," and William Weatherford, while "generally accommodating to whites," became notorious as Red Eagle, the chief of the Red Sticks. The Red Sticks, pro-war faction of the Creeks, allied themselves with Tecumseh.

In retaliation for an ambush of Creeks at Burnt Corn, Weatherford led his Creeks against Fort Mims. "Some 265 militiamen — the majority belonging to a troop called the Mississippi volunteers — under another half-breed, Major Daniel Beasley, were stationed there to defend the fort and its occupants." Beasley was trying to get the gates of the fort closed, and was the first cut down in a bloody massacre. See Derr, pp. 61-62. Derr says that Beasely was a half-breed but does not designate the tribal affiliation.

I hope to present a more complete picture of the Beasely family in a future volume of Indian Blood. If you have the red genealogies of this family, please send them to me.

An Andrew Beasley was a blacksmith for the Ottawas at the Sac and Fox Indian Agency in Kansas in 1851 and 1852. See Barry, pp. 1058, 1137.

BEATTY or BAITY – a Shawnee name.

Among the Shawnees who settled on the lands of the Cherokee nation by 1869 were William, Mary, Ida, and Jane Baity. See JAIFR, vol. IV, #2, pp. 100-111.

W. T. Beatty, listed as a white man, was living with his Shawnee family consisting of Mary E. (age 32), Ida (age 15), James (age 10), Babe (age 3), and Morris Beatty (age 5 months). This Beatty family appears among the Shawnees on the 1880 Cherokee Nation

Census. See JAIFR, vol X, #1, p. 44.

BEAUBIEN – a Potawatomi name.

Article II of the 1832 Treaty with the Potawatomi specifies that land be given to "Josette Beaubien and her children," the land to be located on Hickory Creek. See Watson, pt. 10, p. 43.

The Potawatomi woman, Shaw-we-n-quah, was the mother of Joseph LaFromboise by a white father. He married Therese and their daughter, also named Therese, married Madore B. Beaubien, daughter of the Potawatomi woman, Mannabenaquah, by a white man. John B. Beaubien was the son of Madore and Therese and he married Mary e. Their son, John E. Beaubien married Cora Martin and their son was Virgil M. Beaubien who applied for tribal membership as a 1/8 blood Potawatomi.

Among the 1893 Citizen Potawatomi roll were Charles H., John B., Nellie, Walter, Benjamin, Eliza S., Battist, and Chevalier Beaubien.

BEGGS or BIGGS – a Wyandot name.

William Biggs was a member of Robert George's Company at Ft. Jefferson. Years later, he settled near Kaskakia, Illinois, and he held several territorial and state offices.

In 1826, shortly before his death, he published a narrative of his capture by Shawnees. He was captured while camping with John Vallis in 1788. John Vallis put up a fight and was mortally wounded. William Biggs surrendered and let himself be adopted into the tribe. He says he was given a young, beautiful, "very white" wife whom, he says, he resisted because he was already married.

See Hiram W. Beckwith, *The Illinois and Indiana Indians*; Carl R. Baldwain, *Echoes of their Voices*. For some additional notes on the pioneer Biggs family, see

Leckey, p. 258.

Among the Wyandots listed on the 1900 Federal Census of Indian Territory was Mike Beggs, a white man born in Illinois in 1859. His part-Wyandot wife, Alice Beggs, was born in 1859 in Kansas. Her father had been white, her mother a Wyandot. Peter Shiffhauer lived with them, a half-breed step-son of Mike Beggs. See Prevost, p. 80.

BENJAMIN – a Miami name.

David Benjamin, and perhaps others of his family, were taken captive by Indians. See Thompson, p. 74.

Charley Benjamin (Wa-pe-si-in), "a well-known Miami who is often seen in Wabash and Peru," is a descendant of Pontiac, one of the family of that Ottawa chief having married a Miami woman and their descendants settling in Indiana. This information is from Thad Butler, Indian agent. See Draper 1YY117-119.

On the 1880 Miami census appears James Benjamin, 29, a farmer, living with his wife, Wah-wa-ni-sum-quah (last in water), 33. Susan and Catherine Benjamin appear on the 1893 Miami census.

BENNET or BENNETT – a Wyandot name.

Among the Wyandot households enumerated on the 1860 Federal Census of Wyandotte County, Kansas was that of John Bennett, age 28, born in Ohio. Living in the same household were Hannah Bennett, 40, born Ohio; Henry Armstrong, 17, b. Kansas; Betsy Whiting, 40, b. Ohio; Eliza Lewis, 18, b. Kansas, John Lewis, 13, b. Kansas, and Phoenix Lewis, 24, born Kansas.

Another Wyandot household included James, 35, Jane, 34, and Cyrina Bennett, 12, all born Ohio.

The 1900 Federal Census of Indian Territory lists Jefferson Bennet as a Wyandot, born 1866 in Kansas. His father was a white man, his mother a Wyandot.

His wife, Verna, was a white woman born in 1872.

BENSON – a Creek name.

When very young, Mary Benson was captured by a war party of Creeks. She was taken to their Indian towns, adopted, and grew to womanhood among them. She married the medicine man, In-tak-faht-ky, a full-blooded Creek of the Creek Hillabee Town. In-tak-faht-ky was a serious conjurer, but was said to have a keen sense of humor and stories are told of his practical jokes.

Their children included E-mah-thla-hut-ky (The Hog Meat Man), Nannie, Nancy, Johnie or Tsah-nu-tsee (Town Warrior), Somully, Dick, and Jack. The family name was Benson, somewhat in the manner of the matrilineal Creeks whose ways were being continually modified by the whites among them.

When her children were young, Mary Benson's uncle came to the village on a visit. When he returned, he took two of Mary's boys, Dick and Jack, with him back to his Georgia home. Some time afterwards, they returned to the tribe but they had picked up some white ways, spoke English, and wore white-style clothes. Both Dick and Jack Benson had families.

Jack Benson's family included Mary who married Timothy Barnett. Barnett and his wife operated a trading post, and Timothy Barnett was prominent in the political affairs of the Creek Nation. After the Civil War broke out, Colonel Timothy Barnett was given command of the 2nd Creek Regiment on the Confederate side. He killed a Creek of the opposing political faction, and in retaliation, his house was surrounded by a band of Indians who shot him to death.

One of E-mah-thla-hut-ky's daughters married Daniel Grant Wilson, the trading partner of the half-breed Cherokee, Jesse Chisholm. Wilson's daughter married John McIntosh, the son of Col. Chilly McIntosh.

Johnie Benson sided with the Red Sticks after Tecumseh visited the Creek towns. At the battle of Horseshoe Bend, he made his stand with Man-ah-we against the forces of General Andrew Jackson and was severely wounded. He was carried from the battle by his brother, E-mah-thla-hut-ky, and although he never fully recovered from his wounds, he survived. Johnie Benson married Katy Grayson, the daughter of Robert Grierson (Grayson). See Baird, pp. 21-25.

BENZADONE, BIZAIZON, etc. – a Miami/ Delaware name.

Peter Bezallion was an Indian trader associated with George Miranda, Peter Chartier, and John Burt. Like most of the early traders, he had an Indian wife, and Zimmerman says that his first wife was Iroquois. See Zimmerman, p. 168.

Lawrence Benzadone was a half-breed Indian trader who lived at Vincennes who had an Indian wife. He traded as an agent for Michael Lacassagne of Louisville. He was tried for murdering "a Monsco Indian," apparently one of the Muscogee Creeks who lived among the Miami.

Indian trader Etienne Bizaizon's will is filed in Clark County, Indiana Will Book A, p. 72, witnessed by the Indian traders James Stewart and Joseph Barron.

Joseph Bezion was in Capt. James Swannuck's company in the Florida War, and he later became one of the Delaware free hunters in the Rocky Mountains.

Among the Delawares who moved to the Cherokee Nation and were listed on the 1900 Federal Census were Stephen Bezion, born 1857 in Kansas. His father was born in Ohio. Also there was Mary C. Benzion, born 1849 in Kansas. She said that she was half-Wyandot, that her father was born in Indiana, that her mother was born in Ohio. See Prevost, p. 31.

BIGARMS or STRONGARMS – a Wyandot name.

Ethan Bigarms was allotted land in Kansas in 1855.

Among the Wyandot cases heard in 1871 by Ely Parker, Commissioner of Indian Affairs, was the case of Ethan Bigarms who had died in 1858 or 1859. His wards were not listed. See JAIFR, vol. VIII, #2, p. 20.

In 1872, John Bigarms "assuming that Ethan Bigarms is dead, and if dead left as sole heirs of his half [of his inheritance], Theressa Whitecrow and his niece Maitha [Martha] Driver. John Bigarms went to California in 1859 and has not been heard of in 13 years." See KHC, vol. 15, p. 160.

BIGELOW – a Wyandot name.

"In a conversation with Judge Anderson respecting the Wyandotte Indians, I was somewhat surprised to find that they had a reputation for being strictly honest in all business transactions...

"J. T. Rappee, of Upper Sandusky, who lived among them for many years as a trader, says that when the tribe left Ohio for the West, individual members of of it were indebted to him in numerous small sums aggregating about $5,000, and that in time, as the Indians were able to save money from their annuities and the sale of furs and skins, every dollar due to him was paid, so that he lost nothing at all by reason of the confidence reposed in them. In respect to the honorable fulfillment of contracts of this kind, Mr. Rappee considers them much superior to the average white man. Among the notable Indians of the Wyandotte Nation were the Armstrongs, Walkers, and Garretts. Some of these were educated at Kenyon and one of the Armstrongs married a daughter of Hosea Bigelow, a pioneer Methodist minister." See Ford, p. 142.

Jacob Bigelow was among the Shawnees and Wyandots and was allotted land. His allotment adjoined that of Margaret Zane. See KHC, vol. 15, p. 165.

BIGKNIFE – a Shawnee name.

The Long Knife, or Big Knife, was a term used by Shawnees to designate Virginians or Kentuckians — prior to the Treaty of Greenville, at least. Several council dialogs could be cited, and many first-hand conversations as quoted by Draper and other historians. For a while, the term was used to designate General George Rogers Clark.

The Longknife or Bigknife family among the Shawnees may have derived its name from a family connection with such a white frontiersman as Clark.

The family of the elder Bigknife appears on the muster roll of the company of Shawnees from the Hog Creek and Wapakonetta bands who were led from the Ohio lands to Kansas by Joseph Parks in 1832. His family consisted of one male over 50, one female between 25 and 50, two males between 10 and 25, and three children under 10, one of them a girl.

Tom Bigknife, probably a son of the elder Bigknife, also had a family on the Shawnee muster roll. His family of six consisted of one male between 25 and 50, one female between 25 and 50, one male between 10 and 25, one female between 10 and 25, and two females under 10. See Roy, p. 39.

Both Bigknife and John Bigknife were among the Shawnees who accompanied Capt. Joseph Parks to Florida to engage in the Seminole War.

Among the marriages recorded by Rev. Joeb Spencer in Kansas were that of Nancy Bigknife who married Francis Whitefeather January 8, 1859 and also that of Thomas Bigknife who married Sarah Tooley on June 7, 1859. See The Johnson County (Kansas) Genealogist, vol. I, #1, p. 16.

Among the Shawnees allotted land in Kansas were Thomas, Fanny, Samuel, George, Elizabeth, and

Nancy Bigknife. See KHC, vol. 15, p. 174.

Among the Shawnees who settled on the lands of the Cherokee nation by 1869 were Lewis, Sally, George, Susan, Nancy, James N., Henry, and Mary Bigknife. See JAIFR, vol. IV, #2, pp. 100-111.

Among the Shawnee guardianship cases heard in 1871 by Ely Parker, Commissioner of Indian Affairs, was the case of George Bigknife, but his wards were not listed. See JAIFR, vol. VIII, #2, p. 27.

James (age 36), Susie (age 28), Henry (age 12), Jane (age 3), and Reuben (age 10 months) were members of the Bigknife household listed as Shawnees on the 1880 Cherokee Nation Census. See JAIFR, vol X, #1, p. 45.

BIGTREE – a Mingo name.

Big Tree was the Seneca husband of Madame Montour, who had been raised by the Mohawk. When Big Tree was reported slain in a battle with the Catawbas, John and Thomas Penn sent her a message of sympathy. Some of their children took the name Montour, but the Indian name Big Tree was carried on also.

Big Tree was General Anthony Wayne's Seneca ambassador (and spy) at the peace talks with the Shawnee in 1793. See Gilbert, p. 169.

The 1843 Muster Roll of Wyandots from Sandusky, Ohio, included the James Bigtree family, consisting of one male between 25 and 55, one female between 10 and 25, and three children under 10, two of them boys.

John Bigtree died about 1857 and his sole heirs were his daughter, Catherine Bigtree, and his wife, Mary Solomon Bigtree, daughter of John Solomon. See KHC, vol. 15, p. 160.

BINGAMEN, BINGAMIN – a Delaware name.

The Indians attacked the Bingamen family in Shenandoah County, Virginia in 1755. Most of the family was believed to be killed, but two or three seem to have been captured and later adopted. Lewis (or Christian) Bingamen was one of those adopted and he became "so addicted to his Indian ways" that he refused to leave them when given the opportunity. He was adopted by Delawares and became a notorious "renegade" living sometimes red and sometimes white. His story appears in Draper mss., Glen Lough's works, and Chalkley's Augusta County, Virginia, vol. II, pp. 507-510. Some of his family was later supposed to have settled in Natchez.

Lewis Bingamon, "the white renegade and Indian lover," was at the head of a war party of thirty warriors in pursuit of John Price, who had treacherously murdered a chief. Price said he did it because the chief kept a Christian bible. Bingamen decoyed Price and took him back to the tribe. See Lough, AAT, vol. 1, #9, Jan., 1972, p. 2.

BLACK BEAVER – a Delaware name.

The daughters of Black Beaver, like many of the daughters of the legendary Delaware trappers and scouts, were said to have married white men.

Black Beaver roamed throughout the west with other Delaware and Shawnee hunters, became conversant in several Indian languages, and was in almost constant demand as a guide and interpreter.

When Black Beaver served as interpreter for Col. Richard Irving Dodge in 1834, Dodge wrote, "Of all the Indians, the Delawares seem to be most addicted to these solitary wanderings, undertaken...from pure curiosity and love of adventure..."

It was a hankering for adventure and a curiosity "about the big guns," that prompted Black Beaver to command a company of Delaware and Shawnee Indians who engaged in the Mexican War in 1846. They satisfied their curiosity, but the records show that they were never given money for their service.

In 1849, Captain Randolph B. Marcy engaged Black Beaver as a guide. He found that Black Beaver was familiar with the western and northern tribes, that he "converses fluently with the Comanche and most of the other prairie tribes. He has spent five years in Oregon and California, two years among the Crow and Blackfeet Indians. Has trapped beaver on the Gila, the Columbia, the Rio Grande, and the Pecos; has crossed the Rocky Mountains at many different points, and indeed is one of those men that are seldom met with except in the mountains."

All of the many contemporary accounts of Black Beaver agree that he was an extraordinary man, a master tracker gifted with rare intelligence, perfectly reliable, brave, and modest. Often he told stories, exaggerating his own follies and laughing at them.

The Kickapoos bought a fleet thoroughbred from a Missourian and took him out onto the plains for the express purpose of racing against the Comanche horses. Black Beaver was in on the deal, convinced that the thoroughbred was a sure thing. While a guest of the Comanche chief, Black Beaver foolishly bet all of his possessions, and the chief took all of his bets. After the thoroughbred was badly beaten, the Commanche chief did not have the heart to take Black Beaver's horses, but advised him to never again bet against the Comanches.

The story came up because Lt. John Buford of Marcy's command had one of Abe Buford's Kentucky thoroughbreds along. Black Beaver advised against racing him against the Comanches, having learned his lesson.

Black Beaver settled down and built the first

house at Anadarko near the Washita, less than a mile from the Wichita Agency school. "When Pat Pruner went to Anadarko in 1871, he married Black Beaver's daughter, Mrs. Osborne after her husband's tragic death. Jesse Sturm, a son of J. J. Sturm, married Mrs. Osborne's daughter Mattie."

Judge C. Ross Hume stated that he knew Black Beaver's daughter, Lucy Pruner; his son-in-law, H. P. Pruner; his two grandsons, John R. Osborne and Charles Beaver Pruner; and his two granddaughters, Margaret Osborne McLane and Mattie Pruner Sturm.

BLACKBODY – a Shawnee name.

The family may have intermarried with blacks. Of course, we don't know that they were black/red Shawnees, but it is certainly possible, and they seem to have been dark-skinned traditionalists at any rate. Some of the Shawnees, including Chief Joseph Parks, owned slaves, but there was far more intermarriage between adopted blacks and Shawnees than has been generally believed. In general, if a man acted like a slave, the Shawnees treated him as a slave. But if a man proved himself worthy of being a Shawnee, he was adopted like any other.

At a council in 1775, whites were still demanding that the Shawnee deliver up the blacks among them. Cornstalk was exasperated and said that he could not comply any longer with their demands. But he said that "there is a woman of my Nation, Anipassicowa, who has some of your negroes. As she belongs to my tribe, I will speak to her and doubt not that she will listen to me, but as her children are sprung from my Grandfathers, the Delawares, there may be perhaps some difficulty arise from that.

"It is true that there are two Negro children which were begotten by my people and we are not the only people who have intermixed with Negroes. We are not willing to give up the children." See Thwaites & Kellogg, Revolution on the Upper Ohio, pp. 115-116.

Pompey has been the most famous black Shawnee, and he was certainly among them long enough to have fathered red children. See Belue, pp. 5-12. When Ridout was among the Shawnee in 1788, he noted a black man living comfortably among them named Boatswain or Boosini. See Ridout, p. 16. By the time they moved to Kansas, most of the Shawnees were almost white enough to pass for white, most of the Wyandots were just a shade darker, and some of the darker Shawnees may have intermarried with the more traditional Delawares, among whom there were no slave owners. George Brent, who was half-Cheyenne, said that his people always referred to the Delawares as "black Shawnees."

But there continued to be some dark-skinned traditionalists among the Shawnees and without them, in fact, many Shawnee traditions might have died a hard death. The Bobb and Blackbody families appear to have been among those who best kept the traditions.

Blackbody appears on the muster roll of the company of Shawnees led by Joseph Parks from the eastern reservation lands to Kansas in 1832. His family of three consisted of one man between 25 and 50, one female between 10 and 25, and one female under 10. See Roy, pp. 39.

Blackbody became a counselor among the Shawnee. He went with the Shawnees to the Florida War. John Wolf wrote John Johnston of his death in 1846. See Draper 1YY25.

Kansas trader James Hamilton wrote in his journal, "Blackboddy or Cottawahcothi, one of the Shawnee chiefs or counselors, died on Wednesday morning, the 8th of April, 1846. He was one of the principal medicine men of the nation. He was disposed to do right and pay his debts..."

Among the Shawnees who settled on the lands of the Cherokee nation by 1869 was Elizabeth Blackbody. See JAIFR, vol. IV, #2, pp. 100-111.

BLACKENY or BLACKENEY – a Shawnee name.

Among the Shawnees who settled on the lands of the Cherokee nation by 1869 were George, Kate, Robert, and Emily Blackeny. See JAIFR, vol. IV, #2, pp. 100-111.

BLACKFEATHER – a Delaware/Shawnee name.

Blackfeather attended a council held at Detroit in June, 1778, the only Shawnee there, and apparently the guest of the Delaware village chief, Capt. James. The translation of his name given on the ensuing treaty was Peck-an-dogh-a-lisid, possibly what the Delawares called him.

This was likely the Blackfeather who was the leader of a band of Indians who surrendered at the Wea town to George Roger Clark's men later in 1778. Clark's officers "counselled whether to tomahawk the Indians." John Bailey wanted to butcher them, but Leonard Helm objected, and the Indians were released to take a message of peace back to their village. See Seineke, pp. 247, 532.

Blackfeather apparently sided with Blackhoof against Tecumseh in the Shawnee political disputes of the early 1800s, at least after Tippecanoe. Blackfeather rode with John Logan's band of United States scouts in the War of 1812 along with Capt. Chieska, John Perry, and others of note.

The scout, Blackfeather, was mentioned by Dr. H. McMurtrie in his 1819 edition of Sketches of Louisville (p. 25). Discussing the New Madrid earthquake — when Tecumseh was said to have stamped his feet and made the earth move — McMurtrie argued that the Shawnees were not as naive about earthquakes as had generally been believed. "During the year 1812, Black Feather, a Shawnee chief, and Perry, another Indian of the same rank, on their way to Fort Meigs with the American troops, were sitting in a tent, in company with several of the latter, when the earth began to oscillate. Before any of the whites present perceived it, Black Feather, swinging himself from side to side, observed that the 'earth tottered.' An officer asked him if he ever before felt a similar sensation, to which the chief, counting the number of suns, replied in the affirmative, at three different periods during the last 40 years. This anecdote I have from a gentleman who was present."

In 1835, Capt. Blackfeather was a subchief of the Hog Creek Branch of Shawnees. John and William Perry were the principle chiefs of this band, and the other subchiefs were Little Fox, Henry Clay, and Letho. Marston G. Clark was their agent, and Charles Shane was their interpreter. L. Jones was their blacksmith. See Caldwell, p. 19.

Among the Shawnees who settled on the lands of the Cherokee nation by 1869 were Johnson, Nancy, David, and Eliza Blackfeather. See JAIFR, vol. IV, #2, pp. 100-111.

Charles, Eliza, Frank, Lizzie, and Nan Blackfeather were among the Shawnees on the 1880 Cherokee Nation Census. See JAIFR, vol X, #1, p. 40

Johnson Blackfeather married Wa-pe-pease and their daughter, Eliza Jane Blackfeather, was born in Shawnee, Kansas in 1860. Eliza married Willis Bluejacket and their children included Minnie (b. 1878), Alexander C. (b. 1881), Lula (b. 1882), Lillie Edeth, nicknamed Babe, (b. 1885), Gertrude and Willis G. (b. 1891). Eliza Jane (Blackfeather) Bluejacket lived until 1935 and was buried in the Bluejacket Cemetery in the town of Bluejacket, Oklahoma.

Lillie Edeth Bluejacket married Charles Fletcher

Hudson in 1905. Their children included Earl, born 1908; Carl, born 1911; John, born 1914; and Dale, born 1918. Earl Hudson married Lelia Marie Kincade, daughter of Curtis and Mable Kincade, and their children included Larry (m. Gloria Francisco), Paul (m. Ermadeen Shamblin; served in Korea), June Marie (m. John C. Pitts), Johnny Lee (m. Sherry Stinnett; served in Viet Nam), and Charles Curtis Hudson. Earl also had a son named Richard Hudson by an earlier marriage.

Charles Curtis Hudson, whose great-grandfather was Johnson Blackfeather, was born in 1934. He grew up to love hunting, fishing, and playing the guitar. The Oklahoma Highway Department hired him, and he has worked for them most of his adult life. While on Christmas leave from the United States Army, he married Elizabeth Alice Trundle. His new wife joined the Christian Church where Charles became a deacon. Their children included: Carol Ann, Charles Allen, Christopher, and Cynthia Lynn Hudson. See SOCC, vol. II, pp. 114, 183-184; information from Wilma Bluejacket Huff and Elizabeth Hudson.

BLACKFISH – a Shawnee name.

The Shawnee chief, Blackfish, was one of Cornstalk's lieutenants at the Battle of Point Pleasant in 1774.

Four years later, during the Revolution, it was Blackfish who led his warriors in the siege of Ft. Randolph where Cornstalk had been murdered. They were unable to take the fort, but pinned up the defenders with a small detachment while the larger body of the tribe raided the smaller Ohio valley settlements and farms, causing great alarm and taking prisoners along the way.

Some of those prisoners taken were adopted into Blackfish's own extended family, which included at various times Tecumseh, the Prophet, George Ash, Henry Rogers, Benjamin Kelly, and Daniel Boone. Henry Rogers married one of the daughters of Blackfish, and Chief Blackfish has many descendants with the surname Rogers.

Boone seems to have been a particular favorite of Blackfish, if ultimately a disappointment to him. Abraham Whitaker mortally wounded Blackfish as he was trying to surrender. See Draper 1R143. When the news of the death of Blackfish was told to Boone he became unusually quiet and went off to be alone for a time. See Elliott, p. 156.

The son of Blackfish carried on the name, white-fashion, and he was the (Young) Blackfish from whom Thomas Ridout ran in 1788, when he was "saved" by two Indian women. See Ridout p. 27.

Both (Young) Blackfish and Jo Blackfish were among the Shawnees who accompanied Capt. Joseph Parks to engage in the Seminole War.

See KHC, vol. 9, pp. 170n, 212; C10, 402; for Hiram Blackfish, ibid., pp. 189; C17, 430.

Among the Shawnees who settled on the lands of the Cherokee nation by 1869 were Hiram, Henry, Peter, Mary, Sarah Jane, Willie, and Thatthequaker Blackfish. See JAIFR, vol. IV, #2, pp. 100-111.

Among the Shawnees on the 1900 Federal Census of Indian Territory was Peter Blackfish who was born in Kansas in 1849. He said that both his father and his mother had been born in Ohio. His wife, Mary, was a white woman who had been born in Missouri in 1853. The white father of Mary Blackfish had been born in Missouri and her mother had been born in Virginia. See Prevost, p. 67.

BLACKHOOF, BLACKFOOT – a Shawnee name, and a family which intermarried with whites.

The white-style descent of the surname came

from the chief named Blackhoof (whom Kentuckians often called Blackfoot) who succeeded Blackfish as head chief of all the Shawnees.

"One of the most noted chiefs was the venerable Blackhoof (Cul-the-we-ka-saw, Cuttahecasa, etc.) in the raids upon Kentucky sometimes called Blackfoot. He is believed to have been born in Florida, and at the period of the removal of a portion of the Shawnees to Ohio and Pennsylvania, was old enough to recollect having bathed in the salt water. He was present, with others of his tribe, at the defeat of Gen. Braddock near Pittsburgh in 1755, and was engaged in all the wars in Ohio from that time until the treaty of Greenville in 1795.

"He was known far and wide as the great Shawnee warrior, whose cunning, sagacity and experience were only equaled by the force and desperate bravery with which he carried into operation his military plans. He was the inveterate foe of the white man, and held that no peace should be made, nor negotiation attempted, except on the condition that the whites should repass the mountains and leave...

Blackhoof "was the orator of the tribe during the greater part of his long life, and is said to have been an excellent speaker. Col. John Johnston says he was probably in more battles than any living man of his day, and was the most graceful Indian he had ever seen, and possessed the most natural and happy faculty of expressing his ideas.

"He was well versed in the traditions of his people and no one understood better their relations to the whites whose settlements were gradually pressing them back, and he could detail with minuteness the wrongs inflicted by the whites on his people..." See Lang, pp. 208-209.

As Lang points out, Blackhoof opposed the United States until after the Treaty of Greenville, and then he was a staunch advocate of peace. He was striving to keep peace with the United States at the same time as Tecumseh and the Prophet were threatening war.

During the uneasy summer of 1807, a man named Myers was killed in the woods, and those who examined the signs around the body deemed it to have been Indians. Tecumseh "with sixty or seventy men and Black Hoof with a similar entourage from Wappakoneta met with a gathering of whites at Springfield, Ohio. The inquiry degenerated into a shouting match between Tekamthi [Tecumseh] and Black Hoof, both claiming that they knew nothing about the murder of Myers but that the other did."

In the heat of the argument, Tecumseh put his hand upon Black Hoof's shoulder and said to the whites, in effect, that Black Hoof was the man who had committed the murder. "Black Hoof went for his hatchet, as did the men with him. Alarmed whites, fearing they might be caught up as innocent bystanders in a savage battle, separated them. A compromise agreement was hastily reached to the effect that somebody else other than Shawnee had no doubt killed Myers." See Gilbert, p. 238-239.

The Shawnee Nation, under chief Black Hoof, remained loyal to the United States during the War of 1812. Strange but true. Johnson reported that about 200 of his Shawnees and Delaware left to join Tecumseh's forces, but the larger number of Shawnees stayed with Black Hoof and some of them became United States scouts.

Lang said that Blackhoof lived with only one wife through forty years, that he raised a large number of children who loved and revered him. His eldest son, Lang says, was Quasky who succeeded his father and took his name as a white-styled surname.

Blackhoof (Quasky) appears on the muster roll

of the company of Shawnees that Joseph Parks led from the eastern reservation lands to Kansas in 1832. His age is given as over 25 but under 50. See Roy, p 38. His wife was the Rabbit (Ne-nux-se), a granddaughter of the Big Snake (Major Snake, She-me-ne-to, etc.). She outlived her husband after he died in 1856, and when Draper passed through the Shawnee reservation, he stopped to interview her.

Today in the museum on the old Johnston Farm at Piqua, there are several prints of the actual portraits painted of various Shawnees, most of them perhaps chosen for their exotic looks. An exception is the portrait of the chief, Blackhoof, whose likeness suggests white intermarriage in the Blackhoof family. In the early 1850s, a missionary noted that the Blackhoof family looked to him to be "at least half-white, maybe more." See KHC, vol. 15, p. 184.

Eli Blackhoof, apparently another son of Blackhoof, was among the Shawnees who accompanied Chief John Perry and Capt. Joseph Parks to engage in the Seminole War.

In Kansas, the Rev. Joab Spencer performed the marriage of Thomas Blackhoof to Alice T. Albert, March 29th, 1859. See the Johnson County (Kansas) Genealogist, vol. I, #1, p. 16.

Among the Shawnees who settled on the lands of the Cherokee nation by 1869 were Eli, Thomas, Charles, Nancy, and Willis Blackhoof. See JAIFR, vol. IV, #2, pp. 100-111. John Blackhoof appears on the 1876 payroll of the Eastern Shawnees.

Some of the members of the Shawnee Blackhoof family seem to have intermarried with whites, blacks, and members of other tribes. Living amongst the Peorias and Kaskakias in 1883 were Mary Blackhoof, age 33, her son Silas Tucker, 14, and her daughter Alin Blackhoof, 5.

See KHC, index, for many other references to the

Blackhoof family.

BLANCHARD – a Shawnee name.

Francis Blanchard appears on the muster roll of the company of Shawnees led by Joseph Parks from the eastern reservation lands to Kansas in 1832. His family of five consisted of one male over 50, and four children under 10, one girl, three boys. See Roy, p. 40.

Both John and Charlie Blanchard were among the Shawnees who accompanied Capt. Joseph Parks to the Florida War.

Among the Shawnees who settled on the lands of the Cherokee nation by 1869 were Josiah Blanchard's family. See JAIFR, vol. IV, #2, pp. 100-111.

Listed on the index to 1893 Eastern Shawnee and Citizen Potawatomi Allotments are Agnus, Alice, Caleb, Claude, and Joseph Blanchard.

BLAND – a Wyandot name.

John Bland and his wife (nee Osborne) came to Nelson County, Kentucky and settled near where Bloomfield is now. In 1782, his son, Osborne Bland, and some of the other members of the family were captured at Kinchloe's Station by a mixed party of Shawnees and Wyandots. The Indians turned over the adult prisoners to the British at Detroit, but most of the children were adopted in the tribes and some later established families among them.

In 1872, one of the heirs of Silas Armstrong, a Wyandot, was "Eliza Armstrong now Mrs. Bland." See KHC, vol. 15, p. 161.

Among the Wyandots listed on the 1900 Federal Census was John Bland who was born in Kansas in 1867. He said that his father had been born in Kentucky and that his mother was a Wyandot. John Bland's wife, Lula Bland, was listed as a white woman, born 1870 in Nebraska where her mother had been born, her father having come west from Indiana. Thomas Ormsbee, John Bland's brother-in-law, lived in the household as did George Coon, a boarder who was listed as a Wyandot. See Prevost, p. 80.

BLUE JACKET – a Shawnee name.

Blue Jacket was originally two words. It became a surname and was made one word. The name Blue Jacket appeared more than once, but the most famous Shawnee going by this name, Marmaduke Van Swearingen, could hardly have been the original Blue Jacket.

Other historians have noted this. For example, Helen Hornbeck Tanner wrote that the "erroneous notion that Blue Jacket was actually a white captive named Marmaduke Van Swearingen has received wide acceptance since the 1967 publication of Allen W. Eckert's *The Frontiersman*. The identity is based on a family tradition originating in Kansas in 1877..." Tanner then notes that "Blue Jacket was a recognized chief of the Mequachake division of the Shawnee in 1772, while Marmaduke was reportedly but a youth at the time of his capture tentatively dated at 1778." See Tanner, p. 36.

She's partly right. A Shawnee named Blue Jacket was listed among the Indians by John Owens in his accounts as early as 1756, the name appearing along with Ben Dickerson, the Half King and son, and there was Bluejacket's cousin along with Blue Shadow and the Earl of Hell's brother. And the Rev. David Jones visited Blue Jacket's Town in 1772.

Sometime during the 1770s, Marmaduke Van Swearingen was captured and adopted and given the name Blue Jacket. It is said that his name was given to him due to the color of the jacket he had on at the time, but perhaps he was adopted to replace the original Blue Jacket, in which case Blue Jacket's relatives might have bestowed upon him the same name, as was commonly done.

In 1788, captive Thomas Ridout, enroute to the house of Major Snake in the company of George Ash, passed by "a fine plantation well stocked with cattle belonging to a Shawanese chief called Blue Jacket." See Ridout, p. 27.

Blue Jacket was second in command when Little Turtle engineered the red victories at Harmar's Defeat and St. Clair's Defeat. After General Anthony Wayne took over the white forces and organized the army, Little Turtle recommended reconciliation with the whites. Blue Jacket and Turkeyfoot disagreed, and Little Turtle retired from fight. Then Blue Jacket and Turkeyfoot commanded the red forces at Fallen Timbers and were defeated.

After the Treaty of Greenville, Blue Jacket traveled to the white settlements to deliver up former prisoners. See Knoft, p. 67.

Blue Jacket's first wife was a Clearwater, a half-breed daughter of Deperon Baby and his Shawnee wife. Their children included James Bluejacket, born possibly about 1790. Blue Jacket's second wife was Peggy Moore, a white daughter of the adopted Shawnee James Moore. Among Blue Jacket's other children were Joseph Bluejacket who became a sub-chief or leading warrior under Tecumseh in the War of 1812; Mary Jane Bluejacket who married the French-Canadian trader named Lacelle and later lived in Detroit; James Bluejacket (father of Rev. Charles Bluejacket for whom the town of Bluejacket, Oklahoma was named); and Nancy Bluejacket who married James Stewart and had four children including Joseph Stewart (see MMV, p. 177).

Among the Shawnees given tracts of land in Ohio by the 1817 Treaty of the Miami of Like Erie was Thucuscu or Jim Bluejacket. See Harvey, p. 168.

The muster roll of the Shawnees brought from the Ohio Hog Creek and Wapakonetta bands included the Henry Bluejacket family of seven and the James Bluejacket family of four. See Roy, p. 43.

Among the Shawnees who fought against the Seminoles in the Florida War were Henry, George, and Jim Bluejacket.

Charles Bluejacket, son of James Bluejacket, was born on the Huron River in Michigan around 1816. The family moved in 1822 to Piqua Plains, Ohio. Charles attended a mission school near Fort Meigs (south of Toledo, Ohio) and was again versed in theology by missionaries such as Johnston Lykins upon coming west with the Wapakoneta or Hog Creek bands.

A James Bluejacket appears to have married a Wyandot and lived with his wife's people for some time. On the 1843 Muster Roll of Wyandots from Sandusky is James Blue Jacket's family, consisting of one male and one female 10 to 25, and one female under 10.

The Rev. Charles Bluejacket married Pa-wa-see in 1833. Among others, their children included Robert Bluejacket, born in 1840 and shot to death by William Fish in 1858 in Johnson County, Kansas.

After Pa-wa-see died in 1841, Charles married Julie Ann Daugherty, a member of the Louis P. Daugherty family. The children of this marriage included Sally, born 1844, who married Jonathan Gore; David, born 1846; Price, born 1854; Willis, born 1860; Julia Ann, born 1863; and Richard, born 1866, died 1885.

Charles Bluejacket's extended family seems to have included Amanda, Mary B., Sally, Lucinda, Cora B., and sons David L., Henry C., Lewis, Price K., Richard M., Silas D., and Willis Bluejacket.

Besides the Rev. Charles Bluejacket, James Bluejacket's family included daughter Nancy and sons

Henry and George Bluejacket.

Attending the Ft. Leavenworth Shawnee School in 1847-49 were the Shawnees Robert, Stephen, and Thomas Bluejacket.

Among the Shawnees who settled on the lands of the Cherokee nation by 1869 were Charles, Louisa, Price, Willis, Silas, Henry, Richard M., David, Eliza, Rosella, Katherine, Sally Martin, Joesph, Emma, Sally ("F. E. Bailey's divorced widow"), Stephen, Emily, Francis, Ella, Eddy, Mary, George, Sophia, Monroe, Thomas, Josephine, Willie, Sarah, Issac, Jane, Julia, and Ida — all members of the Bluejacket family. See JAIFR, vol. IV, #2, pp. 100-111.

Twenty-four members of the Bluejacket family of all ages are listed among the Shawnees on the 1880 Cherokee Nation Census. See JAIFR, vol X, #1, p. 40

Dennis W. Bluejacket was among the Shawnees who fought for America during World War II. He was killed in Europe. See JAIFR, vol XI, #1, p. 28.

BOB, BOBB – a Shawnee/Delaware name.

John Bobb (Black Bobb) was a Shawnee village chief.

By the treaty of 1854, the Shawnee Nation ceded to the United States 1,400,000 acres of their 1,600,000 acre Kansas reserve. Their remaining 200,000 acre tract was to be allotted out to them individually, 200 acres per person. This was better for the white-styled capitalists among them, most of whom were part-white or married to whites. But the traditionalists (and those who feared for the existence of the Shawnee Nation), wanted the lands held in common. Two Shawnee settlements — Black Bob's and Long Tail's — elected to hold their lands in common and communual assignments of 200 acres per person were provided to them. The eight Shawnee leaders who signed this treaty were Joseph Parks, Black Hoof, George McDougal, Long

Tail, George Bluejacket, Graham Rogers, Black Bob (Wa-wah-che-pa-e-kar), and Henry Bluejacket. Charles Bluejacket was listed as interpreter. See Barry, pp. 1212-1213.

Many dark-skinned tradtionalists associated especially with the Black Bobb band. During the Civil War, they were harassed by Quantrell and his outlaws. After the war, they were flatly opposed to giving up their tribal identity to join the Cherokee nation. A letter of protest, dated October, 1868, said: "We the members of the Black Bobb tribe of the Shawnees protest Agents Taylor and Abbot who are trying to break up our reservation....We seek protection for our families and for our lands." This letter was signed by the members of the band who included Black Bob, Big Fox. Hiram Fox, the heirs of John Fox, Joseph Blackfeather, Johnson Blackfeather, the heirs of Louis Coffee, Martha McLane and others. See Audrey Wagner,"The Black Bob Indian Lands," in The Johnson County Genealogist, vol. I, #3, 1973, pp. 67-72.

Among the Shawnees who settled on the lands of the Cherokee nation by 1869 were James, Sally, Jane, and George Bobb. Mrs. Jim Bobb is listed on the 1876 Eastern Shawnee payroll. See JAIFR, vol. IV, #2, pp. 100-111.

For Black Bobb or Jim Bobb, the Shawnee chief, see KHC, vol. 16, p. 763; village of, noted, KHC, vol. 8, pp. 93, 94, 96; c10, 391.

Some of the Bobb family crossed over to the Absentee Shawnee band and to the more traditional Delawares. Chief Jim Bobb succeeded Bill Thomas as the Delaware chief of what was basically Black Beaver's band of dark-skinned Delaware traditionialists at Anadarko. A picture of this Jim Bobb, from 1898, is to be found in Weslager's *The Delaware Indians*, p. 434.

BOMBERRY, BUMBERRY – a Wyandot/Seneca name.

Listed on the 1843 Muster Roll of the Sandusky Wyandots was Thomas Bumberry's family, consisting of one male 25 to 55, two males and one female 10 to 25, and one male under 10.

Listed on the 1894 Seneca Census of the Quapaw Agency are Joseph Bomberry, 60; his wife Eliza, 43; his daughters Betsy, 17, and Julia, 15; and his sons Christy, 12, and Louis, 7.

BOONE – a Shawnee/Wyandot/Cherokee name.

Are there people around today who have Shawnee blood and also descend from Daniel Boone? Well, there are certainly people who share that tradition.

Daniel Boone was captured by Shawnees twice. The first time he was captured by Will Emery (Captain Will) who took his furs and sent him home with a warning not to trespass on the Shawnee hunting grounds again.

The second time Boone was captured, he was adopted as a son by Blackfish and given the Shawnee name, Sheltowee (Big Turtle). Boone blended in well with his Indian family, and late in his life he felt secure enough among his white family to speak honestly of the pleasant side of his Shawnee experience.

He spoke of Blackfish as "one of Nature's noblemen," and was particularly attached to two of Blackfish's little daughters, to whom Boone sometimes gave presents. Many years later, in Kansas, one of Boone's granddaughters met one of Blackfish's daughters, then an elderly woman, who remembered Boone from long ago and showered her with affection.

In the best and most recent (1992) biography of Daniel Boone, John Mack Faragher noted that "Some biographers have fixed on vague suggestions in the evidence that Boone may have lived with a Shawnee woman at Chillicothe. `I have been obliged to be married in Indian fashion a couple of times,' a friend quoted him as admitting to Rebecca."

Well, if he did, who can blame him? Boone was among the Shawnees for a couple of years, and Shawnee women found him attractive. Back at Boonesboro, his wife gave him up for dead and married one of his brothers. When Daniel Boone returned to Boonesboro and found that his wife was pregnant, he simply shrugged, saying that at least it was all in the family. See Mastin, p. 119, n. 53. An easy-going nature, an adjustable mind, was Boone's greatest asset.

Later in life, the Shawnees were Boone's "second family," as Faragher points out.

In Missouri, Daniel Boone "encountered a number of friends from his days as a captive, Delawares and Shawnees from the town of Chillicothe on the Little Miami who had emigrated during the 1780s, including a number of former American captives who had chosen to remain and had raised Indian families, like Joseph Jackson, a former salt maker, Charles `Indian' Phillips, and Jimmy Rogers, now the village chief." After moving from Kentucky to Missouri, Boone once again found himself surrounded "by farming people who loved horses and hunting...."

Boone often visited the Shawnees at their village which was not far away, sometimes going on short hunts with them. "One day, before the war, one of Boone's granddaughters, seeing strange horses tied up before the house, asked Rebecca who had come. Boone's grandchildren remembered when the Shawnees would come to visit, seeing the horses tied up outside. 'Who is here,' Rebecca was asked. 'Your grandfather has got some visitors, old friends,' she said, 'some of the identical old Shawnees with whom he was a prisoner.' Sometimes, after they had been on a hunt, they would stay up late, talking in the light of a campfire built outside the cabin. One of Boone's grandsons remembered listening to the Shawnee men tell the same stories that Daniel told, only reflecting their own distinctive point of view. 'Dan, you remember when...our chief adopted you as his son, and you and he made an agreement that we would all go to Boonsboro, and you would make them all surrender, and, all bury the tomahawk and all live like brothers and sisters...then you remember we were all glad." Ferragher says, "There is no mention of Boone dissenting from this version." See Faragher, pp. 170, 300, 313-314.

As with Simon Kenton's sons, the several descendants of Daniel Boone's sons and grandsons associated with Native American tribes either as traders or agents.

On the 1882 Census Roll of Eastern Shawnees is the household of Na-co-quas Parks, 45, with her daughters Delia Thomas, 5, and Fannie Boone, 20. Listed as Na-co-quas grandchildren were George Boone, 1 1/2, and Josephine Boone, 6 months. Of course, maybe these were part of the Bone family or maybe the Shawnee Bone family and the Shawnee Boone family were the same family.

There are undoubtedly answers around, but so little has been written about Indian blood that answers are still hard to find sometimes. On the Eastern Cherokee Roll #2803 is listed Betsie H. Boone, of East Chattanooga, Tenn., the daughter of Mary Hildabrand and the grandaughter of John W. Hildabrand. William H. Boone married a Constance who may have had Indian blood. Of course, some of the Indians may have taken Boone's name as a badge of honor. (If someone has discovered the source of this tradition, please drop me a line.)

The 1914 Wyandot heirship card #267 contains details of the estate of Alice R. Boone nee Walker. A

Wyandot and the wife of W. J. Boone, her heirs included sons Octavius Boone of Julia, Oklahoma and Walker Boone; daughters Alice R. Clark nee Boone of Albeq., New Mexico, Charlotte Boone of Seneca, Missouri, and Ceale Boone.

BOOTH– -a Shawnee name.

Among the Shawnees who settled on the lands of the Cherokee nation by 1869 were Eliza and Franklin Booth. See JAIFR, vol. IV, #2, pp. 100-111.

Frank Booth, age 19, was listed among the Shawnees on the 1880 Cherokee Nation Census. See JAIFR, vol X, #1, p. 40

The Frank Booth listed as a Shawnee on the 1900 Federal Census said that he was born in 1861 in Kansas. His father had been born in Virginia, his mother and father both members of the Shawnee Nation. His wife, Melissa Booth, was listed as a white woman whose father was from Georgia and whose mother was born in Tennessee. Melissa Booth herself was born in Missouri. See Prevost, p. 68.

BOSHMAN or BUSHMAN – a Potawatomi/ Shawnee name.

John Bushman was "a well-known Delaware" guide and hunter, but I suspect that this was yet another case of a Potawatomi being identified as a Delaware and not minding. The Delaware hunters far outnumbered the Shawnees, Potawatomi, and Wyandots who rode among them, and they were often confused for one another.

About the year 1824, Mackinaw Beauchemie [Buschman], an adopted Potawatomi, married the Shawnee Polly Rogers, daughter of Henry Rogers, a son-in-law of Blackfish. Their children included Annie (who married N. T. Shaler) and Julia Ann (who married Thomas Nesbit Stinson), Alexander, William, and

Martha Boshman and possibly others. The Louisa Bushman who married the Shawnee Jacob Turkeyfoot seems to have been part of the family.

John, Alexander, or Mackinaw Boshman may have been the Bossman whose name is attached to the Potawatomi Treaty of 1846 at Potawatomi Creek near the Osage River. The name may also have appeared as Beauchamp, depending upon the ears of the court clerk.

John Bushman served as guide to Captain R. B. Marcy on an expedition to the Red River in 1852. Marcy considered him dignified, reserved, taciturn, self-reliant, and fearless. In 1853, Lt. Whipple endeavored to enlist him as a guide through Commanche territory, but like Jesse Chisholm and Black Beaver, Bushman declined, as the Commanches would scorch the earth behind them, the scouts said. Balduin Mollhausen wrote that Bushman visited the Whipple expedition at Old Camp Arbuckle on August 19, 1953, accompanied by his young son and "a beautiful squaw."

See Mollhausen, Diary, I, p. 95; Whipple, Report, Aug. 18, 19, 1853; Holton, Beyond the Cross Timbers, p. 126; Gordon, p. 240. Through Indian Country to California, John P. Sherburne's Diary of the Whipple Expedition 1853-1854, ed. by Mary McDougall Gordon, Standford, California, 1988.

Alexander Boshman is among the Wyandots and Shawnees allotted land in Kansas. See KHC, vol. 15, p. 175.

BOWMAN, BAUGHMAN, or BOUGHMAN – a Shawnee name.

Issac Bowman's story, as given in a narrative to his grandchildren, is that he was taken prisoner while serving as a lieutenant and quartermaster under George Rogers Clark in November, 1779. At one time, the Indians buried him up to his armpits, as punishment for his trying to escape. But the chief of the Chickasaws became fond of him, and gave him one of his daughters for a wife.

"...The squaw was very pretty and the two of them got along very well together until one day when eating from the same vessel, grandpa took too large a share of the bear's oil, whereupon the squaw slapped him and he slapped her back, with the old chief's consent...and grandpa very soon ran away...."

He was caught and about to be killed, when purchased by the Indian trader John Turnbull for a keg of rum. Turnbull gave him passage to New Orleans, then to Cuba, then back to Kentucky. See Draper mss. 27J95-97.

Back in Kentucky, Isaac Bowman was one of George Rogers Clark's men who served at Ft. Jefferson, where many of the men are said to have had Indian wives.

There were others of Isaac Bowman's family among the Indians. In 1756, Christian Bowman and his oldest son, John, were captured and taken to a Mingo town on the Ohio. The Mingoes sold Christian Bowman to a Shawnee squaw by whom he had three children, a son and two daughters. According to Glen Lough, the Shawnee son was named Neshwa-Neshwa, Two Goose; his father called him Billy.

In 1767, Christian Bowman returned to live among the whites. *The Pennsylvania Gazette* published a narrative of his life among the Indians which is contained in Draper mss. volume JJ and is republished in Glenn Lough's Now and Long Ago, p. 45. Bowman said that "there are about 200 white people living among the Indians at the Mingo, Shawnee, and Delaware camps who have been long among them...few of them are inclined to come away."

Among the Shawnees who settled on the lands of the Cherokee nation by 1869 were William and Mary

Boughman. See JAIFR, vol. IV, #2, pp. 100-111.

BOYER, BOWYER, or BOUYER – a Delaware/ Wyandot name.

A family of Boyers was captured during the French and Indian Wars.

One of the family, Margaret Boyer, was raised as a Shawnee and became the wife of white Indian trader, Richard Conner. Their children mixed with white and red. Two of their sons, John and William Conner, operated trading posts on White River in Indiana territory and had Delaware wives. See Gilbert, p. 193.

Among the Sandusky Wyandots on the 1843 Muster Roll was Bowyer, a male over 55 years of age.

BOYD – a common name of those with Indian blood traditions.

Rhoda Boyd was among the prisoners delivered up to Bouquet in 1764. On the march home, she escaped and made it back to her Indian family. See Gilbert, p. 81. Boyd became a surname among the Wyandots and Potawatomis.

Washington Boyd was a Wyandot to whom land in Kansas was allotted in 1855. See KHC, vol. 15, p. 172.

BOYLE – a Shawnee name.

Five children of Charles Boyle were taken prisoner by Delawares and Shawnees on Jackson's River in 1757.

John Boyle was an Indian trader at Ft. Pitt in the 1760s. In 1775, a John Boyle was at Boonesboro.

Among the Shawnee marriages solemnized in Kansas in 1856 were that of the John Boyle to Polly Captain and that of another John Boyle to Caty Short.

Among the Shawnees who settled on the lands of the Cherokee nation by 1869 were John, Amanda, Margaret, Hugh, Willie, and James H. Boyle. See JAIFR, vol. IV, #2, pp. 100-111.

BRANT, BRANDT – a Mohawk name.

Tehowaghwengaraghkin, a Mohawk of the wolf clan, was one of the Indian chiefs who visited England in 1710. One of his sons was named Aroghyadagha, who represented his tribe at the Treaty of Forty Stanwix in 1768. He had several children, among whom were Joseph and Molly Brandt.

Molly Brandt became the wife of SWJ, English Superintendent of Indian Affairs in America. Johnson was the one most influential forces among the Indians for many years.

Joseph Brant or Thayendanegea, was born about 1742 on the banks of the Ohio River. He made his first appearance as a warrior in the Niagara campaign which was led by Sir William Johnson in 1759. In 1763, Brant participated in the war against Pontiac. In 1771, Johnson sent him to Connecticut to attend Dr. Wheelock's Indian School at Hanover.

At the outbreak of the Revolution, Brant was serving as secretary to Guy Johnson, and like Johnson, he chose to remain loyal to the Crown. He went to England, and upon his return he was employed in predatory raids against the colonies. He is supposed to have been a major factor in many of the major engagements of the day, including the siege of Ft. Stanwix, the Battle of Oriskany, the Cherry Valley and Wyoming raids, Lochry's Defeat, the Long Run Massacre (sometimes called Squire Boone's Defeat), and Floyd's Defeat.

Joseph Brant held a colonel's commission from the King, and after the war, he remained a major factor in the Indian department in Canada. In 1786, he again visited England where he was honored. He returned to build an Indian church in Upper Canada and to translate the Gospel of St. Mark into the Mohawk language. He died at Wellington Square in Upper Canada, October

24, 1807.

Joseph Brant married three times, the first two times to sisters, daughters of an Oneida chief. His first wife's name was Margaret, who died in 1771. Their children included Isaac Brant, who was well-educated but developed a drinking habit. He quarreled with his father in 1795, receiving a wound which led to his tragic death. Isaac Brant left a widow and two children including (1) Isaac, jr. who served with distinction in the War of 1812 but was killed in a drunken brawl, and (2) Christina Brant, who married a Frenchman who was killed toward the turn of the century on the Wabash River.

Joseph Brant married secondly to Susanna, a half-sister to Margaret. She died shortly after the marriage, in the early 1770s.

Joseph Brant married thirdly to Catherine, sister to his first wife and the eldest living daughter of the head chief of the turtle clan of the Mohawk nation. Their children were:

1. Joseph Brant, Jr., born 1783, educated at Dartmouth College. He married and his daughter, Catherine, married the Mohawk, Arron Hill. Joseph Brant, Jr. died in 1830.
2. Jacob Brant, also educated at Dartmouth, married and his children included John; Squire; Christina who married John Jones; Jacob, Jr., who married Mary Jones; Peter; and Charlotte who married Peter Smith.
3. John Brant (Ahyouwaeghs), was born at the Mohawk village on Grand River in 1794. Well educated and well read, he cultivated the manners of an English gentleman.

   He participated in the War of 1812, but settled down again after the war into the life of a refined gentleman, noted for his hospitality. He visited England in 1821 to appeal to the Crown for his people. Upon his return, he became a politician and the leader of the Iroquois Nations.

4. Margaret Brant, who married a Mr. Powles and left children.
5. Catherine Brant who married Peter John.
6. Mary Brant who married Seth Hill and left at least one child.
7. Elizabeth Brant who married William Johnson Kerr, a son of Dr. Robert Kerr. According to one source, Dr. Kerr's wife was Mary Brant Johnson, a daughter of SWJ. The Kerrs had four children.

Joseph Brant's last marriage was to a daughter of Col. George Croghan, the Indian trader. See Engle's Notes and Queries, p. 491-493.

Among those paid for the improvements on their Ohio lands that they were forced to abandon by the 1831 treaty were the Senecas and Seneca/Shawnees Joe Brant, Joe Brant's wife, Jacob Brandt, Powhis Brandt, Powles Brandt, and Thomas Brandt. See Watson, Vol. V, pt. 3, pp. 11-14.

The Brant family intermarried with whites, blacks, and other tribes and became a principal family in many communities. John Anthony Brant signed the 1832 Treaty with the Stockbridge (Mohiccan), Munsee (Delaware), and Brothertown tribes on behalf of the Six Nations (Iroquois) and St. Regis Indians. See Watson, pt. 13, p. 73.

BRASHEAR(S)–a Choctaw/Creek/Chickasaw name.

Benjamin Brashear took his family from Maryland to western Pennsylvania about 1780. In 1779, they traveled by flat boat and settled in what is now Bullitt County, Kentucky. Some stayed behind, but most moved again down the river to Ft. Jefferson and to Illinois. They were one of the first families to abandon

Ft. Jefferson due to the harsh conditions there, and they traveled by flatboat down the river to the Natchez area.

One of Benjamin's sons, Capt. Richard Brashear, became one of George Rogers Clark's officers and served at Ft. Jefferson, although he was not there during the battle. Another son, Marsham Brashears, became one of the original trustees of Louisville.

And another son of Benjamin Brashears, Turner Brashears, may have been one of those captured in the Ft. Jefferson area. Adopted or not, Turner Brashears married a Choctaw woman, and became a trader in the Choctaw Nation. For the next three decades, he appears often in the records as a guide, trader, interpreter, and inn-keeper.

Turner Brashears advertised in the *Natchez Gazette* on December 2, 1806 that he had established "a House of Entertainment on the road leading from Natchez to Nashville." Rev. Jacob Young, a Methodist itinerant preacher, stopped there in 1807 and said of his host, "Although he had an Indian wife, he himself was a gentleman. He had a good many colored people and appeared to be a man of considerable wealth. He treated us well but knew how to make a high bill."

Turner Brashear's many children included Robert Turner Brashear who married Nancy Vaughn, Benjamin Brashear, and Lewis Brashear. Also among the Indians in Mississippi in 1831 were Alexander Brashears, a half-blood Creek, with six children under 10, and three over 10, living on Suckenacha Creek; half-breed Zadock Brashears, with two children under 10, one over 10;; and half-breed Turner Brashears, jr. Also listed is half-breed Rachel Brashears and her child; and Deleley (Delila) Brashears and her six children, half of whom were under ten years of age. Most of these last named Brashears lived on the Tombigbee River. See MGE, vol 18, p. 11-13.

Among the Choctaws given land by the Treaty of Dancing Rabbit Creek in 1830 were Vaughn and Turner Brashears.

BRIGHTHORN – a Shawnee name.

The Shawnee Moses Silverheels told Draper in 1868 that Brighthorn had been a chief, that he had died while still in Ohio, about 1827 or 1828. See Draper 23S165.

John Brighthorn appears on the muster roll of the company of Shawnees that Joseph Parks led from the eastern reservation lands to Kansas in 1832. His family of four consisted of one male over 25 and under 50, one female over 10 and under 25, and two children under 10, one boy, one girl. See Roy, p 38.

BRITIAN, BRITTIAN or BRITTON – a Miami/Shawnee/Delaware name.

Mary Britton was registered as a Delaware in 1867. She was on the 1880 roll as Mrs. C. E. Elkhair, apparently having married into the family of Chief Elkhair. See Prevost, p. 32.

Among the Shawnees who settled on the lands of the Cherokee nation by 1869 were Frederick, Mary, William, Caroline, Randolph, and John Britton. See JAIFR, vol. IV, #2, pp. 100-111.

BROUILLETTE, BRUET, or BRUETTE – a Miami name.

A French half-breed doctor named Michael Brouett (or Brouillette) married a white woman who had been captured, adopted, and raised by the Indians. They lived in Indiana territory opposite The Owl's Town, about 12 miles north of present-day Indianapolis. Most of their children married Miamis and part-Miamis. See Thompson, pp. 204-205. The doctor died in 1801, but among his children was Michael Brouillette,

Jr., who served as an interpreter and spy for General William Henry Harrison during the War of 1812.

Among the Indians on the payroll of the Miamis in 1831 appearing in the Tipton papers was J. B. Bruette, who represented nine members of the tribe at the Mississineway.

Like the Richardvilles, who were closely allied to this family, the Brouillette descendants can be easily traced through the Indiana county records. In Knox County, they intermarried with the Bernard, Sprinkle, and Somes families, among others.

BROWN – a common name among various tribes.

Adam Brown was an Indian trader with a Wyandot wife. He was at Detroit during Pontiac's War. He served from time to time in the British interest at Brownstown and Malden.

Listed on the 1843 Muster Roll of Wyandots from Sandusky, Ohio, were:

1. Adam Brown's family, consisting of one male and one female 25 to 55, three males and one female 10 to 25, and two males and four females under 10.
2. John D. Brown's family, consisting of one male over 25, one female over 25, one female between 10 and 25, and two boys under 10.

Among the Shawnees and Wyandots allotted land in Kansas were Theressa and Thompson Brown. See Kansas Historical Collections, vol. 15, p. 174.

Among the Shawnees who settled on the lands of the Cherokee nation by 1869 were Thenesson, Thompson, Matthew, Elinora, Elizabeth, Margaret, John D., Mary E., and Alphens Brown. See JAIFR, vol. IV, #2, pp. 100-111.

Among the Wyandot cases heard in 1871 by Ely Parker, Commissioner of Indian Affairs, was the case of Isaac W. Brown, who was then dead. Brown had been the guardian for Joseph Arms (killed in the Battle of Wilson's Creek), Daniel Williams, Susan Hill, and William Blacksheep. Blacksheep had gone to New Mexico. Also heard was the case of John D. Brown whose wards included Amos Peacock and Stookey (who had four grandchildren). See JAIFR, vol. VIII, #2, p. 19, 21.

Dick Brown was a Delaware scout who accompanied the Beale expedition. He was a remarkable man, a master tracker and hunter. See Hafen, The Far West and Rockies Series, vol. 7.pp. 58-158.

After the outbreak of the Creek War in 1813, Major John H. Gibson was sent into Creek territory to scout out the movements of the hostile forces. His own forces split up, "Major Gibson to visit a friendly Cherokee, Dick Brown (who was to become a colonel in the liaison forces and to fight alongside Jackson's men), and [Davy] Crockett to visit Dick's father..." See Shackford, p. 21.

BUCK – a Shawnee/Delaware name.

A common name, sometimes short for Spybuck or Killbuck. Among the Shawnees who settled on the lands of the Cherokee nation by 1869 was Josephine Buck. See JAIFR, vol. IV, #2, pp. 100-111.

BULLITT, BULLET, or BULLETTE – a Delaware name.

A John Bullitt was among the Indians and adopted whites dealt with by the Ohio Company traders as early as 1756.

A John Bullet is listed among the Indians in the SWJ Papers (1763) along with John Champion, The White Mingo, Jacob Daniel and King Shingess.

Captain Bullet, a Delaware, took Gorsham Hicks from the Shawnees and sent him to White Eyes during Pontiac's War. White Eyes was already protecting

John Gibson and one Morris, and they are mentioned in Hicks' deposition. See Michigan Pioneer and Historical Collections, vol. 19, pp. 352-355.

Captain Bullet (Missenewand), a Delaware, signed the treaty at Vincennes, Indiana in 1805 which ceded a part of the Delaware, Miami, and Potawatomi land. See Valley and Lembcke, p. 270.

In 1826, in the midst of a Delaware/Osage War, an Osage war party killed George Bullet along with George White Eyes and some other young Delaware free hunters. See Weslager, p. 365.

A Bullit was one of the six Delaware scouts under Capt. Fall Leaf on the Kiowa and Commanche Campaign of 1860 along with Sarcoxie, Bascom, Wilson, and John Williams. See KHQ, vol. 23, p. 395.

Eliza Conner, part-Delaware daughter of William Connor and his wife, Me-king-ess, who was a daughter of half-breed William Anderson, married George Bullette for her third husband. George Bullette was half-white, but was an older captain, having been "among the Delawares who helped the Cherokees in the battle at Claremore Mound in 1818. He also had gone to Mexico in 1839." Sometime after that, he married Eliza Conner Halfmoon Wilson and took her children by her former marriages into his home. Eliza's children by George Bullette included:

1. Simon Bullette who married Saphroni Rogers and had at least one son named Frank Bullette. Frank had two daughters, Lillie Maudie and Sanoma. Lillie married into the Pittsenbarger family.
2. John Bullette who married a white girl, Nellie Helen Conkle, and their children included Mable Zoe Bullette who married Dr. Franklin Duckworth; John Bullette, jr.; George Cleveland Bullette; Mary R. (Nina) Bullette who married Walter Shaw; and Floyd C. Bullette.

John Bullette himself was "assassinated" in Claremore, Oklahoma, in 1909.

3. George Bullette, Jr., who was born in 1853 just before his father died. He married first Eliza Edgar, and they had a son, also named George Bullette. He then married a white girl, Betty Payne, and their children included Alice, John Edward, Nellie Frankie, Laura, Jesse Edith, and George Pocahontas Bullette. This family intermarried with the Baldwin, Johnson, and Morris families.

Also a "Capt. Bullet's son," Joseph Stitler Bullette (We-wa-wah-kee-numd), married Jane Sarcoxie, a daughter of Chief Sarcoxie and his first wife. Joseph and Jane Bullette moved to a place northeast of Lawrence, Kansas, and they had at least two children.

One son of Joseph Stitler Bullette, Baston Bullette, later came to Indian Territory and became a leader in the Big House ceremony of the Delawares. He died in 1886. Baston had married an Edgar and their children included Jane Dora Bullette, Minnie Bullette (who married 1st William Longbone and 2nd Julius Fouts), and George H. Bullette (who married 1st Rosa Big John and 2nd Kate Brown).

For a more elaborate account of this Bullette family including the dates and the names of those who intermarried (the Anderson, Elkhair, and Davis families, among many others), see Ruby Cranor's magnificent book on Chief William Anderson and his descendants.

George (age 20), Henry (age 6), Jane (age 5 months), John (age 26), Mary (age 9) were all members of the Bullet family, Delawares on the 1880 Cherokee Nation Census. A Mrs. Bullett (age 18) is also listed. See JAIFR, vol X, #1, p. 49.

Julia Wise (Julia Bullet), Mary Bullit (Mary Halleck), John Sr., Nancy Louisa, William, Amanda, and Simon Bullit are all on the non-dated list of Delawares appearing in JAIFR, vol. VI, #1, pp. 41-51.

BUNDY, BONDIE, BUNDAY, or BONDY – a Miami name.

There is an Indian blood tradition among the Bundy family. Many of the Bundys in the early records of Kentucky and Indiana appear to have been part-Indian, including Sophia Bundy who married Robert Kelly in Clark County, Indiana in 1834, and the Catherine Bundy who married John P. Clark, "persons of color." These individuals may trace to Antoine Bondy, who had a wife among the Miamis. Bondy was at the Ft. Wayne agency, serving as an interpreter, in 1814. See Indiana Historical Collections, The Ft. Wayne Indian Agency, p. 178, 215.

Ross Bundy, age 82, died at Marion, Indiana, on January 2nd, 1963. He could speak the Miami language, one of the few around with that ability. He normally spoke English, but spoke Miami with other Miamis and to his dogs and cats. Those who knew him spoke highly of his Indian lore as a fisherman, hunter and woodsman.

Ross Bundy was the son of John Bundy (Won-con or Foggy Morning) and his wife Nancy Brouilette Bundy (Az-noc-sim-quah or Prairie Fire). Nancy's grandfather, Jean Baptiste Brouilette or Te-qua-ke-aw) was a doctor, dealing with both white-styled medicine and Indian herbs. Nancy's other grandfather was Peter Bundy, a preacher among the Miami Nation.

Francis Slocum, the great-great grandmother of Ross Bundy, lived with the Miami chief, She-poc-a-nah, the Deaf Man. She had been captured and adopted by Delawares when young, but she stayed with her Miami husband willingly. She was the first lady of their village, Deaf Man's Town, consisting of seven or eight log houses on the south bank of the Mississinewa River about eight miles east of the present city of Peru, Indiana.

See E. Wendell Lamb and Lawrence W. Shultz, *Indian Lore*, pp. 112-115.

BURK, BURKS – a Delaware/Shawnee name.

The Burks name is, of course, a major source of the Indian blood tradition. One major reason is that Thomas Hughes married Niketti, Powhattan's granddaughter, and one of their daughters, Elizabeth, married Nathaniel Davis, and one of their daughters, Mary, married Samuel Burks.

John Burks was a member of Capt. George Owens Company at Ft. Jefferson. At one time he was an Indian trader himself, and he may have been kin to Lawrence and Thomas Burks, two of the older Indian traders.

Lawrence Burks, employee of Indian trader John Martin, had a reputation as "an infamous rogue." He was a scout for General Bouquet in Pontiacs War, but he preferred to live among the Delawares with whom he had a wife.

Thomas Burks was taken prisoner by French and Wyandots at the mouth of the Scioto River. He had been enroute to trade with the Shawnees, among whom he had friends. Burks was taken to France as a prisoner, but later returned, and it may have been this Thomas Burks who was awarded 400 acres by the Jefferson County Court in 1782.

There was a Mary Burks who married Indian trader John Meranda in 1760. Among the whites forcibly delivered up to General Bouquet in 1764 at the end of Pontiac's War was Mary Burks, who had two children with her.

BURNEY – a Chickasaw name.

Thomas Burney, captured and adopted, did blacksmith work while living among the Senecas and Shawnees. He took a message from the Half King (Tanacharisson) to Governor Dinwiddie in 1853, warning of the French danger. See Hanna, p. 368. Some time later, Burney was reported to have been killed (see Gist's Journal). He appears to have been on the English side at Ft. Necessity.

Simon Burney was a guide for Capt. James Willing (along with George Girty, John Ash, Robert George, and a few other rough men) on his expedition down the Mississippi.

In August of 1782, Simon Burney came to Louisville (Ft. Nelson) along with two Chickasaw warriors, seeking to make a peace between the Chickasaw and the Americans. See COVSP, vol. III, p. 282, 298. Simon Burney married Peggy Colbert and their descendants made the Burney name prominent among the Chickasaws.

BURNETT, BURNET – a Potawatomi/Shawnee/ Wyandot name.

"Half-bloods" James, John, Isaac, Jacob, Abraham, Nancy, and Rebecca Burnet were allotted land in Indiana on the lower side of Tippecanoe on the Wabash. See *Public Advertiser*, Louisville, Kentucky, Oct. 20, 1818, copy on microfilm at the Louisville Free Public Library.

Abram and John Burnett were Potawatomi students at the Kentucky Choctaw Academy in 1830. See Foreman, p. 473.

Nancy Davis as heir of Jacob Burnett attempted to sell land to John Shawn in Indiana in 1832. As this was part of the reserve, the sale was disapproved. See Tipton Papers, p. 656.

Listed on the 1843 Muster Roll of Wyandots from Sandusky was Widow Burnett's household, consisting of one female between 25 and 55, two females and one male between 10 and 25, and two male children under 10.

Andson and Henry Burnett were among the

Shawnees on the 1880 Cherokee Nation Census. See JAIFR, vol X, #1, p. 49.

BURT, DEBURT, DEBOLT, DUBERT, or DIBERT

– a Shawnee name.

John Burt was a Pennsylvania Indian trader as early as 1723. In 1728, he lived at Snaketown, forty miles above Conestoga on the east side of the Susquehanna. See Hanna, I, chapter 5; II, p. 328; Engle's Notes and Queries, I, pp. 10, 19, 41, 70; Pennsylvania Colonial Records, pp. 301, 344.

John Burt or de-Burt married Mary Chartier Seaworth, a daughter of Martin Chartier and his Shawnee wife. The name became Dibert in the Bedford County, Pennsylvania records. The large family was attacked on the Pennsylvania frontier in 1732 and seven out of twelve children were killed. Five escaped, however, and Charles Christopher Dibert was one of these and his son Michael took out a land warrant for him in Bedford County in 1766.

Christopher Dibert and his wife, Eve Elizabeth Dibert, had a family including sons Michael and Adam and three other children. Christopher was killed by Indians in 1757. Some members of the family went to Virginia while some others continued to live in the county. They appear in Bedford County, Deed Book A. See *Bedford County: The Kernal of Greatness*, a publication of the Bedford County Heritage Commission, pp. 14-15.

John Crawford, nephew of the Arthur Crawford who was one of White Eyes adopted sons, wrote of his uncle's mode of hunting which was to deceive the deer so that it would come close to the hunter. He wrote, "This mode of hunting has been laid aside before my time, or at least I have not seen it put in practice, but I am told that a Michael Debolt that lived about five miles from my father's when I was a child did practice it. He had been a long time prisoner among the Indians. I think when the Indians used nothing but bows and arrows, this mode [of hunting] would be very important." See Lobdell, *Indian Warfare...*, p. 32.

It seems that Michael Debolt, the great-grandson of Martin Chartier and his Shawnee wife, died in Fayette County, Pennsylvania. His will was filed in 1784. His children included George, Catherine, Michael, Michlin, and Mary. A George Debolt died in Fayette County in 1829, and his will mentions his wife, Elizabeth (Teagarden), and children Teagarden Solomon, William, David, Daniel, Abraham, Elizabeth (Lowry), Rezin, and Jacob Debolt. A George Debolt bought land from Michael Debolt (wife Apolonia) there in 1799.

Also the George Debolt of Greene County, Pennsylvania, was apparently of the same family. This man married Ann Long, the daughter of John Long. The children of George and Ann (Long) Debolt included: Noah, Jacob, Jeremiah, George, Elizabeth (m. Amos Herrington), Charity (m. Nathan Thompson), Priscilla (m. Morgan Herrington), Rhoda (m. Ezekiel Calvert), Harriet (m. John Herrington), Mary (m. Teagarden Solomon Debolt of Fayette County, apparently her cousin), Catherine (m. Patrick Baily), Martha (m. Francis Hupp), and Sarah (m. John McFarland).

Further generations of this family married into the Knotts, Mesterzat, Bare, McCurdy, Lynn, Bayard, Whitlatch, Riggle, and Sherich familes, taking the Shawnee blood tradition along. See Leckey, pp. 621-622.

BUTLER – A Shawnee name.

There were Indian traders named Butler on the frontier very early in colonial history. James and Thomas Butler were both Indian traders in 1747. See Hanna, II, p. 328. Thomas Butler had two sons, Richard and William, who also became Indian traders. Listed among the Indians in the Ohio Company Papers of the 1760s were Indian Butler, John Butler and "Betty's Son Will." It was "well known that General Butler had an Indian wife named Betty" at the time, according to Rev. James B. Finney.

John Butler, or Col. or Gen. John Butler as he became known, was an Indian trader associated with Sir William Johnson in New York and Pennsylvania. John Butler (Sugantah or the Lodging Tree) married a Seneca and raised an Indian family. When James Smith was taken captive by the Senecas, he was adopted into John Butler's family to replace his son, Walter Butler (Duxea or the Leader), who had been killed by Oneidas allied to the colonists.

These two, the father and son, made the Butler name notorious and they were the villains (along with the Mohawk, Joseph Brant) in Walter D. Edmonds' famous historical novel, *Drums Along the Mohawk*, and the movie of the same name, still one of the best historical movies involving the frontier.

Both John Butler and his notorious son, Walter, appear to have had families among the Senecas. John Butler's children included a son who was also called John Butler but whose Indian name was Gandiogah or Hot Ashes. Hot Ashes sometimes served as an interpreter. He may have been the man to whom the irreverent Indian trader John Owens referred to in his Indian accounts as the Hot Arse and Hot Turd's Son.

The United States General Richard Butler formerly lived among the Indians with his brother, William, whom the Rev. David Jones encountered at the Indian towns in 1772. Richard Butler was said to have had one of Cornstalk's sisters as a wife. The two brothers were at St. Clair's defeat where Richard Butler was killed — and where his Shawnee son, Capt. Butler, was said to have been a significant warrior in the opposing army.

Indian Agent John Johnston said that the Polly Butler who lived with the Shawnees "was the daughter of Richard Butler by a Shawnee woman. A son, also, was the offspring of the same union, who became a distinguished chief in peace and war among the Shawnees — being in authority during the whole of my agency over this nation — a period of almost thirty years. General Butler was an Indian trader before the Revolutionary War and spoke the language of the natives and, as was customary with persons of those pursuits, took an Indian woman to wife. His son and daughter bear a striking resemblance to the Butler family, many of whom I knew in early life."

Capt. Butler, the Shawnee warrior, is mentioned in several early journals, and seems to have gotten along well while in white settlements. Capt. Butler and The Glaize King had Christmas Eve dinner with Andrews at Ft. Defiance (Ohio) in 1795. In 1809, Capt. Butler (along with the Shawnees Old Snake, the Young Snake, Blackhoof, the Wolf, and the Delawares Wahappi and Beaver) was one of the seven chiefs signing letters to the United States government complaining of mal-treatment. See Thornbrough, pp. 46-48.

Polly Butler, the daughter of General Richard Butler, is described as "half-white...her skin was not dark...[and she had] large blue eyes, long black hair...tall and well-proportioned." This daughter married the Shawnee chief Capt. Shigster, according to Finney. This man was likely Capt. Chieska, as Finney had some difficulty with names, and if so, she was probably the mother of Spybuck.

Henry Harvey said that Polly Butler left Ohio and went to Kansas where she was residing among the Shawnees in 1854, "married to one of the best men of that tribe, and is mother of a large family. Her husband has a large, good farm, good houses, out-buildings, orchard, stock...She is a good-looking, intelligent, and nice woman."

A William Butler was one of the Long Hunters in Kentucky who had Indian blood himself.

"He must have lived on the frontier all his life for he was a great woodsman...As late as 1783, he took up land on the waters of Clinch River in southwestern Virginia. In a few years he and his family, sons William, John, James, Issac, and Elcanah were in [what would become] Lincoln County, Kentucky."

William Butler and his family became prominent in the affairs of Green and Adair counties (Kentucky). He was one of the first scouts on the payroll of Green County, and participated in several campaigns against various tribes. While in Adair County in 1844, Draper interviewed Zachariah Hollady "who told him about an outing which Colonel Casey, Captain Butler, and their men went on across the Cumberland River in the direction of Obey's River to hunt for horses which the Indians had stolen. They found a camp with one Indian whom Captain Butler killed and they recovered their horses.

"On the return trip, the Indians pursued them as far as the Cumberland, firing on them, but not inflicting fatal injuries. One of the Indians was killed, and possibly two. After the men crossed, to quote, 'There was some blackguarding across the river, and Butler, who could talk Indian, asked them if they liked horses and said that he liked hair (scalps).' Judge Rollin Hurt, in his history of Adair County, stated that William Butler was part Indian..." See Burdette and Berley, p. 29.

See Leonard Hill, John Johnston and the Indians, pp. 170-171; Harvey, pp. 180-181; Finney, p. 513; Draper Mss. 4S23, 4S79; Kenneth Bailey, The Ohio Company Papers; Judge Rollin Hurt, History of Adair County, Kentucky; and Thornbrough, pp. 46-48.

The 1860 Census of Wyandotte County, Kansas

listed the family of Franklin Butler, an adopted white/ Shawnee born in Virginia, age 42. His family included Harriet Butler, age 29, born in Canada, and Ellen, age 13, Juletta, age 9, and Thomas, age 7, born in Kansas. See Prevost, p. 8.

Among the Shawnees who settled on the lands of the Cherokee nation by 1869 were Francis, Julietta, and Thomas Harrison Butler. See JAIFR, vol. IV, #2, pp. 100-111.

CAESAR, CESAR, SEZSAR – a Shawnee name.

During Pontiac's War, returned captives told of "a large, lusty, Negro" living with the Indians along with James Sherlock, O'Brian, and Vause. Some of the returned captives did not like Sherlock, but they all liked the negro who treated them well. They said that he worked with the horses among the Indians, doing blacksmith work. Possibly it was Caesar who was meant.

"Black Caesar" dealt with the Ohio Company traders as early as 1756. See Bailey, p. 57.

At the settlement of Pontiac's War, Sir William Johnson demanded that Cut the Pumpkin (Squash Cutter), Long Coat, Sherlock and the negro blacksmith be turned over to him, but Johnson wrote General Thomas Gage on June 28th, 1765, "As for Sherlock and the negro, I am assured by the Senecas, they fled southward several weeks ago...when it was learned that they would be delivered up..." See SWJ Papers, vol. XI, p. 833.

The creek on which Caesar made his camp was called Caesar's Creek (near Caesarville, Ohio) and it retains the name today. See Archer Butler Hulbert's Military Roads, p. 94. Allan Eckert made Caesar a character in his book, *The Frontiersman*, (p. 169, 175) but I cannot believe that the man was the stereotype that Eckert makes him out to be.

See Draper 1NN2: "Richard Butler, August 23, 1774, deposes...speaks of some Shawnees, among them the son of an old negro called Caesar..."

In 1776, Indian agent George Morgan expressly requested that the Shawnees bring Caesar, "the old mulatto interpreter," with him to the conference so that the commissioners and the Shawnees might "understand each other perfectly." Morgan sent a message to Cornstalk inviting Caesar to the council. Caesar, "an old mulatto who had been among them for twenty years," spoke English and Shawnee. See Schaaf, pp. 163-164, 166.

The whites again demanded the return of all whites and blacks, whether they lived among the Indians willingly or not. After some delays, Cornstalk, the Shawnee chief, told the white authorities that they "had now delivered all whites and blacks up except for one old negro woman who you can have back if you will come and carry here, for she cannot walk," and another black who has "run away from the north of Hockhocking and who threatens to kill either white man or Indian who threatens to molest him." See Thwaites and Kellogg, Rev. on the Upper Ohio, p. 105; Draper mss. 22J193.

If it was Caesar who ran off, he came back. Of course, it's possible that after Cornstalk was murdered, a son of this Caesar went down the Ohio River and was captured by Chickasaws. The Colberts, traders among the tribe, considered captured blacks as white plunder, kept some as servants, and sometimes traded them among the settlements. I cannot believe that the son of Caesar would remain a slave to anyone, and would probably run off or be killed trying. But that's just an opinion.

In 1787, William Colbert of the Chickasaw Nation sold Caesar to trader Jeptha Higdon. Caesar then passed to Col. Stephen Minor who employed him to work with his horses and lent him out sometimes as an interpreter. His services were in demand by traders traveling north to Kentucky. See McBee, p. 101.

In 1797, Caesar was employed by Governor Winthrop Sargent of Mississippi Territory. On April 9th, 1800, Gov. Sargent wrote of the necessity of keeping him in the government service..."I know of no other adequate to the purpose who could be engaged...His name is Caesar. He was placed under my direction in the service of the United States in October of 1798 by Mrs. Minor..."

On May 14th, 1800, Gov. Sargent wrote that "The negro interpreter has been taken from his duty by a Mr. Nolan, a dealer in horses, who means to use him for their safe passage through the Indian Country to Kentucky..." See Mississippi Territorial Archives, p. 220-221, 233.

Indian trader Phillip Nolan recruited Caesar (John Caesar or Juan Bautista Caesar) to serve as a guide and interpreter for his band of rebels in the Revolution against the Spanish authorities in 1800. Mordicai Richards deserted and led the authorities back to Nolan and his command. Nolan then wanted to make a stand and fight to the death. John Caesar saw the folly of that plan and was among the first to desert, and when the others surrendered, no action was taken against Caesar.

There were many blacks among the Indians, and Caesar was a common name.

See Fayette County, Kentucky affidavit, Sept. 26th, 1800..."Robert Mayes deposes that...Caesar, now in the possession of Nathaniel Lowry; James, now in the possession of Charles Wilson; Nancy, now in the possession of William Lyttle; Lucy and her 3 children, now in the possession of Buck Nunnally, are all descendants of Indians...illegally reduced to slavery...were removed from Dinwiddie County, Virginia to Camden, South Carolina...and brought to this country by Richard Coleman and the widow Nancy Gillaspie..." See Weiss, Kentucky & Pio. Gen. Records, vol. 1, #3, July, 1979, p. 7.

Among the Shawnees on the 1880 Census of the Cherokee Nation were James Saesar (age 45) and his Shawnee family who included Nancy (33), Lucy (6), Mary (2), and Dick Saesar (7 months). Also on the census was another Shawnee named George Saesar (age 22). See JAIFR, vol. X, #3, p. 15.

CALDWELL – a Potawatomi name.

William Caldwell, a British officer, came to Kentucky with a detachment of Potawatomi braves and helped to defeat the Kentuckians at Blue Licks in 1782. His son by a Potawatomi (or Mohawk) woman called Billy Caldwell (Sauganash, the Englishman). Another son by a white woman was called William Caldwell, jr. and the father and two sons are often confused with one another. All three were connected to the British Indian department and were Indian partisans during several battles.

At the River Raison, a white prisoner, Major Benjamin Graves, had concealed a knife and opted for martyrdom. He hung back as the prisoners moved along, and after Billy Caldwell told him to move faster, he turned on Caldwell with the dirk and plunged it into his neck. Graves was immediately shot down. Blackbird said to "kill the dogs," and the Potawatomis commenced killing the white prisoners.

This, more than anything else, established the battle cry of the war, "Remember the Raison!", in the minds of Kentuckians, and set the forces in operation which would affix the names of Simpson, Allen, McLean, McCracken, Hickman, Hart, Ballard, Edmondson, Meade, and Graves Counties in Kentucky. Of all the continental United States, Kentucky is the only one which did not name one of its counties for an Indian chief or an Indian tribe. But Kentucky has had several counties named for men who had Indian blood, such as Floyd County, and several others, such as Caldwell county, who bring the memories of half-breeds to mind.

Billy Caldwell recovered and became a valued assistant to Tecumseh. He survived the war, and later came to Missouri and then Kansas with the Potawatomi Nation. He married La Nanetta, a daughter of White Sturgeon and a niece of Mad Sturgeon. She died young, and he married the daughter of Indian trader Robert Forsyth by his Objibwa wife. At her death, he took a third wife, said to have been a French woman but possibly a mixed-blood. Altogether, his wives gave him at least eight children, including Alexander and Elizabeth Caldwell.

See Clifton, pp. 185-210; Edmunds, pp. 172, 250-251.

CALLOWAY, CALLAWAY – a Shawnee name.

Micajah "Cager" Calloway was one of the saltmakers captured in 1778 with Daniel Boone. Like Boone, he was adopted into the Shawnees and adapted well to his Indian life.

Calloway was with a war party of his tribe who accompanied Joseph Brandt on the 1781 expedition into Kentucky. Ezekial Lewis and four others who had been captured at Lochry's Defeat fell to Calloway's party and Lewis later referred to him as "the most savage amongst them." Calloway marched them five days without any food at all, and then when he gave them food, he ordered them to eat it all and threatened to kill them if they did not. They took the threat seriously and ate so much that they were in much distress afterwards. It appears the Calloway was a leader of the war party. See the interview with Ezekial Lewis in Draper 30J80-81.

This is incongruent with Calloway's deposition requesting a pension for his captivity and service to his country in which he talks of "hunger and cold, the privations incidental to a prisoners life among the savages are impossible to describe." Well, the man was trying to get a pension.

"Micagah Callaway" did serve twenty days as

an interpreter when Daniel Boone worked out the prisoner exchange with the Shawnees at Limestone in 1787. See Bushnell, p. 5. He may have come back to live among the whites then, for at least by 1794 he had changed sides again and was a scout and interpreter for General Anthony Wayne. See Draper 30J80-81.

How long was Calloway living red? At least five years, at least long enough to have a wife and several part-red children.

Micagah Calloway filed his Revolutionary War pension claim with Virginia, but he moved to Washington County, Indiana and he was the Micajah Calleway listed on the 1830 Washington County, Indiana Census, a head of a household which included one male between 70-80, one female 50-60, two males 20-30, one female 20-30, two females 15-20, and two females 10-15.

CAPTAIN – a Shawnee name.

Of course, there were many captains among the Delawares and Shawnees. Sometimes it was simply a title: Captain Killbuck was John Killbuck, Captain Parks was Joseph Parks, Captain Swannock was James Swannock.

But sometimes it was a name: Captain Pipe was simply Captain Pipe, Captain Johnny was simply Captain Johnny.

A Shawnee named simply Captain signed the ratification treaty in 1819. A Shawnee named Captain married Phiby (or Phoebe) Perry on the Kansas reservation in 1848. Of course, the Perry woman may have been a daughter of Chief Perry, and the Captain may have been James Captain.

The James Captain whose name appears on the 1842 census of the Shawnee Nation is said to have given his name to Captain's Creek which runs through Shawnee, Kansas. His daughter, Betsy Captain, attended a Quaker mission school when young and later married a member of the Chouteau family who ran the trading post. Their children included William A. Chouteau.

Mr. Chouteau died, and in 1853, the widow Betsy Captain Chouteau married the "white" (or part-Wyandot) wagonmaster Sam Garrett. Anyway, the couple settled down on 900 acres just south of the Kansas River across from where Bonner Springs is now located. The Garretts were farmers and stonemasons and house-builders. Sam and his brothers, Elias, Uriah, and Jack built a historic home for wagonmaster (and part-Wyandot) Dick Williams, a friend of the family.

In 1870, Betsy Garrett died in childbirth and was buried alongside Sam's parents, Edward and Elizabeth Garrett, on a hillside overlooking Captain's Creek. Sam then took his six children to Indian territory, there joining his friends Dick and Margaret Williams. Margaret Williams, a daughter of Capt. Joseph Parks and his Wyandot wife, helped to raise the children. Sam Garrett later remarried, lived until 1891, and was buried in the Garrett-Williams cemetery.

Among the children he brought to Indian Territory was Frederick Garrett, a farmer, who in 1889 married Sarah Carr in a ceremony performed by Rev. Charles Bluejacket at his home in what is now Bluejacket, Oklahoma. The couple had ten children including son E. O. "Babe" Garrett, a farmer and stockman, born in 1903. Among his children was Bertha Garrett Cameron. This information on the Captain/Garrett/Williams connection comes from Descendant of Shawnee Indians, Pioneer Developer Witnessed History, a newspaper article by Marsha Bennett, appearing in the *Journal-Herald*, February 25, 1986, Shawnee, Kansas.

But then, there were other members of the Captain family. When Nicholas Boilvin visited Kansas to explore lands for a Winnabago reserve in December, 1839, Tom Captain rented him a horse. See Barry, p. 386.

From 1845 through the early 1850s, Joseph Captain was employed as a blacksmith for the Osage Agency, and Augustus Captain sometimes served as miller for the same agency. See Barry, pp. 533, 569, 661, 730, 792, 896, 977, and 1058.

From an examination of the Eastern Shawnee Census Rolls in the records of the Miami and Quapaw Agencies, it appears that there was a Tom Captain (born 1852) who lived (in 1882) with "La-ki-wi-pe-a Blackfish or Captain" (born 1850), who may have been his wife or sister and a relict of the Chief Blackfish. Also living with Tom Captain was his niece, Julia Bobb (born 1874), likely a relation of Chief Black Bobb.

Through the years, Tom Captain must have been married, for sons and daughters begin to be listed for him. His wife is not listed, but by 1888 the family is listed as: Thomas Captain, father, 35; L. A. Captain, son, 4; Cordelia Captain, daughter, 2; and Mary Ellen Captain, daughter, age not given.

CAPTAIN JOHNNY – a Seneca/Delaware/Shawnee name.

Capt. Johnny married a white girl who had been adopted by the Shawnees. William Wells, a white Miami, married Capt. Johnny's sister.

The first Capt. Johnny of which I find record was a son of the Seneca chief, Tanacharisson, the Half King. Did this Capt. Johnny consider himself to be a Seneca? If his mother was Shawnee or Delaware, by tribal custom, he would follow the tribe of his mother, but he could be adopted by any tribe. And Capt. Johnny's tribal affiliations and political views possibly changed over the years of his life, several times. Or maybe the name was constantly "risen up" in the memory of the older one. Either way, the name Capt. Johnny, like the name Silverheels, continued on and crossed tribal lines.

It would seem that the old Capt. Johnny would be more attached to his uncles rather than his father, but the records show that the Half King and his son, Johnny, traveled together. During the French and Indian War, Capt. Johnny was known as Mr. Johnny, or Little Johnny or simply as Johnny, the Half King's son. The accounts of Indian trader John Owens show that Owens gave considerable credit to his father-in-law and brother-in-law, "the Half King and son."

Right before Braddock's Defeat, General Braddock insulted his Indian allies and ordered them all off except for the Half King, who would be loyal to the English until death, and the Half King's loyal band of eight warriors which included his son, Johnny, and Silverheels. See Weslager, p. 225.

After Tanacharisson's death, Johnny, more often referred to as Capt. Johnny, served as an express rider, taking messages through the woods on behalf of George Croghan and Sir William Johnson. Johnson's account itemized funds allotted to Silverheels and Johnny, two Senecas who were sent out as spies. Later, Johnny was said to have been "very much disgusted" that he was not "more particularly noticed and rewarded" for his services to the English. But he was just a boy, probably still in his early teens at this time.

A Capt. Johnny is listed as a Delaware warrior at the Ft. Pitt Treaty of 1764 along with the chiefs The Beaver, Capt. Pipe, Turtle Hart, White Wolfe, Thomas Hickman and Simon Girty. Capt. Johnny appears in the Indian trader accounts.

Capt. Johnny's name translated as Straight Arm according to the Pennsylvania Colonial Records, vol. 6, p. 589. Capt. Johnny was also known as Israel, Assilcius, Heylepacheion, and Welapochchon according to Thwaites and Kellogg, Frontier Adv. on the Upper Ohio, pp. 225, 282, 321, 338, 353. It is not certain if this is a case of multiple men or of multiple names for the same man. If Captain Johnny changed tribes, his name must have changed also. Draper interviewed the Shawnee Charles Tucker in 1868 who remembered the last Capt. Johnny's Indian name as Ah-old-ka-wah (he who scares game up).

The Captain Johnny who spoke to James Sherlock at the 1785 council was said to have been the Shawnee in whom Alexander McKee and Matthew Elliot placed the most trust. Although the United States was convinced that the Northwest Territory had been won from the British, Captain Johnny envisioned a separate, independent nation, unconquered by either British or Americans.

After Molunthy was killed in 1786, the Shawnees turned to Captain Johnny for leadership. It was Captain Johnny who worked out the prisoner exchanges with James Sherlock, Benjamin Logan, and Daniel Boone. Capt. Johnny's wife was a white woman, Rachel Kiser, who had been adopted into the tribe. She was apparently among the women captured when Molunthy was killed, and Capt. Johnny did not see her again until she was exchanged at Limestone. Before the exchange, Capt. Johnny sent some tobacco on ahead as a present to her (this was a custom, and it does not mean that the lady chewed tobacco). They were again united and she continued to live with him after the peace.

Thomas Ridout described Captain Johnny as the principal Shawnee chief in 1788.

Like Black Hoof, Little Turtle, and several others, Capt. Johnny fought the United States bitterly until the Treaty of Greenville and then, he changed sides and worked actively on behalf of the Americans. Perhaps there was a father and a son, both called Captain Johnny, or perhaps the name was "risen up." I am not certain where one left off and the other began.

In 1791, it had been Captain Johnny's war party

who surrounded Simon Kenton's camp. Later, like Captain Tommy (Chieska), he befriended Kenton. According to one account, it was Captain Johnny instead of Capt. Tommy who captured two horse thieves, both white men, and turned them over to the whites, thus freeing Kenton from debtor's prison.

Captain Johnny did business at McClure's trading post (1804-1810) along with Chieska, Simon Kenton, the Shawnee James Sanders, and others.

During the War of 1812, a Captain Johnny served with William Wells' scouts, and he was with Logan in the skirmish with the Potawatomis when Logan was mortally wounded. Shane interviewed one of Wells' scouts, William Curry jr., who told several anecdotes of Wells and Captain Johnny.

For additional notes on the men named Captain Johnny, see Pennsylvania Colonial Records, vol. XIV, p. 256-257; WVHQ, vol. 32, p. 238-241; OHQ, vol. 70, p. 204-207; VMOB&H, vol. 25, p. 1-11; Bailey, p. 51, 146; Draper Mss. 13CC146-153; History of Shelby County, Ohio, 1883, p. 61; SWJ Papers, Post-War Period, vol. 5, p. 354; Milo Quaife, ed., Hay's Journal, p. 20; Harvey, p. 113.

CARPENTER – a Shawnee name.

The Carpenter name became one of the most prominent names among the Shawnee population over the years, and in the main population it is a common source of the Indian blood tradition.

Several members of the Carpenter family were captured and adopted during Pontiac's War, and Solomon Carpenter was among the captives delivered up to Bouquet in 1764.

Solomon Carpenter was in Capt. John Lewis's Company in Dunmore's War. In Kentucky, Solomon Carpenter built a cabin on the head branch of Paint Lick Creek in 1776. He was with William Harrod on his expedition to the Shawnee towns in May, 1779.

In 1781, Solomon Carpenter enlisted in the Virginia Militia — along with Amos Carpenter, Samuel Lyons, and others — but they were deceived as to what the conditions of service would be and deserted, leading a company of scouts into the forest.

A letter to Governor Thomas Nelson in the Calendar of Virginia State Papers (1781, p. 184) said of them: "...they have deserted and laid in the mountains for a long time...[they number] about forty or fifty...I have used my best endeavors to disperse the party and have the leader apprehended, but every measure has proved ineffectual. The men above mentioned are now at my house, under the sanction of a [white] flag...they propose that they [are willing to] serve two years with the militia of this county, whenever called for, or join General Clark for the same term.

"I would only observe that Solomon Carpenter, the leader of the party, was captivated by the Indians when young & remained with them a number of years, that he is a bold, daring, active man and intimates that if his terms are not complied with, he will seek refuge among the Indians..."

Jeremiah Carpenter was also among those adopted by Shawnees, having been captured when he was nine years old. He was taken to the village of Oldtown, opposite the mouth of the Kanawha. There he lived with them until he was eighteen.

McWhorter said that Carpenter began to romance one the chief's daughters and might have married her — but the affair was broken up when the peace was made and he was forcibly given up. The white world made him uncomfortable and he returned to live on the edge of the frontier in what is now Braxton County, near Sutton, West Virginia. He was the first settler in the area. The next neighbor was Adam O'Brien. See McWhorter, pp. 464-465.

Christopher and David Carpenter were scouts for Harrison County, Virginia in 1792.

Among the Shawnees who settled on the lands of the Cherokee nation by 1869 were Rad, Mary, William, Joseph, Lizzie, and Benjamin Carpenter. See JAIFR, vol. IV, #2, pp. 100-111.

Mary (age 50), Ben (age 21), Ben jr. (age 6), Fannie (age 22), Lenia (age 2), and William Carpenter (age 25) were among the Shawnees on the 1880 Cherokee Nation Census. See JAIFR, vol X, #1, p. 51.

When James H. Howard was among the Oklahoma Shawnees investigating tribal customs, he met Ranny Carpenter who became one of his main informants and who was quoted extensively throughout his book. Regarding the tradition of Shawnees when it came to ceremonial paint, Howard asked Ranny Carpenter, who was the drumkeeper at Whiteoak, if the different face-painting designs used by the men in the Shawnee dances had any significance. Carpenter told him that, "Some people are very particular about the way in which they are painted, but the only way I know for Shawnee men is a single red line going out from the corner of each eye. This is done so that the Creator will recognize the worshipper as an Indian, a Shawnee. They are painted the same way at death. With so many Shawnees mixed with whites now this is necessary. Take me, for example, I look like a white man." See Howard, pp. 70-71.

CARTER – a Mingo/Shawnee name.

Sarah, Eliza, and Nathaniel Carter were captured and adopted by Delawares during Pontiac's War. Eliza Carter, then ten years old, was purchased for five pounds by the mulatto blacksmith (possibly Caesar) who made axes for the mixed Shawnees, Delawares, and Senecas then at Chenussio. Gaastrax was the main chief there; and James Sherlock, Cut the Pumpkin

(Squash Cutter) were there as well. Even though the Indians were starving, Eliza Carter said that the black man treated her well. Both Eliza and Sarah were among those captives who were returned and gave their depositions which appear in the Sir William Johnson Papers, 1763-1774.

All attempts to get Nathaniel Carter to return to his family failed, and Nathaniel grew up and married among the Indians. Some of his Indian family is supposed to have kept Carter as their surname; and one of the sons of Nathaniel Carter, a half-breed, returned to Cornwall, Ohio to attend missionary school. After graduating, he left to become a preacher among his people. Nathaniel Carter is supposed to died when about seventy years of age in the Cherokee Nation. See Ohio Arch. & Hist. Soc. Pub, vol. 18, pp. 584-589.

What was Nathaniel Carter's Indian name? I do not yet know. He could have been the Pheasant, who accompanied George Washington on his 1770 tour down the Ohio River. But there is much I have not yet seen.

Among the Shawnees who settled on the lands of the Cherokee nation by 1869 were George Carter and his family. See JAIFR, vol. IV, #2, pp. 100-111.

George Carter (age 55) is also listed among the Shawnees on the 1880 Cherokee Nation Census. See JAIFR, vol X, #1, p. 51.

CASTLEMAN – a Wyandot name.

Some of the children of William Castleman were adopted, including Mary and Margaret who were adopted by Wyandots. Margaret "was married to Williams, a half-Indian." Some of the family later lived in Jefferson County, Ohio. See Draper 16S291.

CHAMPION, CAMPION – a Mingo name.

A family of Campions were Indian traders at

Detroit before the Revolution and were closely associated with several tribes.

John Champion is listed among the Indians in the SWJ Papers, 1763-1774, along with Jacob Daniel, King Shingess, Turtle Heart, and Thomas Hickman.

After Frederick Stump murdered several of the leading Delawares in 1768, Newahleeka sent word of it to Pennsylvania Governor Thomas Penn via the Indian messenger, Billy Champion.

CHARLEY – a Delaware/Miami/Peoria name.

Charley was an Eel River Miami who later resided among the Shawnees and Delawares, becoming a diplomat among them. Charley (Ki-tun-ga or Sleepy) signed several treaties for the Eel River, Wea, Miami, and Delaware nations, and he was on a peace mission for them when the Battle of Tippecanoe occurred. He arrived at the village and found the people scattered and fearful that "the Great Spirit had turned against us."

Charley may have had a Shawnee or Delaware wife because his son, Little Charley, is identified as Delaware Charley who went to Kansas with Joseph Parks and the Shawnees in 1832. At the time, "Chawwee's" family of eleven consisted of one male between 25 and 50, one female between 25 and 50, two males between 10 and 25, two females between 10 and 25, and five children under 10, four of them males.

Delaware Charlie (Chah-la-wees) went to Kansas with the Shawnees and Delawares. A Delaware Charlie was among the scouts in Capt. James Swannock's band who served with John C. Fremont in 1845 and during the Mexican War. He was a medicine man, a mystic who could converse with the spirits of the departed. See Weslager, pp. 379, 408, 409, 443.

Among the Delawares on the 1880 Cherokee Nation Census were Delaware Charley (age 76), Mrs.

Charley (age 19), Sam Charley (age 17), and Sarah Charley (age 14). See JAIFR, vol X, #1, p. 52.

CHARLOW, SHARLOW, CHERLOE, CHARLIEU

– a Mingo name.

Charlieu was a mixed-blood Mohawk, a cousin of Joseph Brant (Brandt). He married a French/Indian half-breed, but mixed freely with the French and Wyandots and came to Ohio in 1829 to live among the Senecas and Shawnees. When a young man, Charlieu was one of the Mohawks with Montcalm, and thereafter he was in many engagements, usually on the side of the British. He moved out west in conjunction with the others but died on the journey at St. Louis in 1832. He wore his hair long, and had little silver crosses strewn into it. See Butterfield, p. 171.

On the 1843 Muster Roll of Sandusky Wyandots were:

1. Jacob Charloe's family, consisting of one male over 25, one female between 10 and 25, and one boy and one girl, both under 10.
2. James T. Charloe family, consisting of one woman over 55, one man between 25 and 55, one woman between 10 and 25, and one girl under 10.
3. John Charloe's family, consisting of one male between 10 and 25, four females between 10 and 25, and one boy under 10.

Among the students attending the Ft. Leavenworth Shawnee Indian School in 1851 were the Wyandots George and Peter Sharlow. Among the Wyandots given land by the 1855 treaty were Joseph, Mary, George, David, Henry, Elizabeth, and Peter Charloe.

Among the guardianship cases reviewed by the Commissioner of Indian Affairs in 1871 was the case of Mary (Amelia) Cherloe, a Wyandot. Mary Cherloe's maiden name had been Peacock and she was the guardian for both her sister, Elizabeth Peacock, and her nephew, Issac Peacock. See JAIFR, vol. VIII, #2, p. 19.

CHARTIER – a Shawnee name.

Martin Chartier was a French outlaw who sought and found refuge among the Shawnee, with whom he married and raised a family. A son, Peter Chartier became a chief among them, a hunter wise in the trading ways of whites, who led them west to escape the encroachment of civilization. See Hanna, II, pp. 328, 329.

Martin Chartier's only crime was that he had gone among the Shawnees "that owed him some beaver" without the permission of the colonial authorities, "and when he came back, the Governor put him in prison and in irons, where he continued for several months; but at last got loose, made his escape, and ever since hath used the woods." He told it this way before the Maryland Provincial Council in 1692, at which time he was residing there with his Shawnee wife. He died in 1718, master of a huge trading house and plantation on the Susquehanna River. He might have had several children, but only one son, Peter Chartier, handled the estate. Peter Chartier went to live with his mother's people and learned to see the English trader from a red perspective.

A man who is drunk, or in need of a drink, can more easily be taken advantage of in a financial transaction. This was an axiom in the Pennsylvania Indian trade. With George Miranda, Peter Chartier drew up a petition for a ban on all liquor trade between the English traders and the Shawnees and the entire village pledged to smash any existing kegs and spill the rum, and to remain dry for a period of four years. The names of niney-eight Shawnees are attached to this contract, which was submitted to the Pennsylvania authorities. It does not appear to have been carried out, however. Peter Chartier, apparently disgusted at the way the white traders took advantage of the Shawnees, led them away from the English trading posts. When the Shawnees returned, Peter Chartier was not with them.

John Burt (de-Burt), another early trader, married Mary Chartier Seaworth, a daughter of Martin Chartier and his Shawnee wife. Their descendants carried the name on as Dibert or Dubert. Part of this family stayed in what would become Bedford County, Pennsylvania and some went to Virginia. See *Bedford: The Kernal of Greatness*, written and published by the Bedford County, Pennsylvania Heritage Commission, pp. 14-15. There are many stories of John Burt and his dealings with the Indians in the colonial records.

A well-documented account of Martin Chartier and his half-Shawnee son, Peter Chartier, appears in Hanna's Wilderness Trail. An undocumented account appears in *The Horn Papers*. Horn says that Peter Chartier associated with the Delawares in later years and married among them. He gives a rather elaborate account of Peter Chartier's family, but so much of what Horn says conflicts with more reliable records, you don't know when he can be believed. According to Horn, Peter Chartier is supposed to have died at Chartier's Post, near Canonsburg, October 24, 1774, apparently leaving descendants among both the whites and the Indians.

A Michael Chartier served under George Rogers Clark in the Illinois Regiment and is mentioned in the Court Martial Book in the Thruston Papers, copies at the Filson Club in Louisville.

Mary Chattaire, a half-breed, was delegated land in 1818 on the Wabash River below the mouth of Pine River in Indiana. See the *Louisville Public Advertiser*,

October 20, 1818, on microfilm at the Louisville Free Public Library.

CHOUTEAU, CHOTEAU, etc. – a Shawnee/Osage/Sioux name.

In 1825, Francis and Cyprian Chouteau built a trading post on the south side of the Kansas Shawnee Reservation near Muncie. Then when the Fish or Jackson band of Shawnees moved to the new reservation, Frederick Chouteau came with them and re-established a Chouteau trading post among them. See Caldwell, p. 7.

In 1830, Frederick Chouteau married Nancy Logan, a relative of the Shawnee scout, James Logan, and their children included William (born 1833), Benjamin (born 1835), Amanda (born 1837), and Francis X. Chouteau (born 1839). See Barry, p. 166, 453.

Another of the Chouteaus married the Shawnee girl, Betsy Captain, and became the parents of William A. Chouteau.

Among the Shawnees who settled on the lands of the Cherokee nation by 1869 were William, Mary, Anna, John, Benjamin, Edmond, Julia, Benjamin F., Sterling P., Amanda, Grant, Charles, Alexander, Franklin, and Victoria Cheautou. See JAIFR, vol. IV, #2, pp. 100-111.

Among the Shawnee guardianship cases heard in 1871 by Ely Parker, Commissioner of Indian Affairs, was the case of Cyprian Chouteau, who was then living in Kansas City at the time of the hearings. Among his wards were James and William Francis, the half-brothers of his wife. James Elliott and Maria Francis were also wards. See JAIFR, vol. VIII, #2, p. 25.

There are thirteen members of the Chouteau family listed on the 1880 Census of the Cooweescoowee District of the Cherokee Nation. They are listed variously as mixed-blood Shawnees, Blacks, and Cherokees. The Chouteaus were a big family and the name appears in conjunction with many other tribes as well. See JAIFR, vol X, #1, p. 53.

CHIESKA – Like Tecumseh, a Shawnee concept name.

The name means the end-of-the-tail, the end-all, the most terrific, the ultimate. "Ne plus ultra," Charles Tucker told Draper, but he said that there was no exact translation. It was a reoccurring name, and Chieska and such other heroic names as Tecumseh, Black Fish, and Cornstalk were "risen up" in memory of the old heroes, and perhaps even other heroes of the same name back into time. There was a Shawnee warrior named Chieska as early as 1756 and he was probably the same man Indian trader Pat Mullen listed in his accounts as Cheesecake. Below this name in Mullen's account book was Little Johnny, possibly Chieska's adopted nephew who later became known as Capt. Johnny.

In 1785, along with Capt. Johnny, Major Snake, and Thomas Snake, Chieska sent a letter to Alexander McKee which detailed how the Hurons and eastern Delawares had "sold their land and themselves with it" to the Americans, how the Wyandottes "gave them from Little Beaver Creek, the whole Shawnee Country," and how the Americans were "settling our country and building cabins in every place." In a postscript to the letter, Chieska requested McKee to pass on the information his brother, "who is Capt. Brant's great friend."

This Chieska was often called Capt. Tom, and his Indian name was variously given as Chicksea, Shigster, etc. People said he looked to be part-white, raw-boned and lean. His wife might easily have been Polly Butler, the daughter of Richard Butler and his wife, a sister of Cornstalk.

Like Captain Johnny and Little Beaver, Chieska and his sons, Captain Tommy and Spybuck, endorsed the American side after the Treaty of Greenville.

Chieska or Captain Tommy joined Little Beaver in the War of 1812 as one of William Henry Harrison's elite band of scouts. Chieska also rode with William Wells' scouts, and after Wells was killed in the shootout with Winnemac's Potawatomis, he became the captain of the company. It was Chieska who killed Winnemac.

Those who knew him said that Chieska was a natural comic, and kept the troops entertained with his wry talk and mischievous pranks. The Rev. David Jones remarked on Shawnee humor, writing in his journal that "it appears as if some kind of drollery was their chief study," and ranked some of the Shawnees among the greatest laughers he had ever known.

There is the story that, while in the white settlements, Chieska was saved from a lynch mob by Simon Kenton. Later, he went west with his tribe and he died in Kansas during the cholera epidemic of 1833. See Draper 23S and 11YY2.

For the additional record of some of his descendants, see SPYBUCK.

CHISHOLM or CHISM – a Cherokee name.

John D. Chisholm, a white trader, moved from Charlestown to Savannah to St. Augustine to Pensacola. From there he went to the Creek Nation of Georgia. By 1777, he left the Creeks to go north to Cherokee country in the eastern Tennessee area. There he married Betsey Fauling, nee Sims, widow of William Fauling.

Among the children of John D. Chisholm and Betsy Fauling were Ignatius, Elizabeth (who married William Massengill), and Deborah (who married John Sommerville). The marriage ended, or perhaps Betsy died, and John D. Chisholm married Martha Holmes, a mixed-blood daughter of a British officer named Holmes and his part Cherokee wife. The children of this marriage included Thomas Chisholm, and possibly James, Joseph, Dennis, and Issac. Evidence indicates that by 1796 John D. Chisholm was then married to Patsy Brown, a sister to the Cherokee chief, Richard Brown.

Thomas Chisholm, a part-Cherokee son of John D. Chisholm, married Martha Wharton and their children included Martha, Jane (who married J. B. Lynde), Alfred Finney Chisholm, William Wharton Chisholm, Thomas Chisholm, and Narcissa (who married Robert L. Owen). The children of Narcissa Chisholm Owen included William O. Owen and United States Senator Robert L. Owen.

Ignatius Chisholm, son of John D. Chisholm, married Old Tassel's sister and their children included Jesse, William, and John Chisholm. The last named son married Polly and had Toby, Nancy, Betsy, David, Jane, James, Thomas, Elizabeth, and Lewis Chisholm.

Ignatius Chisholm afterwards married Martha Rogers whom some accounts say was a sister to Diana Rogers, the Cherokee wife of General Sam Houston of Texas. The children of Ignatius and Martha included sons George and Nelson, and a daughter also named Martha. This daughter married Dave Biggs and their children included Dewitt C., Bennett, Margaret A., Mary I., John, David, Jacqueline, Christopher, and Narcissa Biggs.

Jesse Chisholm, the half-Cherokee nephew of Old Tassel, became one of the most famous scouts in American history. He often associated with such notable Shawnee and Delaware scouts as Black Beaver and Fall Leaf.

Jesse Chisholm's first wife was Eliza Edwards, the half-Creek daughter of Indian trader James Edwards. Hoig says that Jesse's second wife was "another halfblood Creek woman, Sah-kah-kee McQueen, in 1847."

Among the children of Jesse and Eliza Edwards Chisholm was William Edwards Chisholm who married (1st) Hester Butler (Cochran) by whom he had a daughter named Caroline. William married (2nd) Julia Ann McLish by whom he had Eliza, Angeline, Mary V., Alice, Cora Ann, Estella, Julia Ann, and William, jr.

The children of Jesse and Sah-kak-kee McQueen Chisholm included Jennie Chisholm who married (1st) Buck Beaver by whom she had Cora, Lucinda, and Frank Beaver. She married (2nd) Albert Harper by whom she had at least one son, Albert Harper, Jr. She married (3rd) Sam Davis.

Among the other children of Jesse and Sah-kak-kee McQueen Chisholm were Lucinda, Mary, and Frank (Jesse) Chisholm. Lucinda married a Whiteturkey. Mary married Jesse Cochran and had sons Rocky and Walter. Frank married Lucy Little Bear and their children included Jesse and Nellie Chisholm.

Jesse Chisholm was about sixteen years senior to Sah-Kak-kee when they were married, and after his death she married Jackson Chisholm and had Sallie and William Chisholm. Previously, Jackson Chisholm had been married to a woman named Amy and had Shawnee Bob Chisholm. Shawnee Bob, sometimes listed as Shawney Chisholm, was listed as a trader on the old Creek roll of 1857 and his name appeared in 1879 when he was listed as a freighter for the Sac and Fox Agency along with his relatives White Turkey and Buck Beaver.

Later, Jackson Chisholm would marry a third time to "a Caddo woman" by whom he had a son named Charlie Chisholm. In a footnote, Hoig says that "statements by Charlie Chisholm indicate that his mother was a Caddo but that he was an Absentee Shawnee. Whether this means he was adopted into the Shawnees or that his father Jackson was of the Shawnee blood is not clear.

"The most famous of cattle trails bore the name of Jesse Chisholm, a half-breed Cherokee trader who set up a trading post on the Canadian River in Indian Territory about halfway between the Texas border on the Red River and the Kansas state line. His father was of Scottish descent and his mother a full-blood Cherokee. In 1865, Chisholm charted a straight, level, wagon road through the wilderness from his trading post near present-day Wichita into the middle of Indian territory. Chisholm died in 1868, at about 63, before the 'old Chisholm Trail' became a part of western lore. His epitaph says of him, No One Left His Home Cold Or Hungry."

See Hoig's excellent history of Jesse Chisholm, as good a history as you can find anywhere.

CICOTT or CICOT – a Miami/Potawatomi name.

The Cicotts were French residents of the Indian towns very early and the Indian blood in some of the family predates the Revolution. Hays saw Cicott at the Glaize (now Ft. Wayne, Indiana) and mentions him in his journal in 1789. See Quaife.

Both George and Zachariah Cicott became chiefs. The 1828 Treaty with the Potawatomi stipulates that land be given to "Me-shaw-ke-to-quay, wife of George Cicot." See Watson, vol. 5, pt. 11, p. 50.

CLARK – a common source of Indian blood traditions.

Draper inquired about John Clark near Essex, Ontario. His respondent answered with, "All I know of the John Clark you speak of, he lived within the vicinity of Chicago — or Skunktown, as some Potawatomi Indian named it, when it was a sort of Potawatomi headquarters in earlier days. All I knew about him, when I was a boy, I heard some of my full brothers speak about him as a half-brother of ours and called him Yankee John.

"My grandfather's name was Thomas Alexander

Clarke and was born within the vicinity of Harrisburg, Pennsylvania. When he was about 18 years of age, he came to his uncle [his mother's brother], Col. [Alexander] McKee at Detroit who took him in as a sub-agent in the Indian department. He was a British militia captain in the battle Mad Anthony Wayne fought with the Indians at the Maumee rapids some 16 miles above Toledo. He was taken prisoner at the siege of Ft. Meigs and whilst on a scout with some Indians. My father died here in Canada in March, 1840 in the 76th year of his age.

"My mother's name was Mary, daughter of chief Adam Brown [a Wyandot chief]. She died in August, 1863, in her 88th year. My father...was a white man, My mother being half-English and half-native which makes me quarter-Indian by birth like our deceased friend, William Walker. Ever yours, R. L. Clarke."

Clarke was the author of *The Origin and Traditional History of the Wyandots,* 1870. See Draper 8YY8-10.

By no means was this the only Indian blood connection with the Clark and Clarke families.

Another letter to Draper appears in Draper mss. 8Y43:

"Dear Lynn Draper, Your letter of May 11th read, and will now reply as best I can in regard to Tecumseh the famous Indian chief. I have often heard my father speak of him. Yes, his brother, Andrew Clark, was Tecumseh's aid-de-camp. My grandmother Clark was taken prisoner by the Shawnee tribe and remained with them twelve years and married a British officer by the name of John Clark.

"Three children were born while she lived with the Indians: My father, John H. Clark the eldest, born June 12th, 1792; Andrew Clark and sister Sarah born March, 1794. They were twins. They were all born at Ft. Wayne. Then they moved to Malden, Canada and my mother's father heard where his daughter was and went after her and took her home in Virginia. She took my father and his sister with her but his brother Andrew and grandfather Clark preferred to remain with the Indians.

"Andrew, my uncle, became associated with Tecumseh at Ft. Wayne and went with him on his exploits. When Tecumseh was killed at the Battle of the Thames, my uncle was by his side. Aunt Sarah Clark married William Eahart and had ten children..."

There are many people in this country who have the tradition that they have Indian blood and also descend from General Clark. Of course, there is more than one General Clark from whom to descend.

There is General William Clark of the Lewis and Clark expedition, later an Indian agent and the Governor of Missouri. People usually wonder about this man and Sacwajacea, the Shoshoni guide of the expedition. Clark seems to have had warm feelings for her, and a lot of people wonder if her son, whom he adopted as his ward, was truly his. It wasn't. But Clark probably had affairs with a number of Indian women.

Other researchers have found that General William Clark had a son by a plains woman, a Flathead, who was aware of his paternal heritage and boasted of it. And William Clark also had some black/white or mixed-blood children who claimed him as a grandfather, and they may have been part red also and not known it.

But by far the most Indian blood traditions I have heard involve William Clark's brother, General George Rogers Clark. Over the past ninety years, people have sometimes written letters to the Filson Club and the Kentucky Historical Society noting such a tradition. They usually received a pointed letter back simply stating that the genealogy of George Rogers Clark has been firmly established, that he never married and therefore could not possibly have had children. But that doesn't necessarily follow. In fact, as we say in Kentucky, that is not the way to bet.

Some of the people sending such letters were too important to be cast aside so curtly. There was, for instance, the letter from Esther G. Clarke, dated April 24th, 1944, from Los Angeles. The lady was the daughter of Dr. C. C. Godshaw, of a prominent Louisville family. Her husband was Frank Clarke whose family tradition was that he descended from George Rogers Clark and had Indian blood. Frank Clarke's father, who added the "e" to the name, had a brother and a sister with marked Indian features and straight black hair. John W. Clark's father used to say that his own father brought home an Indian girl from the wars.

A similar tradition was carried down to Lynn H. Clark of Deland, Florida. An intelligent and reflective man, Mr. Clark was aware that George Rogers Clark never married, and his strong tradition puzzled him. In an effort to clear up the mystery, he had his own lineage independently researched. It leads, as many red traditions do, to the Miami River Valley in Ohio. George P. Clark married Barbara Waggoner (Wagner) there. Barbara Waggoner may have been a part-red descendant of Peter Waggoner, as the Indian blood tradition is also strong in the Waggoner family of the Miami Valley.

Anyway, George and Barbara Clark moved to St. Joseph County, Michigan. Their Ohio born children included Sarah (b. 1825, m. Mr. Johnson), Mary (b. 1828), Archibald (b. 1830), Samuel (b. 1832), (b. 1834). Their Michigan born children included Eliza Jane (b. 1836, m. Charles M. Reed), Elizabeth (b. 1838), Catherine (b. 1841, m. Mr. Baird), and George Henry Clark sr. (b. 1844, d. Feb. 2, 1924).

George Henry Clark, Jr., born 1868, married Emma Kate Bolender, and their children included Berenice, Helen, Wayne, and Lynn Clark, who carries on the tradition.

Another relative of General George Rogers Clark, a half-brother named Marston Green Clark, lived at Clarksville and associated with Robert Stewart, the Cleghorns, Peter Smith, the Owens, and other interesting men. He too became a general and played significant roles at Ft. Meigs, Tippecanoe, and elsewhere. Made an Indian Agent, he associated with the Shawnees and Delawares in Kansas. He understood that reservation life tended to make the Indians bankrupt, not in terms of dollars, but in terms of spirit and self-respect.

John Treat Irving, nephew of Washington Irving, met Marston G. Clark when he was the Indian agent at Ft. Leavenworth. Irving found him "a tall, thin man, of that hardened appearance which rather denotes extreme toughness than great muscular strength. His hair was snowy white. His forehead was high and narrow, and his nose aquiline. His light blue eyes, half-extinguished by two heavy lids, betokened calm reflection. His mouth was large, firmly set, and surmounted by two or three deeply furrowed wrinkles. There was something in his look that betokened a man of resolution, bordering on obstinacy. He was dressed in a deerskin hunting shirt, trimmed after the Indian fashion with a border of bear's hair and ornamented with porcupine quills. His pantaloons were of course cloth such as universally worn by frontiersmen. In his hand, he held a large cap of foxskin, so constructed that the snarling head of the animal was preserved and appeared to be keeping guard over the cranium of the wearer."

When Irving met Marston Clark at Independence, Missouri, in 1832, he noted in his journal that Clark "thinks the clergymen the only class of people on earth that he hates," and belittling the government policy of penning the Indians up in reservations and then setting missionaries upon them. He railed against the policy of degrading them, advising that the government "must not shut up the only road left them to honor and promotion..." Irving, p. 90

The Presbyterian missionary, D. W. Smith, met Clark at the Shawnee village in Kansas and found him "an open and avowed infidel, and I may add, foul mouthed, a man of inordinate self conceit...as might be expected of such a man, he is in heart opposed to all religious instruction and expresses himself as having no confidence in schools or any attempt to civilize the Indians." See Irving, pp. 239-240.

After Marston G. Clark resigned from the Indian Agency, he came back to Indiana and raised a large family. I have not yet seen a good account of his children, one of whom, George B. Clark, rode express through the Indian lands and was at one time licensed as an Indian trader in Kansas. See Barry, pp. 263, 276, 279, 282.

Information found in Draper's papers indicates that a Robert Clark was captured by Shawnees along with two black men and a woman who escaped. He was with them 18 months. Robert Clark was at Piqua when George Rogers Clark's forces invaded in 1786, and he told the story later that there was a white man who rode on ahead of the army to warn the village.

Listed on the 1843 Muster Roll of Wyandots from Sandusky, Ohio, were:

1. Thomas Clark's family, consisting of one male and one female over 55, one female 25 to 55, two females 10 to 25, and three females under 10.
2. William Clark, a male between 25 and 55.
3. George I. Clark's household, consisting of one male and one female 25 to 55, and three children under 10, two of them female.

Among the Wyandot guardian cases reviewed in 1871 was the case of George I. Clark or Clarke. He died in 1857. He had been the guardian for his three children: Charlotte, Richard, and Mary. He, his wife, and Mary all died in a three week period. Son Richard lived in Wyandotte, Kansas, but did not testify. See JAIFR, vol. VIII, #2, p. 19.

Charlotte Clarke, daughter of George I. Clark, seems to have been the same lady who was then the ward of H. M. Northrup. His wards included Charlotte Clarke who was then living with her husband near Lafayette, Indiana in 1871.

Living among the Wyandots in 1855, in Wyondotte County, Kansas, were George I. Clark (born 1803 or 1804), with wife Catherine Clark, 47; son, Richard W. Clark, 18; daughter Harriet, 15; and daughter Mary J., 13. Also listed were Peter D. Clark, 35 and Sebra Clark, 19.

Listed on the 1883 Ottawa Census is the family of Emeline Clark, age 55, including John, 27, James, 26, Harry, 23, Charles, 21, Richard, 33, Emaline, 8, and Esther, 6.

John Clark, listed as a forty-year-old white man, was living with his Cherokee family in the Cooweescoowee District in 1880. The household included Nancy (age 36), Alice (age 11), Mary (age 3), and William (age 6 months).

Other Clarks on the census included the Cherokees Martha (age 5), Sabra (age 42), and Johnson Clark (age 28). See JAIFR, vol. X, #1, p. 53.

CLAY – a Shawnee/Ottawa name.

The Shawnee councilor and sub-chief, Henry Clay, was a son of Capt. John Wolf and a grandson of Cornstalk. Henry Clay was educated under the supervision of Indian Agent John Johnston at Upper Piqua, at the expense of the Quaker Friends. Lang, in his *History of Seneca County, Ohio*, says that Henry Clay "married the daughter of Jeremiah McLain, formerly a member of Congress from the Columbus District." See Lang, p. 210.

General Jeremiah McLene, to whom Lang referred, was born in Pennsylvania about 1765. He went to Tennessee where he appears to have had some dealings with the Cherokee. He came to Ohio, apparently as an Indian trader, and became one of the first sheriffs of Ross County, Ohio. He served in Congress and died while in office, about 1835.

Jeremiah McLene's son-in-law, Henry Clay (Nolesimo or Onessimo), signed the 1831 treaty, and was then among the Shawnees listed on the muster roll of the Hog Creek and Wapakonetta bands who came to Kansas with Joseph Parks in 1832. His family then consisted of one female over 50, one male between 25 and 50, one female between 25 and 50, and three boys under 10. See Roy, p. 40.

In 1835, John and William Perry were the principal Shawnee chiefs of the Hog Creek band; Capt. Blackfeather, Little Fox, Henry Clay, and Letho were subchiefs. Marston G. Clark was their agent, and Charles Shane was their interpreter. L. Jones was their blacksmith. See Caldwell, p. 19.

Henry Clay was among the Shawnees who went with Chief John Perry and Capt. Joseph Parks and served in the Florida War. Clay was employed as the Shawnee and Ottawa interpreter by the Kansas Agency in 1835 and 1836, serving in various official capacities on behalf of his people up until his death in 1846. James Gillespie Hamilton wrote in his notebook that Clay was an educated and talented man but, in his opinion, lacked the "moral honesty" to become a strong leader of his nation. See Barry, pp. 284, 300, 573.

William Clay was allotted land as a Shawnee in Kansas in 1855. He may have been white enough to pass for white, and he may have moved off the reservation entirely. Although there was a Susan Clay listed, no males appeared with the Clay surname among the Shawnees who settled on the lands of the Cherokee nation in 1869. Maybe they all left the reservation. But the Clay name appears in later years to have been carried on as an Ottawa name, so perhaps the Shawnee Henry Clay, in his capacity as "Shawnee and Ottawa interpreter," met and married a woman belonging to an Ottawa clan.

Among the Ottawas on the 1883 Census was Henry Clay, age 50, Martha, 34, David, 13, Catherine Walker (step-daughter of Henry Clay), 10, Angeline Clay, 7, Lewis Dagenett (step-son of Martha Clay), and an infant son of Martha and Henry Clay, not named. See JAIFR, vol. IV, #2, pp. 100-111; and the 1883 Ottawa Census in the Quawpa Agency Records, on microfilm, National Archives, Texas.

CLEGHORN – a Potawatomi/Otoe name.

In 1783, two of the eighteen original trustees of Clarksville (later Indiana) were John and Joseph Cleghorn. Like David Owens, John Owens, Martin Carney, Robert George, and the others who dared settle in the Indian territory at the time, they appear to have engaged in the Indian trade and at least some of the eighteen people listed had Indian wives. White women were in short supply, and having a red wife facilitated the trade and certainly made it safer to live on the Indian side of the river. See Baird, p. 44.

One member of this family, John Cleghorn, was captured by Indians in 1792. See Putnam, p. 311. There may also have been other members of the family captured and adopted.

W. W. Cleghorn and Robert Polke, both apparently the sons of adopted whites, were living as traders among the Potawatomis in the 1830s. See Barry, p. 341.

The Laport County, Indiana, Willbook A, p. 122, contains the will of Ann S. Cleghorn (Akat), a member of the Potawatomi Nation. It was dated February 13, 1849; probated August 3, 1852, and names husband W. W. Cleghorn, son William M. Rice (apparently by a previous marriage), and her mother Anawanka, "a good and ample support in food and clothing and a comfortable home." The executor was W. W. Cleghorn and the witnesses were Johnston Lykins and Noediah Dille. The will was also presented in Jackson County Court, State of Missouri, as abstracted in the Hoosier Genealogist.

Some of the Cleghorn family intermarried with other tribes. James Cleghorn was interpreter for the Council Bluffs Agency in Kansas in 1853. On the Otoe Allotment Roll, 1891-1907, are listed James Cleghorn, age 40, Jane Cleghorn (O-chay-tom-me), 28, and William Cleghorn (Chee-naw-ruch-ee), 12. See JAIFR, vol. IX, #3, p. 49.

COHON, COLHOON, CALHOON – a Shawnee/ Delaware name.

Thomas Calhoon was an Indian trader who lived among the Delaware whose name sometimes appears as Colhoon. In 1762, Heckewelder attended the funeral of the wife of the Delaware chief, Shingass, and Thomas Calhoon was living at the town and also attended the ceremony. See Heckewelder, pp. 270-275.

Cohon was one of the legendary Delaware trackers and free-hunters who resided among the Shawnee.

In 1805, Pierre Chouteau and Lt. George Peter hired Cohon and his brother as hunters and guides on a peace-making mission to the Osages. During the next thirty years, Cohon became noted as among the most expert of hunters, guides, and express riders. William Clark wrote Richard Graham about Cohon, affirming that he was a Delaware who lived among Fish's band of Shawnees and endorsing his character and reputation for honesty.

Johnston Lykins, a Baptist missionary, writing some recollections in 1858, remembered fondly his association with the Delaware free hunters including Cohon, "who annually wintered in the mountains" and would call on Lykins and tell him of "his romantic adventures. He spoke English well and stood high in the estimation of all..."

It is likely that Cohon was involved in many of the expeditions involving Delawares for which we have not yet discovered a muster. For a more complete account of Cohon's career, see the excellent "A History of Shawnee's Fabled Mountain Man," by Rodney Staab, *Shawnee Journal-Herald*, September 23, 1992, p. 8D. Cohon married into the Rogers family and Rodney Staab says that as late as the 1880's Shawnees with the surname of Cohon could be found in Oklahoma.

Among the Shawnees who settled on the lands of the Cherokee nation by 1869 were George, Margaret, and Edward Cohon. See JAIFR, vol. IV, #2, pp. 100-111.

COLBERT – a Chickasaw/Choctaw name.

The original Colbert (George, James, or Alexander) was a Scottish trader who married the daughter of a Chickasaw chief and started the name among them. Through intermarriage, the name also became common among the Choctaws, Creeks, Cherokees, Shawnees and other tribes through the years.

The Cherokees, Choctaws, and Chickasaws formed an alliance in 1780 in their attempt to repulse George Rogers Clark's forces from their land. Clark built Ft. Jefferson at the confluence of the Ohio and Mississippi Rivers. The adjacent town was named Clarksville. Allan W. Eckert (in *The Frontiersmen*) missed this completely and confused Ft. Jefferson with Ft. Nelson at the site of Louisville. Years after Ft. Jefferson was abandoned, another Ft. Jefferson was built in Ohio.

Another Clarksville was later established across from Louisville. Historian Margery Heberling Harding makes the same mistake in her excellent compilation, *George Rogers Clark and His Men*. She says that the company of Capt. George Owens marched against the Shawnees in 1780. It never happened.

Anyway, Capt. Robert George commanded Ft. Jefferson and Capt. James Piggot headed the land company who sold lots in the town. In June, 1780, a hunting party of whites were attacked on the Ohio river, some were killed, and two were made captives. Then in September, a large force of Cherokees besieged the fort. They were joined (or replaced) with a force of Chickasaws and Choctaws with some Potawatomis and Delawares.

While the colonists held the fort, the Chickasaws burnt the town and destroyed the crops and grain stores. There were red allies with the whites and white allies with the reds. Colbert and Whitehead came out with some of the red chiefs under a white flag. Capt. Robert George sent out Leonard Helm with David Owens, the interpreter, and James Piggot, who represented the interests of the town. Colbert said that if they surrendered, all would be permitted to leave and go back east, "except for a few the Indians had determined to kill." They knew that they had little food and little ammunition, Colbert said, information taken from one of their captives.

There was firing from the fort, and Colbert was wounded in the arm. His party dropped the white flag and dashed behind a tree for protection. Leonard Helm apologized for this treachery, and promised that it would be dealt with severely. The men who fired from the fort were William Musick and Jefferson Ducoigne. Of course, nothing was done to either of them.

Capt. Robert George refused to surrender. That night a relief party arrived and slipped into the fort with some ammunition and food. The whites fired their swivel several times, thus refuting Colbert's evaluation of their condition. Eventually, the red forces returned to their villages. Most of James Piggot's land company who had bought lots in the town were ruined and went down the river. Many of them — the Shilling, Grafton, Hutsel, and Iller families among them — settled in Natchez. Some went on to Kaskakia, some came back to Kentucky. At great expense, George Rogers Clark maintained Ft. Jefferson until 1781 when it was abandoned. There are many accounts of the battle, but for the best eyewitness account, see Robert George's letter to John Montgomery appearing in Seineke, pp. 457-459.

The Colbert family became known as "river pirates," attacking and looting flatboats and keelboats that descended the river until Capt. Robert George and James Sherlock made a peace with them in 1782. Thereafter, they were among the tribes most friendly to the interests of the United States. James Colbert brought a war party of Chickasaws to assist Anthony Wayne at the Battle of Fallen Timbers. General Wayne put the Chickasaws into the thick of the fight, and the unit was cut to pieces, Chief Piomingo being among the fallen.

Among the Choctaws given land by the Treaty of Dancing Rabbit Creek in 1830 was Susan Colbert (formerly Susan James).

Listed on the 1885 Census of Boktucklo County in the Choctaw Nation were Sampson Colbert, 66, with Sarah Ann Colbert, 25, Silvesta Colbert, 4, and Ellis Colbert, 1. Also listed is Davidson Colbert, 17, who may have been boarding with Benjamin Allen, 40, and Eliza Ann Campbell, 30, and her family which seems to have included Leana Campbell, 16, Liddia Campbell, 10, Anderson Campbell, 8, and Simeon Nakeshi, 16. See JAIFR, vol. IV, #2, p. 91.

COLDWATER – a Shawnee name.

John Coldwater was with Capt. Lewis during the War of 1812. See Draper 23S175. Simon Kenton's family learned the Shawnee language from long association with Chieska, Spybuck, Cornstalk, John Coldwater and Pa-mo-tee, who was John Coldwater's son. See Kenton, p. 253. "John Coldwater was a big, heavy set fellow, jovial and funny." See Draper 17S105.

Stephen Coldwater was among the Shawnees listed on the muster roll of the Hog Creek and Wapakonetta bands who came to Kansas with Joseph Parks in 1832. His age was given as between 10 and 25. See Roy, p. 40.

Among the Shawnees who went with Capt. Joseph Parks and served in the Florida War were Stephen and John Coldwater.

COLLET – a Shawnee name.

George Collet was captured, adopted, and lived among the Indians. He fought on the Indian side during the Battle of Pt. Pleasant. Collet was conspicuous amongst his company of Shawnee, echoing Cornstalk's cries of "fight on, fight on" and encouraging his companions throughout the fight. David White shot him and he fell. After the battle was over, White and some of his company washed some of the warpaint off of George Collet's face and he was recognized by his brother, Thomas Collet, a member of the white forces. See McWhorter, p. 358. See Draper 8ZZ71.

COLTER – a Wyandot name.

Among the guardianship cases reviewed by the Commissioner of Indian Affairs in 1871 was the case of John Colter, a Wyandot, who was guardian for his brother, Amos. Amos Colter died in 1869 or 1870, but John Colter had been murdered while serving in the military during the Civil War. See JAIFR, vol. VIII, #2, p. 19.

COMPASS – a Delaware name.

Joseph Compass was among the Indians as early as 1756. He served as an express rider. His name often appeared in the Indian trader accounts, and he signed several treaties. See SWJ Papers, vol. V., p. 356. For Joseph and James Compass, see Hanna, I, p. 282.

Jim Compass was a "friendly Indian" who attended a shooting match in Ohio — but is said to have killed Thomas Burbridge for his rifle, a story told by A. W. Patterson in *The Backwoods.*

CONNER, CONNORS – a Delaware name.

One of the Indian traders that the Rev. David Jones saw at the Indian towns in the 1770s was Richard Connors who was living with his wife, Margaret Boyer Connor who had been captured when young and adopted into the Delaware Nation. She spoke only broken English, and the family conversed in Delaware normally. This household included their sons, William and John, who stayed on the edge of red society like so many others mentioned in this work, and became scouts, interpreters, and traders. See Weslager, p. 334.

I'm not certain what happened to Richard Connors and his wife. They may have moved to Nelson County, Kentucky. William and John Connors moved to Indiana and operated trading posts there. William Connors settled in Chief William Anderson's town and married Me-king-ees, the chief's daughter. During the War of 1812, William Connors commanded a company of 30 Delaware scouts on the side of the United States. They were at the Battle of the Thames against the British and the forces of Tecumseh.

In the absence of her husband, Me-king-ees ran the trading post along with their business partner, William Marshall, a white man who also had married a Delaware.

The children of William Connors and Me-king-ees included John (Jack), Eliza, Nancy, William M., James, and Harry Hamilton Connor. When her father, Chief William Anderson, took the Delawares west, Me-king-ees took her children and went with him. William Connors stayed behind, remarried a white woman, and became a prominent Indiana politician. He died a wealthy man with over 6,000 acres of land, and his red family was involved in a suit against his white family in 1861 over the vast estate.

John Connors, a son of William and Me-king-ees, became a scout and interpreter in Texas for General Sam Houston. He became chief of the Delawares who located on the Brazos River and associated with the Caddos who included Jack Harry and Jim Shaw. Connors married a Delaware in 1828 and they became the parents of George Washington Connors in 1829. John Connors continued to serve as a scout on several expeditions in the southwest, including the Eldridge expedition into Commanche country in 1843. He returned to Kansas after the death of Chief Ketchum to become the head chief of the Delawares in 1858.

The family of John Connors then included his wife Nancy, 33, his son, John Q, age 16, and his son by his previous wife, George, age 29. John Connors' family intermarried with the Bullette, Haff, and Ketchum families. Also in the household were some members of Harry Hamilton Connors' family.

Harry Hamilton Connors, son of William and Me-king-ees, appears to have accompanied his brother John at least in some of his adventures in Texas. Harry married a Caddo woman and his children included Alexander and Diogenese. Alexander came from Texas with his uncle, John Connors, and married Elizabeth Thomas and they had two girls, Elizabeth and Lucy Connor. The family married into the Zulkey, Yellowjacket, Swope, and Keys families.

Nancy Connors, a daughter of William and Me-king-ees, married first a Delaware named Wilson and they had a son, called Young Wilson, and then she married John Quincy Adams, a son of Thomas Roylston who was the third son of President John Quincy Adams. The President sent his grandson to the Delawares as a goodwill ambassador and the young man accompanied the Delawares during the Florida War in 1836-1837. The children of Nancy and John Quincy Adams included Mary and William. See ADAMS.

William (Bill) Connors, a son of William and Me-king-ees, also accompanied James Connors to Texas and served as a messenger to the Commanches there. He seems to have died in Kansas in 1861, but before then he fathered at least two children, William McEwin Conner and William (Washer) Marshall Conner. The Conner was apparently dropped from the names of these two.

William McEwin's wife was named Susan and their children included Lily (who married a Wilson), Sarah (who married a Cherokee, Charlie Williams, and their children included Anna and Nannie Williams). Anna Williams married William Greathouse and their daughter Margaret married Kenneth Gougler.

William Marshall married first Susan Whiteturkey and their children included Ida Mary Marshall who married first Fredrick Metzner and second D. N. Broadbent and had nine children altogether. William Marshall married second Lizzy Secondine James and their children included Andy, James, Jane Anna, and Maggy Marshall.

James Connor, the youngest son of William and Me-king-ees, was born in Indiana and went west with his family. He became the interpreter for Marston G. Clark. While still a young man, he went to Florida and served in the War with the Seminoles in 1836-1837. He was one of James Swannuck's band of ten Delaware scouts and accompanied James C. Freemont west in

1846. In 1854, he accompanied Chief Ketchum on a trip to Washington and they stopped by to see their relatives in Indiana.

Eliza Connor, youngest daughter of William and Me-king-ees, was only two years old when the Delawares left Indiana. She was raised Delaware and married Bill Halfmoon. Their daughter, Sarah Halfmoon, was born in 1839 and that same year Bill Halfmoon died. Eliza then married Tom Wilson, who was later killed by a buffalo bull. She then married George Bullette (Pen-dox-ie), a much older man who was half-French, half-Delaware, a village chief. See BULLETTE.

My reference here is Ruby Cranor's wonderful work on Chief William Anderson and his descendants. For a more elaborate account of these families, including dates and more specific information, please see her work.

CONWAY, COPWAY – an Ojibwa name.

Among others, John Conway, his wife, and seven children were all captured at Ruddle's Station in 1780. Among the children were Elizabeth, Sallie (then six years old), John (then twenty-two), and Joseph (then fifteen). Elizabeth married W. M. Daughtery. Sallie returned to Kentucky when she was fifteen. Lafferty also lists Samual Conway, a brother, his wife, two daughters and a son, Joseph. Joseph had been wounded by Indians two weeks before his capture, and partially scalped. He survived but his head was bandaged. See Lafferty, pp. 321-322.

Were any of these children adopted by the Indians?

According to McCutchen, George Copway (Kahgegahkowh) presented a book on the origins and traditions of the Ojibwa Nation. He was supposed to have been a chief as well as a Christian missionary, but

I have not yet seen a copy of his book. It was published in Philadelphia by James Harmstead, 1847.

COON, KUHN, COONHAWK – a Wyandot/ Delaware name.

An Abraham Kuhn, "a Wyandot who could read," appears in the colonial journals of several early traders including that of Richard Butler. See Williams, p. 44n. At one time, he served as the war chief of the Wyandots, and he served as the deputy Half King after Tarhe was wounded at Fallen Timbers.

"Coo-na-haw, otherwise old John Coon, calmly settled down on Kenton's farm with his squaw, his son William Moses, and his two daughters Katy and Betsy and lived there for years; a little son Abraham died early and was buried on Kenton's place. Coo-na-haw was a full-blooded white man, captured when a boy of three and reared by the savages. He used to say he was 'an Indian, but a white Indian.' When John Downden came up from Kentucky to visit his mother the second summer after the migration, he found Coo-na-haw already settled at Kenton's, and recognized him as the Indian who had nearly shot him on paint Creek in 1793. Coon told him then, as he had told Kenton, that in the Little Miami skirmish of 1792, it was the splashing on the Indian children and squaws making off through the stream which made the whites believe that reinforcements were coming up." See Kenton, pp. 252-253.

John Coon was a white man adopted by the Indians. He got into a fight with another Indian, and both shot. John Coon's gun misfired and he was killed. See Draper 17S287.

On the 1843 Muster Roll of Wyandots from Sandusky, Ohio, were listed:

1. Auren Coon's family, consisting of one male 25 to 55, one male and one female 10 to 25, and three males and two females under 10.

2. George Coon's Widows, between 25 and 55.

In 1855, among the Wyandots in Kansas was the family of Sara Coon, age 40, with children Thomas, 11, Mary, 9, Joseph, 7, Henry, 6, and William, an infant. George Coon, age 21, apparently also lived in the household and may have been another son or step-son. Among the Wyandots allotted land in Kansas were Thomas, Mary, and Henry Coonhawk. See KHC, vol. 15, pp. 110, 134.

Among the Wyandot guardianship cases reviewed by the Commissioner of Indian Affairs in 1871 was the case of Sarah Coon, who had been the guardian for William and Henry Coon.

Also heard was the case of John L. Coon who had died about 1860 in Sandusky, Ohio, leaving heirs that included four children and his ward, George Whitewing. One of Coon's children, William, testified. Whitewing was the step-father of Coons. See JAIFR, vol. VIII, #2, p. 20, 22.

A James Coon (Merumdahhese) appears on the Delaware rolls appearing in the JAIFR, vol. IV, #1, 1985, pp. 31-52.

Among the Delawares appearing on the 1880 Cherokee census of the Cooweescoowee District were Sallie Coon (age 59), James Coon (age 40), Rosa Coon (age 20), Wane Coon (age 4), and Whale Coon (age 2). See JAIFR, vol. X, #1, p. 56.

COOK – a Mohawk name.

John Cook (a white man adopted by the Mohawks) became a leading warrior of the western Iroquois living among the Delawares and Shawnees. These disgruntled Iroquois were commonly referred to as Mingoes, and John Cook was given the name, the White Mingo, and his name appeared frequently on traders' ledgers, travelers' diaries, and he usually signed treaties. Edward Cook, probably related to John

Cook, was given the name Telinemut. Telinemut sometimes served as an interpreter and messenger for the Pennsylvania Indian Department in the 1700s. Mention is made of him in the Sir William Johnson Papers, the Pennsylvania Colonial Records, and elsewhere.

Andrew Cook was among the Mohawks who fought for America during World War II. He was killed at Manila. See JAIFR, vol XI, #1, p. 27.

Basil (Buddy) Cook, a Mohawk, became the co-owner of the Mohawk Bingo Hall and involved in the controversy at the heart of the 1990 Mohawk Civil War. See Rick Hornung, One Nation Under the Gun: Inside the Mohawk Civil War.

CORNATZER – a Shawnee name.

Samuel Cornatzer was a white man who married a Shawnee, Caroline Suggett, and was officially adopted into the tribe in 1847. His brother, Calvin Cornatzer, also married a Shawnee woman.

During the time when the Rev. Charles Bluejacket was head chief of the Shawnees, Samuel Cornatzer served as clerk of the tribal council. In 1864, prior to Charles Bluejacket abdicating his position, Cornatzer testified in defense of the chief and his methods. He said that Blue Jacket had his own ceremony of marriage, but would perform either the traditional or the newer custom depending upon the desires of the couple to be married.

Among the Shawnees who settled on the lands of the Cherokee nation by 1869 were Samuel M., Caroline, Lyeurgus, Ninie E., Adelia A., Samuel, Cyrus, and Lidia Cornatzer. See JAIFR, vol. IV, #2, pp. 100-111.

Among the Shawnee guardianship cases heard in 1871 by Ely Parker, Commissioner of Indian Affairs, was the case of Samuel M. Cornatzer. Most of his wards were not listed, but he distributed money to several members of the Black Bob band of Shawnees who are listed as Thomas Pierce, Harriet Pierce, Perryann Henry, and Ship Tuckless. He gave money to Henry Blackfish that was meant for Ship Tuckless. See JAIFR, vol. VIII, #2, p. 26.

For the more complete family data on Samuel Cornatzer, see SUGGETT.

Cyrus C. Cornatzer, son of Samuel and Caroline (Suggett) Cornatzer, a member of the Rabbit Clan, was given the Shawnee name of See-tah-way-see-coh. Cyrus owned a horse farm and trained race horses, having a string of his own horses and also training for other owners. Cyrus married Lydia Boggan in 1871, and their children included Caroline B., Nanya Jane, Cornelia, and Walter C. Cornatzer.

Walter C. Cornatzer helped his father on the family farm in Indian Territory. Walter had bay colored hair, brown eyes, and a fair complexion. He met and married Grace Patterson, a daughter of the Rev. William G. Patterson, in 1901. Their children included Winifred (b. 1902), Rachel (b. 1903), Warner (b. 1905), Cornelius (b. 1906), Carlotta (b. 1908), Carol (b. 1910), and Catherine (b. 1912). See SOCC, vol. I, pp. 307-308; information from Patricia M. Chambers.

CORNSTALK – a Shawnee/Miami name.

The powerful Shawnee chief named Cornstalk had several white connections in his extended family.

Silverheels, Keeweton, and Cornstalk were supposed to be brothers or half-brothers. Their sister was Nonhelema, also known as Catherine, Kate, or the Grenadier Squaw. Said to have been among Cornstalk's extended family were Elipinissco, the Walker, the Black Wolf, John Wolf, Aracoma, Henry Clay, Young Cornstalk (Nern-pe-nes-he-quah, Stout Body), and Peter Cornstalk. Maybe two Peter Cornstalks.

Cornstalk's son (or son-in-law), Elinipsico, was with him and another Shawnee on a diplomatic mission to Ft. Randolph in 1777. The commander of the fort, Capt. Matthew Arbuckle, undiplomaticly imprisoned Cornstalk and his son for reasons that are unclear. A mob decided to vent their hatred on the unarmed Shawnees, and as they approached the prison cabin, a white woman ran to warn the prisoners.

Elinipsico was afraid, but Cornstalk was calm and said stoicly, "I can die but once, and it's all the same to me, now or another time."

"Cornstalk's son fled into the loft and his father shamed him. Told him he had but once to die and ought to die like a man. Cornstalk opened his breast, and said if any man had anything against him, to avenge himself. Several bullets were shot through his heart. The Indian who had climbed up the chimney was pulled down and killed."

See Draper 5S11; Thwaites, Dunmore's War, pp. 347, 432, 433; Rev. on the Upper Ohio, p. 26, 103, 126; Gilbert, p. 97; Williams, The Journal of Richard Butler, WPHM, vol. 47, notes 23 & 69.

Among those present at Cornstalk's death was Henry Aleshite, whose pension declaration S.29579, was taken 24 Sept., 1832, in Page County, Virginia, when he was 78. Aleshite said that he was present at Ft. Randolph when Cornstalk and "a white man who had married Cornstalk's daughter" were killed.

It should not be surprising that Elinipsico was white. The name "Elinipsico" was a "beloved name" among the Shawnee, a name given to outsiders who have become "special friends," and according to Indian agent John Johnston there were several the name was bestowed upon at different times. See, for instance, Draper 11YY30.

It would not be surprising if Cornstalk himself were found to have been part white or black. His father "was the White Fish or Sunfish," and the former was a re-ocurring name given to white captives and the latter name was, in fact, given to a black man adopted by the Senecas.

Cornstalk and his sister, Nonhelema, were both exceptionally large people, especially for Shawnees. The Rev. David Jones noted that the Shawnees were not even so "well-made" as the Delawares, and all reliable accounts indicate that Shawnees tended to be relatively small-boned and short. "Cornstalk was large and tall and heavily formed, of commanding, noble appearance. The Grenadier Squaw was also tall. Her daughter, Fanny, was slender, not very pretty. Mother and daughter always rode elegant horses." See Draper 5S11.

One traveler noted that among the attractive faces to be found on Shawnee women was that of the "Mistress Grenadier" who "lives in a house of her own, built after the European manner in the orchard of the fort. She is no longer young but still shows the traces of a faded beauty which formerly elevated her to the companionship of an English, and later of an American General. Her daughter, with all the advantages of youth, is not so attractive as her mother." See Schoeff, p. 277.

I'm not certain which American general was referred to by Schoeff. General Richard Butler or his brother, William, Indian traders and known to have had red children, seem to be obvious choices and Richard was, indeed, supposed to have married one of Cornstalk's sisters, but Nonhelema was almost as famous as Cornstalk, and I have not seen this mentioned elsewhere. But maybe that was how it happened.

If so, then Capt. Butler, the Shawnee, must have been Nonhelema's son. See BUTLER.

By 1785, however, Richard Butler was back with his white wife and Nonhelema was living with Moluntha. She was present when that peaceable chief was murdered, and she was among the women captured and held at Danville, Kentucky. She might also have been the woman who tried to work out the prisoner exchange with James Sherlock.

According to the Virginia Calendar of State Papers, May 21st, 1784, p. 586: Speaks of "the frequent observations of Young Cornstalk, the son of that great chief of the same name, whose tragical end at Point Pleasant fixed the Shawnee nation our inveterate enemy. While at Louisville...he would frequently say, as if with a wish to be informed, that he did not know why our warriors had come there after the war between us and Great Britain was over, but that he hoped all would be peace..."

Peter Cornstalk was possibly taken captive by whites at the same time that Moluntha was killed and John Logan was taken. See the interview with Charles Tucker, 23S175. More likely, I suspect, he was taken on John Hardin's expedition together with Blue Bird who later became the wife of Logan, but further research needs to be done on this.

Was Peter Cornstalk a son of Cornstalk? Some of the Kansas Shawnees whom Draper interviewed thought so, some did not. Possibly there were two generations of Peter Cornstalk's. Or possibly Peter Cornstalk had a Miami mother. Or possibly there were two Peter Cornstalk's, one a Shawnee and the other a Miami.

Peter Cornstalk's Shawnee name was given as Peitehthator on the 1817 treaty and as P. H. Thawtaw when he signed the Shawnee treaty in 1831. Charles Bluejacket told Draper in 1868 that Peter Cornstalk's name was Pe-et-tha-ta or "he comes flying," and that he died about 1842 when in his mid-sixties. According to Harvey, p. 244, Peter Cornstalk was a warchief.

Charles Bluejacket said that the Old Cornstalk was "some the oldest" of the two, which suggests that the young man having political conversations at Louisville in 1784 was the Young Cornstalk rather than Peter Cornstalk.

This young man, the Young Cornstalk referred to, must have been a teenager in 1784, and perhaps did not have many memories of his father but was raised by one of his uncles, and possibly by Major Snake. Young Cornstalk was at the falls, painted, in 1784. See Draper 11S186.

It was probably the Young Cornstalk (Nern-pe-nes-he-quah, Stout Body) who was among the Shawnees who went with Capt. Joseph Parks and fought against the Seminoles in the Florida War.

Living among the Shawnees and Wyandots in Wyandotte County, Kansas in 1855 were John B. Cornstalk, age 35, and Mary Cornstalk, apparently his wife whose age is not given on the Wyandot census.

The Black Wolf (Biasieka) and John Wolf (La-wa-tu-cheh) were both supposed to have been sons or adopted sons of Cornstalk. John Wolf was the father of Henry Clay.

Pete Cornstalk, the Miami, was called Peter Cornstalk and he may have actually been a son of Cornstalk by a Miami wife, but his Miami name was Ah-san-zang (Sunshine). He is the man for whom Pete Cornstalk Creek was named. He was an Eel River or Wea Miami, and lived in Indiana until his death. It is around Pete Cornstalk the Miami that most of the Indiana legends have grown. Bridgie Brill Brelsford has a marvelous time sorting out the Peter Cornstalks, and I recommend Brelsford's work.

COTTER or COTTIES – a Wyandot name.

A John Cotter was among the whites delivered up to General Henry Bouquet in 1764. Perhaps he went back to the Indians. A James Cotties (or James Cotters or Catas) was supposed to have been "the Indian who killed Capt. Hambus and Martin."

On the 1843 Muster Roll of Wyandots from Sandusky, Ohio, were listed:

1. Francis Cotter Sr.'s household, consisting of one male and one female over 55, two males and two females 10 to 25, and one male and one female under 10.
2. Francis Cotter Jr.'s family, consisting of one male and one female between 10 and 25.

Among the Wyandots allotted land in Kansas in 1855-57 were Nicholas, 33, Caroline E., 6; John, 31; Hiram, 20; Francis, 36, Elizabeth, 31, Bernard, 9, James W., 6, and Cassils Cotter, 4. See KHC, vol. 15, pp. 110, 134. Nicholas Cotter was also a distinguished, intelligent-looking individual. For his picture, see Tooker, p. 404.

COX – a Shawnee name.

Rumleco Cox was listed among the Shawnees and Delawares dealing with the Indian traders in the Ohio Company Papers in the 1760s. See Bailey.

A young man named Cox was captured with the Armstrongs on the Ohio River in 1794. See the Narrative of Jeremiah Armstrong in the *Old Northwest Historical Quarterly*, p. 151.

A black Delaware named Cox was the interpreter for Chief William Anderson when the missionary Issac McCoy came to see him.

Among the Shawnees who settled on the lands of the Cherokee nation by 1869 were Mary, Claude, and Hubbard Cox. See JAIFR, vol. IV, #2, pp. 100-111.

Claud (age 27) and Margaret Cox (age 53) were among the Shawnees on the 1880 Cherokee Nation Census. See JAIFR, vol X, #1, p. 56.

COYLE, CROYLE – a Shawnee name.

The original English spelling may have been Croyle, but the Shawnee always had trouble pronouncing the "R" sound.

In early Bedford County, Pennsylvania, "Thomas Croyle cleared land and raised crops thereon in 1752, building a cabin of logs, three or four perches from the Snake-Spring. He married Judith Stoneking, an Indian woman," and he traded with the Indians, running a blacksmith shop and a tavern for many years. Their sons, George and Thomas, ran another blacksmith shop in the same county. See *Bedford: The Kernal of Greatness*, compiled and published by the Bedford County, Pennsylvania Heritage Commission, p. 18.

George Croyle (Coyle) and his descendants have passed on this Indian tradition. There are Indian blood traditions from every point on the compass which lead back to this Bedford County, Pennsylvania family. Those who intermarried include the Sorrell (Sorel, Sowell), Redmon (Redman, Dedman) Stringer (Tringer, Springer), and Cartmill (Cotmill, Carpmell) families.

Of course, there is more than one source of Indian blood in most families whose American histories precede the 1770s. What are the common denominators? Well, in this case, one of them seems to be Bath County, Kentucky, and from there back to Augusta County, Virginia and western Pennsylvania, on back to the common denominators of most Indian blood traditions: Indian traders and adopted white captives. A Peggy and Molly Cartmill, a Margarett Carpmill, and a Mary Tringer and her two children were among those who were forcibly delivered up to Bouquet in 1764.

(If you know more about the basis for these traditions, why not sent the details to me so that I might present them with documentation in a future volume of *Indian Blood*.)

COZINE, CONSEEN – a Cherokee name.

I believe that there is a basis for most family traditions of Indian blood. The Indians share the same blood types as the rest of humanity, and by Indian blood, I mean direct descent of a member of a Native

American tribe, either by blood or adoption.

There are lots of people who have the Indian blood tradition and find that they descend from an adopted white who lived among the Indians and married another adopted white among them. This situation was fictionalized in the movie *Dances With Wolves*, and in real history it happened many times. The descendants of these unions will have the Indian blood tradition, and probably that is true of those adopted captives who returned with habits learned while living red.

"Grandpa was the best hunter in the county; he was part-Indian, you know." The basis for such traditions is sometimes corrupted, but the point here is that when there is a strong tradition like that, there is usually a basis for it. These traditions may be embellished or mistold, but the tradition has a basis to be found in history.

It would not surprise me if such a tradition would not develop around Sarah Cozine, orphan of Cornelius Cozine, step-daughter of Samuel Demaree. Sarah was captured in Kentucky when still a child in 1790 and she did not return to her family until after the Treaty of Greenville, in 1795. She married a white man and raised a large family. Family tradition says that she was regarded as somewhat eccentric for following Indian habits learned during her days living red — such things as the way she kindled a fire, and moving out of her cabin into a wigwam during the summer. See Demarest, pp. 110, 506-507.

Among the Cherokees listed on the 1880 Census of the Saline District were Frank Conseen, 34, his wife, Josephine, 30, and their family which included Susie, 8, Josephine, 7 Thomas, 4, Joseph, 2, and Nancy, an infant. See JAIFR, vol. VI, #2, p. 20.

CRANE – a Wyandot/Delaware/Shawnee name.

The Crane (Tarhe), was a Wyandot chief whose

last wife was an adopted white girl named Sally Frost. The Crane was sometimes referred to as the Half King. To at least some degree, the Crane deserved the title, as several other tribes seemed to have occasionally bowed to his will, and he was yet powerful enough in the years prior to the War of 1812 to dissuade most of his tribe from following Tecumseh, Roundhead, and the Prophet.

Like the Miami chief Little Turtle, the Crane fought the United States until the Treaty of Greenville, and then he changed sides, once and for all. The Crane went by many names, usually Tarhe, a concept name which might have meant "the crane in the tree," but also meant "the tree of being," or "at the tree" or "the tree personified," take your pick. There were maybe six other names he went by, but he was usually called Crane, Tarhe, or the Half King.

Tarhe's wife was Sally Frost, a white woman who had been captured and adopted when young, with whom he raised a large family. One of Tarhe's daughters married Issac Zane. The family intermarried with whites, Wyandots, Miamis, Shawnees, and Delawares, and among the surnames of Tarhe's descendants are Zanes, Armstrongs, McCullochs, Gardners, Robetailles, Dawsons, and many, many others.

A Crane was listed on the payroll of the Miamis in 1831, receiving payment for thirty of the Miamis residing at Mississineway.

A younger Crane was the name of one of Jim Swannock's select band of Delaware and Shawnee hunters, and Crane was with Swannock when they scouted for John C. Fremont. The younger Crane may also have had a white wife, an adopted Shawnee. Indian agent John Johnston told Draper that "a Miss Sharp was taken prisoner when a child and adopted and "she grew up pretty and became the wife of the

Crane." See Draper 11YY11.

Among the Shawnees who settled on the lands of the Cherokee nation by 1869 were Mary Crane, Edward Crane, and a young child. See JAIFR, vol. IV, #2, pp. 100-111.

CRAWFORD – a Shawnee/Wyandot/Delaware/ Ottawa name.

Several Crawford descendants have told me of their Indian blood traditions, and I do not doubt them. The Crawfords were a family of Indian traders turned politicians that lived on the Pennsylvania and Virginia frontiers, and there were several sources of Indian blood in the family.

Hugh Crawford, who seems to have been one of the earliest traders, was captured during Pontiac's War but was treated well and later released. Arthur Crawford was captured by Delawares in 1756, was adopted by White Eyes into his extended family, and Crawford lived red by choice from age 14 to age 21. See Lobdell, Indian Warfare..., pp. 31-34.

Among the Senecas and Wyandots on the 1881 rolls were Lucy Crawford, age 28, and her family which included Ellen Crawford, 10, George Crawford, 8, Joseph Crawford, 6, and Julia Crawford, 3.

CUAPEA – a Shawnee name.

On the Hog Creek and Wapakonetta bands who travelled from the Ohio lands to Kansas in 1832, he appears to have been listed as Kewapa. His family then consisted of two males between 25 and 50, one female between 25 and 50, one male between 10 and 25, and three children under 10, two of them boys.

On the list of Shawnees given money for their Ohio lands they were forced to leave behind, Kewepea is listed with property worth $241.50, not nearly as much as Spybuck, but considerably more than was given for the property of such notable Shawnees as Peter Cornstalk ($162), John Coldwater ($117), or Henry Clay ($103). See Watson, vol. V, pt. 3, pp. 14-15.

Cuapea was in Capt. Joseph Parks's company of Shawnees in the Seminole War. He seems to have been one of the few casualties among the Shawnees and Delawares there. He was shot in the wrist, but recovered to tell of his adventures there. Cuapea was the only Delaware or Shawnee injured there, it appears, except for the death that was mentioned in Buchanan's journal.

"December 11th...One of the Delawares died today, and at night one of their chiefs came to Col. [Zachery] Taylor to say that it was their custom to fire off guns...and that he wishes permission to do so." Permission was granted and the Delaware was buried with Delaware military honors.

James Cuapea (Kewapea, Quaspea, etc.) lived on among the Shawnees who settled on the lands of the Cherokee nation by 1869 was James Quawapea. See JAIFR, vol. IV, #2, pp. 100-111; Buchanan, p.140; and Staab.

CUNNINGHAM – a Shawnee name.

Several members of the Cunningham family were captured and adopted by Shawnees. The story of the three-year captivity of Thomas Cunningham's wife is told in Withers, p. 370-373.

One of Thomas Cunningham's sons may have been Joseph Cunningham. "There was among the Cunninghams one Joe, captured by the Indians when a small boy and retained by them until grown.

"The traits of forest life were indelibly fired. He wore rings in his ears and in many ways retained the Indian dress. A hunting knife always hung at his belt and he had an unpleasant way of slipping up upon people unawares and, suddenly whipping out his knife, feign stabbing them, accompanying the motion with a guttural `whoa!' He was known as Indian Joe." See Comstock's West Virginia Encyclopedia, supplement volume #12-13, p. 419.

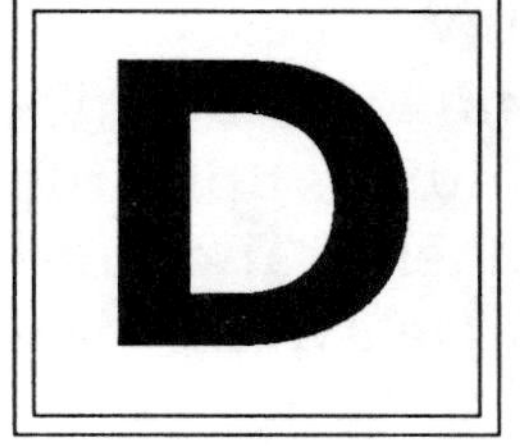

DAGENETT, DAGENEY, DASNEY, etc. – a Miami/Peoria name.

When George Croghan visited the Wabash settlements, he found that most of the residents were intermarried French and Indians. One of these original families was the Dagenett family which has many relicts living in the general population, some of whom have the Indian blood tradition.

There was a Dagenett living at Tippecanoe in 1789 (see Quaife, Hay's Journal). The family had been long associated with the Wea and Eel River groups, and some of its members became leaders of their respective tribes.

Noel Dagenett (Wis-ron-cah) was born in 1799, the son of Ambrose Dagenett and Me-chinqua-me-sha (beautiful shade tree). She was the sister of Jacco Godfroy (Tac-ke-he-kan, the tall oak), a Wea chief who lived near present-day Terre Haute, Indiana. Noel (Christmas) Dagenett married Mary Ann Issacs, a New York Brothertown Indian, and their children included Noel, Edwin R., Lucian, and Emma E. who married Thomas Hedges.

Noel Dagenett went to the Treaty of St. Mary's in 1818, and was allotted land on the Wabash along with his sister, Mary Dagenett Shields. Thereafter, Noel Dagenett became a leader of his tribe when negotiating with the United States. He was described as being quite handsome, "nearly, if not altogether, six feet high, weighing about 175 pounds, features of classic mold, the carriage of a soldier and a resonant voice with a touch of music in its modulation...he was a chief in truth...through most of his active years, he was rich —had lands, and horses, and money, and cattle..." See Valley and Lembcke, pp. 179-181.

DAVIS – a common name among many tribes.

John "Powder-maker" Davis, a mixed-blood descendant of Powhatan, lived with the Indians upwards of twenty years in the upper Monongahela Valley and intermarried with the Shawnees and Delawares. See Lough's AAT.

A Davis family was captured at Ruddle's Station in 1780, and at least one them intermarried with a fellow prisoner when Sarah Ruddle married Thomas Davis. Two of the Davis daughters and Issac Davis, a lad of six, were among those of the family known to have been taken captive by Shawnees at Polke's Station in 1782 in what was then Nelson County, Kentucky. In general, the adults captured at these two stations were sold to the British, the children were kept and later adopted. In all, there were 37 people captured at the Polke's Station, few have been identified, and there may have been other members of the Davis family among them.

Among the scouts who were the core of William Wells company of scouts was Benjamin Davis. He may have been a white or mixed-blood, as most of the others in the outfit had lived with the Indians and could pass for red or white.

Among the Shawnees who went with Chief John Perry and served in the Florida War was Bill Davis.

A Joseph Davis married Selekwa, a Shawnee woman, on the Kansas reservation in 1849, a marriage recorded in the Steward's Book.

Among the Shawnees on the 1880 Cherokee Census of the Cooweescoowee District was Willie Davis. See JAIFR, vol. X, #1, p. 59.

In 1867, when the Peorias bought land from the mixed Seneca/Shawnee band, Lewis Davis, a Seneca/Shawnee served as an interpreter. See Valley and Lembcke, p. 73.

Among the Senecas listed on the 1894 Quapaw

Agency Roll were Taylor Davis, 36, his wife Eliza, 38, and their children Eliza, 13, John, 12, Rosa, 8, and an infant daughter whose name is not given.

DAWSON – a Wyandot name.

A Peter Dawson was captured during Pontiac's War. A Mathias Dawson was delivered up by the Shawnees at the Treaty of Greenville.

A Dawson descendant from Ohio told me of her Indian blood tradition but could tell me nothing concrete, not even the tribal affiliation. That's not unusual. I made a note of it at the time and later, at the Filson Club in Louisville, I took a look through the excellent book on the Dawsons (*A Collection of Family Records & Biographical Sketches of the Dawson Family*, compiled by Charles C. Dawson, Joel Munsell Co, Albany, New York, 1874).

The genealogy of the Ohio Dawson family was there, but there was no mention of Indian blood. Typical. But when I compared the Dawson's listed in the book to those 1855 Wyandot census, the whole thing cleared up for me.

Jared B. Dawson was one of the founders of Bellefountaine, Ohio. He built a mansion for his family which stood "at the corner of Detroit and West Chillicothe streets," and which later became the City Building. He married the part-Wyandot Catherine (Kitty) Armstrong, a granddaughter of Issac Zane and his wife, who was a daughter of Tarhe (the Crane, the Wyandot Half King). See MMV, vol. 1, pp. 178-198.

Listed on the 1855 Wyandot Census was Jared S. Dawson, age 47, with his wife, Catherine, 47, and his children Eudora, 15, Robert, 14, Jordania, 13, Catherine, 10, and Oella, 5.

Charles C. Dawson said that Jared S. Dawson was the son of Peter Dawson and Jane (Rankin) Dawson of Cynthiana, Kentucky. Among the eight children of

Jared S. and Catherine L. (Armstrong) Dawson were: Wilhelmina who married a Mr. Cook and was then (1874) widowed with two children; Robert A. (possibly Armstrong); Kate Florence; Oilla C.; and Jordena H. who married T. J. Weakley and lived at Dayton, Ohio. See Dawson, p. 280, 297.

As with the Rankin, Armstrong, Zane, Punch, Peacock, Walpole, and other Shawnee/Wyandot families, some of the Dawsons moved west, some remained in Ohio. Some went to Kansas and then returned to Ohio. Others scattered out across Indiana, Kentucky, Tennessee, and eventually the four points of the compass, taking an Indian blood tradition with them. Of course, a few stayed with the Indians.

An R. A. Dawson was the captain of police at the Quapaw Agency in 1894. This was likely Robert A. Dawson, a part-Wyandot, and his six deputies on the list were Joe Bigknife (a part Shawnee), Moses Pooler (a part-Ottawa), Louis Miller, Amos Vallier (probably part-Peoria), John Faber (probably part-Shawnee/Wyandot), and Alfred Whitecrow (probably part-Seneca/Wyandot). See JAIFR, vol. VIII, #4, p. 41.

A Robert Dawson appears on the 1900 census of Indian territory as a Wyandot. According to the information listed, he was born in August, 1842, in Ohio. He lists his father as a white man, born in Kentucky, and his mother, a Wyandot, born in Ohio. See Prevost, p. 81.

DECKER – a Delaware/Seneca name.

A daughter of Cobus Decker was living at Capt. Bull's Delaware town in the early 1760s. See "Proceedings and Collections of the Wyoming Historical and Genealogical Society," vol. VIII, p. 179.

John and Moses Decker were early Indian traders associated with Moses Henry. They moved from western Pennsylvania and re-settled among the Indians near Vincennes, Indiana. They were among the first to enter land claims there.

Thomas Decker was chief of the Delawares at Chugnut in 1781 on the British side. See *The Nanticoke Indians* by C. A. Weslager, p. 89.

John Decker (Deckhart, Dickey, Deeker, etc) was a Seneca chief who told Draper his Indian name was Dah-gan-non-do, "he who patches." He was born near Franklin and spent his life on the Allegheny...His ability to speak English made him a useful member of Cornplanter's delegation in 1790-1791. Chi-ti-aw-dunk (Hummingbird) was Kyashota's sister and the mother of John Decker. Decker participated in the attack on Hannastown on the British side in the Revolution.

In 1850, Draper had a lengthy interview with him at which time he had his wife, a son, and a daughter living with him on the Allegheny reservation. See Kent and Deardorff, pp. 305, 464.

DEMUTH – a Seneca name.

According to one observer, "a rather surprising number of white men were settled among these Indians [the Genesee River Senecas]...with Indian wives and families..." and among them were Nicholas Demuth and Elijah Matthews who often served as interpreters. See Kent and Deardorff, p. 303.

DICK, DICKIE, or DICKEY – a Shawnee/Delaware name.

Several members of the Dick or Dickey family were captured by Indians during the early colonial Indian wars.

Thomas Dean associated with Jacob and Thomas Dick and their sons. He mentions them in his journal along with Peter Cornstalk, William Marshall, and many of the Brothertown Indians who had moved to Indiana.

Ruxton wrote that Jim Swannock, Big Nigger (Big Nichols), Little Beaver, and Jim Dick or Dickie were the "remnant of a band who had been trapping for several years in the mountains."

James Swannock's band originally consisted of a about 15 Delaware and Shawnee hunters. Most of them were killed when they were set upon by a much larger number of Sioux and Cheyenne on the Smokey Hill River in 1844. Capt. James Swannock vowed revenge, and he gathered a large war party, returned to the Smokey Hill country and destroyed the Sioux villages. The Delaware and Shawnee war party probably included the likes of Fall Leaf, Black Beaver, Spybuck, Little Beaver, John Sarcoxie, Jim Secondine, Killbuck, Jim Simond, Crane, Big Nigger, Tom Hill, and Jim Dickie.

Harvey L. Carter, who wrote a sketch of Capt. Swannock and three of his men, says that the Indian trader logbooks show that Jim Dickie hunted and traded extensively in various places including Fort Bent, Fort Barclay, Taos, Hardscrabble, El Pueblo, and especially the Wet Mountain Valley.

In 1849, trader Alexander Barclay gave Jim Dickie a tomahawk pipe when he left Ft. Barclay in the company of Charles Kinney, a white trapper. The Kinney family intermarried with the Delawares, and these trapping partners may have been related. See Ruxton, p. 271; Carter, p. 300; Kan. Hist. Quar., vol. 30, pp. 78-79.

In 1852, Mar-mar-trish-ey, the "recent widow" of Jim Dickie, the Delaware hunter, was traveling home from the mountains with her cousin, a young man about eighteen years old, taking a train of "some 13 horses and mules" loaded with deer and elk skins, and other valuables including $450 in cash. They were set upon by four United States Army deserters who killed the man and left Mar-mar-trish-ey for dead after cutting her throat.

"The criminals made for the Missouri border

with their loot; disposed of the animals as best they could; and three of them took a steamboat for St. Louis. Meantime Mar-mar-trish-ey recovered enough to travel..."

She managed to get to the authorities and report the crime. All of the killers were arrested, one at Liberty, Missouri, and the other three at St. Louis. One of the killers turned states evidence, one was acquitted, and two were hanged. Mrs. Dickey recovered and a few of the stolen animals were returned to her. See Barry, pp. 1111-1112.

Among the Shawnees who settled on the lands of the Cherokee nation by 1869 were Joseph and Juliana Dick. See JAIFR, vol. IV, #2, pp. 100-111.

Listed on the 1880 Absentee Shawnee roll were Billy Dick, 49, and his wife, Lucinda, age not given. James Dick, an Absentee Shawnee, administered the estate of Lucy Secondine (perhaps his sister), who died Sept. 19, 1898.

Among the Dick family on the 1880 Cherokee Census of the Cooweescoowee District were the Shawnees Angeline Dick (age 36), Big Dick (age 28), George Dick (age 27), James Dick (age 22), John Dick (age 4), Polly Dick (age 45), Sallie Dick (age 20), and Willie Dick (age 9 months). Apparently living with these Shawnees were Lucy Dick, listed as a white woman (age 28), and Jacob Dick, a Cherokee (age 28).

Also on the census were the Delawares Lucy Dick (age 15), Richard Dick (age 12) and Emily Dick (age 3). See JAIFR, vol. X, #1, p. 58.

DICKENS – a Shawnee name.

George Dickens was a member of Col. William Oldham's Company, Colonel William Linn's battalion, on the 1780 expedition against the Shawnees. On the pay abstract, it is stated that George Dickens deserted to the enemy. See Harding, p. 72.

George Dickens gave his power of attorney to others in Kentucky and he left Louisville to go live among the Shawnees. In Draper mss. 8J200, another pioneer remembers him as having been flogged in Louisville for selling whiskey to the soldiers. He is supposed to have gone to the head of the Miami where he resided with Shawnees. Returned captives often spoke of him.

George Dickens had a land claim in northern Kentucky adjoining that of George Clark.

According to Draper Mss. 44J4-5, Joseph Dickens was captured by Shawnees in 1780, 5 years a prisoner, settled in Mercer County (Ky) and raised a large family.

According to Papers from the Spanish Archives 1783-1800, vol. 9, p. 120-121: "Declaration of Simon Burney, Oct. 9, 1784, deposed that Henry Dickins lived in the woods, that is, he went from one nation to another, and in America, where his business was to steal negroes and horses. Henry Dickins, a native of South Carolina, had told him on the road that he had stolen a valuable race horse from General Clark that was shut up under lock and key before running him in a race in which the prize was a hundred loui and carried the said horse to the Talapuches where he sold him to a trader for forty louis."

In his answer to the charges, Henry Dickins admitted that he had broken out of jail in Louisville, but said that he taken the horse to enable him to get away.

DIXON – a Miami/Creek name.

Hannah Thorpe, daughter of Moses Thorpe, was "stolen by the Indians" in southern Indiana. Her father searched for her but did not find her until years after the War of 1812 was over. Hannah was then the wife of a Miami warrior, Me-tack-ke-quah, known to the whites as Captain Dixon. The father of Captain Dixon was Chief Me-to-cin-yah whose village was on the Mississinewa River. The Dixons lived about three miles from the village of Ashland, now Lafontaine, Indiana. Their children, Charles and Hannah, were educated after the white fashion, but they kept their Miami tribal status and, in the land divide of 1873, Charles Dixon and three of his daughters received their shares.

Hannah's children included Charles Marks, Hannah's son by Abe Marks, a white man. Charles Marks lived in Wabash County near the Miami County line, and had a large family. See Winger, pp. 68-69.

DODGE – a Shawnee/Delaware name.

Israel Dodge and John Dodge were early pioneers and Indian traders. John Dodge was closely associated with Baptist Ducoigne's family and the Kaskakia tribe during the Revolutionary war.

Among the Shawnees who went with Capt. Joseph Parks and served in the Florida War in the 1830's was a "Dodge."

Listed on the 1900 census was Arthur Dodge, a white man born in 1853 in Nova Scotia, Canada. His wife, Sara Dodge, was a Cherokee, daughter of a Cherokee woman and a white man. Apparently Arthur Dodge had previously been married to a Shawnee woman, because Ada M. Dodge, born 1884, lists him as her father and says that her mother was a Shawnee. See Prevost, p. 70.

Also listed on the 1900 Census of Indian Territory was a William Dodge, listed as a white man. His Delaware wife, Susan Dodge, had been born in Kansas in 1857. Her mother was a Delaware and her father had been born in New York. See Ibid., p. 50.

DOLEMAN – a Shawnee name.

Charles Doleman was among the 23 men in Squire

Boone's company at the Painted Stone. He next appears in Kentucky records in Lincoln County in 1782 where he was beset by debts and his property was confiscated. In Jefferson County in 1784, he was sued by Ezekial Trammel Hickman, nephew of William Hickman, sr.

The Doleman who left Louisville with James Sherlock and the Shawnee delegation in September, 1785, probably became familiar with Indian ways before that, somehow. He is mentioned in Butler's journal elsewhere as an Indian messenger. In 1789, John Hamtramck wrote to Gen. Josiah Harmar, "I enclose a number of papers which I got from one Dolman who lives with the Shawnees. He tells me that he had been with you last summer." Enclosed was a list of white prisoners among the Indians.

See Craig, vol. 2, p. 511; and Draper 14S216, the deposition of William Doleman, resident of the Shawnee towns. It identifies the British emissaries as Simon Girty, Thomas Smith, Robert Surplus, Capt. Caldwell, and Gillis or McGills.

DONAHOE – a Delaware name.

Among the captives delivered up to General Henry Bouquet in 1764 was John Donahoe. See New York Colonial Documents, vol. VII, p. 746.

Listed on the 1858 Chippewa / Munsee Delaware allotment roll are Henry, Polly, and Mary Anne Donahoe.

Listed on the 1886 Chippewa / Munsee Delaware annuity payroll were Jane Donahoe (age 40), her sons William (20) and Walter Donahoe (15), her daughter Ellen Donohoe (10), and her grandson Enoch Jones (3). Also listed is Tressia Ewing nee Donahoe (23). See JAIFR, vol. VI, #1, pp. 53-57.

DONALSON or DONALDSON – a Shawnee/

Cherokee name.

William Donalson was a white man who served as an official blacksmith in the Shawnee Nation for over twenty years. A William Donaldson married Rachel Rogers on the Shawnee reservation in 1847. Either by this marriage or another, Donaldson became the son-in-law of Capt. Joseph Parks, who served a term as chief of the tribe.

Among the Shawnee students enrolled in October, 1848, at the Kansas Methodist Mission School were Catherine Donaldson, age 10 and Rebecca Donaldson, age 7.

Rev. Gideon Seymour performed the marriage ceremony of John Swatzel to Catherine Donaldson on July 5th, 1858, in Shawnee, Kansas. See Shonkwiler, p. 15.

Among the Shawnees who settled on the lands of the Cherokee nation by 1869 were John, Katherine, and Charles Swatzel. These Swatzels were probably all related to Capt. Joseph Parks. See JAIFR, vol. IV, #2, pp. 100-111.

DOUGHERTY, DAUGHIRTY, DAUGHERTY, DAUGHTERY – a Shawnee name.

The Detroit prisoner list included Dudley, Andrew, and Robert Daugherty, listed as being captured in Pennsylvania in May, 1780. See McHenry, p. 24.

Arline Stith Dougherty, writing in the newsletter of the Daughterty Family Association in 1984, told of her family tradition which had often been told to her by her father: "I heard this story many times but remember best the last time I heard it. It was my Grandmother Stith's version, as she told it to me. I was in Indiana for my father's funeral in January, 1959, and it was the last time I saw her before she died.'

"From the first time my grandmother met my husband, whenever the Doughterty name was mentioned, she always said that she had cousins named

Dougherty, but they spelled their name with an "a." This time she told the story about "one of those Daugherty's" who lived after "running the gauntlet." These Daughtery's had been captured by the Indians, and they were taken somewhere on a river by boat. The Indian chief had a son and both the son and the Daugherty child became very ill. The Daugherty wife took care of both children and they recovered. As a reward, the chief told them that they could be free if Daugherty would run the gauntlet, which he agreed to do. When it came time for the event, the Indian chief ran beside him, taking half the blows, so that Daugherty survived...

"My grandmother was almost eighty-four years old when she told me this story. Although she was elderly, she was clear of mind and memory. Although legends often become distorted by time, I believe there is always some basic foundation of truth within them."

So do I.

There were members of the Daugherty family captured by the Indians during Pontiac's War in 1763. Among the whites delivered up to General Henry Bouquet in 1764 was Ann Daugherty. Gen. Bouquet wrote of the genuine love that appeared to exist between these whites delivered up and their "Indian captors." Some of the women appeared with their children in arms. Often there were children who were white, often there were mixed bloods. Some of the mixed bloods came along and were raised among the whites as white. Some of the white children managed to escape along the way and made it back to their Indian families and were raised red.

Some members of the Nelson County (Ky) Daugherty family appear to have been captured at the Kinchloe's Station. As with those captured at other stations, the adults were taken to Detroit and turned over to the British. The children were adopted into

Indian families and raised red.

During the years before the War of 1812, Tecumseh and the Prophet were busy making enlisting allies. From Ft. Wayne came a report that the Indians were gathering at Greenville, and Simon Kenton "felt the situation was serious enough to warrant a dangerous trip into the enemy camp." He left for Greenvlle in the company of James McPherson and some other frontiersmen. Their report to the governor said that, if things looked too dangerous, they had planed to send Alexander Dougherty, "one of the men with us, and who was related to the Indians," in to discover their designs. See Kenton, p. 269.

The experience of the red/white Daugherty family was probably similar to that of the Walker, Barnett, Quick, Ruddle, and Ash families, just to name a few. Some came back, some stayed with the Indians. Some tried coming back, then left again when things became uncomfortable. Some adapted well to life on the edge of the red/white frontier and became Indian traders, scouts, or interpreters.

One of the most famous of interpreters among the Shawnees and Delawares in Missouri and Kansas was John Dougherty (or Daugherty) who long associated with the Shawnees as an agent and trader.

In the Daugherty family file at the Kentucky Historical Society in Frankfort, there is a letter from Mrs. Jack Daugherty of Liberty, Missouri:

"Oct. 28th, 1939...I am writing for some information regarding this family of Daugherty – came from Va. to Ky. The lived at one time in Franklin Co. and again Nelson Co. John Daugherty was born in Nelson Co. Apr. 12th, 1791. He came to Missouri when 17 years of age and connected with the Missouri Fur Company...was a member of the 2nd Lewis & Clark Expedition & Long Expedition & was Indian agent and interpreter...his wife, Mary Hertzog...His father's name

I do not know. Major John Daugherty had brothers Wm., Hannibal, Robert...and one sister Annie...."

In 1819, John Dougherty was interpreter for Indian agent Benjamin O'Fallon who recommended him as an assistant agent, and wrote that "he is a Kentuckian but has lived between this [outpost] and the Yellowstone for the last 8 years and speaks several Indian languages tolerably well..." See Carter, vol. 15, pp. 563-564.

Lewis Bissell Dougherty, the son of Indian agent John and Mary (Hertzog) Dougherty, was born in 1828 and he died at Liberty, Mo. in 1925. See Barry, 155.

Among the Shawnees listed on the muster roll who went from Ohio to Kansas in 1832 were:

1. Charles Daugherty. His family of five included one male between 25 and 50, one female 10-25, and three males under ten.
2. Lewis Daugherty, with one male over 50, three males between 10-25, one female over 50, and two females 10-25.
3. John Daugherty, with one male and one female 10-25, and three children under ten, one of them male.
4. Jacob Daugherty, with one male and one female 10-25, and five children under ten, four of them male.

Among the Shawnees who went with Chief Perry and Capt. Joseph Parks and served in the Florida War were Black Daugherty and Joseph Daugherty.

The Black Daugherty family may have been part black, as the Daugherty families captured in Kentucky may have had black slaves captured with them. The Daugherty family among the Shawnee seems to have been divided into two segments, one segment so light-skinned and so oriented toward white ways that people sometimes took them for white, and the other segment consisting of dark-skinned traditionalists.

Ranny Carpenter said that, "Many years ago, when the Shawnees were living near present Kansas City, there was a medicine man, a mixblood like myself, named Daugherty. He had only one eye. He had been blessed by many spirits and was known as a great healer by his people. There were many such healers in those days. They were like saints."

Carpenter tells the story of Daugherty and his encounter with the Great White Buffalo who took him beneath the surface of the Missouri River on a journey to another country. There, Daugherty was taught the Buffalo Head Dance, used by traditional Shawnees today as an addendum to the Green Corn Dance of the Cherokee Shawnee. See Howard, pp. 288-289.

According to Wolfe, an Indian named Doughty lived with a band of thirty others in early Guernsey County, Ohio. Some of the early white settlers were afraid of them, but their fears turned out to be unjustified.

Attending the Ft. Leavenworth (Kansas) Shawnee School in 1841 was Mebzy Doughtery, a Shawnee.

The Shawnee James Daugherty married Sarah B. Tiblow in 1848 on the Kansas reservation. Etta Tooley, daughter of William Tooley, married William Daugherty.

Among the Shawnees who settled on the lands of the Cherokee nation by 1869 were David, Ellen, Charles, Joseph, Matilda, Josephine, Jane, John, Angeline, Nancy, George, Mary, Ridley, Margaret, Issac, Thomas, Alice, Joshua, Hiram, Susan, Elizabeth, Martha, Ella, Mabel, Eddy, James A., Marion, and Lucy Daugherty or Daughtery. See JAIFR, vol. IV, #2, pp. 100-111.

Among the Shawnee guardianship cases heard in 1871 by Ely Parker, Commissioner of Indian Affairs, were the cases of Lewis, David, and George Daugherty.

Their wards were not listed. See JAIFR, vol. VIII, #2, p. 26.

The Daugherty family intermarried with the whites, the Cherokees, the Shawnees, and the Delawares. Among the Daugherty's on the 1880 Cherokee Census of the Cooweescoowee District were the Shawnees William and Nancy Daugherty, the Delaware Hetty Daugherty, and the Cherokees Charlie, Ellis, Jane, Lizzie, and Lydia Daugherty. See JAIFR, vol. X, #1, p. 58,

DRAGOO – an Ottawa name.

William Dragoo, the son of John Dragoo and his first wife, Elizabeth Straight, was captured on Straight's Run (in what is now West Virginia). William was taken to the Indian towns in Ohio. He grew to manhood among them, married an Ottawa woman and had four children by her. After the death of his Indian wife and an unsuccessful Indian war, he took his two sons and went back to live among the whites.

Glen Lough says, "There are several versions of the William 'Indian Billy' Dragoo story.... One version has one of the half-Indian sons of William marrying and fathering children." See Glenn Lough's AAT, vol. 3, #4, pp. 3, 5.

"Billie Dragoo lived with the Indians as one of them in their towns in Ohio. He married an Indian girl, who bore him two sons and two daughters. He was, after some years, divorced from his Indian wife...he received custody of their sons, and she custody of their daughters. The son's names were John and Issac. John became a carpenter; Issac, tutored by Rev. Levi Shinn, became a Methodist preacher and went west of the Mississippi River to preach to the Indians. He was never heard of after leaving on his journey. Billie visited his old home in the Barrackville area and brought his sons with him, but the sons, young men then, 'were uneasy here,' and soon rejoined their Indian relatives."

Billie Dragoo married a Licking County, Ohio woman named Rebecca Metheny and lived "in the roughest part of the county." They had seven children. See Lough, pp. 560-561.

Carl N. Thompson, who compiled *The Historical Collections of Brown County, Ohio,* says that Billy Dragoo "was eventually adopted by an Ottawa chief. Nobody knows how far west or northwest the Indians took him, but he was soon taught to be an excellent hunter and fisherman." It was dangerous for returned whites to talk of fighting against their neighbors, and Billy Dragoo told people that he had stayed behind with the women and old men while his foster father led some Ottawa braves against St. Clair. See Thompson, p. 74-75.

The Rev. Thomas Bacon was in Ohio in 1802, and on the Miami at an Ottawa camp, he found "an excellent interpreter, in whom the Indians place the utmost confidence, and who served me faithfully for a much less sum than what either of the others would have asked. His name is William Dragoo. He appears to be a very worthy man considering the advantages he has enjoyed — was taken prisoner on the Monongahela when he was ten years of age and adopted into the head family of the nation and is considered a chief..." See Knapp, pp. 103-105.

A John Dragoo located in Nelson County, Kentucky, on Wilson's Creek near Deatsville. His wife was named Elizabeth, and their children included Peter, Thompson, Ephraim, Silas, Harrington, Mahala, and Nancy. An Ephraim Dragoo served with General George Rogers Clark and his will was filed in Nelson County Records (see Bullitt County Will Book 1, p. 816).

The daughters who stayed among the Ottawas may have retained Dragoo as their English surname for their families. For one reason or another in any event, the name was carried on among the Ottawas. As late as 1883, the Ottawa Census (of the Quapaw Agency) listed Lucy Dragoo, 16, living with Petah, 35, Rose Ann Thomas, 5, and Wa-ka, a new born.

DRENNON – a Shawnee name.

I have not yet discovered exactly how the Indian blood tradition in the Drennon family came to be. There are several possible sources.

In colonial times, the Indians captured Thomas Drennon's family including a three-year-old boy named Charley Drennon.

William Drennon was on the payroll in 1788 as a Jefferson County (Ky) scout.

Jacob Drennon was an Indian trader and a scout. He served in Dunmore's War, at the Battle of Point Pleasant; in several engagements in the Revolution, often as a scout. He maintained to his last day that Simon Girty was a good man, that his notorious reputation was undeserved.

"In 1777, Capt. White Eyes came to Ft. Pitt and told them that the Indians were going to take Wheeling home. White Eyes was sometimes thought to be of both sides...Jacob Drennon said he would go and ask Girty. If he knew, he would tell him..." He went to the Indian towns and asked Girty to tell him. Girty replied that "if he was going home, not to go into the fort until after dark, for he be damned if they wouldn't be attacked." Drennon went back to Wheeling and spread the alarm, and Wheeling prepared for the upcoming siege. See Draper's interview with Jacob Drennon's last wife in 12CC236-238. Also see Thwaites and Kellogg, Rev. on the Upper Ohio, p. 60, 62, 65.

James Drennon, who discovered Drennon's Lick in Kentucky, had previously lived among the Indians. See Draper 12CC73.

DRIVER – a Wyandot name.

On the 1843 Muster Roll of the Wyandots from Sandusky, Ohio, were listed:

1. Francis Driver's family, consisting of one female over 55, one male and one female between the ages of 25 and 55, three females between the ages of 10 and 25, and one boy under 10.
2. Issac P. Driver's household which consisted of one male between the age of 25 and 55, and one boy under 10.
3. James Driver's family, consisting of one male and one female, both between 10 and 25, and two females under 10.

Among the Wyandots listed on the 1855 census were Issac P. Driver, Magee 46, Catherine, 46, Sarah, 19, and Susan, 18.

Francis Driver had married Matilda Stephenson, an adopted Wyandot from Lancaster County, Pennsylvania. A few months after Francis Driver died (January 24, 1847), his widow married Francis A. Hicks, then the chief of the Wyandot Nation in Wyandotte County, Kansas. See Barry, pp. 662, 686.

Among the students at the Kansas Methodist Mission School in 1848 was Susan Driver, a Wyandot, age 14.

DROUILLARD or DREWYER – a Shawnee name.

Pierre Drouillard was interpreter for the Hurons at Detroit in 1778, Seineke, p. 285. He assisted Simon Kenton in obtaining his release after he had been captured by Indians and taken to the Sandusky towns. By his Shawnee wife, he became the father of George Drouillard. This son went with his mother to the Missouri territory.

In 1803, George Drouillard was recruited to go on the Lewis and Clark expedition. Lewis found him with his uncle, Louis Lorimer, who had married the Shawnee sister of the wife of Pierre Drouillard. Peter Louis Lorimer (Loramie, Lourimer, etc.) was a half-breed himself, being the son of Don Louis Lorimer and "a Canadian Indian." See Draper 1YY129, including some information from a Mr. Penney (or Perry?), who was a clerk in Lorimie's store.

In May, 1810, on another expedition for the Missouri Fur Company, George Drouillard was trading with the Crows in Blackfoot country. He left the main party and went on a hunt with two Delaware hunters. When they didn't return, the company went in search of them.

They found the bodies of the two Delawares "pierced with lances, arrows, and bullets and lying near each other. Further on, about one hundred and fifty years, Druyer and his horse lay dead, the former in a horrible manner. His head was cut off, his entrails torn out, and his body hacked to pieces. We saw from the marks on the ground that he must have fought in a circle on horseback and probably killed some of his enemies, being a brave man and well armed..." See George Drouillard by M. O. Skarsten, pp. 20-21, 310-311.

DRUM – a Shawnee/Delaware name.

Listed as a Delaware in 1867 was Ahpahmala Drum, age 43. See Prevost, pp. 33, 77. Listed on the 1880 Cherokee Census were the Alex Drum, a Shawnee, age 35, and his Delaware children George and James Drum. William and Josie Drum might also have been his children. See JAIFR, vol. X, #1, pp. 61.

DUCHANE, DUSHANE, DASHADE, etc. – a Shawnee name.

The name comes from the French-Canadian Indian trader Isodore Chene or Deshane who accompanied Blackfish and Captain Will on the expedition to besiege Boonesboro. Chene's half-breed sons Anthony Shane (by an Ottawa wife) and Joseph Dushane (by a Shawnee wife) carried on the name in different forms. See SHANE.

Among the Shawnees who went with Chief John Perry and Capt. Joseph Parks and served in the Florida War was Joseph Deshane.

Among the Shawnees who settled on the lands of the Cherokee nation by 1869 were David, Nancy, Andrew, and Louisa Duchane; also Jemima, Henry, Polly, Cornelias, Peggy, David Franklin, Napolis, Eliza, Spencer. Eli, Martha, Francis, and Caleb Duchene. See JAIFR, vol. IV, #2, pp. 100-111.

Among the Shawnees on the 1880 Cherokee Census of the Cooweescoowee District were David Dashade jr. (age 57), Martha Dushade (age 32), and children Frank (18), Napoleon (16), Lewis (13), Dennis B. (6), and Antonia Dushade (2). See JAIFR, vol. X, #1, p. 58, 61.

Howard S. Dushane, the Shawnee superintendent of the Ft. Belknap Agency, served in Manila in World War II. He married Leona E. Wilkie of Belcourt, North Dakota, and their children included Linda Jeanne and Lawrence Dushane. See Gridley, p. 54.

DUCHOUQUET, DOCHOUQUET – a Shawnee name.

The name has many variations, all derived from Francis Dochouquet, a French-Canadian trader who resided among the Shawnees. Over the years, he assisted several white captives including, in 1790, Charles Johnston who later wrote a narrative of his captivity. Johnston was ransomed through the efforts of the Crane (Tarhe) and Francis Dochouquet.

In 1802, Dochouquet was part of a delegation of Indians who traveled to Washington to negotiate with the government. On the way, he stopped by Charles Johnston's estate in Roanoke County, Virginia. Johnston was delighted to see him again and a dinner was held for Dochouquet and the Shawnee Tom Lewis, who had been one of Johnston's captors. The acquaintance was renewed again in 1826, when Dochouquet was interpreter for another Shawnee delegation. See *Three Came Back: The Narrative of Charles Johnston, in Captured By Indians,* ed. by Frederick Drimmer, pp. 183-215.

Francis Dochouquet was an interpreter in 1814 at Ft. Wayne, then again at the 1817 treaty talks at the Miami Rapids.

Henry Harvey said he accompanied "Francis Duchequate" and a delegation of Shawnees to Washington in an effort to voice certain grievances of the nation. The chiefs were John Perry, Wayweleapy, Blackhoof (Quaskey), and Spybuck. Duchoquet and Joseph Parks were along in the capacity of interpreters.

Harvey says, "When we arrived at Cumberland on our way to Washington, Francis Duchequate was taken very sick; so we had to leave him...It was affecting to see him take leave of the chiefs...he told them he had been with them ever since they were little children...was then an old man and should soon die, and he thought they would never see him anymore...at parting with him they were affected into tears. His prediction was verified, as he died in a few days...he was a very honest, upright man..." See Harvey, pp. 209-210.

DUCOIGNE – a Kaskakia/Peoria name.

Baptist Ducoigne, sometimes Battise Decoign, chief of the Kaskakia Indians, was at Ft. Jefferson with his small tribe on the side of the Kentuckians there. It was his son, Jefferson Ducoigne, who shot and wounded Colbert under the white flag. See Draper Mss. 31J17.

Baptist Ducoigne's father, Jean Baptist De

Coigne, was an interpreter for Sir William Johnson during Pontiacs War. He visited the Senecas and Delawares while James Sherlock was living among them in 1763. See SWJ Papers, Vol. IV, p. 286.

According to one account, the elder De Coigne married the sister of Black Dog, chief of the Kaskakias. Another one of Black Dog's sisters married Pontiac. The younger Baptist Ducoign was with Black Dog and Walkshingau when they argued with Pontiac over the way he was treating his wife. A fight developed and one of them stabbed Pontiac, who later died. See the letter of June 23rd, 1766, Ibid., pp. 278-279; Parkman, pp. 328-329; Draper 1Z99.

During the spring of 1775, Ducoigne took his small tribe (they could only furnish 140 warriors) to the White River in Spanish Arkansas. They were welcomed by the Spanish and the local tribes and lived there in peace for three years, until George Rogers Clark convinced them to join the American cause.

Decoign had his tribe at Ft. Jefferson and one of them slipped out of the fort with Jack Ash during the night and went for help. It was likely Jefferson Ducoign who shot Colbert as he was parleying under the white flag.

Baptist was well remembered by several of the old pioneers interviewed by Draper and Shane. See Draper Mss. 1Z98: "I was quite a boy at the time of his death, yet I remember him well. His father, I think, was a French Canadian and his mother was of the Kaskakia tribe...His manner and deportment was that of a Frenchman...his height was but five-foot seven-inches, rather corpulent, at least in his old days. I have been told by my father who knew him as a young man that he was an extraordinary...hunter and ran fast races in which he was never excelled...

"Baptist had two wives. By the first, he had two daughters; by his second, who was all French, he had two boys. One, Lewis Jefferson [Ducoign] succeeded him as chief. He was fine looking and intelligent. His brother, Jean Baptist [Ducoigne] was the best made man that my eyes ever beheld. He was about six foot, very white, hair long and wavy and as black as pit."

Baptist Ducoigne became disenchanted with the Americans treatment of the Indians who had assisted them during the Revolution. He again took his tribe to the Arkansas, but his village was raided by Chief Menoquet's warriors and he lost some of his people, including one of his daughters who was captured, and later ransomed.

He was a spokesman for the Kaskakias, Weas, Eel River Shawnees and Piankashaws at a Vincennes council on September 24, 1792. He told the American agent, "I should be glad if matters had remained as they were in the days of the French. Then, all the country was clear and open...These are the sentiments of the Indian tribes. We would regret the loss of our beds. The author of life created us on these lands, and we wish to live and die on them...I tell you the plain truth. It is best that the white people live in their own country and we in ours...We desire you to remain on the other side of the river Ohio..." See Putnam, pp. 342-363.

"Baptist Ducoigne died in the lands of his tribe on the Wabash above Vincennes. Silver ore had been found near the mouth of the Vermillion River and to this the chief attached much importance. When about to die, he directed that his body after death should be placed in a sitting position overlooking the silver mine, an enclosure and shelter placed about it, his hands placed upon his loaded rifle, it being pointed toward the mine that he might shoot any white man who came to silver." See Draper Mss. 11YY31-33.

Baptist Ducoigne seems to have died before October, 1832, when the Treaty of Castor Hill, Missouri ceded to the United States the last of the Illinois Indian lands east of the Mississippi, except for one 352 acre tract, reserved for a daughter of the Baptist Ducoigne, named Ellen Ducoign, who married a white man.

DUNN – a Shawnee name.

There is an Indian blood tradition in the Dunn family.

Jack Dunn was one of the saltmakers captured with Daniel Boone, Benjamin Kelly, Joseph Jackson, Micagah Calloway, and others in 1778. An adopted Shawnee, Jack Dunn "was never able to resolve the conflict he felt about his identity, and he later returned to Chillicothe to warn his Shawnee family of an impending American attack. Captured by Kentucky rangers soon afterward, he was tortured to death as a turncoat." See Faragher, p. 165.

See Ebenezer Denny's journal: "We were surprised by the arrival of Mr. Abner Dunn, an old officer who had been to the Shawneetowns. He arrived with five Indians...spent the winter with the Shawnees."

EDMUND, EDMOND, EMMONS

– a Shawnee name.

The part-Shawnee Anna Harvey, a daughter of Martha Captain Fish, married Henry W. Edmonds (or Edwards, or Emmons) a white man about 1863. Their children included Mary, Samuel, and David Emmonds.

The part-Shawnee, part Wyandot grandchild of Hanna Zane, Eudora Fish, married Dallas Emmons about 1860. He was an engineer who built bridges. They lived in several places, including the Cherokee Nation, Memphis, Tennessee, and Thayer, Missouri. Their children included Bertie J. Emmons (b. 1861, d. 1891 in the Phillipines), Theodore Pascal Emmons, Hettie Emmons, Adelia Adair Emmons (b. 1871, m. George Parks in 1892 at Thayer, Mo.).

Theodore Emmons married (1st) Clara M. Hopkins at Thayer, Mo. Their children included Dallas, Clarence, Vivian, and Warren Emmons. Theodore married (2nd) Sarah Caroline Hall of Virginia. Their children included Jerome M., Eudora, Majorie, and Grace Evelyn Emmons.

Warren Emmons, son of Theodore and Clara, worked for a company at Broken Arrow, Oklahoma, then moved to Michigan where they lived for thirty years. By his first marriage, Warren had two daughters. His second marriage was to a woman named Mary Elizabeth by whom he had at least one son, Warren, jr. The younger Warren Emmons served in the Air Force and he and his wife, Nancy, had at least one daughter, Dawn Emmons. See Long, p. 5A.

Among the Shawnees who settled on the lands of the Cherokee nation by 1869 were Endora, Theadora, Bertie J., and Dallas Emmons.

Among the Shawnees who settled on the lands of the Cherokee nation by 1869 were Henry, Anna,

Mary, Samuel, David, and Charles Edmund. See JAIFR, vol. IV, #2, pp. 100-111.

All of these people are the descendants of the Shawnee chief, Blackfish, whom Daniel Boone called "one of Nature's noblemen," and also of Tarhe, the Wyandot Half King, a powerful warrior, yet in easy circumstances, a warm, friendly man, beloved by all.

ELLIOT – a Shawnee name.

Matthew Elliott was a native of Ireland who came to America as a young man in 1761. He served in Bouquet's Expedition during Pontiac's War, and became an Indian trader after the peace. He allied himself with Alexander McKee and Simon Girty, going to the British side at the outbreak of the Revolution. He participated in many of the Indian campaigns, including the invasions of Kentucky in 1780 and again in 1781. He died at Burlington Heights in 1814. See The John Askin Papers, I, 257-258. He is supposed to have married Sarah Donovan, daughter of Matthew Donovan of Detroit.

For Capt. James Elliott and Nancy Ward, see Draper mss. 10S163-166.

For the deposition of Daniel Elliott, an Indian trader who lived at the Shawnee towns in 1785, see Draper Mss 11S201.

A John Elliott, apparently an Indian trader, was closely associated with the Shawnees in Ohio at the time of their planned removal to Kansas. Sums were allotted to him for various services. While the Shawnee chiefs were attending the council at Wapakonetta, they stayed with John Elliott. His name is attached to the 1831 treaty.

Among the Shawnees who settled on the lands of the Cherokee nation by 1869 were James, Emily, Emma, and Mary Elliott. See JAIFR, vol. IV, #2, pp. 100-111.

James Elliot (age 37) and Emily Elliot (age 28) with children Emma (13), Mary (10), Dora (5), and Nancy (2) all appear among the Shawnees listed on the 1880 Cherokee Census of the Cooweescoowee District. See JAIFR, vol. X, #2, p. 12.

James Elliot was one of the twenty men who comprised the core of William Wells' band of scouts and Indian spies. Many of the men on the list had lived with the Indians, and Elliot seems to have been one of them.

James Conner (a mixed-blood, part-Shawnee grandson of the Delaware chief, William Anderson) married Nancy (a part-Delaware daughter of a French missionary). Nancy had previously been married to "James Elliot, an army officer from Ohio," by whom she had two children including Lucinda Elliot. Her step-father, James Conner, adopted Lucinda and she took the Conner name. See Cranor, p. 151.

Lucinda Elliot Conner (1850-1923) married:

1st. George O. Collins (1843-1871) and their children included Ida May, Willie V. and George O. Collins. Ida May Collins married Clinton L. Goodall.

2nd. Jordon Journeycake (1843-1875) and their children included Lenora Aurora Journeycake (b. 1873) who married into the Quinn and McCreary families.

3rd. Dr. Andrew J. Lane and their children and grandchildren married into the Mattherson, Johnstone, Alexander, Hauburson, Cushenberry, Robbins, Smart, and Henry families.

For a much elaborated account of the family of Lucinda Elliot Connor, see Ruby Cranor's magnificent book on Chief William Anderson and his descendants noted elsewhere.

ELLIS – a Shawnee name.

John Ellis, a son of a Spaniard and a Shawnee or Creek woman, became chief of the Long Beard or Absentee Band of Shawnee around 1840. He had a brother named Jack Ellis and a sister named Susie Ellis. John Ellis favored his white father a good deal, having straight black hair and blue eyes. See Draper 1YY.

The Shawnee named Edwin Ellis might have been a son of John Ellis. Information garnered from the Absentee Shawnee heirship cards shows that Edwin and Anna Ellis's heirs included their son Jesse Ellis, born 1891, as well as Walter Ellis, Lucetta Ellis Snake, and Thomas, John, and Anna Sampson.

EMORY, EMERY. EMMERY, etc. – a Cherokee/ Shawnee name.

William Emory was an early Indian trader who married a Cherokee woman and from whom a multitude of Americans now trace their lineage. Their children included:

1. Mary Emory who married Ezekiel Buffington, a Scotch trader, and started the prominent Buffington line among the Cherokees which would include Chief Thomas Mitchell Buffington.
2. Elizabeth Emory who married John Rogers, another Indian trader, and started the prominent Rogers surname among the Cherokee which would include Chief William Charles Rogers, Diana Rogers Houston (Sam Houston's wife), and Will Rogers, the noted journalist.
3. Susannah Emory who married the colonial Indian agent, Capt. John Stuart, and from whom descends many Cherokees of note including Chief Dennis Bushyhead.
4. Will Emory, the renegade Cherokee who ran

with the Shawnees and became known as Captain Will. The name is somewhat famous in frontier Kentucky annals because of Captain Will's relationship to Daniel Boone and the attack on Boonesboro. Captain Will doubtlessly has many mixed-blood descendants around today.

Will Emery's original village was called Will's Town, and it was located on Will's Creek in what is now Maryland. As the settlements of whites crept westward, Captain Will was forced to utilize the Kentucky lands as hunting grounds. He and his Shawnee/Cherokee hunting party surprised and captured Daniel Boone on his first trip to Kentucky. Captain Will released them with a warning never to return.

In 1774, when Logan's band of Mingoes were raiding the white settlements on the the Virginia frontier, "a large man much whiter than the rest" who "talked good English" was reportedly in the war party. "Some think Capt John Logan is about yet — others that it is Will Emery, a half-breed Cherokee...he is known to be...in the Shawanese interest...he was the interpreter when Col. Donelson run the line, and it was he robbed Knox and Skaggs..." See Draper 3QQ117.

Captain Will spoke excellent English, and seems to have had a hearty sense of humor. He was on good terms with Daniel Boone during Boone's second captivity and discussed the prospects of taking Boonesboro with him. Captain Will and Blackfish led the Indians during the siege. See Faragher, pp. 80-82, 156-57, 164, 179.

According to a history of Bedford County, Pennsylvania (*Bedford: The Kernal of Greatness*, p. 17), some of the women of the county were captured by Shawnees and Captain Will was believed to have been the leader of the war party. These warriors and their captives were tracked by a company of their relatives. The main party was not overtaken, but one of the pursuers, George Powell, later waylaid Captain Will at his campsite on Will's Knob, took his scalp, and buried the body there.

Some of Captain Will's "immediate descendants intermarried with white people...early in the past century they were living in Pennsylvania, near the Allegheny County line." See Marye, pp. 162-164,

EVERET or EVERETT – a Delaware name.

Solomon Everett was a Delaware scout, serving with Capt. James Swannuck on the Freemont expedition in 1845. He may have been on other expeditions also. See Weslager, pp. 379.

Calvin Everett was also said to have been a Delaware scout. Both men probably rode on several campaigns with the likes of Black Beaver and Fall Leaf. Calvin Everett's age was listed as 48 on his 1867 registration card. His wife's name was Sarah.

Mary (age 30), Caroline (age 29), and Nancy (age 29) are among the Everet family of Delawares listed on the 1880 Cherokee Census of the Cooweescoowee District. See JAIFR, vol. X, #2, p. 13.

FAIRFIELD – a Shawnee/Delaware/Cherokee name.

Among the marriages in the Recording Steward's Book for the Shawnee Mission was that of Julius Fairfield who married Mary Blackhoof in 1856.

Among the Shawnees who settled on the lands of the Cherokee nation by 1869 was Eliza Jane Fairfield. See JAIFR, vol. IV, #2, pp. 100-111. Amelia Fairfield was a sister, or perhaps a half-sister, to Silas Hamilton Connor, and was a descendant of the Delaware Chief William Anderson. See Cranor, p. 121.

FALL LEAF, FALLEAF, or FALLINGLEAF – a Delaware name.

These surnames are carried by the descendants of Capt. Fall Leaf (Panipakuxwe, "he who walks when the leaves fall"), a Delaware who was a guide for Col. John Fremont and was with Major Sedgewick in the Civil War. There are many stories about this exceptional man, far too many to recount here. Verna Lerdall says that Fall Leaf was born in Ohio in 1807, and that sounds about right.

Capt. Fall Leaf was one of the Delaware free hunters, and as such, he participated in the many skirmishes the Delawares had with other tribes. An expert shot and a renown horseman, Fall Leaf led bands of Delawares across the west as far as California. In 1860, Capt. Fall Leaf was the leader of five other Delaware scouts in Major Sedgewick's expedition against the Commanches and Kiowas. The other Delawares were identified as Sarcoxie, Bascom, Wilson, Bullit, and John Williams. And there was also a band of Pawnee scouts along.

The expedition was confronted by a large band of Cheyenne, estimated between 900 and 1000. Peck, in his journal, says that the soldiers were greatly outnumbered and he became especially fearful when he noticed that the Cheyenne were stretching out their ranks and outflanking them on both sides of the river, their ranks three-deep.

Peck says that they were still out of rifle range when "we say our old Delaware chief, Fall Leaf, dash out from our line 'til he got about midway between the two sides, when he suddenly halted his horse, raised his rifle and fired at the Cheyennes." He circled around and rode back, while the Cheyennes returned fire.

"A large party of the Cheyennes had turned their left, and some were coming up in the rear behind the pack-horses." The order was given to draw sabers, Peck says, "and our three hundred bright blades flashed out of the scabbards."

At this, the Cheyennes hesitated. "At their first checking of speed, a fine-looking warrior mounted on a spirited horse, probably their chief, dashed up and down in front of their line with the tail of his warbonnet flowing behind, brandishing his lance, shouting to his warriors...evidently urging his men to stand their ground....Many of us found time to admire his superb horsemanship, for he presented a splendid sight as he wheeled his horse, charging back and forth, twirling his long lance over his head now and then."

The soldiers charged and the Cheyennes scattered. Peck estimated that thirty of them were killed in the running fight. Peck says, "Old Fall Leaf and his Delawares went into the fight with us and did good service, but the cowardly Pawnees that Colonel Sumner had brought with him from Fort Kearney, only followed in our wake, scalping the dead Cheyennes and gathering up their ponies..."

See *Relations with the Indians of the Plains, 1857-1861, Journal of R. M. Peck,* ed. by Leroy R. Hafen and Ann W. Hafen, Aurthur H. Clark Company, Glendale

California, 1959, p. 106, 120-126, 196.

Capt. Fall Leaf's band of scouts on the Wichita expedition against the Commanche, Kiowa and Cheyenne included George and Fred Fall Leaf, George and Ice Wilson, Charles Washington, John Kiney, Jim Coon, Elk Hair, Jacob Parker, Sam Williams, Lenowese, John Silas, Young Marten, George and John Swannock, Yellow Jacket, and Calvin Everett. See Chalfant, p. 247. Chalfant quotes a manuscript diary of W. C. Brown, who was on the expedition.

Captain Fall Leaf has a large number of descendants living today, and although the family was traditionalist, many of the Fall Leaf's intermarried with whites and with other tribes. The children of Captain Fall Leaf and his wife, Katy, included Kathy, Silas, Sally (m. Jackson Simmons), Talahwhanumd (m. Martha Jacobs), George (m. Martha Curlyhead), Suhohluxqua, and Lucy (m. John P. Beaver).

Silas Falleaf, as the name came to be spelled, married Tundia and their children included Nellie (m. Dutch Whiteturkey), Henry (m. Amanda Thompson), Simon, and John Nelson (m. 1st Ida Yellowjacket, 2nd Sally Elkhair). John Nelson Fallleaf's children included Fred (m. Fern Whetstine), George, Ruby, William, Richard Franklin, Numerous Marion, Myrtle May, Irene, Alona Fay, and Mona Verna Falleaf. Weslager published a picture of John Nelson Falleaf, taken in the 1920s, with his five daughters Irene, Myrtle, Mona, Alona, and Nancy Falleaf. See Weslager, p. 148.

Among the Delaware members of the Fallingleaf family appearing on the 1880 Cherokee census of the Cooweescoowee District were Geroge (age 26), Lizzie (20), Cyrus (35), Mrs. C. (30), Aus-cus-quee (16), Henry (13), Charles (5), Lizzie (18), Fugerson (14), Mary (6), Nancy (4), Sulus, jr. (age not given), We-che-lon-kon (2), and the Widow Fallingleaf (80). See JAIFR, vol. X, #2, p. 13

FISH – a Shawnee name.

William Jackson was an adopted captive who lived with the Shawnees. After the Treaty of Greenville, life became difficult for William Jackson and the other whites living red. Traders hooked a large proportion of the red population on alcohol, created a sub-nation of alcoholics, and thereafter demanded furs for whiskey. The land was already over-hunted by both reds and whites, and game became even more scarce. Those with eyes clear enough to see what was happening were disgusted by the general discenegration of red society and were ripe for the political movement of the Prophet when it came along.

During this time, many of the whites living red despaired and like George Ash, Bill Cunningham, Christopher Miller, and many others, they tried to come back to live with their white relatives. One of these was William Jackson. But he soon felt too uncomfortable among the whites and went back to the Shawnees.

William Jackson's Shawnee name was Fish, and he became the leader of a band of Shawnees that became known as the Fish Band.

The missionary Issac McCoy wrote that he tried to convince Capt. Cornstalk and Capt. William Perry, the Shawnee chiefs, to agree to the establishment of a mission school among them. McCoy says that they replied negatively, saying that "they felt little desire for schools and still less to hear preaching."

However, McCoy made a deal with "a white man by the name of Fish, who had lived with the Shawnees from a small boy and was in all respects identified with them, had become a principal of a clan which had lived many years in the state of Missouri and which was a good deal civilized." See McCoy, p. 404.

George Vashon, the Indian agent, wrote of his

approval for the mission at the request of Fish, who was also called William Jackson, a white man raised with the Shawnees...Fish, the Shawnee chief, has a son by the name of Paschal who was put to school when he was a boy. He can speak English very well. He is a sober, steady, moral, good man. He had an Indian family and is industriously employed in farming..." See KHC, vol. 9, pp. 166-167.

Historian Rodney Staab of Shawnee Mission, Kansas, has furnished me with an excellent account of Chief Fish written by Fern Long. Her information conflicts somewhat with other sources, but it should not be missed by anyone doing research on the Jackson / Fish family.

According to her 1978 article on Chief Fish, she agrees that he was captured as a youth and raised by the Shawnees in the band of Lewis Rogers whose daughter he married. Paschal Fish was "a large-framed man" who "also acquired the Indian ways seeming to be totally Indian." But at the same time, she says "these Shawnees had associated with white people for generations and desired a settled life with homes, schools, churches, and agriculture."

Known children of Chief Fish (William Jackson) were:

1. Paschal Fish, born 1804, probably in Missouri, died 1894 in Oklahoma.
2. Charles Fish, born 1813, died 1869.
3. Jesse Fish, born circa 1827, died 1866.
4. William Fish, born circa 1839.
5. John Fish (who served in the Civil War in 1863).
6. a daughter who married Josephus Paschal or Pascal. They had 2 sons and another child and seem to have joined the Delawares and later the Peorias.

One of the son's of Paschal Fish was Leander

Jackson (Jack) Fish. His Shawnee name was Leading Turtle, but was usually referred to in the records as Jackson Fish. A picture of white-looking Jackson Fish accompanies Fern Long's 1978 newspaper article and the caption says that "Jackson Fish's father was half Shawnee, one-eighth Miami and one-sixteenth Delaware; his mother was one-fourth Wyandotte (Huron)."

Jackson Fish became a storekeeper in Baxter Springs, Kansas. His married 1st Julia Parks; 2nd Rosa Fish; 3rd Mary Katherine Large, the mother of Joseph P. T. Fish; and 4th Josephine Heitz of New Glotz, Maryland. He died July 23, 1937.

Leander Jackson Fish's son, Joseph P. T. Fish, married Lily E., and among their children was a daughter, Dorothy Fish Hall, who was living in Oklahoma in 1978.

Paschal Fish succeeded his father as chief of the Fish Band. He married Hester Zane, daughter of Hannah Zane of the Wyandot Nation. Hester was 1/4 Wyandot, a cousin of John M. Armstrong, and "related to the Conley sisters who saved the Wyandot Indian Cemetery in Kansas City."

Besides L. J. Fish, Paschal Fish's children included Andrew Fish and Susan Zane. His niece's husband, Samuel Wheeler, served in the Civil War.

A James Allen Fish served with Chief John Perry in the Florida War, and it is not yet known if this was a brother or a son of William Jackson Fish.

Josephus Paschal or Pascal, a nephew of Paschal Fish, born circa 1827, had a brother named Lucas or Locust, a sister named Mary, and a sister named Quahlas-se who left the Shawnees in 1839 to join the Delawares. Locust Pascal married Elizabeth (Eliza or Nake-ase). Their children included sons, Lewis and James Pascal, and they lived in Desoto, Kansas. Locust Pascal served in the Civil War. An Issac Fish, of Desoto, also served.

Locust Pascal's wife Elizabeth, apparently widowed, married George Ironsides and their children included at least one son, Charles Ironsides.

A William Fish left the Shawnees and married into the Delaware tribe. This was certified by the deposition of H. L. Taylor in 1863, but he may have been speaking of the son of Chief William Jackson Fish.

Charles Fish, a brother of Paschal Fish, married Mary Henry Barnett, apparently the child and sole heir of Nancy Henry. She had a child by her previous marriage, Sally Ann Barnett, and her children by Charles Fish included Elizah, Margaret, John W., William, and Thomas.

Charles Fish was the interpreter at the Wakarusa Mission. He died in 1869 — from drinking, according to Rev. Abram Still's daughter, Monrovia Clark.

Among the Shawnees who settled on the lands of the Cherokee nation by 1869 were Paschal, Jane Q., and Leander J. Fish. See JAIFR, vol. IV, #2, pp. 100-111.

Among the Shawnee guardianship cases heard in 1871 by Ely Parker, Commissioner of Indian Affairs, was the case of Charles Fish and Paschal Fish (who was said to be unreliable). See JAIFR, vol. VIII, #2, p. 26, 27.

Some of the Fish family, probably the Paschal Fish family, seem to have intermarried with the Peorias. Frank Fish was one of the Peoria councilors in 1881. See Valley and Lembcke, p. 147.

Among the Delawares on the 1880 census of the Cherokee Cooweescoowee District were Jake (age 50), Mary (30), Minnie (5), and Malinda (4) Fish. See JAIFR, vol X, #2, p. 14.

FISHBACK – a Shawnee name.

Among the captives delivered up to Bouquet in 1764 were Barbara and Margaret Fishback who had been living among the Indians since 1755. See Hanna.

Among the Shawnees allotted money for property that they were forced to leave behind in Ohio in 1833 was Granny Fishback, who was allotted $9. See Watson, pt. 3, p. 16.

FISHER – a Shawnee name.

"Fisher was no doubt one of a Shawnee party who captured Mr. Purviance's boat in the spring of 1788 — as there was a Fisher among the Shawnees who made the capture..." See Draper 3YY6; Draper's Clark notes, 1788.

In 1799, the British Indian Department was "in some shape connected with this tribe [the Shawnees] either by marriage or concubinage which occasions that partiallity so manifest in their favor, and which has been the cause of that nation...being more insolent and troublesome than any other...Mr. Elliot has left...for Lower Canada...He is acccompanied by three Shawnee chiefs and one Fisher, an interpreter, who acted in that capacity..." See Mich. Pio. & Hist. Col., vol. 12, pp. 305-306.

Frederick Fisher was an Indian trader on both the Canadian and American sides and he served as a spy for the British against General Anthony Wayne. See Gilbert pp. 237-247.

Matthew Fisher, a mixed blood, said that his uncle, John Fisher, knew John Naudee (Sha-wah-wan-noo) who fought at the Monroviantown (as other accounts confirm) and who had buried Tecumseh's bones on Walpole Island, next to St. Anne's Island. He used to fly a flag over the grave. This was also confirmed by Edward Jackson, John Naudee's grandson. See Sugden, p. 218.

FITZPATRICK – a Shawnee name.

Among the Shawnees who settled on the lands of the Cherokee nation by 1869 were Joseph, Rebecca, Oliver, and Willis Fitzpatrick. These people seem to have been related to Chief Joseph Parks. See JAIFR, vol. IV, #2, pp. 100-111.

FLINN – a Shawnee name.

Members of the Flinn family were captured and adopted by Shawnees, including Chloe Flinn, her sister, Polly, and her brother, John. Chloe Flinn, when still a child, was among the whites delivered up in the prisoner exchange worked out by Daniel Boone, Micagah Calloway, Peter Cornstalk, Noamohouoh, and Captain Johnny. Both a John and a Thomas Flinn came back to the whites and became scouts and interpreters. Thomas Flinn was an interpreter for John Hardin and was killed with him, at least according to one source.

Part of Chloe Flinn's family remained among the Indians including a sister who "grew up to marry a Shawnee man and raise an Indian family." See Faragher, p. 258; Draper 14C50.

I'm not certain how Thomas Flinn came to live with the Indians, but John Flinn was Chloe Flinn's brother and later became a scout, interpreter, and an early settler of Miami County, Ohio, where he entered a claim for his land in 1805. He is supposed to have gone from there to Indiana and had a family of fourteen children, some of whom seem to share an Indian blood tradition.

See the information in the Flinn family files at the Kentucky Archives and the Kentucky Historical Society. The name may also have been corrupted to Flint.

FLINT – a Shawnee name.

Jo and Silas Flint were two of the Shawnees who served with Captain Joseph Parks, Chief John Perry, Henry Bluejacket, and others in the Florida War against the Seminoles.

Attending the Ft. Leavenworth Shawnee School

were the Levi Flint (17 years old in 1842), Lazarus Flint (15 years old in 1842), Jacob Flint (10 years old in 1848), Samuel Flint (12 years old in 1851), and William Flint (15 years old in 1851). All of them are listed as Shawnees.

Among the Shawnee guardianship cases heard in 1871 by Ely Parker, Commissioner of Indian Affairs, was the case of Lazarus Flint, whose wards were not named. See JAIFR, vol. VIII, #2, p. 27.

Among the Shawnees who settled on the lands of the Cherokee nation by 1869 were Joseph, Levi, Stella Ann, George, Ann, Sarah C., Jane, Katherine, Auburn, Mary Jane, and Lazarus Flint and their families. See JAIFR, vol. IV, #2, pp. 100-111.

Among the Shawnees listed on the 1880 Cherokee census of the Cooweescoowee District were Alice (age 26), Jake (38), James (35), Julia A. (37), Kate (6), Susie (9), and William Flint (25). See JAIFR, vol X, #2, p. 15.

FLOYD – a common source of the Indian blood tradition.

Did Col. John Floyd of early Jefferson County, Kentucky, have Indian blood as his descendants claim? Yes. He descended from Powhatan through Thomas Hughes and his wife Niketti, and through their daughter Elizabeth who married William Davis. He looked the part, and even the Victorian histories commented on his looks, "with a complexion unusually dark, his eyes and hair were deep black." See L. A. Williams, p. 79.

The Powhatans were — like their one-time neighbors, the Shawnee — a branch of the Algonquins. We're not sure what amount of pride or shame, if any, that John Floyd felt about this, but something said about his heritage must have made the family angry in 1783, when Mylissa and Micagah Mayfield felt compelled to publicly state and enter it into the public records that "whereas, certain malacious persons have propagated a report of my having said that Robert Floyd and the rest of the family were of the Mustic Breed or mixed with mulatto blood, I do hereby solemnly swear that I never reported any such thing respecting said family..." See FCQ, vol. 3, p. 181-182.

Col. John Floyd was in command of the Jefferson County Militia in the fall of 1781 during Boone's defeat, more renown locally as the Long Run Massacre, and the defeat which followed and became known as Floyd's Defeat. In September, Squire Boone opted to evacuate his station in the face of the Indian threat, and he sent a request to Floyd for an escort to accompany the families to the more secure stations on Beargrass Creek. Floyd dispatched eight men out under the command of James Welch.

Early in the morning of September 13th, the families started out, with cows and packhorses, men, women, and children. There were twenty-one miles to travel to Linn's Station, the closest of the Beargrass Stations. The trail was often narrow and dark. Some of the families were slower than others and straggled behind. After nine miles, Lt. James Welsh became sick and had to turn off the trail until the sickness passed. Many of the militia men stayed behind with him as a guard. The families became even more scattered out. Just after midday, those in front approached the main branch of Long Run Creek. Very suddenly, they were set upon by Indians.

These Indians were Miamis who had broken off the main invasion force which was commanded by Joseph Brant and consisted largely of Miamis, Wyandots (or Hurons), and Ottawas with about twenty Mohawks from Brant's own band. James Girty, Alexander McKee, and some other whites were along.

If the families had stayed together, they might have made a stand, but scattered as they were, there was no chance. The fleeing families tried to make a run for it to Linn's Station, about nine miles away. People began being shot down. There was general confusion and panic. Painted warriors appeared out of nowhere with tomahawks. Some of the small children nearly drowned crossing the creek. Personal property was dumped and left behind.

Thomas McCarty and Bland Ballard "were particularly active in cutting off the packs and getting the women and children onto the horses. One cowardly young man was caught in the act of driving a woman off her horse so that he might ride it. Ballard and McCarty cursed him, one of them shouting, `Touch another woman and I'll blow a hole through you.' The young man was next seen trying to ride a wild colt without either a bridle or saddle. The colt threw him into the air heels over head. The young fellow was frantic with fright." Most of the men put up a brave resistance, or rather, a running fight, protecting as many as they could as they fled.

As the terrified survivors straggled into Linn's Station with the accounts of the carnage that had taken place at the Long Run, runners were sent to the other stations, and Col. John Floyd collected all the men he could enlist to take the offensive, or at least to search for survivors and to bury the dead. Early the next morning, before daylight, he started out with a party of twenty-eight men, including John Dyal, Samuel Murphy, Aquilla Whitaker, and Bland Ballard. Floyd rode his favorite mount, "a fine black horse named Shawnee."

Floyd expected that the Indians had gone to Squire Boone's Painted Stone Station and expected to arrive at the station to find it under seige. He failed to send out advance scouts. In fact, the entire body of Joseph Brant's forces had camped at Long Run, and when Floyd's company came riding up fast along the wagon road between Floyd's Fork and Long Run, as they passed through a divided ridge, they were suddenly caught in a cross-fire.

"Nineteen-year-old John Dyal had his horse shot out from under him. The wounded horse plunged through the Indian line. Dyal jumped up and scrambled away, bullets whizzing all around him." The bullets stopped as he ran through the Indian lines. Dyal told Draper that the Indians spoke English and told him to surrender, that he would not be hurt.

Floyd's horse, which had been acting up, became partly unmanageable and ran under a low-limbed tree, knocking Floyd off, and running into the woods. Floyd lost his gun in the confusion, but was saved by young Samuel Wells who gave him his horse.

In all, of the twenty-seven men who rode out with Floyd, only ten returned. From Linn's Station at 10:30 pm that night, Floyd wrote to General George Rogers Clark, briefly telling of his defeat, his men being "cut to pieces," and requesting assistance.

The Indians, having their hands full with captives and booty, returned north, refusing to attack the additional stations as Joseph Brant urged them to do.

Many months later, John Floyd was waylaid by Indians near Manslick and mortally wounded. Before he died, he expressed sorrow that he hadn't been riding Shawnee, his fine black horse who could sense an ambush and who might have warned him of the impending danger.

The Floyd family, like the Davis and Hughes families, were blessed with many sons who propagated the family name along with the Indian tradition. It is now probably even more common than the Pocahontas tradition, despite the many descendants of the huge Randolph family. Because, in the early days, cousins and second-cousins often married cousins, it is not unusual to meet a fellow researcher today who has four or more crosses back to Powhattan.

See Vince Akers, *The American Revolution in Kentucky 1781*. Akers has done the best job by far on the Long Run Massacre and his account is minutely detailed and documented. And see for yourself Draper's and Shane's interviews with John Dyal, 13CC226-227, Samuel Murphy, 3S1-67, and Bland Ballard, 8J162-163.

FOLSUM or FULSOM – a Choctaw name.

David Folsom was a half-breed Choctaw chief. He was at the council of Choctaws when Tecumseh came to persuade them to join a confederation of Indian tribes. Colonel David Fulsom was given land by the Treaty of Dancing Rabbit Creek in 1830. Jacob and Israel Fulsom were also given land.

David Folsom's father was Nathanial (or Ned) Fulsom, a white Indian trader who married a Choctaw woman in Mississippi. Their children, in no special order, included:

1. Mollie Fulsom who married a man named Sam Mitchell and had two children, including Sophia who married at least three times — first to a Hancock, then to a Moore, then to a Tiner.
2. Delia Fulsom who married a Cameron and had at least two children, Margaret and Alex.
3. David Fulsom who married Mary Nail and had children Corneilius, Henry, Loren, Simpson, Nora, David, and Rhoda.
4. Rhoda Fulsom who married Peter Pitchlyn who was at the time chief of the Choctaw Nation and a delegate to Washington.
5. Israel Fulsom married Tobitha Nail.
6. Rebecca Fulsom who married first to a man named Black, then to David Mitchell, a white man, by whom she had a son named John Mitchell (whose descendants petitioned for

admission into the Choctaw Nation in 1896-1906).

The descendants included Andrew J. Mitchell, John Mitchell, Milton Welsh, Dosia A. Welsh, Luella Pyburn, Emma J. Welsh, Alfred H. Mitchell, John W. Mitchell, William J. Mitchell, Robert H. Mitchell, Docia A. Mitchell, Myrtle Lee Mitchell, Ollie Mitchell, Benjamin H, Pyburn, Milton H. Pyburn, James B. Pyburn, Mary L. Pyburn, Odelia B. Welsh, John M. Welsh, Christian P. Welsh, Milton Welsh, David Welsh, Roy Addus Mitchell, Jessie Lee Mitchell, and Mattie Mitchell. This petition appears along with other family information in JAIFR, vol. V, #3, 1984, pp. 619-623.

FOSTER – a common name among those with Indian blood traditions.

Elizabeth Foster was among the whites delivered up to Bouquet in 1764. James Foster signed the treaty with the Miami in 1826. David Foster was a trader living amongst the Miami lands who platted the village of Kokomo, Indiana. See Anson, p. 206.

In the 1700s, John Adair, from Ireland, married Mrs. Ge-ho-ga Foster, a full-blood Cherokee of the Deer Clan. See Woodward, p. 85.

Among the Choctaws given land by the Treaty at Dancing Rabbit Creek in 1830 were Moses and S. Foster.

A James Foster was a half-breed living in Mississippi on Black Creek with three children under 10 in 1831. At the same time, Hugh Foster and William Foster were listed as half-breeds living on the Mississippi River. Hugh had four children under 10 years of age living with him, and William had two of his own. See MGE, vol. 18, Spring, 1972, p. 11-13.

FOULKES, FOLKS – a Wyandot/Shawnee name.

George Foulks and his sister, Elizabeth, were

captured in 1780 along with Lewis and Polly Tucker. Polly married an elderly Frenchman at Sandusky named Wine (Christian Wine?) and had several children by him. After some time, she came back to live with her father, "old Mr. Tucker." Some of the Turners were taken. The adopted father of George Foulks used skunks on him to ward off the smallpox.

George Foulks lived with them for eleven or twelve years. Elizabeth Foulkes married James Whitaker who had been adopted by the Wyandots. See Draper 16S273, 292.

FRAME, FRIMM, FROMM – all Shawnee/Seneca names.

Isera Frim was listed among the white people given up by the Senecas to General Henry Bouquet in 1764. She was described as being "born in Bolton, Connecticut...about 15 years old...captured at Lackawack in Pennsylvania." See SWJ Papers, 1763-1774.

Margaretta From was an interpreter for the New York Senecas and Delawares in 1830. See Watson, vol. V, pt. 8, p. 34.

"It was a drizzly, rainy day. That day two men came over. One on the men was shot with twenty-three bullets in the breast. He had called not to shoot, for he had been a prisoner last fall. He snapped his gun, however, and they all fired. Both of them, I believe, were white men. Both were blue eyed. Bill Frame and Archibald Frame some said they were." See Draper 13CC156.

FRANCIS – a Creek/Shawnee/Miami name.

In 1771, John Brown wrote Sir William Johnson, "There was a squaw here a few days ago who formerly had a child to Mr. Francis late of the 44th Regiment.

"She had consented to send the boy to his father,

thinking that he would be taken care of, but she has been informed that the boy is now living with the Indians...near Montreal. She left a string of wampum with me, begging that I would write, so as the boy might be returned to her...The mother is a sister to Silverheels." See SWJ Papers, vol. 8, p. 235.

Josiah Francis, a mixed-blood Creek whose father ran a trading post, joined Tecumseh and the Prophet and advocated the evangelical Shawnee doctrine. See Wright, 60, 168-169, 172, 174, 179-180, 184; for Joseph and Milly Francis, 201, 312; Gilbert, p. 267.

Among the Shawnees allotted funds for their Ohio property which they were forced to leave behind in 1831 was Joe Francis. See Watson, vol. V., pt #3, p. 12.

After Chief John Perry died in 1846, he was succeeded in the traditional way by his sister's son, John Francis (Ta-pa-ta-ca-tha). Francis died a year or so later, the last traditional chief of the Shawnee Nation. See Draper 23S167-176.

Among the Shawnee guardianship cases heard in 1871 by Ely Parker, Commissioner of Indian Affairs, was the case of George Francis who had settled his account in 1860. His wards were not listed. See JAIFR, vol. VIII, #2, p. 28.

Among the Shawnees who settled on the lands of the Cherokee nation by 1869 were Richard, George, John, Rebecca, Anna, John, Nancy, Angeline, and Sally Francis. See JAIFR, vol. IV, #2, pp. 100-111.

Among the Shawnees on the 1880 census of the Cherokee Cooweescoowee District were Richard (age 32), Lizzie (24), Edmon (5), and David Francis (3). See JAIFR, vol X, #2, p. 16.

Francis was the surname of a Miami chief. See Anson, p. 136.

FRANKLIN - a Shawnee name.

Among the Shawnees who settled on the lands of the Cherokee nation by 1869 were George, Louisa, Mary E., Francis M., John, Alexander, Benjamin, and Alminia Franklin. See JAIFR, vol. IV, #2, pp. 100-111.

FROST – a Wyandot name.

Some members of the Frost family appear to have been captured during Pontiac's War. Sally Frost, a white girl, was captured and adopted by Wyandots and she willingly married Tarhe, the Crane, and had several children by him. Lang says she outlived her husband and "was among the white pioneers of the Sandusky country."

William Frost was a settler of Miami, County, Ohio, at least as early as 1807, a time when many of his neighbors were mix-bloods and white men with mixed-blood wives.

Listed on the 1843 Muster Roll of Wyandots from Sandusky, Ohio, was Sally Frost's household, consisting of one female over 55, one female 25 to 55, and one female and two males between 10 and 25.

Listed on the 1855 Wyandot Census were Michael Frost, age 31, with Hannah, 31, and Eady, 7.

Among the guardianship cases reviewed by the Commissioner of Indian Affairs in 1871 was the case of Michael Frost, a Wyandot, who was guardian for Baptiste and William B. Bigtown. Frost died in 1863, leaving three daughters. Baptiste Bigtown was Frost's uncle. See JAIFR, vol. VIII, #2, p. 22.

FROMAN – a Miami/Peoria name.

Some of the Froman family may have been captured from Nelson County, Kentucky at Kinchloe's or Polke's Station. The Froman name appears among the Miami at an early date. Guy Froman was a Peoria chief.

William Henry Froman, a half-breed Miami and

a descendant of Little Turtle, married Angeline Eddy, a Peoria.

One of their sons, Guy Willis Froman, played professional baseball from 1921 to 1932, mostly in the St. Louis Cardinal's organization, and thereafter worked for the Eagle-Picher Mining Company until 1967. He was elected chief of the Peoria tribe in 1947 after the death of George Skye. Chief Froman married Gertrude Helm and their children included Elizabeth Froman Hargrove, William Henry Froman, Robert Guy Froman, John Edward Froman, David Wesley Froman, Ronald Froman, and Donald Froman.

See Valley and Lembcke, pp. 206-207; Anson, p. 256.

An Eliza Foman (or Froman) and Sam Buck were Indians residing in Louisville, Kentucky in 1847. See the *Louisville Daily Democrat*, Feb 3, 1847.

GAMELIN – a Miami/Peoria name. Both Antonine and Pierre Gamelin were residents of Vincennes and had Wea or Miami wives. See Anson, pp. 103-104, 112-113. Antoine and his Wea wife, Assapho, later sold land off the reserve in Indiana.

Antoine Gamelin was employed by General St. Clair as a messenger to the Indians in 1790. After visiting Kickapoo and Piankeshaw villages, he went to the Wea and the Miami. Gamelin was well received by his kinfolk, but the Shawnees and Miamis largely ignored St. Clair's peace message. See R. David Edmunds, Wea Participation in the Northwest Indian Wars 1790-1793, FCQ, vol. 46, p. 244.

GARDNER – a Wyandot name.

A Mrs. Gardner was living among the Indians in 1792 at the time that Tecumseh's band skirmished with Simon Kenton's company of frontiersmen. Among these Shawnees, besides Mrs. Gardner, were John Ward, his Shawnee wife, and several of their children, and Coonna-haw. See Kenton, pp. 224-225.

From Draper Mss. 3YY62-63: DeGraff Buckeye, Dan S. Spellman, ed. "Ka-los-i-tah, the celebrated Indian wrestler was well known to the old settlers, but whether he belongs to the Shawnees or not I cannot say. The McCollochs and Zanes and Gardners influential citizens of this county had off of them Indian blood. A few of the children are still living in the county. My brother now living at Danville, Illinois married a Miss Tennery who was 1/16 Indian and related to the McColloch's. Rev. George McCulloch is still living near Bellefontaine. He is perhaps 74 years old but he is quite active. Gardner is yet living in Bellefontaine upwards of seventy — but is quite active. Each of these are `tainted with Injun.' A. J. Lippincott is still living here, a brother-in-law of mine...Very respectfully, Dan S Spellman...."

GARRETT – a Wyandot/Shawnee name.

Several members of the Garret(t) family were captured and adopted, including Phineas and Eli Garret. When John D. Shane interviewed Mrs. Sarah Graham, she told him that the Garret boys had been sent after the cows and while out were taken by Indians (about 1781). The boys were separated and went with different bands. Eli returned to Kentucky after three years, but Phineas (who was apparently much younger), remained with the Indians. See FCQ, vol. 9, p. 231.

There is an Indian blood tradition among some of the descendants of the early Bullitt County, Kentucky, Garrett family.

Listed on the 1843 Muster Roll of Wyandots from Sandusky, Ohio, were:

1. Charles B. Garrett's family, consisting of one male and one female 25 to 55, four males 10 to 25, and two males under 10.
2. George Garrett's household, consisting of one female over 55, one male and one female 25 to 55, two males and two females 10 to 25, and one male under 10.

Among the Garretts listed on the 1855 Wyandot Census were Charles B., 61, Maria, 48, Russell, 26, Cyrus, 24, Henry, 22, Nancy, 50, Nancy, 16, Theodore F., 27, Edward, 24, Mary, 21, Joel W., 29, Eliza J., 26, Mary Ann, 29, and Bryan, 8. The ages given should be taken as approximate because the year that they were taken seems to have been approximate. See KHC, vol. 15, p. 111.

Among the Shawnees who settled on the lands of the Cherokee nation by 1869 were Samuel, Richard, George, Robert L., Frederick, and Mary Garrett. See

JAIFR, vol. IV, #2, pp. 100-111.

The Shawnee Garretts and Wyandotte Garretts were almost certainly of the same family and intermarried with whites. In 1871, the guardianship cases of Henry, Cyrus, and Mary Ann Garrett were reviewed in the Wyandotte Nation and reveal some information about them. Henry Garrett had gone back east and died — in Cincinnati or St. Louis. Charles and Mary Garrett were his parents and Russell Garrett was his brother. He had been the guardian for John Punch.

Cyrus Garrett, another brother, had been guardian for Catherine Young who was then living in Indian Territory. Mary Ann Garrett (now Mary Ann Zane) was the guardian for William Long, her brother. See JAIFR, vol. VIII, #2, p. 18, 22.

In 1853, the widow Betsy Captain Chouteau married the wagonmaster Sam Garrett. The couple settled down on 900 acres just south of the Kansas River across from where Bonner Springs is now located. The Garretts were farmers and stonemasons and housebuilders. Sam and his brothers, Elias, Uriah, and Jack built a historic home for wagonmaster Dick Williams, a friend of the family.

In 1870, Betsy Garrett died in childbirth and was buried alongside Sam's parents, Edward and Elizabeth Garrett, on a hillside overlooking Captain's Creek. Sam then took his six children to Indian territory, there joining his friends Dick and Margaret Williams. Margaret Williams, a daughter of Capt. Joseph Parks, helped to raise the children. Sam Garrett later remarried, lived until 1891, and was buried in the Garrett-Williams cemetery.

Among the children he brought to Indian Territory was Frederick Garrett, a farmer, who in 1889 married Sarah Carr in a ceremony performed by Rev. Charles Bluejacket at his home in what is now Bluejacket, Oklahoma. The couple had ten children including son E. O. "Babe" Garrett, a farmer and stockman, born in 1903. Among his children was Bertha Garrett Cameron. This information comes from an newspaper article by Marsha Bennett, "Descendant of Shawnee Indians, Pioneer Developer Witnessed History," appearing in the *Journal-Herald*, February 25, 1986, Shawnee, Kansas.

GEORGE – a common Indian name.

Captain Robert George was in command at Ft. Jefferson during the siege.

He was from Alexandria, Virginia. He is probably the same Robert George who snapped a pistol at James Smith's head during "the black boys affair" at Paxton.

Robert George became an Indian trader and the Indian trader John George who was listed on the 1761 census of Ft. Pitt was probably kin. It was a tradition that Robert George's first wife was part-Indian, and several half-breeds with the last name of George appear, for one reason or another. John George, an Indian from Conoy, was living among the Delawares in 1763. Billy George, "a notorious half-breed, who boasted that he had killed two captains, Captain Thomas Harrod and Mr. David Wolf." Billy George was half-Cherokee.

Capt. Robert George is also said to have been a cousin of George Rogers Clark through the Rogers family.

In 1778, Lt. Robert George joined Capt. James Willing's expedition down the Mississippi on the marine ship Rattletrap as second in command of the rough-hewn company which included such rough men as ensigns George Girty and John Ash. More like pirates than soldiers, they shot up the neighborhood and plundered some of the rich merchants. Robert George took command of the company on their return trip. There was some difficulty with the company's ensign,

George Girty, and Robert George personally escorted him to the guardhouse at Ft. Nelson in May of 1779 (see The Thruston Papers, A-2-331-334). Shortly thereafter, George Girty was released (or escaped) and returned to the Indians.

It was certainly Capt. Robert George who commanded the militia at Ft. Jefferson during the siege, and his letters contain the most reliable accounts of the battle.

In 1782, Clark sent him to the Chickasaws along with James Sherlock to make a peace with them. On the 24th of October, 1782, he held a council with the Chickasaw main camp. Present were the chiefs Piamattihaw, Piomingo (the Mountain Leader), Mingohamah, Chambeau, and The Red King, two or three of whom were white or half-white.

The Revolution was explained to the Chickasaws in the words of Robert George, with James Sherlock interpreting as needed. "...the English and Americans were even as one family, but the English grew proud and thought themselves our superiors, that we should be deprived of our liberties and rights and, like servile slaves, support them with our labor. But our spirits would not permit us to condescend to such impositions. In opposition to their tyrannical proceedings we took arms in defense of ourselves..." See *Calendar of State Papers* (of Virginia), Vol. III, pp. 356-357.

Magee, in her major work on Ft. Jefferson, says that Capt. George "fraternized with the Indians" (p. 27); and in a footnote, she says, "He not only fraternized, he led them in battle." I do not know the source of her information, but I feel certain she did not make this up.

Robert George was one of the original settlers of Clarksville along with John, George, and David Owens, Enoch Springer, Moses McCan, the Cleghorns and a few others. A good many of the early settlers in the Clarksville/Charlestown area were related to him by blood or by marriage, including most probably Buckner Pittman, Martin Carney, and Peter Smith. On December 8, 1785, Richard Butler came to Clarksville and noted in his journal, "was very kindly received by Mr. Dalton and Mrs. & Captain George, who pressed us to stay for dinner." See L. A. Williams, *History of Ohio Falls Counties*, p. 196.

Robert George's wife, Nancy, ran off to Natchez with one of his Clarksville neighbors, Stephen Richards.

John Murphy, whose interview appears in Draper Ms. 8J193, said: "Robert George married his first wife for a given number of years at the expiration of which they separated according to contract and he then married a woman who was related to the wife of Major John Dunn of this city [Louisville]."

The nature of his marriage contract was similar to some Indian marriages, but this just may have been one of Robert George's own personal quirks. In Lewis C. Baird's *History of Clark County,* (1909) p. 898, it is noted that Ann Wood "often told of the peculiarities of Robert George."

Heckewelder, on his journey to the Wabash in 1792, stopped at Clarksville and noted seeing "the well-known Indian murderers, David Owens and Robbin George, now Capt. George, who had once stolen some of our horses on the Muskingum." See PM of H&B, vol. 12, p. 174.

Johnny George, a half-breed Cherokee, appeared on the frontier. Although he was not liked by the frontiersmen, he was not afraid to associate with the Kentuckians and the white settlements. One day, a couple of white men found his attitude too threatening, and they killed him. See Kenton.

Listed on the 1883 Ottawa census was the family of Edwin [Edwaize?] George, age 30, with Mary George, 35, Sampson George, 5, Phillip George, 4, and Jane George, 2.

GIBSON – a Shawnee/Wyandot name.

John Gibson, a brother of Indian trader George Gibson, was taken prisoner in 1763 and adopted. He was released to Gen. Henry Bouquet in 1764.

He continued to trade with the Indians and to live on the edge of Indian society. Travelers found him a genial host. "Mr. [John] Gibson, a trader here [at Logstown or at Newcomers Town], was taken prisoner last war by the Indians and was adopted into one of their chief families, and was well respected by them..." See the journals of Nicholas Cresswell and David McClure, among others.

At Ft. Pitt in 1772, Rev. David McClure was preparing a missionary journey to the Indian towns. He rode with John Gibson to the trading post at Logstown and noted in his journal, "The greater part of Indian traders keep a squaw, and some of them a white woman, as a temporary wife. Was sorry to find Friend Gibson in the habit of the first."

Hanna says that John Gibson's wife was a Shawnee woman, sister-in-law to Logan, the Mingo Chief, who lived, in 1773, at a small Mingo village called Logan's Town, at the mouth of Beaver Creek."

After Logan's family and John Gibson's wife were wantonly slaughtered by Daniel Greathouse and his party, it was John Gibson who took down Logan's message and brought it back to the white settlements. Only Logan, who was away, and John Gibson's son by his Indian wife had also escaped the massacre. After gathering up a war party, Logan began raiding the white settlements and killed many settlers in revenge. The killing did not really come to an end until the Treaty of Greenville, although there were uneasy truces in the intervening years.

The Indians often requested to have John Gibson as their go-between in red/white negotiations, and he was named Indian Agent, then Secretary of Indiana

Territory until it became a state, and he was at one time its acting governor. See Sipes, p. 502. In 1803, John Gibson interpreted a treaty to the Delawares while William Wells was the interpreter for the other tribes present.

After the death of his Shawnee wife, John Gibson remarried at least once, and possibly two or three times. The Rachel Gibson who married Peter Smith may have been his daughter, for it was certainly this John Gibson who gave his name for bond and witnessed the marriage.

John Gibson returned to Pennsylvania and died at the home of his son-in-law, George Wallace. His will, dated February 8, 1822, was probated February 24, 1825. It names his wife, Mary, sons Joseph, John, James, Hugh, and Elezer; daughters Mary, Esther, and Ellcy. The witnesses were James Weir and Evan Barrickman. Joseph Gibson, his son, was executor.

Some of his family must have remained associated (or semi-associated) with Indian life. A John Gibson and his family were among the Shawnees and Wyandots living in Wyandotte, Kansas in 1855.

Among the Wyandots on the 1843 census were John Gibson and his family, consisting of two males between 25 and 55, one female 10 to 25, and four children under 10, three of them boys.

Among the Shawnees who settled on the lands of the Cherokee nation by 1869 was William Givson. See JAIFR, vol. IV, #2, pp. 100-111.

Was the George Gibson who went on the Lewis and Clark Expedition related to John Gibson?

Quite possibly.

Historian George Yater wrote a sketch of this George Gibson in 1992. Gibson was from Pennsylvania, Yater says, a fine hunter and horseman. "Sergeant Ordway, in his journal, indicates that Gibson was something of an Indian interpreter and that there was some rivalry with George Drouillard in this regard. That is difficult to accept, however. If Gibson were acquainted with some Indian dialects it would have been that of the Ohio Indians — the Algonquin language family and a knowledge useless west of the Mississippi."

I wouldn't say that, but my point is here that both George Gibson and half-Shawnee George Drouillard knew some Indian dialects, if only Delaware and Shawnee.

Yater says that "Gibson was married after the expedition and died in St. Louis in 1809. That is the extent of present knowledge. His story, like that of so many other Expedition members, belongs to the short and simple annals of the poor."

In the Clark County, Indiana records there is a deed concerning Maria Gibson, "the daughter of Jacob Reager and the wife of George Gibson of St. Louis." Another deed is there wherein Peter Smith (the notorious Peter Smith) gives a black girl named Matilda to "his beloved sister-in-law, Margarite Gibson."

In the early Clark County, Indiana, Circuit Court records there is a dispute concerning the indenture of John (or Jack) Green, who was either an Indian or a "free man of color." The participants were Indian trader Francis Vigo, said to have married a part-Shawnee, and George Gibson who was probably a son of Col. John Gibson.

GILLIS or McGILLIS – a Delaware name.

According to a 1786 report by Doleman from the Indian towns, there was a renegade named McGillis or Gillis who lived among the Shawnees. See Draper 14S216.

William Gillis, a white man, born in Maryland about 1797, went to Kaskaskia about 1817 and lived there about ten years. He later moved to Missouri, and then to Wyandotte County, Kansas. One of the founders of Kansas City, he amassed a fortune before his death there in 1869. His will named his two daughters of Delaware women, Sophia and Mary Gillis, but he only gave them ten dollars apiece. The rest of his estate was given to his niece, Mary A. Troost.

Well, as often happens when rich men die, the will was contested beyond all reason. The subsequent testimony revealed some interesting things about William Gillis. About 1829, while living at the James Fork Trading Post on the White River, he married Kahketoqua, a daughter of a Piankashaw/Peoria chief. She died about 1863. Their daughter, Nancy Gillis, died about 1862, leaving two children, Francis Boyer and James Charlie, jr., the son of Chief Charlie of the Peorias. It turned out that Sophia Gillis (born 1826), Mary Gillis (born 1829), and Nancy Gillis (born 1830) were each daughters of William Gillis by a different Delaware (or Piankashaw) woman.

This is what the court ruled, anyway. There were other claimants to the rich man's fortunes, however.

Anthony (Nat) Gillis claimed a part. Frank Morrison, of Randolph County, Illinois, deposed: "I am 66 years old and am a younger son of Matilda, the mother of Nat Gillis. There are three or four children that were born between us. Matilda was of white, Indian, and some negro blood, a mulatto brighter than a quadroon. She had long black hair. It touched the floor when she walked. She was a slave belonging to General [John] Edgar and had her freedom before I was born. She died many years ago. William Gillis, a white man, was the father of Nat, and always recognized Nat as his son."

Morrison goes on to say that William Gillis and Matilda lived together except when Gillis was away trading with the Indians. That she had two children by him, Nat and Pamelia Gillis. That afterwards, she lived with a white man named Lemons, with whom she had one child, then later, she lived with a mixed-blood named Osborn, with whom she had two more children. After that, she lived with "my father, Frank Morrison, a mulatto, of whom three children were born; and afterwards, with Michael Brandemore, of whom one child was born." The depositions of 82-year-old Eliza Briggs and 95-year-old Raphael Francis were taken and they substantiated that of Morrison. But all agreed that Matilda was never officially married to William Gillis, and the claim was disallowed.

The Shawnee woman, Mary Ann Gillis Steele, the daughter of a Shawnee woman named Sophia McLane, claimed a part. She was the wife of John Steele. The court ruled that her claim had no basis, but the testimony is interesting.

Nancy Dougherty, a daughter of Lewis Dougherty, married James McLane. After James McLane's death in 1864, she married Tom Bigknife, sr. But pertinent to this case, among her children by James McLane was Sophia McLane. Sophia had an illegitimate child named Mary Ann. Shortly afterwards, Sophia married William Gillis. The ceremony was performed by a missionary named Francis Barker. Tom Bigknife was married to Fanny Logan at the same time. Gillis provided food and clothing for Mary Ann, caused her to be sent to school, always recognized her as his child, and she was called Mary Gillis.

But while Mary Ann Gillis was still a child, her parents split up and her mother, Sophia, married Abraham Grandstaff, a white man.

And that's just half the testimony on this issue. The other side presented testimony which refuted that of Polly Rogers, one of the witnesses for Mary Ann Gillis Steele, splattering mud upon Polly's reputation for both chastity and veracity. The combined testimony of Charles and Jane Journeycake, Elizabeth Rogers, Samuel Cornatzer, and Abraham Grandstaff cast doubt upon her word.

The deposition of Mary Gillis Rogers, age 57, was taken in May, 1883. She said that her mother's name was Maria, a part-Delaware, part-French woman. She lived with her father, William Gillis, in Kansas City until she was 13. She married William Rogers in 1843 and had four children, the last born in 1852. She knew Polly Rogers who testified in this case, as Polly was her sister-in-law, the widow of Wilson Rogers. Polly's reputation for truth was bad.

The deposition of Mrs. Nary Carpenter, age 60, was taken in November, 1883. She was Shawnee, the daughter of Jake Dougherty, a son of Lewis Dougherty. She stated that Nancy Bigknife, her aunt, was the mother of Sophia McLane. In her opinion, Sophia McLane never had an official marriage before she married Grandstaff, and for that matter, the same was true of Fanny Logan and Tom Bigknife, jr., who just "took up at a dance at Polly Rogers' house north of Shawneetown; got together and went home together. When Tom brought Fanny home, his mother, Nancy Bigknife, asked Tom why he brought such a woman, a runabout, ragged, and barefooted...." See Gillis.

GIRTY – the most famous renegade name ever.

Yet a family who has been so maligned by popular history as to be virtually unknown.

The Eckerlin brothers, evangelical missionaries of the Euphrata or Dunkard sect, robbed their Church treasury and moved to the wilderness — land that is now a part of southwestern Pennsylvania. Here, they helped to establish one of the first white settlements in the area. Their settlement, on Dunkard Creek, is shown on Shippen's "Draught of Braddock's Road, 1759." John Owens settlement is also shown.

One of the Eckerlin sisters, Rebecca Ann Eckerlin, married Adam Doane of "The Terrible Doanes," who later robbed and murdered throughout the area of the Upper Ohio and Monongahela Rivers.

Another sister, Mary Eckerlin, married in 1736 to Thomas Newton, who left her a widow when he drowned in the Susquehanna River near present Harrisburg, Pennsylvania. She then married, in 1737, Indian trader Simon Girty, Sr., and they became parents of several children, including Simon Girty jr., George Girty, and James Girty. These three were captured and adopted by Indians when young, and later all became Indian traders and infamous on the frontier during the Revolution. They were not necessarily by the same father, as Mary Eckerlin was said to play around when her husband was away. According to one story, Simon Girty sr. was killed by one of her lovers, John Turner, whom she subsequently married. See Lough, 54-64.

Simon Girty Jr. was born in Pennsylvania in 1741. At the age of fifteen, he was captured and adopted by Senecas. He subsequently became an interpreter and Indian trader. He served as a scout and guide during Lord Dunmore's War. He went to the British and became the most notorious of all the Loyalists. He participated in all British Indian affairs until his death, February 18, 1818. See the John Askin Papers, I, 308-309.

George Girty and a few Delawares were also along with the party of Hurons, Wyandots, Chippawas, Shawnees, and Ottawas who accompanied British Captain Henry Bird and his men on the campaign into Kentucky in 1780. On the trek back, food was scarce, but George Girty killed some deer and brought them in. The British officer purchased the deer for himself and his officers, but gave none to his prisoners. Members of the Breckinridge family, who were among the prisoners from Ruddles' and Martin's Stations, told the Rev. Shane that George Girty cursed the British for their conduct, for "having plenty of rations but carrying his prisoners back to starve without them." See Lafferty, p. 25.

George Girty is said to have had several children by his Delaware wife. He died about 1810 near Ft. Wayne at James Girty's trading post, and his family is said to have stayed among the Delawares. For years after his death, his Delaware friends told stories about his bravery and heroism at Blue Licks and the other conflicts of his day. See Butterfield, p. 315. George Girty, the son of George Girty, stayed among the Delawares after the War of 1812 as an Indian trader.

Michael Girty was a son of Simon Girty. He was "born of a squaw and spent his early life among the Indians of Ohio. He came to this country [Illinois] soon after 1821, and was employed as interpreter by the fur company. Here he married a squaw and raised a number of sons. Michael tried hard to gain the confidence of the Indians, but they did not trust the treacherous half-breed.

"On the 21st of June, 1827, Gen. Cass, as Indian agent, held a council in Bureau County with the Indians. Girty acted as interpreter. Cass gave him a silver medal, as a token of friendship...." After the Blackhawk War, Michael Girty's Indian family returned to Bureau County, Illinois, but he was not with them. "His fate at the time was unknown." See Lang, p. 139.

Simon Girty's "respectable" children included Ann (b. 1786), Thomas (b. 1788), Sarah (b. 1791), and Prideaux (b. 1797). Besides Michael, he is also said to have had a son named Simon among the Shawnees who may have taken Simonds as a surname. Some of the Girty family appear to have moved into the Cherokee Nation. Shares of the money granted by the treaty of 1828 to the Arkansas Cherokees went to Issac Girty and his family of five, and to John Girty and his family of five. Another share went to a woman listed as "Girty's mother-in-law." See JAIFR, vol. VI, #4, p. 15, 17.

GIST, CIST, GUESS or GUEST – a Shawnee/ Cherokee name.

Christopher Gist was a Pennsylvania Indian trader with a Shawnee wife. His son, Nathaniel Gist, was sent on a mission to the Cherokees by Governor Dinwiddie of Virginia to ask the them to join in a battle against the Shawnees. While there, Nathaniel Gist met and married Wurteh, the Cherokee sister of Chief Doublehead, Onitositah, and Pumpkin Head. Their son was born about 1760 and named George Gist (or Guess) — more famous by his Indian name, Sequoyah.

Woodward says, "In the Great Island treaty of 1777, the Cherokees reserved Great Island for Nathaniel Gist, Sequoyah's father. The Cherokees said that they desired that Gist 'might set down upon it when he pleased, as it belongs to him and them to hold good talks on.' But Gist by then had decided to join Washington's army and so did not use Great Island." He was commissioned a colonel in the continental army on the recommendation of George Washington, with whom he had been friends for years. Seventeen Cherokees, led by the Pigeon, accompanied Gist back to Washington's army to serve as scouts. See Woodward, p. 98.

GODFROY or GODFREY – a Miami name.

Jacque Godfroy was living among the Miami Indians in 1790. One of his letters is in Hays Journal; see Quaife, p. 40-41.

According to Quaife, this was possibly Jacques Godfrey, Sr. He figured in the events attending Pontiac's siege of Detroit in 1763, and the following year he saved the life of Captain Thomas Morris. He was at Miamitown when Harmar fell upon it in October, 1790, and Godfrey carried to Detroit an account of the ensuing battles. The following spring his goods to the value of 500£ were destroyed by the American army that raided the Wea villages. See Mich. Pio. & Hist. Col., VIII, 283-85; XXIV, 100, 107, 166, 273; XXXVII, 448, 453.

Lewis Godfroy appears on the 1831 payroll of the Miamis in the Tipton Papers.

Alexander D. Godfroy and Richard Godfroy, "adopted children of the Pottowatomie tribe," were given land in the 1817 treaty held at the Miami Rapids on Lake Erie.

Francois Godfroy was a French-Miami half-blood who married Sakwata, a Miami woman, and became a chief of a small band of the tribe in Indiana. He signed the 1838 treaty as "Paw-law-zo-aw," which was thought to have been his Indian name. As other historians have pointed out, the Algonquins had trouble with the "R" sound, and this was merely a Miami attempt to pronounce the name Francois.

A son of Francois Godfroy, Gabriel Godfroy, traced his maternal ancestors and found that "his grandfather was a white man who was captured in Kentucky when about seven years old by the Shawnee Indians. Two other children were taken at the same time he was captured. His right name he had forgotten, but thought it was Coe or Coleman. This boy grew up among the Indians and became a skillful trader, and was the Shawnee interpreter at the Treaty of Greenville. He married a woman among the Miamis who was half French. They raised a large family, and at an old age the father died near where he was captured in Kentucky. His widow then came to live among her own people, the Miamis, near Ft. Wayne."

And who was his grandfather? Many men almost fit the description, but this was most probably

Alvin Coe who was one of the many interpreters at the Treaty of Greenville. The Coe family has a strong Indian blood tradition and it could be that brothers and sisters of Alvin Coe were also captured and adopted and that, together with his other children, they have spread the tradition. Many members of the Coe family moved to the Miami River valley and associated with others who had red connections in the early Ohio, Kentucky, and Indiana area.

Godfroy was a war chief among his people, and he took part in several battles. According to Stephens' account, Harrison sent a detachment of 600 mounted men to burn all the villages on the Mississinewa. Col. Campbell, who commanded, was ordered not to molest the Delawares or Miamis, but the expedition reached the Mississinewa valley on the 17th of December and immediately fell upon them, despite the orders. Francois Godfroy quickly collected about forty or fifty braves and scouted the woods. They found the soldiers encamped on a high bluff of the river, and "they began to plan their assault, Indian style. They skulked around the camp, howling like wolves so they could recognize each other and keep together."

The Miamis attacked the camp a half-hour before daybreak. Eight of the soldiers were killed, including two officers, with forty-two wounded. Fifteen dead warriors were found by the soldiers after the fight. As always, the red forces were badly outnumbered and felt their loss more severely than did the larger force. And the Miami and Delaware Nations were at peace.

By his first wife, Francois Godfroy's children included: (1) Poqua, (2) Tac-con-ze-quah, (3) Catherine who married a Mr. Goodboo, (4) Louisa who married a Mr. Hunt, (5) James R. Godfroy, and (6) William Godfroy. By his second wife, Sac-kah-quet-tah, his children included: (1) Sallie, (2) George W., (3) Thomas, (4) Gabriel, (5) Clemmance, and (6) Frances. See

Stephens, pp. 29-34.

One of Francois Godfroy's great-grandsons, Lawrence Godfroy, was a leading chief of the Miamis in 1972 when settlement checks of about $1200 were paid to each of the 4000 or so enrolled members of the Miami tribe. A picture of Lawrence Godfroy, who was then 76 years old, appears in an article in the Indianapolis news. Godfroy said he was nominated and elected a principal chief at a council in Peru, Indiana, a position that his father, Peter Godfroy, and his brothers, Sylvester and Clarence, had previously held.

See the newspaper clippings in the Indian File at the Public Library of New Albany, Indiana. See Anson for Clarence Godfroy, p. 281; for Francois Godfroy, pp. 161, 170, 178, 190, 199, 204, 206, 300; for Gabriel Godfroy, pp. 18, 279; for Ira Sylvester Godfroy, p. 283; for Jacques Godfroy, pp. 55, 65, 68, 71; for Peter Godfroy, p. 279; for William A. Godfroy, p. 283.

GORE – a Shawnee name.

Jonathan Gore, a lawyer from Nelson County, Kentucky, married Sallie, a Shawnee, the daughter of Charles Bluejacket. See the *Louisville Daily Journal*, Nov. 27th, 1858, copy on microfilm at the Louisville Free Public Library.

Among the Shawnees living on the Cherokee Reserve in 1869 were Jonathan Gore, Sally Gore, Eva B. Gore, Hattie Gore, and H. Blake Gore. See JAIFR, vol. IV, #2, p. 106.

Born in Bullitt County, Kentucky, to Enoch and Hattie Gore on Feb. 23, 1833, Jonathan Gore was probably named for his more famous relative, the Jonathan Gore who was a lawyer and judge for Nelson County. He wandered around the country for a while, but settled in Johnson County, Kansas, where he became a county attorney in 1858. He married fourteen-year-old Sallie Bluejacket, the daughter of Chief Charles

Bluejacket. Gore was the lawyer for the tribe, and he accompanied them to the Cherokee Nation when they moved there. He was a friend of the Cherokee Chief Tom Buffington, and his son, Jonathan Gore, jr., was the boyhood companion of Will Rogers, the famous part-Cherokee humorist.

The children of Jonathan and Sallie (Bluejacket) Gore included:

1. Eva, b. 1860.
2. Hattie, b. 1867.
3. Henry Blake, b. 1869.
4. Jonathan jr., b. 1875.
5. Mary (Mamie), b. 1877, m. Alexander McKinzie.
6. Daisy, b. 1879, m. Sam Crockett. She lived until 1965.
7. Nathaniel S., b. 1886.

Will Rogers, when a student at Willie Halsell College, wrote to a friend, Charley McClellan on March 28, 1893, "My little friend...do you ever go to see your girl...her big sister Mamie is my girl and the little one is yours. I have got the prettiest girl in the country. She is Jon Gore's sister and lives at Bluejacket, 12 miles from here." Mamie Gore, however, was to marry Alexander McKinzie, and their children included Lacy McKinzie who became a lawyer and later a judge in Vinita, Oklahoma. See SOCC, vol. I, pp. 369-370. A picture of Jonathan Gore's beautiful daughters appears on page 369, and Gore appears in a picture with Chief Tom Buffington on page 370.

GRAHAM – a Shawnee name.

Among the Shawnees who settled on the lands of the Cherokee nation by 1869 was John Graham. See JAIFR, vol. IV, #2, pp. 100-111.

GRAVES – a Shawnee name.

Among the Shawnees who settled on the lands of the Cherokee nation by 1869 were Charles and Albura Graves. See JAIFR, vol. IV, #2, pp. 100-111.

Living among the Shawnees in 1880 was Charles Graves, a white man, age 35. He was living with the Shawnee woman, Abby Graves, age 34, and Clarence Graves, age 8, probably their child. See JAIFR, vol X, #2, p. 18.

GRAY – a common name with Indian blood traditions.

John Gray's wife was captured when Bingham's Fort was attacked on June 11, 1755. See WPHM, Vol. 7, p. 73. Several other members of the Gray family appear to have been captured during the French and Indian War.

James Kenny saw John Gray at Ft. Pitt in the early 1760s and noted in his journal that, "One John Gray, an old trader, came up from ye lower Shawnee Town and says that ye Shawnees were so cross that he wa afraid to stay there, that ye Mingoes had sent a belt amongst them advising them to mischief against ye English..."

Sam Gray, a half-breed, was the leader of the party of Indians who captured William Boggs (the same Boggs who, with Lewis Wetzel, had tomahawked Killbuck) near Wheeling in 1781. See Lobdell, Indian Warfare..., p. 110.

A James Gray was with the Shawnees who served with Chief John Perry and Capt. Joseph Parks in the Florida War. A James Gray signed the Delaware Treaty. This man appears to have been a Mohawk or part-Iroquois scout that came to Kansas with the Lagotherie's and was a free hunter in the Rocky Mountains for a time.

Charlotte Gray, the part-Iroquois daughter of John and Marienne Gray, married the part-Mohawk

Benjamin Lagotherie, son of Victor Lagotherie, in Kansas in 1836. See Barry, p. 312. John Gray sometimes hired on as a hunter for wagon trains going to California and Oregon.

In 1841, Father Nicolas Point, a Belgian priest and artist, left Westport Missouri for California with a wagon train headed by Thomas "broken-hand" Fitzpatrick. Along with Fitzpatrick was half-Iroquois scout John Gray (Ignace Hatchiorauquasha). They spoke of Gray as a man of "extraordinary courage and dexterity."

In 1849, John Gray was a gunsmith for the Osage River Agency. See Barry, p. 896.

Among the Shawnees who settled on the lands of the Cherokee nation by 1869 was Issac Gray. See JAIFR, vol. IV, #2, pp. 100-111.

GRANT – a Cherokee name.

Ludoric Grant was an Indian trader who lived among the Cherokees in the early 1700s. His quarter-blood grand-daughter married John Stuart. Many of his mixed-blood descendants are among the Cherokees today.

GREEN – a Delaware name.

Thomas Green is listed among the Indians in the accounts of the SWJ Papers in 1763, along with Wechimboughwa, Toghgache, Capt. Pipe, Kishecima, John Owen's Son, and Thomas John.

Tom Green, "one of ye Delawares," appears in the journal of James Kenny, an Indian trader operating out of Ft. Pitt in the early 1760s. Green told Kenny that he had been up on the Susquehanna where his mother and brother were and had taken them to the Delaware towns "at Cuscuskies Salt Licks." See Kenny, p. 152.

Greentown was apparently a Delaware town

near Anderson, Indiana. In William C. Smith's *Indiana Miscellany*, that author speaks of an Indian whose English name was Green saying he had "killed enough white people for himself and his pony to swim in." See Thompson, p. 202.

Cherry says that Greentown was named after "the renegade Thomas Green. He was a Tory in the bloody Wyoming Valley. There he had been associated with the cruel Mohawks in the wanton murder of his countrymen and to escape vengeance, [he] fled with Billy Montour, Gelloway, Thomas Lyons, Armstrong, and others to the wilds of Ohio. He founded a town among the Delawares, which in honor of this renegade, they called Greentown. This village became well known in Northern Ohio annals." See Cherry, p. 249.

There is the account of a fight between Peter Killbuck and John Green, both Delaware Indians, in which Peter Killbuck was killed. "Green is the man who lately attempted to stab William McClelland of Hamilton." See Ohio's Newspaper Extracts, vol. II, #67, p. 52 (Wednesday, 15 October, 1800).

In the early Clark County, Indiana, Circuit Court records there is a dispute concerning the indenture of John (or Jack) Green, who was either an Indian or a "free man of color." The participants were Indian trader Francis Vigo, whose wife was possibly part-Indian, and George Gibson, who was possibly a son of Col. John Gibson, and possibly the man who went with Lewis and Clark.

(The) GREY-EYED MAN, GREY EYES – a Wyandot name.

Eckert says that Grey Eyes (Tayauendottoontgraw) and another Wyandot (Tsoondoweneo, or Spliced Arrow, probably George Punch) went as ambassadors to the tribes in the south to get them to join the alliance against the forces of General St. Clair.

See Eckert, Tecumseh, p. 735, note 392. According to Mrs. Walker, a half-blood Wyandot, Grey Eyes helped Tecumseh compose an eloquent speech he made before the British. See Sugden, p. 223n.

Grey Eyes was a Methodist minister for the Wyandots. He opposed the sale of Wyandot lands but was not strong enough to resist the whites and went west with his tribe under Chief Jacques. See Lang, p. 210. Margaret Grey Eyes, the daughter of John Grey Eyes, was also long associated with the Wyandot mission in Ohio. She married John Solomon and went west with him in 1843, but after he died, she returned to Ohio.

On the 1843 Wyandot Muster Roll were listed:

1. Doctor Grey Eyes' family, consisting of one male and one female 25 to 55, two females 10 to 25, and two males and one female under 10.
2. Esquire Grey Eyes' family, consisting of one male over 55, one male and one female between 25 and 55, one male and one female between 10 and 25, and one boy under 10.
3. John M. Grey Eyes' family, consisting of one male and one female, both between 10 and 25.
4. Robert Grey Eyes' family, consisting of one male between 25 and 55, and two females between 10 and 25.
5. Widow Grey Eyes' family, which included two males 25 to 55, one female 10 to 25, and one female under 10.

Among the Wyandots allotted land in 1856 was Henry C. Greyeyes.

Among the guardianship cases reviewed by the Commissioner of Indian Affairs in 1871 was the case of John W. Greyeyes, a Wyandot, guardian for the John Williams family among others. See JAIFR, vol. VIII,#2, p. 17.

GRIFFIN – a Shawnee name.

Among the Shawnees who settled on the lands of the Cherokee nation by 1869 was Sally Griffin. See JAIFR, vol. IV, #2, pp. 100-111.

GRILLS – an Ottawa name.

William Grills was a frontiersman who was captured and adopted by Ottawas when a child. He lived with them six years, then left on his own and went to Maryland for a time, but later returned.

Eckert, who made him a character and recounts some of Grill's stories in *The Frontiersman*, quotes him as saying that there were "many traits of the Indian that were considerably more admirable than those of the white man." Eckert has him, in 1774, deserting the Greathouse party as they were torturing Chief Logan's family:

"No one had even noted that Bill Grills was no longer with them. From fifty yards away in the heavy darkness of the woods he had been watching, but now he turned and slipped silently away. His association with both Jacob Greathouse and the frontier had just ended permanently."

Eckert's reference was *The Journal of William Grills*, which I have not seen; but even without seeing it, I think that Eckert may have jumped to the wrong conclusion. I have no doubt that Grills made a return trip to his Maryland family. But later, Bill Grills came to the Ohio falls area (present Louisville) and resumed his trapping and trading. His name appears in the early Jefferson County Kentucky Common Law Court records.

John Sanders and William Grills appear to have been trading partners, possibly also with George Owens. William Grills had a suit against George Owens in the Jefferson County Common Law Court dated May 9, 1785, Case #861. Enclosed in the suit is a running account against Owens for various items and services. The suit was still pending when Grills and Sanders were killed.

See Draper Mss. 13J33-36: "...My father and his comrades left the main shore and went on to an island and stayed all night without fear and in the morning my father returned for his trap alone, his comrades refusing to accompany him, and got his traps and a beaver in each one and on their way home to Louisville met Grills and Sanders, two great trappers and hunters [who were] going to the same island and creek to trap for beaver. They informed them of the presence of Indians but Grills and Sanders, heedless of their warning, went to the island [probably eighteen-mile island] and camped and built a fire. The Indians in the night crept up on them and killed them but their camp boy made good his escape and, although late in the fall, swam to the Kentucky shore and went to Louisville and told the news."

GUTHERIE – a Wyandot/Shawnee.

John Gutherie was among the whites delivered up by the Wyandots and Shawnees to General Henry Bouquet in 1764.

Abelard Gutherie worked for the Indian Agency in Ohio. He married Quindaro Nancy Brown, a part-white daughter of the Wyandot chief Adam Brown and Theresa, his Shawnee wife. Gutherie was adopted by the Wyandots and he became a Wyandot politician, being a delegate to Congress from the Nation. The one-time town of Quindaro, now a part of Kansas City, was named for his wife. See Barry, pp. 520, 939, 1129, 1134, 1173-74, 1184.

The 1855 Wyandot Census lists the Gutherie family including Abelard, age 41, Nancy, 35, Abelura, 10, Morsona, 8, James, 5, and Jacob, 3.

Among the guardianship cases reviewed by the

Commissioner of Indian Affairs in 1871 was the case of Abelard Guthrie, guardian for the John Bigtree, a Wyandot. Gutherie lived at Quindaro, Kansas, in 1871. Bigtree had died about 1857, leaving Mrs. John Spicer (formerly Eliza Bigtree) as his heir. Her husband was a Seneca chief. See JAIFR, vol. VIII, #2, p. 22.

Among the Shawnees who settled on the lands of the Cherokee nation by 1869 were James, Nancy, Jacob, and Narsonia Guthrie. See JAIFR, vol. IV, #2, pp. 100-111.

The children of Abelard and Nancy (Brown) Guthrie included:

1. James who m. Grace—, and they had four children who included Lucy, Percy, Hugh, and Ray Guthrie.
2. Abalura who m. Charles Graves, and they had a son named Charles Graves jr.
3. Narsona who m. Edward Lane, brother of H. J. Lane, editor of the *Kansas City Herald*. Their children included Marsh and Vernon Lane (m. Julia Bodenhommer).
4. Jacob who m. Dora—, and their children included Robert and Wade Abelard Guthrie. See SOCC, vol. I, p. 375, from information supplied by Retha Miller.

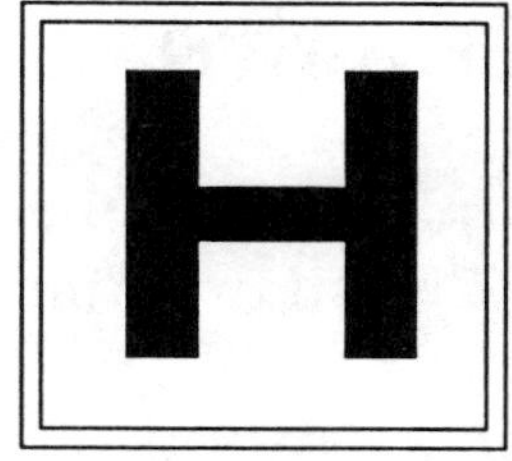

HACKLEY – a Miami name.

The first wife of noted scout William Wells was Anahquah, a sister of Little Turtle, the great Miami chief. Their children included Ann (Ahpezzahquah), who married Dr. William Turner; Rebecca (Pemesahquah), who married Captain James Hackley; Mary (Ahmahquauzahquah), who married Judge James Wolcott; William Wayne Wells; and Samuel G. Wells.

Capt. James Hackley was from Hardin County, Kentucky, but seems to have lived for a while in neighboring Nelson County where some of the Hackley daughters and nieces later attended the Nazareth Academy. He was a clerk for James Audubon (the famous Audubon Society namesake) in Elizabethtown where Haycraft described him as "one of the most starchy and fine dressing men who ever lived in our town." He is supposed to have committed suicide in later life by cutting his own throat.

Ann Wells Turner, the daughter of William Wells and the widow of the former Indian agent Dr. William Turner, was educated at the Catholic seminary (Nazareth) in Bardstown, Kentucky. See Indiana Historical Collections: Fort Wayne, p. 31; Tipton Papers, 1824, p. 398.

The 1826 Treaty with the Miami specified that sections of land between the Maumee and St. Joseph Rivers be given to Ann Hackley and Jack Hackley, to Ann Turner alias Hackley, to Rebecca Hackley, and to Jane S. Wells "under the direction of the President of the United States."

Some of the Hackley children went white, and some went red. Jack Hackley (Lanapincha) was a Miami delegate in the 1850s. See Anson, p. 239. He was a miller for the Miamis in 1853, and he signed the treaty in Washington in 1854. See Barry, pp. 1190, 1220.

HAHN, HONN, HORN, HAUN, or HAWN – a Shawnee/Delaware/Shoshoni name.

There is a strong Indian blood tradition in the family, say some of the descendants of Christian Hahn of early Nelson County, Kentucky.

Among the 127 prisoners taken in the capture of Ruddles' and Martin's Stations in Kentucky in 1780 were Joseph Honn, his wife, and their children Katherine, Polly, Margaret, and Joseph.

"Mrs. Honn and her daughter, Katherine, were among the captives from Ruddles'. Katherine, a fleet-footed girl of eighteen, was chased by the Indians a half a mile while running the gauntlet and was knocked down by an Indian club. She married first, Charles Munger (a Munger family was also captured at Ruddles' Station), then Joseph Fenis. The mother, Mrs. Honn, was placed in Blue Jacket's family where she kept the cows and made the butter, esteeming herself fortunate to be so well placed." See Lafferty, p. 33, 26.

According to Lafferty, the family returned to Kentucky and resided in Montgomery County.

Ex-slave Harry Smith says that Worden Hahn was "a half breed," who claimed he could get the best of any white or black man alive. Worden Hahn lived in Louisville, Kentucky in the 1850s and he was an interesting man, running a horse stable until his barns caught fire and burned in January, 1853. In March, 1853, he was the entrepreneur who towed ice down the river from Pittsburgh and sold it for ice cream that could be made in the spring. In the records, he looks like a wealthy white man. So why would Harry Smith refer to him as a wealthy half-breed? See Smith, pp. 151-152.

Many of the Kentucky Indian blood traditions lead to the Miami River Valley in Ohio. The 1818 Warren County will of Jacob Hawn mentions brother Christian, his wife, Peggy, his unnamed children, and

Lewis Davis who became the guardian of the children in lieu of Christian Hawn.

Many of the Kentucky Indian blood traditions lead to the Miami River Valley in Ohio. The 1818 Warren County will of Jacob Hawn mentions his wife, Peggy, and his brother Christian as guardian of his unnamed children. Lewis Davis became the guardian of the children in lieu of Christian Hawn.

A Christain Hahn with a part-Delaware wife is listed on the 1900 census of Wyandot County, Kansas. He is listed as a white man born in 1864 in Michigan. His wife, Mattie Hahn, was born in Kansas in 1868, her father a white man, her mother a Delaware. See Prevost, p. 45.

A Frank Hahn married the half-breed daughter of mountain man Jim Bridger in Westport, Missouri, but the Hahn Indian blood tradition has an earlier source than this. Perhaps I can follow up on this in a future volume of *Indian Blood*.

HALE – a Miami name.

"Thirty years ago in an evil hour the Miamis were induced by the prospect of immediate gain and by the persuasion of men whom they regarded as friend to concede to the abrogation of the treaty under which they were to receive and annuity forever and be to accept in lieu thereof the gross sum of $221,000 to be paid to the Miamis in 26 annual payments...White speculators speedily gained control of their holding and the Miamis became...wanderers, refugees, and vagabonds.

"An exception was to be found in the case of Meshingasiens band, just south of this town. Me shin go mena was the last chief of the Miamis and his family as well as others that were with him were of a high order of intelligence. They tilled the soil with success and had many fertile acres and lived comfortably and they were too shrewd and provident as a rule to be taken in by designing white men.

"For many years the Miami maidens have been sought in marriage by white scoundrels and adventurers who knew of their wealth in land and expected to make something out of the transaction...

"Much surprise was caused here a few years ago when an advertisement appearing in a local newspaper announced that 'Nancy Wa-ca-c-had, a young Miami maiden, good-looking, amiable and neat, and the owner of two hundred acres of excellent land,' would marry a white man if the right one presented himself. Efforts were made to head the girl off, and the sad fate of her sisters was pointed out to her, but she would not be advised, and the ad stood as written.

"From a score of suitors, Nancy selected a young man named Charlee Hale, and this marriage was speedily celebrated. Hale was a man who had never made a success of anything, and he was indolent and without experience of any bread-winning pursuit, but he was fairly good looking and for a time Nancy was the happiest girl in Indiana.

"She and her husband settled on her farm but Hale had no intention of working. On one pretext and another he induced her to sell or mortgage the hand and to give him the money until all was irretrievably gone, and then with nothing but the charity of her people to rely upon, he abandoned her, taking up with a white woman and leaving the country.

"Nancy could hardly believe that the land which had been hers and her fathers and her grandfathers had passed from her control forever and the white husband for whom she had paid so dearly had abandoned her.

"Some of the older members of the tribe who still retain their lands took this girl in and gave her a home and through the kindness of a Wabash attorney an action for divorce has now been brought in the bill. Hale is charged with cruel and inhuman treatment and drunkenness and unfaithfulness...and there are plenty of witnesses."

See Draper Mss. 9YY18, a newspaper article from the *Madison Indiana Democrat*, 1887: "Wedded To Adventurers – Indian Maidens Shamefully Deceived by the Principled White Men."

Good husband or not, she is supposed to have had two children by this man named Hale. The Hale name became prominent among the remnant Miami in Indiana and in recent years men with the surname have been vying for leadership for the entire Miami tribe.

According to a 1972 newspaper article, William F. Hale, 80, a retired building-contractor in rural Eaton, Indiana, claimed to be the head chief of the Miamis on the basis of having been elected to that position by "the Indiana Miami Group in Wabash in 1960."

"Hale, whose age permitted him to be listed on the 1895 Miami roll, said that he had spent his entire life working to get justice for the Miami who were stripped of their land. And in 1972, President Nixon signed a five million dollar settlement which had been negotiated with the tribe, to be distributed to every individual on the rolls, about $1000 per person.

See "Miamis Await Wampum," by Barry Henderson, a newspaper story appearing in the *Indianapolis News*, July 17, 1972, p. 4. There is a copy in the Indian file of the New Albany, Indiana Public Library.

HAMPTON – a common name among several tribes.

Some of the Hamptons intermarried with the Creeks, Choctaws, Chickasaws, and Shawnees.

Listed on the 1900 Indian Territory Census was William Hampton, a Shawnee born in 1866 in Missouri. He said that both of his parents were Shawnees born in Kentucky. His wife, Shalot Hampton, was a Potawatomi. Also listed were Cora Hampton, a Shawnee born in Kansas, and her children Bill, age 15, Ora, 14, Zeralda, 13, Nellie, 8, Fred, 6, and Mark, 2. The father of the children was born in North Carolina. See Prevost, p. 71.

Wade N. Hampton was granted permission in 1867 to establish a tollgate in the Chickasaw Nation to be called the Buffalo Station on the west side of Buffalo Creek at what is now known as Pulcher, in Pittsburg County, Okla. See M. H. Wright, p. 815.

HANEY – a Shawnee name.

Among the Shawnees on the 1880 census of the Cherokee Cooweescoowee District were Anna (age 36), Robert (26), Malinda (26) Runabout (3), and Saproney Haney (7 months). See JAIFR, vol X, #2, p. 16.

HARDIN – a Shawnee name.

Serena Harden was captured at Ruddle's Station at the age of seven. She was adopted by Wyandots, but later she returned to live among the whites. She married Thomas Hutton. See Lafferty.

Some of the other Hardins were apparently captured and adopted and stayed with the tribes. Among the Shawnees allotted money in payment for improvements on property that they were leaving behind in 1833 was Martin Hardin. See Watson, pt. 3, p. 16.

HARPER – a Shawnee/Cherokee name.

On July 4, 1753, Peter Harper and Eve Deal were married in the Lutheran Church in Philadelphia. They went to the frontier, and there Peter was killed and Eve and her children were captured and taken to the Ohio towns by Shawnees, among whom Eve later took a husband. She had by her Shawnee husband at least one child, Peter, whom she named for her first husband. After the peace of 1764, she was delivered up to Bouquet and the family went to Ft. Pitt. Half-breed Peter Harper became a valuable frontier scout at Boonesboro and elsewhere. There are many references to him in other histories, but see Drapers interview with William Clinkenbeard. Also see Draper 12CC17; Sir William Johnson Papers, vol 11, p. 486.

A Peter Harper is listed among the Arkansas Cherokees in 1828. When a share of the treaty money was paid to him he was listed as having a family of three. See JAIFR, vol. VI, #4, p. 23.

HARRIS, HOLLIS – a common name associated with Indian blood traditions.

John Harris, an adopted Seneca and later a trader, was influential among the Indians for many years. He was connected with the John Harris whose trading post was located at what later became Harrisburg, Pennsylvania. He might also have been related to Mary Harris.

Mary Harris, an adopted captive, was called the White Woman and her village was known as White Woman's Town. The site is nearly opposite the mouth of Killbuck Creek. See Hanna, vol. II, pp. 148-149; Williams, p. 394; Darlington, p. 41, 114.

Jemmy Harris was among the Indians at Conestoga in January, 1755. PA Archives, p. 242.

A John, James, and Joseph Hollis were among the Mingoes, Wyandots, Shawnees, and Delawares on the frontier, listed in Indian trader accounts and involved in several frontier incidents related in Draper Mss. and elsewhere. These people were quite possibly of the Harris family but anyone whose native language was Algonquin usually had trouble pronouncing the "R" sound. A James Harris was among the whites delivered up to General Henry Bouquet in 1764.

A John Harris was among the Wyandots on the 1900 Census of Indian Territory. He was born in 1859 in Kansas of a white father and a Wyandot mother. His wife, Jane Harris, was listed as a white woman born in Illinois in 1867. Her parents were born in Illinois. See Prevost, p. 82.

HARRY– a Delaware name.

Dee Brown, author of *Bury My Heart at Wounded Knee,* also wrote a work of fiction entitled *Creek Mary's Blood,* which illustrated the way that some members of the eastern tribes were pushed west and there intermarried with other tribes. Their descendants took part in the local conflicts until some of them, too, were pushed west, where they again intermarried with the local population until some of them were pushed further west yet again. In this way, some of the descendants of tribes of the eastern seaboard became affiliated with tribes in Montana and California.

This happened in many cases, but it seemed too far-fetched for many experts, people who demand that the lines of demarcation be clearly drawn. They want their Cherokees in the Smokey Mountains, their Shawnees in the Kentucky woods, and their Seminoles in the Florida swamps. To these people, it seems a sacrilege to think of Little Turtle as part-Mohican. They read the book, and the last of the Mohicans died a long time before.

Among those whose descendants crossed the continent as the tribes were pushed west, some possibly carried the surname Harry. Jo Harry was an early interpreter among the Conestogas in Pennsylvania.

In 1785, John Harry had a house at the Delaware town and was involved in the peace negotiations there. See Draper 14S195-196.

In 1857, the Delaware Joe Harry, his wife, one

son and two daughters, were with the families of Jim Shaw and John Conner at the Brazos Agency in Texas. See Staab, List of Delawares...

Jack Harry (Wy-a-wa-qua-cum-an,"Walking everywhere") was a Delaware scout, at one time residing on the Brazos Reservation, who led a company of Indian scouts with Shawnee Jim just prior to the Civil War. They were under orders from Van Dorn not to engage the Commanche, but they plunged into the Crooked Creek fight anyway. The members of their company wore white bands around their heads that they might more easily be distinguished in battle. See Chalfant, pp. 51, 90.

In 1876, Jack Harry's farm was near Black Beaver's on the Anadarko Reservation. See Weslager, pp. 433, 518.

In 1891, Jack Harry, a part-Delaware, was involved with John Wilson and Sitting Bull in the Sioux ghost dancing religion. See Mooney, p. 903.

HART – a Shawnee/Potawatomi name.

A son of Israel Hart was captured in Kentucky and adopted by Shawnees.

"About 15 or twenty years after this, young Hart was exchanged. He had been sold to some of the Indian traders. His father went to Detroit to see if he was living and brought him home. He went about shooting arrows, and in three months went off, and was heard of afterwards by his father as living among the Indians. The Shawnees had taken him. He had afterwards lived among the Potawattomies..." See Draper 12CC59-60.

HARVEY – a Shawnee name.

Among the Shawnees who joined the Cherokee Nation in 1871 were Robert, William, Lizzie, John, Rhoda, and Nattie Harvey. Among the Shawnee guardianship cases heard in 1871 by Ely Parker, Commissioner of Indian Affairs, was the case of Caleb Harvey, whose wards were not listed. See JAIFR, vol. IV, #2, p. 106; vol. VIII, #2, p. 27.

HAT – a Wyandot name.

John Hat (Tauromee) is listed on the accounts of the Ft. Wayne Agency in 1813. See Thornbrough, p. 184. He married a woman who had previously been married to a McKenzie, as Russell and Livery B. McKenzie were his step-sons, not his wards.

Among the Wyandots allotted land in 1855 were John Hat, 45, and his family which included Mary, 40, William, 19, Henry, 9, Matilda, 7, Virginia, 5, and Francis, 4.

Among the guardianship cases reviewed by the Commissioner of Indian Affairs in 1871 was the case of John Hat or Tawroomu, guardian of Jacob Stookey, Moses Peacock, Margaret, Jonathan, and John Spybuck. John Hat died in December, 1869, leaving daughters Margaret Punch, and Sarah and Eliza Hat. See JAIFR, vol. VIII,#2, p. 20.

HAVERSTOCK, HAVERSTICK, HOVERSTOCK, etc. –a Delaware/Conestoga name.

The Indian blood is from John Haverstock and his wife, Sweet Corn.

Haverstock guarded Sweet Corn during the bloody massacre of the Christian Indians. After it had come to an end, Haverstock took Sweet Corn to the "settlement of Mercertown where she became the bride of her protector and the mother of a respected line of descendants." See OA&HC, vol. VI, pp. 145-146.

See Joseph B. Doyle, *The History of Jefferson County and Representative Citizens*, for the story of the massacre, John Haverstock, and Sweet Corn "from whom the Haverstock family of Belmont County [Ohio] and the late W. T. Campbell were descended."

HAWKINS – a Shawnee/Cherokee name.

In 1781, when Link's blockhouse was captured on the Ohio frontier, a Miss Elizabeth Hawkins was captured, taken to the Ohio towns and later adopted. Draper's notes say that she married a Shawnee. Later she returned to the white society, but was "bored by the monotonous life," and returned to her Shawnee family.

Historian Jared C. Lobdell wrote of this, "Miss Hawkins married a Frenchman (possibly part Native American) at Detroit and remained with him till his death, then returned to the Ohio, but returned again to her husband's country after a few years. According to Hupp's notes, she married into the tribe of her Shawnee captors in the interior of Ohio, and Mrs. Cruger has her return after her visit to her semi-barbarous life. These stories are not contradictory. My seventh great-grandfather was a part-white Shawnee in the Ohio Country, in a war centered on Detroit, and I daresay, for all that he was part Irish (and perhaps Spanish), his life was semi-barbarous." See Lobdell, Indian Warfare..., p. 26.

Among the Shawnees who settled on the lands of the Cherokee nation by 1869 were John, Susan, Eliza, and Jane Hawkins. See JAIFR, vol. IV, #2, pp. 100-111.

The Hawkins surname also arose very early among the Cherokees. Benjamin Hawkins was a white trader who lived among them.

Listed on the 1835 Cherokee census of North Carolina was the family of Walter Hawkins, a farmer. His family consisted of "six quarterbloods and one half-blood." On the same census, living near the mouth of Valley River, were other Hawkins families who owned farms. The family of John Hawkins consisted of one halfblood and four quarterbloods. That of James Hawkins consisted of one fullblood, one halfblood, and eleven quarterbloods. The family of Sally Hawkins consisted of three halfbloods and two people whose degree of Cherokee blood was unknown. A quarterblood Cherokee name Rose Hawkins was also living in North Carolina, and her farmhouse was located on Shewting Creek.

See Tyner, pp. 125, 128-129, 148.

HENDRICK, HENDRICKS – a Mohican/Shawnee/Kickapoo/Delaware name.

According to the SWJ Papers, vol. I, p. 237, Henry Peters or Hendrick was a Mohican by blood, a Mohawk by adoption. The story of Hendrick is to be found in the New York Colonial Documents.

Hendrick (Thaneloqueston, sometimes called Whitehead but usually called King Hendrick by the English), was the half-breed son of a Dutch trader and a Mohican/Mohawk woman. One of his sons was Paulus Hendricks, one of his brothers was Abraham Hendricks, and one of his daughters became a mistress of Sir William Johnson.

King Hendrick was taken to England in 1710, donned a white wig, and was paraded in front of the European elite as a curiosity. He returned to America and was employed in the Indian Agency. It was Hendrick who said of Braddock's forces, "If they are to be killed, they are too many; if they are to fight, they are too few." This quote was uttered by Russell Means in the recent movie, "The Last of the Mohicans," for which Means played the part of Chingahcook, James Fenimore Cooper's fictional character.

Hendrick was too old and out of shape by the time of Braddock's Defeat to have been of much service, but he enthusiastically rode into the fray. "He lost his life by riding on horseback on one of General William Johnson's horses. His horse was shot under him, and he being unwieldy and not able to disengage himself and get away," was stabbed and died on the battlefield.

George Hendrick's captivity is detailed in *Kentucky Pioneer Genealogy and Pioneer Records*, Vol. 8, 1987, p. 65-66, an abstract of *George Hendricks: Illinois Pioneer and His Descendants* by Josephine F. Moeller.

According to this well-documented account, he was captured with Daniel Boone, two other men, and about 20 boys while they were out making salt at Blue Licks in February, 1778. The Indians took them north of the Ohio to their town, which Boone called Old Chilicothe. Daniel Boone's account of the capture, his adoption, and his return to the whites is interesting, and probably honest in most regards. George Hendricks was taken to live at the Pickaway towns and was adopted by a Shawnee family.

Several times, he later traveled with the Shawnees on their raids to Kentucky. After he was with the tribe for about a year, he went with a raiding party against the white settlements on the Ohio River. He says that during this trip he and two other white men, Ansel Goodman and Aaron Forman escaped and got within a short distance of the settlements. George Hendricks, in advance of the other two, saw a large band of Kickapoo Indians coming toward them. He knew he could not avoid being recaptured, but he shouted to the other two to run and they made their escape.

The Kickapoos carried Hendricks back to Pickaway where he was whipped for trying to escape. The Kickapoos were afraid that the Shawnees would kill him, and took him off with them to their own towns. Hendricks remained with them for about six months when he was bought by Indian trader Issac Zane for $100. He then worked for Zane until he paid off the debt, and then headed for the settlements of Kentucky in company with Abraham Chapline. He warned the settlements in May of 1780 of the pending invasion by British General Henry Bird and his Indian allies to attack the Kentucky settlements.

George Hendricks was a member of Capt. William Oldham's company on the 1780 expedition against the Shawnees. He is listed on the pay abstract as "left the country." See Harding, p. 72.

A Munsee Delaware named Thomas J. Hendrick signed the 1832 Treaty with the Delawares, settling a dispute with the Menominees. See Watson, vol. V, pt. 13, p. 73. Among the members of the Stockbridge (Mohican) Tribe allotted land in 1848 were Lewis, Mary and Susannah Hendrick. See JAIFR, vol. XII, #3, p. 35.

HENRY – a Shawnee/Delaware name.

Moses Henry was a gunsmith and an Indian trader with a Shawnee wife, "a white daughter of Major Collins" who had been adopted. The Rev. David Jones visited Moses Henry and his wife at Chillicothe in 1773. Later, Moses Henry moved his trading post and his Shawnee family to the O'Post (Vincennes, Indiana). It was Mrs. Henry, a Shawnee, who assisted Capt. Leonard Helm at Vincennes when he was a prisoner of the British.

Among the Shawnees, Senecas, and Wyandots paid for their property that they were forced to leave behind when moving west in 1833 were John Henry (paid $20) and John Henry and his niece (paid $20 jointly). See Watson, pt. 3, p. 11.

"Some years ago [from 1922], a Mr. Henry came to my house [near Crawfordsville, Indiana]. He had the general appearance of an Indian. He told me he was here to find out what he could about the Cornstalk Indians. He said he was a son of Peter Cornstalk's sister and was born at Piqua, Ohio...He was with me for a part of two days and visited the site of Cornstalk town and sat a long while under a tree..." See Brelsford, pp. 151-152.

HERRON – a Wyandot/Shawnee name.

George Herron was an Indian trader and interpreter whose base was at Detroit, but who apparently played both sides during the Revolultionary War. He was associated with Issac Williams. Richard Butler mentions him in his journal. Herron had a family among the Wyandots. See Williams, p. 36n.

Both George Herron and "Old Mrs. Herron" were allotted money for improvements they had made on their Ohio lands when the Wyandots left their Ohio reservation lands. See Watson, vol. V., pt. 3, pp. 11, 27, 38.

This Herron family seems to have intermarried with whites, Shawnees, Delawares, and other groups. Among the Shawnees who settled on the lands of the Cherokee nation by 1869 was Dick Heron. See JAIFR, vol. IV, #2, pp. 100-111. Among the mixed Chippewa and Munsee Delaware band in 1886 are listed Julia Bittenbender, age 30, and her children who included Peter Herron, 10, Mary Ann Herron, 9, Matilda Herron, 7, and Harry Bittenbender, five months old. See JAIFR, vol. VI, p. 53. Among the Ottawa were Alpheas and Joshua Herron. See Ibid., p. 18. George Herron was interpreter for the Neosho Indian Agency in 1855.

HICKMAN – a Delaware name.

Thomas Hickman lived among the Delawares and Shawnees along with David Owens and Simon Girty as early as 1757. He sometimes served as interpreter and signed treaties. In 1761, he was known as "a friendly Delaware" when it was reported that he had been wounded by a drunken white man.

Joesph Hickman was an Indian trader on the first tax list of Conestoga County, Pennsylvania in 1718.

John and Joseph Hickman were captured when young, adopted, and became leading Delawares. Their band was living at Kittanning until September 8, 1756, when Col. John Armstrong burnt the town. See *The Delaware Westward Migration* by Westlager, p. 6.

In 1856, it was a son of John Hickman who captured John Baker, a servant of George Croghan, and took him to the Indian town of Kittanning. See Pennsylvania Archives, first series, vol. II, p. 569.

One of the Hickmans served for a time as a guide for General Bouquet forces during Pontiac's War. "It seems that Capt. Buckner disagreed with Hickman the Indian, my sheet anchor, so that I'm afraid that I'll have little good of him." See Bouquet Papers, ed. by Kent, p. 206.

Indian trader James Kenny noted in his Ft. Pitt journal, "We hear that Bill Hickman, a Delaware Indian, has informed Patterson and ye inhabitants about Juniata that ye Indians intend to break out in a war against us next spring; but as we know him to be a rogue and a horsethief, we judge his report to be more for self ends than truth or good will to us..." See James Kenny's Journal, PMOB&H, vol. 37, p. 184.

Also according to James Kenny, Thomas Hickman was a leading Delaware counselor. He joined in a raid on a settlement at John Penn's Creek in 1755 in the company of Joseph Compass, Kalasquay, Sochy, Katoochquay, and others. One of these Hickmans, "a man of some consequence" among the Indians, was reported killed in 1761. See SWJ Papers, vol. 10, p. 318; vol. 11, p. 436, 724.

Listed among the Indians in the Ohio Company Papers are Joseph, John, Joshua, Mary, and Phillip Hickman.

William Hickman and Francis Hickman "enlisted in Captain Stephenson's company in 1775. William Hickman again enlisted in Captain Shepard's company in 1776, but was drafted into some other company in August of that year. In 1779, he was in Kentucky, went with Colonel Bowman on an expedition against the Shawnee towns."

Dr. Lyman F. Draper thus spoke of him in his account of the failure of that expedition: 'The Indians, although surprised, gathered into their council house, which they held for defense. A man of the company, William Hickman by name, who had served with Bedinger under Captain Stephenson at the siege of Boston and who during Dunmore's War was strongly suspected of having stealthily killed a white man below Pittsburgh, now met his fate. He was seen at early dawn, peeping around the corner of a cabin to the left of Bedinger's party...was shot by the Indians in the council house, and died instantly. He had said the evening before that he had a presentiment that he would be killed in the expected attack in the morning..." From Dandridge's *Historic Shepherdstown*, p. 323.

See Draper Mss. 8J179-180: "Capt. Lewis Hickman deserted on the campaign of 1780 and went to the Indians." His family later turned up in Hamilton County, Ohio.

A Hickman was one of the two men who discovered that the Shawnees were about to attack just before the Battle of Point Pleasant. His companion, Robertson, made it back to Colonel Andrew Lewis to warn him, but Hickman was reported killed.

Paschal Hickman, a son of William Hickman, became familiar enough with Indian ways that William Wells chose him to be among his elite company of scouts along with such valuable men as Robert McClelland, John May, William Smalley, William Polke, Christopher Miller, and others who had lived among the Indians. Hickman County, Kentucky, is named for this Paschal Hickman who later, like Christopher Miller, became a captain in the War of 1812. Hickman was killed by Potawatomis at the River Raison.

HICKS – a Delaware/Wyandot name.

There were Hicks among the Indian tribes very early, several men by that name being on the frontier as Indian traders or settlers.

In 1764, Gorsham Hicks came back from the Indians and made a deposition, saying that he was the servant of Indian trader Patrick Allison, that he was made prisoner by the Shawnees who gave him to a Delaware known by the name of Captain Bullet. He was kept on the Muskingum River until Capt. Bullet sent him to White Eyes to help him build a house. He spent the winter there, along with John Gibson and one Morris who were also captives under White Eyes' protection.

The Indians sent him off on a hunt up the Hockhocking, and he decided to escape and turned his canoe downstream and came back up the Ohio.

Hicks spoke Delaware and understood some Shawnee and the Indians had great confidence in him from his having been a prisoner once before, and he had friends among them. From what he saw, the Delawares could muster about 150 fighting men with about 30 or 40 boys who could also go to war, leaving about 30 or 40 old hunters home to take care of their families and planting. About the Shawnees, he is not certain, but he estimated their fighting force as not over 200 warriors, with about 20 Mingoes. Hicks said that King Shingass had died last winter, and that King Beaver and Custaloga were for peace. See MP&HC, vol. 19, pp. 253-255.

Later, during the Revolution, Gosham Hicks was captured again, taken from his Bedford County, Pennsylvania farm along with Moses Hicks in the spring of 1778 by Mingo warriors and taken to Detroit. See McHenry, p. 3.

On the 1843 Wyandot roll are listed:

1. Francis H. Hicks' family, consisting of one

male over 25, and five females, three of whom were under 10.

2. John Hicks sr.'s family, consisting of one man and one woman over 55, one woman between 25 and 55, one male and one female between 10 and 25, and two boys under 10.
3. John Hicks jr.'s family, consisting of one male and one female 25 to 55, one female 10 to 25, and one male under 10.
4. Rivia Hick's family, consisting of one male and one female both between 25 and 55, and also one male between 10 and 25.
5. Susan Hick's household, consisting of two males over 55, one female between 10 and 25, one male between 10 and 25, and two males under 10.

Among the Wyandots allotted land in 1855 were Catherine Hicks, 72; John Hicks, 53, and his family which include Mary, 40, William, 19, Henry, 9, Matilda, 7, Virginia, 5, and Francis, 4; James Hicks, 21; Betsy Hicks, 22; Francis A. Hicks, 50; Matilda Hicks, 50; Jane Hicks, 20; Maria Hicks, 18, and her infant, Phillip H. Hicks.

Among the guardianship cases reviewed by the Commissioner of Indian Affairs in 1871 was the case of John Hicks, a Wyandot. Hicks died in Wyandot, Kansas about 1867. He had been the guardian for Susan Hicks, his niece, and also for George Coke, Karrie Rodgers, Adam Young, and Anthony Hat. See JAIFR, vol. VIII, #2, p. 17.

Among the Wyandots on the 1900 Census of Indian Territory was Francis Hicks, a Wyandot, born in Kansas. Both of his parents were born in Canada. His wife was Lucinda (Miller) Hicks, a Delaware. Also listed on the census is Henry Hicks, born 1847 in Kansas. Both of his parents were Wyandots born in Ohio. His wife, Malissa Hicks, was a white woman born in Missouri in 1860. Her father was born in Virginia, her mother in Kentucky. See Prevost, p. 82.

HIGGINS – a Shawnee name.

According to Rev. David Jones, a Mr. Higgins accompanied him, George Rogers Clark, and their guide David Owens on his first trip down the Ohio River. See Jones.

There is the account of the mirthful marriage of a Robert Higgins to an Indian woman reprinted in Hanna's *Wilderness Trail*.

A letter in the Calendar of Virginia State Papers, July 28, 1785, refers to one "Higgins" who had been a trader in the late war, had been compelled to assist the British against his wishes, had escaped from them and went to live with the Shawnees and as he now has "great influence" among the Indians, he offers himself to the American service.

Returned captives spoke of Higgins who lived among the Shawnees, saying that he was helpful in obtaining their release. See More, pp. 287-296.

After the war, being regarded with suspicion by both the English and the United States, Higgins went to reside with the Shawnees.

HILDABRAND – a common Cherokee name.

Peter Hildabrand was a member of George Owens Company at Ft. Jefferson during the siege. He was an early resident of that part of Youghioghany County which became Washington County in southwestern Pennsylvania (see *Pennsylvania Traveler*, vol. I, #2, February, 1965).

Peter Hildabrand served there in the American Revolution with his neighbor Jacob (Polser) Shilling and the two of them were among the defenders during the siege of Wheeling (see Draper Mss. 1S89). Early in the Illinois campaign, he served first under Capt. John

Williams and Lt. Richard Brashear. In Kentucky in 1778, he claimed 400 acres on Harrods Creek; David and John Hildabrand made adjoining claims. In 1780, Peter Hildabrand assigned his land to his former neighbor, William Linn, and Hildabrand took his family to Ft. Jefferson.

It may have been then that Peter Hildabrand jr. was captured near Ft. Jefferson by the Cherokees who were there assisting the Chickasaws and Choctaws. Perhaps it was Peter Hildabrand jr. who gave them the information concerning the condition of the fort.

The older Peter Hildabrand was among those who returned to Louisville where he engaged in the original drawing of lots, taking lot #56 on the old plan. Then after an apparent peace was made with the Chickasaw and Choctaw nations, he returned to the Mississippi.

According to Goodspeed's *History of Missouri*, pp. 371-373, "Peter Hildabrand settled on a tract of land near Maddox Mill, but on the opposite side of the river. In that year [1784], he was out hunting and was shot and killed by Indians on the bank of the river...and his family immediately removed to a settlement for protection."

The younger Peter Hildabrand stayed with the Cherokees and married Nancy Harland, the grandaughter of Nancy Ward, the storied "Wild Rose of the Cherokees." Hence, Peter Hildabrand's wife descended from the famous Cherokee chief, Oconostota. Chief Peter Hildabrand became one of the most prominent men of his tribe, and he was joined there by other members of the Hildabrand family. He erected a trading post "at the north end of the twelve mile portage from the Ocoee to the Conasauga River," near the present site of Benton, Tennessee. See *Chronicles of Oklahoma*, Vol. XI, #3, 1933, pp. 939-941.

HILL – a Mohawk/Wyandot/Delaware name.

Members of the Hill family were captured and adopted during the French and Indian War. William Hill and his son are listed as among the Indians in the Ohio Company Papers as early as 1756. Arron Hill was a half-breed Mohawk.

"The Indians had encamped along the shore...Among them was a renegade white scoundrel named John Hill. As soon as the Indians discovered the boat coming down the Ohio, they quickly concealed themselves, while renegade John Hill, acting as a decoy, sat on the bank and pleaded with the boatmen" to come ashore and save him. By this ruse, the Indians often captured boats with a minimal loss of life. See Thompson, p. 67.

Thomas Hill was a white man who was taken in and adopted when young. He grew up to be a famous Delaware scout out west, associating with such master scouts as Black Beaver, James Secondine, and James Swannock.

The famous scout, Kit Carson (who also had an Indian wife) and Tom Hill made an excursion into Commanche country with a small party of six hunters, three of them Delawares. Attacked by an enormous band of Commanches, they "cut the throats of their mules and forted behind the animals. With three firing while the other three reloaded, they held off a dozen attacks, killing 42 Commanches. The horses of the attackers shied at the fresh blood from the dead mules and would not approach very near. When night came, the six defenders headed back for the Arkansas on foot, abandoning their beaver." See Carter, *Kit Carson*,p. 109.

A fair report of his Thomas Hill's adventures would probably require a book. He rode as far west as California where he fought alongside Fremont and James Swannuck, and he went as far north as Oregan where he is supposed to have married a Nez Perce woman.

He married several times, probably, but one marriage was to Nancy Washington, a Wyandot, and among their known children was Sarah Hill, through whom they have many descendants. Thomas Hill appears to have divorced Nancy, and she soon married another famous Delaware scout, James Secondine.

Listed on the 1843 Wyandot Census were:

1. Thomas Hill's family, consisting of one male between 25 and 55, one female between 25 and 55, four females between 10 and 25, and one male under 10.
2. Rapid B. Hill's family, consisting of one male and one female 10 to 25, and two males under 10.

Tom, John, Milisa, Nicholas, Betsy, Virginia, and Saly (Oh-quain-chis) Hill appear on the Delaware rolls (not dated, but probably circa 1860) appearing in the JAIFR, vol. IV, #1, 1985, pp. 31-52.

Jacob Hill was a Delaware who served with M Company, 6th Kansas Volunteer Cavalry, in 1864. Elizabeth A. Hill was a ten-year-old Delaware student at the Baptist Mission School in 1867.

Jasper Hill (Big White Owl) from Toronto, a Canadian Delaware born and raised on the Monroviantown Reservation in Ontario, was visited by Weslager in 1963. Weslager says that "in recent years there has been considerable intermarriage with both whites and members of other tribes," mainly Mohawk, Oneida, Cayuga, Seneca, Chippewa, and Tuscarora who also share the the land in Ontario. It could be that this Delaware Jasper Hill also descends from the Iroquoian Hill family. See Weslager, pp. 17, 20-26, 512, 514.

John and Mary Hill (both age 21) and Ben Hill (age 5) are among the Delawares listed on the 1880 Cherokee Census of the Cooweescoowee District. See JAIFR, vol. X, #2, p. 22.

HOLMES – a Shawnee/Delaware name.

"Johnny Holmes, an odd fellow, was raised with the Indians and was possibly a half-breed. He married an Indian squaw and they lived with Williams, an Indian." After the War of 1812 broke out, Johnny Holmes, Williams, and their wives went to the safety of Upper Sandusky for the duration. But after the war, Holmes returned and lived in Wadsworth, Ohio, in a cabin "in Holmes Hollow. Holmes Brook and Holmes Brook Hill were named after him and retain their names to this day. Holmes was very helpful to the early settlers and helped build the first settlers' houses." See Cherry, pp. 242-245.

John Holmes served as interpreter for the Senecas at Sandusky in June, 1831. See Watson, vol. V, pt. 4, p. 15.

HOOPER – a Wyandot name.

Among the Wyandots allotted land in 1855 were Jacob and Rebecca Hooper, both 22; Rebecca Hooper, 26, and her family which included Mary, 10, and Peter, 7.

HUFFMAN – A boy named Peter Huffman was captured in southern Indiana at the Pigeon Roast Massacre in the War of 1812. Huffman was transferred to some other Indians who took him to Canada. Huffman was located by some interested parties and returned to Indiana in 1824. However, he did not adjust well to the white-styled civilization, he got on a flatboat that was taking some Indians west, and was never heard from again by his family in Indiana. Does anyone know what happened to him?

HUNTER – a Shawnee name.

Some members of the Hunter family were captured and adopted during the French and Indian Wars.

Joseph Hunter bought land near Ft. Pitt in 1761 from the Cayuga chief, Catfish, who was Peter Chartier's father-in-law. This is the same Joseph Hunter who was later at the Battle of Ft. Jefferson. During that siege, when food was running out, Hunter led a buffalo-hunting party which sneaked out of the fort by night. See Draper 12J31.

Joseph Hunter, an Indian trader and hunter, was involved in several scrapes with the Indians during times of war. He may have been the leader of the party who chased Henry Jackson.

Jackson, captured by the Senecas, but traded to the Shawnees and adopted, returned eventually to Kentucky and lived out the remainder of his life there. He told the story of how, when he lived among the Shawnees, he joined a horse-stealing party. Near the Kentucky settlements, they were discovered and fled. The Kentuckians pursued and overtook them all until Jackson was the only one left. He outran his pursuers and made it back to the safety of the Piqua towns. See Draper 11YY40 and also Draper mss. 9J.

After some Indians had stolen horses from Mann's Lick on Salt River, Joseph Hunter led the pursing party. The Indians got to their canoes but had some trouble getting the stolen horses to take to the water. Hunter gave directions so that each of his men would fire at a particular Indian. John Doone, who told the story that appears in Draper's papers, 31J78, thought that every Indian fell within sight except the leader of the party who was "a little behind on the watch, and when the guns fired, he ran below a little distance, and then ran out upon a sand bar, evidently intending to go as far as he could and then swim over to the north side of the river. But he was hotly pursued by Joseph Hunter who had reloaded as he ran except to crest the patch, and the chief, seeing that he could not escape without an encounter or lose his life without an effort, stopped deliberately, stamped the sand firmly under his feet, and both he and hunter raised their guns at the same moment and took very deliberate aim and both fired simultaneously..."

The Indian leader was believed to be the last Indian of the party to fall. Of course, Henry Jackson possibly ran on ahead and escaped notice.

One of the sons of Joseph Hunter, Joseph Hunter jr., was also supposed to have gone to Kaskakia and become an Indian trader.

Among the Shawnees who settled on the lands of the Cherokee nation by 1869 was Samuel Hunter. See JAIFR, vol. IV, #2, pp. 100-111.

ICE – a Shawnee/Cherokee name.

Among the captives delivered up to Bouquet in 1764 were Eve Ice, William Ice, Lewis Ice, John Ice, Thomas Ice, Catherine Ice, and Elizabeth Ice.

John Ice (sometimes Jice, Eice, Ese, etc.) was one of the family, and he spent many years among the Indians. John Ice was turned over to Bouquet in 1764 as a deserter along with a black man and a white Delaware named Rojer (Rogers). The trio was committed to the New Albany jail briefly, then allowed to go on their way.

Later, John Ice and his brother, William (Indian Billy) Ice became two of the most adept trackers and scouts on the frontier. John was called Old Lonely Ice because he kept mostly to himself and did not mix too well with society. Their brother, Andrew Ice, married Tecumseh's white mother according to one account. See SWJ Papers, vol. IV, p. 439-440; vol. XI, p. 201; Lough's *Now and Long Ago*, p. 124-125; *Tecumseh and the Bayles Family Tradition*, by G. H. Bayles in the KHQ, vol. 46, p. 647-655.

A John Ice was a member of an Indian Company (M Company, 3rd Regiment) in 1868 along with Washburn, Jackson Martin, Jesse Paris, Alick Martin, John White, Jo Bryant, and others, mostly Cherokees. See JAIFR, vol. XII, #2, p.24.

Among the Cherokees listed on the 1880 Saline District Census of the Cherokee Nation were six members of the Ice family: Sallie F. (age 32), John F. (20), Walker F. (18), Jeter F. (14), Joseph F. (9), and Samuel F. Ice (8). See JAIFR, vol. VI, #2, p. 28.

INGLES, ENGLISH – a Shawnee name.

"Thomas Ingles, son of William and Mary Ingles, was captured in 1755 when four years old and raised red. His parents did not recover him until 1768 "when he was found to be practically a young Indian in his habits and his manner of living. Sent to Dr. Thomas Walker of Albemarie County, he acquired something of an education during the next three or four years; but he never became entirely accustomed to civilized life. During his winter at Point Pleasant, where he remained in garrison after the battle, he visited his Indian friends on the Scioto." His wife was captured by Indians in 1782. He later moved to Tennessee and then later to Mississippi. See Thwaites and Kellogg, *Dunmore's War*, pp. 179-180n.

IRONSIDES – a Shawnee name.

George Ironsides, born in 1760 and educated at King's College, Aberdeen, was a prominent trader of the Maumee Valley in the period subsequent to the Revolution. In 1789, he had an establishment at Miamitown, which was destroyed at the time of Harmer's invasion the following year. During the next few years, his trading post was at the Glaize (modern Defiance, Ohio), which was destroyed in turn by General Wayne in 1794. At this place, Ironside had an Indian wife, whose mother, Coo-coo-chee, presided over an extended family which included Oliver Spencer during his captivity. Coo-coo-chee was a remarkable woman, a Mohawk who lived among the Shawnees and Delawares on the Maumee River.

George Ironsides, sr., was witness to the power of attorney from the Miamis Company of Detroit to John Askin to recover payment from Baptist and Charlie Reaume, Degniau Dequaindre and Joseph Guilbeau, and signed by George Leith, William Park, James Abbott, and other Indian traders almost all of whom had their Indian connections. See p. 332.

Dr. C. C. Graham, a veteran of the War of 1812,

went to Canada some years after that war to search for some slaves who had run off from his Kentucky plantation. Matthew Elliot threatened to imprison Graham for kidnapping, and Graham was nearly mobbed by blacks, but he says that General George Ironsides came to his rescue and demanded that he be treated with respect. Graham credited Ironsides with saving his life there. According to Graham, Ironsides was Tecumseh's brother, but the actual relationship was that Ironsides' wife and Tecumseh were both members of the same clan.

Among the Shawnees living on the Cherokee Reserve in 1871 were several members of the Ironsides family including George, Colin, Robert, Susan, Maggie, and Margaret Ironsides. See JAIFR, vol. IV, #2, p. 106.

The Shawnee C. C. Ironside (age 40) and Louisa, his white wife (age 35), were living with Margaret Ironside (age 65), a Shawnee, all listed on the 1880 Cherokee Census of the Cooweescoowee District. See JAIFR, vol. X, #2, p. 23.

Robert Ironsides was born in 1843, and died in 1916. He married Susan Shawn King. They were farmers, and Robert worked for the coal mines and cowboyed some. Among their children was a son named Beverly Ironsides, a white/Shawnee born in 1871, died in Vinita, Indian Territory, in 1908. His wife was Cora Lee, born 1873, died 1950.

Included among the children of Beverly and Cora Lee Ironsides was Elmer T. Ironsides, born January 23rd, 1898. Elmer donated the land for Ironside School, a portion of his Shawnee allotment. He married Mary E. Hildabrand, a great grand-daughter of the the Cherokee, Peter Hildabrand. See SOCC, vol. II, p. 190, information from Carolyn Ironside James.

JACK, JACKS, JACQUIS, JACQUES, etc. – a Delaware/Shawnee/Wyandot/Miami name.

Joseph Jack "an Englishman who had gone over to the Indians and lived among the Delawares" was noted by Charles Stewart while living among the Indians during Pontiac's War. See "The Captivity of Charles Stuart," in MVHR., vol. XII, #1, p. 61. Other members of this family appear to have been among the Delawares also, one of them known as Delaware Jack.

Listed on the roster of Shawnees who came from Ohio to Kansas in 1832 was the family of Jim Jack family of seven, consisting of one male and two females between 25 and 50, and four children under ten, three of them boys.

Chief Jacques (Jack, Jacko, Jocko, etc.) was one of the leading Ohio Wyandot chiefs in 1834. On the 1843 Wyandot Census is listed the Henry Jaquis household, consisting of one male and one female 25 to 55, and one male 10 to 25.

David Jack married the part-Shawnee Mary Owens at the Shawnee Mission in 1857.

JACKSON – a Shawnee/Delaware/Seneca name.

A Henry Jackson was a white prisoner adopted by the Senecas on the upper part of the Big Miami River in what is now Logan County, Ohio. He took a Seneca wife by whom he had several children. "Two sons in maturity were very large men like their father and immigrated with the tribe to Missouri in 1825."

Henry Jackson, adopted by the Shawnees, returned eventually to Kentucky and lived out the remainder of his life there. He told the story of how, when he lived among the Shawnees, he joined a horse-stealing party. Near the Kentucky settlements, they were discovered and fled. The Kentuckians pursued and overtook and killed them all except Jackson. He outran his pursuers and made it back to the safety of the Piqua towns. See Draper 11YY33-40 and also Draper 9J.

Joseph William Jackson, an adopted white man, was raised with the Shawnees. Like many other whites among the Shawnees, especially after the Treaty of Greenville, he left his tribe about 1799 and went back to Kentucky to live with relatives. But although many others adapted to white-styled society, Jackson could not and he returned to the Shawnees, and became chief of the Fish band. He was seen living among the Shawnees Anthony Shane, Capt. Cornstalk, and John Owens in 1830. See Faragher, p. 165; KHC, vol. 9, p. 166. Also see FISH.

Among the Shawnees who settled on the lands of the Cherokee nation by 1869 was the family of Anna Jackson. See JAIFR, vol. IV, #2, pp. 100-111.

Betsy (Pa-mah-tah-oh-qua) Jackson, Colonel Jackson, and General Jackson appear on the Delaware rolls appearing in the JAIFR, vol. IV, #1, 1985, pp. 31-52.

Colonel Jackson (age 56) and his wife (45), and a girl named Lizzie (13) who was probably their daughter are the only Delaware Jacksons listed in the Cooweescoowee District on the Cherokee census of 1880. There were many other Cherokees and intermarried whites among the Jacksons, however. See JAIFR, vol. X, #2, p. 24.

JACOBS – a Delaware/Mohawk name.

There was a Delaware chief named Jacobs whose Indian name was Tawea, but he was usually called Captain Jacobs. He was a brother of Nometha.

Capt. Jacobs lived among the Delawares very early and was reputed to have taken part in raids on white settlements.

He was reportedly killed in 1756 at Kittanning, Pennsylvania. According to Draper Mss. 7J71: "Capt. Jacobs, chief of the Indians, gave the war whoop, and defended his house bravely through loopholes in between the logs. And the Indians generally refused quarter which was offered [free], declaring that they were men and would not be prisoners. Col. [John] Armstrong (who now received a wound in his shoulder from a musket ball) ordered their houses to be set on fire...which was immediately done. When the Indians were told that they would be burnt if they did not surrender, one of them replied that he did not care as he would kill 4 or 5 before he died, and as the heat approached, some of them began to sing. Some, however, burst out of the houses and attempted to reach the river, but were immediately shot down. Capt. Jacobs in getting out of a window was shot and scalped and also his squaw and a lad call the King's Son."

But a Captain Jacobs was among the Indians after that, and sometimes served as interpreter and signed peace treaties, at least once the name appears as Capt. N. Jacobs.

The Jacobs surname survived among the New York and Pennsylvania Seneca and Mohawks, some of whom intermarried with the neighboring Delawares. During the violence that shook the Mohawk Nation in 1989, L. David Jacobs was the principal chief and spokesman for one faction of the tribe.

Rich Hornung, in his book *One Nation Under the Gun*, described David Jacobs as "a New York-based Mohawk who left the reservation to earn a doctorate in psychology and teach at universities across the country. After an absence of two decades, he returned in the 1980s and entered tribal politics on a pro-gambling platform." See Hornung, p. 21.

JAMES – a common name associated with Indian blood traditions.

In January, 1757, Thomas James was paid a sum by Pennsylvania "for Indian services." Pennsylvania Archives, 8th series, vol. 5, p. 4375.

Capt. James (Ma-mat—tee-at, The Spotted Fawn) was the name of a Delaware chief whose name appeared occasionally in frontier annals. He signed a British treaty, listed as the second ranking Delaware/ Shawnee village chief to Blackfeather in 1778. I think that Blackfeather was just a Shawnee guest in the Delaware village where Capt. James was chief. None of the other reds there were listed as Shawnees, and when British Lt. Gov. James Hamilton rose to speak to the Delawares, he addressed Capt. James, not Blackfeather.

Hamilton said, "I have not forgotten the conduct of White Eyes who came with speeches to this council last year...I hope that my children the Delawares will be wise...and that I may give them my hand that I refused to White Eyes. You, Captain James, took hold of your Father's axe yesterday. Hold it fast, be wise and remember...all the words of war..."

Capt. James spoke for the Delawares present, saying, "You have cleansed my heart and the hearts of those who live at my village. There are sixty of us for whom I will be answerable, 'tho I cannot say anything for the rest of the Nation." He then danced the war dance, sang war song, and Lt. Gov. Hamilton dismissed the council. See Seineke, pp. 247, 251, 255.

Living among the Indians on Sand Creek in 1831 were Adam James, his Indian wife (probably Choctaw), and their four children, all under ten years of age. Benjamin James was a member of the Choctaw Nation in 1830 and was given land by the Treaty of Dancing Rabbit Creek.

Charley James married Mary Gutherie at the

Shawnee Mission in 1846.

Joseph James was the official interpreter for the Upper Missouri Indian Agency in 1831 and at the Kansas Indian Agency in 1867-69.

Among the Shawnees who settled on the lands of the Cherokee nation by 1869 was the family of Anna James. See JAIFR, vol. IV, #2, pp. 100-111.

JAMISON, JIMMERSON, JAMESON – a Seneca/ Wyandot/Ottawa name.

Mary Jamison, captured and adopted by Senecas north of Pittsburgh, chose to remain with the Indians. Over some time, she married two different Indians and had children by each. See OA & HSP, vol. 26, p. 505.

There were Jamisons captured in the attack on the house of Thomas Jamison from a Frenchman and six Shawnees in 1758. Betsy Jamison was among those adopted and became known as the White Woman of the Genessee. The Jamison name in varying forms (Jimmerson, Jamerson, etc.) had become one of the most common among all of the remnant Iroquois nations as well as the Delaware and others through intermarriage.

JOHNSON – a Mohawk/Wyandot name.

Sir William Johnson is, by himself, a major source of the Indian blood tradition in the general population. As the colonial Indian Agent, he held a powerful position among the tribes, and he had children by several Indian women. The mixed blood children he had by Molly Brant (Brandt), the sister of Joseph Brant, included Peter (later killed in a duel), Elizabeth (who married Robert Kerr), Magdelene (who married John Ferguson), Margaret (who married George Farley), George, Mary, Susannah (who married Henry Lemoine), and Anne (who married Hugh Earle).

Among the Wyandots allotted land in 1855 was

William Johnson, 35, and his family which included Catherine, 35, Ellen, 15, William, jr., 13, Richard, 9, Job, 4, and Alexander, 8 months.

Among the guardianship cases reviewed by the Commissioner of Indian Affairs in 1871 was the case of William Johnson, a Wyandot, guardian for Granville Peacock. Peacock had died in 1858 or 1859 and William Johnson was suppose to be dying of consumption at the time. Peacock's heirs lived with the Senecas, his male heir was a young boy and hismother had married a Seneca named Jim Bigtail.

Also reviewed was the case of B. F. Johnson, guardian for the Cherloe family and of Josiah Scott Coon. Among those who testified was David Cherloe. See JAIFR, vol. VIII, #2, pp. 21-23.

Among the Shawnees who settled on the lands of the Cherokee nation by 1869 were Berry, Mary, Hiram, George, Angeline, Thomas, Susan, and Stonewall Jackson Johnson. See JAIFR, vol. IV, #2, pp. 100-111.

JONES – a common name; one with many Indian blood traditions.

John and Mary Jones were captured on June 13, 1777, in the Dunkard valley near the Jacob Jones settlement. They were taken to the Ohio towns and adopted into different families of Wyandots near Sandusky. Mary liked her Indian life, but John became dissatisfied and left the tribe after five years.

John Jones then went to Detroit where he was taken into the home of a physician named Harvey who gave him an apprenticeship in medicine. John Jones later came back to Pittsburgh and became a scout and interpreter. In 1796 he married Nancy, daughter of James Thomas Goff, and made his home near Grafton, West Virginia. His children included Lunceford, Stanton, Charity, Elizabeth, Rebecca, and Mary.

Mary Jones remained with the Indians and was "much esteemed" among them. In 1787, she went to Detroit and became associated with the family of General McCoombs. Three years later, she married Peter Malotte and became the sister-in-law of Simon Girty. See Glenn Lough's AAT, vol. I, #12, p 1&2, Fairmont, West Virginia, 1972.

Griffith Jones, from Wales, was a run-away indentured servant from Joseph Reed of Trenton, New Jersey in 1732. He joined the band of Chief Oppekhorsa (White Day) on White Day Creek. His wife was an Indian. See Glenn Lough's AAT, vol. 3, #8.

JOURNEYCAKE or JOHNNYCAKE – a Wyandot/ Delaware name.

Elizabeth Castle was listed among the white women delivered up to General Henry Bouquet at the close of Pontiacs War in 1864.

"A white woman of the Castleman family" was captured when young and adopted, and later married one of the half-breed sons of Issac Williams. One of their children, Sally Williams, married Solomon Johnnycake.

The children of Solomon Johnnycake and Sally Williams Johnnycake altered the surname to Journeycake and became leading members of the Delawares and most eventually became absorbed into the white society around them. Two of these, Charles and Issac Journeycake, were assistant chiefs to principal Delaware chief John Connor in 1866.

One of Charles Journeycake's daughters married Lucius Pratt, the eldest son of Baptist missionary John G. Pratt. Weslager wrote that "Following the death of her husband, Lucius Pratt, in Kansas, Nannie Journeycake Pratt married Jacob H. Bartles. The couple moved to Indian Territory, bringing with them Nannies's three half-white daughters by her first marriage. The site of their home in the horseshoe bend of the Caney grew into a busy settlement named after Nannie's second husband — Bartlesville. Her daughters by her first marriage and her children by Bartles married white spouses. Other daughters of Charles Journeycake also married white men and separated themselves from the Indian world to become absorbed into Oklahoma's white society." See Weslager, pp. 387, 445.

Alexander, Emma, John, Sally, Issac (Sr. and Jr.), Nancy, Mary (Mrs. Dr. Allen), B. S. (Mayeses), Angeline, Joseph, Robert J. E., Rachel, Narcissa, Charles, Jane Soeia, Emeline, Adeline E., Annie E., and Cora Lee Journeycake appear on the Delaware rolls appearing in the JAIFR, vol. IV, #1, 1985, pp. 31-52.

KELLY – a Delaware name.

"John Kellys Son" is listed as living among the Indians in the Indian trader accounts listed in the Sir William Johnson Papers 1763, along with King Shinges, Turtle Heart, Capt. Jacobs, Thomas Hickman, John Owens Son.

Benjamin Kelly, one of the salt makers captured with Daniel Boone and adopted by the Shawnees, lived among his adopted people for four years. According to historian Bil Gilbert, he left only a short narrative of his captivity, saying only that he enjoyed it.

"Rev. Mr. Kelly," who was captured in 1778 and taken to the Shawnee towns, knew Tecumseh and said that he was about 11 to 12 ears of age in 1778. If 12 in 1778, he was born about 1766. This is from Draper's notes in 1YY7.

KILLBUCK – a Delaware name.

The name Deerslayer, the hero of James Fennimore Cooper's novels, is of course a synonym for Killbuck, and although there is not much resemblance, I hardly think that the Deerslayer of the novel resembles the historic Captain Samuel Brady either, as some have suggested.

Killbuck was a spokesman for the more peaceable Delawares at the conclusion of Pontiac's War. He earned a good reputation among the traders, and it was Killbuck who had protected John Gibson. He summoned the Squash Cutter (Cut the Pumpkin) and turned him over to Sir William Johnson. The peace was made, and Killbuck was among the significant chiefs to sign.

The Rev. David Jones visited him at his cabin in the early 1770s. Killbuck asked Jones about one of his people who had married a white English officer and had gone with him to Maryland near Joppa. It was rumored that she had been sold into slavery. This would have been contrary to English law, and Jones told him so.

Gelelemend or Killbuck, sometimes called William Henry Killbuck, was living with his three sons at Zeisberger's town of Goshen in Ohio.

After White Eyes was treacherously murdered by Lewis Wetzel in the fall of 1778, Killbuck became the leader of the Turtle division, and hence head chief of the Delawares. Killbuck met with the representatives of the Continental Congress in 1779. At the same time, John Killbuck (then age 16) and Thomas Killbuck (Killbuck's half-brother, age 19) were enrolled as students at Princeton along with George White Eyes. The two Killbucks had some trouble adjusting to school, and it was said that Thomas Killbuck became addicted "to liquor and to lying," and although John Killbuck took some interest in his studies, he took more interest in one of Colonel George Morgan's maids and became the father of her child. The Killbucks, along with John Killbuck's new wife and child, returned to the Delawares after a few years.

Peter Killbuck was killed by John Green in 1800 at Ft. Hamilton. See Ohio's Newspaper Extracts, Vol. II, #67, p. 52 (Wednesday, 15 October, 1800).

In 1802, Issac McCoy found Billy Killbuck in jail for getting drunk and killing a man.

In 1824, the Delawares roamed west in small bands of free hunters, mixing with Shawnees and white men. One of these free hunters, a son of Chief William Anderson, was killed in a skirmish with Osage warriors. A sporadic war between the Delawares and Osage broke out. The Killbuck who was then a war captain launched "a bloody campaign against the Osage to avenge the death of Anderson's son." See Weslager, pp. 341, 365.

A Killbuck was one of the mixed-blood Delaware free hunters that Ruxton met and wrote about (circa 1832). He quotes Killbuck as saying, "From the Red River, away up north amongst the Britishers, to Helly [Gila] in the Spanish country — from old Missoura to the sea of Californy, I've trapped and hunted.... For twenty years I packed a squaw along. Not one, but a many. First I had a Blackfoot—the derndest slut as ever cried for fofarraw. I lodge-poled her on Colter's Creek, and made her quit. My buffer hoss, as good as four packs of beaver, I gave for old Bull Tail's daughter...Thar wasn't enough scarlet cloth, nor beads, nor vermilion in Sublette's packs for her. Traps wouldn't buy her for all the fofarraw she wanted; and in two years I sold her to Cross-Eagle for one of Jake Hawkin's guns — this very one I hold in my hands.

"Then I tried the Sioux, the Shian [Cheyenne], and a Digger from the other side, who made the best moccasins as ever I woe. She was the best of all and was rubbed out by the Yuta [Yutes] in the Bayou Salade. Bad was the best; and after she was gone under I tried no more." See O'Meara, p. 196.

Some of the family entering the general population seems to have shortened the name to just Buck, but among the tribes the Killbuck name lived on. The 1859 allotment list for the Chippewa and Munsee Delawares includes Naoma, Moses, Jeremiah, Joseph, Rachel, Julius, Rosanna, and John Thomas Kilbuck.

And among the mixed Chippewa and Munsee Delaware band in 1886 are listed William H. Killbuck, age 48, with his wife Catherine, 44, daughters Rachel, 7, and Vida Saul Killbuck, 11. Also listed is John H. Killbuck, 22. See JAIFR, vol. VI, p. 53, 57.

A William Killbuck, a Delaware, and his wife, Mary, were the parents of Mary Killbuck (who married Israel Haff) and Sarah Jane Killbuck, born in 1847. Sarah Jane married John D. Marker, a white man. She had previously been married to John J. Connors and had a daughter, Elizabeth Connors. The children of John and Mary (Killbuck) Marker included: John B. (b. 1871), Robert J. (b. 1875), Sarah Ellen (Marker) Woodall (b. 1877), Josephine Marker Rogers (b. 1879), Charles J. (b. 1881), and Eliza.

Sarah Ellen Marker married William Woodall, jr. in 1892 at the home of Thomas Buffington, who later became chief of the Cherokee Nation. Their children included: James (b. 1893), Lida (b. 1895, m. Virgil Tipton), Stand Watie Woodall (b. 1898, m. Agnes LeSuer), Vera (b. 1900, m. Emmett Cleghorn of the Otoe Nation), Charles (b. 1902, m. Adaline Henry), Hazel (b. 1907, m. Paul Legg), Alma (b. 1909, m. William Burris). See SOCC, vol. I, pp. 671-672; information from Hazel Legg and Virgil Tipton, jr.

KINKEAD – a Miami/Piankashaw/Shawnee name.

Samuel Kinkead, prior to Braddock's Defeat, was tomahawked by the Indians on the Potomac River in Virginia. His wife, two sons, and a daughter were captured and carried away to Ohio territory. Another son, Samuel Kinkead jr., escaped. Mrs. Kinkead was separated from her children and taken away to Illinois.

Among the captives listed in the SWJ Papers as being delivered up to Bouquet were Elinor Kinkead and two children.

Among the captives delivered up to Bouquet in 1764 were the two boys and their sister who had, during her captivity, become the wife of one of the chiefs. Samuel Kinkead jr. who was then an officer in the United States army, discovered them among the returned whites. He persuaded the two boys to remain among the whites (although they seem to have become Indian traders and may have married women who were red or part-red). But their sister refused to stay among the whites and ran off and rejoined her Indian husband.

The mother, among the Illinois tribes, eventually married a frenchman named Larsh, an Indian trader who was probably part Piankashaw himself. They later moved to Ohio and some of their descendants became residents of the Miami Valley.

See *History of Henderson County, Kentucky*, pp. 616-621; *History of Bourbon County, Kentucky*; Veech's Monongahelia of Old, pp. 130-131.

Ernest Rex (Jim) Kincade, born early in the century, married the part-Shawnee Emma Big Knife and their children included Earnestine, Helen, twins Arma and Mary, John and Nancy. Jim Kincade died in 1963 and was buried in the Big Cabin cemetery near Vinita, Oklahoma. His son, John, was later killed in an automobile accident and was buried near his father. See SOCC, vol. II, p. 198.

KINNEY – a Delaware name.

A white man named John Kinney who had a Delaware wife was living on the Delaware reservation in the year 1858, when he tried to erect a saloon there, which was illegal. See Wesleger, p. 411.

John Kinney served in Capt. Fall Leaf's band of Delaware and Shawnee scouts. John and Eliza Kinney appear on the Delaware rolls appearing in the JAIFR, vol. IV, #1, 1985, pp. 31-52.

John (age 43) and his wife Eliza Kinney appeared on the 1880 Cherokee Census of the Cooweescoowee District. John is listed as a white man and Eliza as a Cherokee. See JAIFR, vol. X, #2, p. 26.

KINZIE – a Shawnee name.

John Kinzie was an Indian trader in 1792 at the Glaze and later at Detroit. He married a white woman who had been adopted by the Shawnees. His wife's father came from Virginia and took Kinzie's entire family back with him. Kinzie later married an adopted

Seneca captive whose husband had been killed in the Battle of Fallen Timbers.

Some of his children from both marriages participated in Indian Affairs in one form or another. See "The Glazie in 1792" by Helen Hornbeck Tanner, p. 35; Milo M. Quaife's Chicago and the Old Northwest 1673-1835, Chicago, 1913: 246, 269, 280, 347, 361-364.

KITCHEN – a Shawnee name.

Among the Shawnees who settled on the lands of the Cherokee nation by 1869 were John and Elizabeth Kitchen. See JAIFR, vol. IV, #2, pp. 100-111.

KISER, KIZER, KEYSER, or KYSER – a Shawnee name.

Jacob Kyser and his mother were captured by Shawnees in Kentucky. See Draper 11CC201. A Jacob Kinzer took up land as early as 1805 in Miami County, Ohio, and a John Kizer is on the first tax list there. Most of the residents of the county at this time were Indian traders who dealt with the Shawnee, and many of them married part-Shawnees or part-Wyandots.

A Keiser family may have been captured at Ruddle's Station in 1780.

A Polly Keyser was said to have been a part of the family of Col. Lewis, of the Lewistown, Ohio reservation. "She had been taken prisoner in early life near Lexington, Kentucky, and had been adopted into the tribe. She had an Indian husband and two half-breed daughters." *The History of Logan County, Ohio,* p. 206. Several pioneers remembered her but could not recall if she had been married at the time of her capture. She came back to Kentucky and lived among the whites for awhile, but she felt uncomfortable and soon moved back to Ohio. One of her daughters, Rachel, was also said to have been white and she became the last wife of Captain Johnny and had children by him.

John Keiser (Kiser, Keizer, etc.) was settled near the Ohio Indian towns as early as 1807.

Among the Shawnees who settled on the lands of the Cherokee nation by 1869 were James, Sally, Louisa, Molly, and Henry Kyser. See JAIFR, vol. IV, #2, pp. 100-111.

Among the Shawnees in 1880 was the Kiser family which included Henry, age 30, July (Julie?), 20, Thomas, 16, and Nancy, 11. This household was Shawnee as listed 1880 Cherokee Census of the Cooweescoowee District. See JAIFR, vol. X, #2, p. 26.

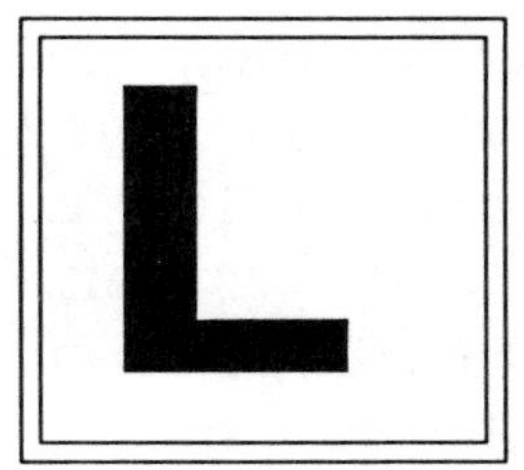

LAFALIER – a Miami name.

Black Raccoon was a "risen up" name among the Miami and their Indiana relatives, the Eel River and Wea bands. In 1880, the Miami Colla-see-pee or Black Raccoon had taken on the name Jarvis (or Servis) A. Lafalier. He lived on his farm with his Shawnee wife, Sara, and their sons Frank and Homer.

Also listed on the 1880 Miami allotment roll was Peter Lafalier (age 55) and his family which included Emma (17), Oscar (12), Henry (10), Nelly (7), Edmund (5), and Daniel, an infant.

Among the Shawnees listed on the 1900 Federal Census of Indian Territory was Louis Lafalier, born in 1857 in Indiana. His mother was born in Indiana, but he lists his father as being born in Michigan. Both of his parents were listed as Shawnees. His wife, Flora Lafalier was listed as a Shawnee, her mother a Shawnee, her father a Miami. Grover C. Paschal, a Peoria, was listed as Louis Lafalier's step-son. They had lived in the Ottawa Nation. See Prevost, pp. 72-73.

LAFLAND – a Wyandot name.

Among the Wyandots listed on the 1900 Federal Census was Louis Lafland, a white man born in Ohio in 1839. He lists his parents as having both been born in Ohio as was his wife, Caroline Lafland, born 1843. Her mother was a white woman, her father a Wyandot. A step-son named Frank Kirkland also lived in the household, his father a white man born in Kentucky, his mother a Wyandot; so probably he was Caroline Lafland's son by her previous husband. See Prevost, p. 83.

LA FONTAINE, LAFONTENNE, etc. – a Miami name.

Hays saw the Indian trader La Fontaine at the

Glaize in 1790. The diarist noted: "A very bitter cold day, froze hard all night. Yesterday evening arrived here a Mr. Lafontenne a trader." Hays noted that La Fontaine had been trading down the Wabash and brought back 80 deerskins and about 500 raccoons "which he brought upon the horses he took out his goods upon. However, he did not trade all his goods away, for he fetch'd some back." Game was so scarce during the cold weather that La Fontaine and his red assistant had to live on acorns for a few days. After five days, Lafontaine sent him out to look for Indian huts where they could obtain meat, and the assistant found "a large Rackoon Tree which he cut down and found five in it." Hays surmised, "Nothing extraordinary in the Indian County."

Quaife notes that this was probably Francis La La Fontaine who had been engaged in the Indian trade at least since 1780. La Fontaine's son, Francis La Fontaine, jr., married a daughter of Chief Richardville and upon the death of his father-in-law, Francis La Fontaine became the chief of all the Miami Nation. See Quaife, pp. 50-51.

LAIL, LAIR, LAIRY – a Shawnee name.

Anyone whose native language was Shawnee would have trouble pronouncing the "R."

George and Johnny Lail were captured at Ruddle's Fort. George married an Indian woman. Johnny later returned to the whites and lived in Harrison County, Kentucky. See Lafferty, p. 322.

Living amongst the Cherokees, Shawnees, and Delawares in the Cooweescoowee District of the Cherokee Nation in 1880 were John, Elisa, James, Willis, and Martha Lairy. See JAIFR, vol. X, #2, p. 26.

LANCISES – Among the captives delivered up to Bouquet in 1764 were Mary Lancises and her child whom she had among the Indians. She had spent nine years with the Indians.

LANE – a Shawnee name.

Martin Lane served as an interpreter for the Senecas and Shawnees in 1831. See Watson, vol. V, pt. 4, p. 15.

Among the Shawnees listed on the 1900 Census as living in the Cherokee Nation were Edward Lane, a white man born in Pennsylvania in 1846, and his Shawnee wife. His father was born in Pennsylvania, his mother in Virginia. His wife, Narsona Lane, was born in Kansas in 1848; both her white father and her Shawnee mother were born in Ohio. Margaret Brown, listed as an aunt, lived with them, born in Ohio as was her Shawnee mother. Her father was born in Virginia. See Prevost, p. 72.

LARSH, LASH, HARSH, LEHARSH, LEHASH, etc. – a Miami/Piankashaw/Peoria name.

La Lache was a half-breed Wea (Miami) mentioned in Hays Journal at the Glaze in 1790. See Quaife, p. 40.

Laharsh (also spelled Larharsh, Laharst, Lehash) was a chief of the Piankeshaws who moved from the Indiana/Illinois region to southwestern Missouri where they were living on Cowskin Creek in the late 1820s. The chief was said to have been "from a family of good moral people." See Valley and Lembcke, p. 181. His Indian name was The Axe.

One of the Kinkead women who had been captured and adopted, probably among the Piankashaws, married a man named Larsh or Lash, an Indian trader who was probably part Indian himself. They later moved to Ohio and some of their descendants became residents of Cincinnati. See KINKEAD. This is the same family as the Lash or Larsh who made a claim on

Ten Mile Creek near David Owens and James Meranda. According to information provided by Glenn Lough, Dr. Jehu Lash was a brother of Paul Lash, the part-French trader who lived with the Indians. See Lough, *Now and Long Ago*, pp. 22-23, 338. Some of the children of this family seem to have lived with the Indians long enough to have children, and some of the family, for one reason or another, were among the first to reside next to the Indian towns in Ohio.

Kercheval, telling a version of this story in *A History of the Valley of Virginia*, p. 373, spells the name as Lease.

A Samuel Larsh lived in the Ohio's Miami Valley among several others known to have Indian connections. His 1823 will mentioned "his present wife" Elizabeth, son Charles, daughter Elizabeth, and his brothers Solaver and Lewis Larsh. Paul Larsh was one of the executors of the will.

LASSALLE, LACCELLE – a Shawnee name.

Francis Lasselle was a nephew of Antoine. His father, Jaques Lasselle, was Indian agent at Miamitown from 1776 to 1780. When La Balme attacked the place in the latter year, he fled by boat down the Maumee River with his family. They later relocated at the Glaize, however.

Jacques Lassalle married a daughter of Blue Jacket and lived near his father-in-law at Ft. Wayne, Indiana territory, in 1795. He sometimes served as interpreter. Mr. Coco Lassalle is talked about in Hays Journal, living amongst the Indians in 1789. La Lache (Lash) told the Indians that Lassalle had informed on them, which was untrue. See Quaife.

Part of the family, like the Richardville's and Godfroy's, stayed among the whites in Indiana, but some relocated to the Munsey Delaware Reservation in Ontario. The five Lacelle households listed on that 1881 Census were:

1. Adam Lacelle, age 62, a member of the Monrovian Church, and Lucy Lacelle, 61. They were living with Colin Jackson, 35, born in the United States, and his family included Polly, 28, Ann, 9, Nancy, 7, Thomas, 3, and Ellen, 1. Also living in the household was Charlotte Wilson, 29.
2. Caleb Lacelle, 27, and apparently his wife Susan, 23. Living in this same household was the family of Edward Whiteeye, 62, a Methodist born in the United States. It included Jane, 52, Absalom, 28, Ennos, 11 — all Whiteeyes.
3. George Lacelle, 30, a member of the Church of England, with Louise, 34, Francis, 9, Fred, 7, Eliza, 4, and Nancy, an infant. In the same household was Nancy Lacelle, age 65, born in the United States. Also living in the same household was Julia Johns, 25, with Mandy Johns, 7, and Alfred Johns, 4.
4. Samuel Lacells (Lacelle), 55, is head of a household which included Peter Lacelle, age 1.
5. Seth Lacells (Lacelle), 38, is listed with Nancy, 38, Julia, 15, Alice, 10, Robert, 8, Charlotte, 6, Samuel, 4, and James, 2. Louise Anthony, 10, also lived in the household.

See Prevost, p. 121.

LEE – a Delaware name.

John Lee was taken captive on Reed Creek in March of 1756. He is listed as having been killed, but apparently he was just captured and adopted. John Lee and Thomas Lee were among the captives delivered up by the Delawares and Shawnees to General Bouquet in 1764. According to Sipe's Indian Wars of Pennsylvania, p. 676, Thomas Lee did not want to leave his adopted family when delivered up.

A John Lee was living in Indiana and in 1805 was charged with assault and battery in Clark County, Indiana, for attacking George Washington (the Shawnee scout who lived among the Delaware) in Clarksville. The court records show the indictment, but do not show what action was taken, so apparently the indictment was dismissed.

Thomas Lee (age 30) had a household which included Lizzie (22), Daniel D. (2), Susie L. (2 months). These, as well as Mary (40) and James Lee (36), were all listed as Delawares on the 1880 Cherokee census of the Cooweescoowee District. See JAIFR, vol. X, #2, p. 27.

LEITH – a Delaware name.

John Leith was reportedly from South Carolina; he hired himself out to an Indian trader, but was adopted by a Delaware chief who had a white wife. He became a respected trader amongst his adopted tribe. Then in 1776, he was captured by a war party of Shawnee who sold him to the Wyandot. They released him because he was an adopted Delaware. Leith then returned to the Delawares and resumed trading, marrying Sally Lowry, a white woman who had also been captured and adopted. He wrote a biographical account of his life which exists today. One of his wives was said to have been Sarah McKee. See Reuben Gold Thwaites, Leeths Narrative; Consul Willshire Butterfield, Expedition Against Sandusky, Cincinnati, 1873, 178-179n; Loskiel, History of the United Brethren, pt. 3, pp. 140-141.

LEWIS – a Shawnee/Wyandot name.

"A reservation of 40,300 acres around Lewistown, in Washington township, in this county [Logan County, Ohio], was granted also to the Shawanoes and Senecas jointly. The name of the principal town on the reservation was given for a noted

Shawanoe chief, who made it his place of residence...

"The reservation life of the Shawanoes was as peaceful and happy as could be...The natives were frequent visitors among the whites, and it was a common thing to see them with their families during the summer, encamped in some shady spot on the bank of a stream..." See *The History of Logan County, Ohio*, p. 206.

This was Lewistown and John Lewis was the leading man of the town. He accompanied Tecumseh to the Wyandot council in 1808. But after Tippecanoe, he stood staunchly alongside Blackhoof against Tecumseh. Capt. Lewis led a company of scouts during the War of 1812 on the side of the United States, and he seems to have been rewarded for his service at the peace. He married one of the adopted sisters of Jonathon Alder, and Polly Kiser was in his extended family and may have been his last wife.

On the muster roll of Shawnees who went from Ohio to Kansas in 1832 is listed the family of George Lewis, consisting of two males and one female 25-50, and three females under ten.

Among the Wyandots allotted land in 1855 were John Lewis and his family who included Jane, David, John, jr., William, Sarah, and Noah Lewis.

LILLY, LILY, LILLIE, etc. – a Susquehanna/ Conestoga name.

William Lilly, who previously lived in Nova Scotia, moved to Pennsylvania and lived for some time with the remnants of the Susquehanna/Conestoga tribe that lived in the valleys of the Susquehanna and Juanita Rivers. William Lilly's wife, tradition says, was the sister of the hereditary chief.

In 1796, a traveler crossed the flooded Juanita on a flatboat and noted that he camped on the east side "near Mr. Lilly's." A Joseph Lilly appeared on the 1790 census of Bedford County made from tax lists. See PMBH, vol. 71, p. 64.

Chief Piercing Eyes (David J. Turnbull) heads the Pan American Indian Association, a non-profit organization which is made up mostly of people with a tradition of Native American descent but also includes card-carrying BIA Indians and others who simply identify with any one of the various Native American ethnic traditions. Like a large number of Americans off the reservation, Turnbull seems to have several red lines in his genealogy, but he is also a direct descendant of William Lilly and carries on the traditions of the Susquehanna/Conestoga.

I know Piercing Eyes only through his publication, but he appears to be a chief of the old style, leading mainly through sage advice and by example. He and his wife, Early Spring, editorialize in their *Pan-American Indian Association News* published from Nocatee, Florida. Being a chief has never been easy, but Turnbull strives to accent the positive side of Native American culture and to stay free of the negativism and degrading sellouts that have ensnared many others. Their growing organization provides an intelligent forum through which the various conflicts between factions might be diplomatically aired and resolved.

For information on the Pan American Indian Association, write Chief Piercing Eyes, POB 244, Nocatee, FL 33864. There is a nominal membership fee, but those engaged in the search for their Native American heritage will find it cheap at the price. "Many Indians spend as much for beer in one day," the chief writes. "Lifetime membership in Pan-Am would be more valuable than a case of beer. We offer them the methodology to discover themselves, while bartenders offer them the methodology to lose themselves."

LINCTOT – a Piankeshaw/Miami name.

Godfrey Linctot (or DeLinctot) was at Ft. Jefferson with his forty mounted men, most of whom were Indians (Piankeshaws and Ottawas) and French half-breeds. He was not there during the battle, however, for George Rogers Clark had sent him against the Shawnees elsewhere.

Sieur de Linctot was a French commander at the Ouitan Outpost (on the Wabash River) in 1738. After the English kicked the French out, Linctot (or his son) lived on with the Indians and became a bitter enemy of the English.

Godfrey de Linctot, a half-breed, was raised among the Shawnees and Delawares; was at Ft. Pitt in 1780; had a confrontation in the presence of Capt. Pipe and other chiefs during which his life was threatened by the English; was commissioned a major in the Virginia militia in recognition and reward for his assistance with the Indians.

Leonard Helm wrote from Ft. Jefferson on February 14th, 1781: "Maj. Linctot with a party of Piankeshaws and Ottawa Indians arrived here a few days ago...[speaks of] an extended expedition against the Ouia [the Wea town], which will be conducted by Maj. Linctot. I am pleased with this gentleman's conduct, as he has given singular proofs of his unwearied diligence to cultivate the good sentiments of our friendly Indians..."

Apparently during one of his company's raids, Major Godfrey de Linctot was killed near Cahokia, June 2, 1781. A notice of his death appeared in a Virginia newspaper.

Draper referred to Godfrey de Linctot as "an honest energetic man," mentions his service at Ft. Jefferson. See *Ill. Hist. Collections*, vol. 18; Draper Mss. 31J72.

Bernard Linctot was his oldest son, and he took

the family to Natchez. A daughter married Stephen Minor who became a magistrate of Natchez. Another daughter later married the notorious Phillip Nolan.

LINN or LYNN – a Delaware/Shawnee/Cherokee name.

Issac Lynn was captured by Delawares near the Ohio River about 1756 and was still living with his adopted people several years later. It was Lynn who warned the Delawares of Arthur Crawford's plans to run off, causing bad feelings between the two youths. See Lobdell, Indian Warfare..., p. 32.

Near Louisville, five school-boys, including William Linn Jr. and Asahel Linn, were captured by Indians while out playing (or hunting). All of them returned to the whites except Abram Pope, who would not abandon his adopted people and married among the Indians. Asahel later married Nancy Hunter Dodge, daughter of Joseph Hunter. William Linn jr. married the widow of Absalom Keller, who had been killed by Indians, and became Joseph Hunter's son-in-law. Linn's first wife may have died as he later was named as the notorious Peter Smith's son-in-law.

Col. William Linn Sr. was killed near Louisville by Indians while going to court. His will is dated July 18, 1780; probated April 3, 1781 and concluded August 2, 1797. Mentions wife Letitia; youngest daughter Ann; oldest son William, land 1000 acres below the mouth of the Miami River; son Asabel, son Benjamin, daughters Theodotia and Luoruania; and says "if the daughters return from the Indians" they are to have certain lands, but if they do not return, the land is to be divided amongst his sons. See FCQ, vol. 6, p. 15.

Theodosia and Lavina Lynn were both among the captured at Ruddles Station in 1780. Theodosia married George Ruddle.

Col. William Linn Sr.'s brother, Col. Benjamin

Linn, spent four years living with the Delawares and Shawnees, among whom he had many good friends. He married Hannah Severns, who had been adopted by Shawnees and was living among them. When they celebrated their marriage at Harrodsburg, George Rogers Clark, in his journal, noted the "much merriment" which accompanied the event.

There are many stories about Benjamin Linn. Once, when he was overdue and it was feared that he had been killed by Indians, a search party was sent to comb the area. One by one, the party returned and as each man passed, he would report, no Linn, no Linn. That's how Kentucky's Nolin Lake and resort area got its name.

Benjamin Linn had always felt safe among the Shawnees and Delawares, hunting at will on both sides of the river. But things changed, and the Indians began to look at him differently while he was hunting in Indiana with Samuel Moore. One of his friends who lived among them warned him of the impending danger, telling him to run south to the river and to keep going, as the Indians would send a running party after them. Linn and Moore ran all night, crossed the river by the light of a full moon, and returned safely.

Subsequently, Benjamin Linn settled down with his wife, and he became a preacher. His name does not appear on many military rosters, but he did go with the 1782 expedition against the Shawnees, scouting ahead on his gray horse. He tried preaching, but his "hardshell" Baptist church found his views too liberal, and they eventually "cold-shouldered" him. In 1810, he and his wife moved from Green County, Kentucky to Madison County, Alabama, and lived with their daughter, Esther, and her husband John Chisholm. His other family included daughter Rachel, who married Marshall Despain, and daughter Milly.

See Beattie, p. 221.

LITTLE TURTLE – a Miami chief with a white wife who has many descendants in the general population.

Little Turtle was chief of the Miamis during their greatest military victories. He was the son of the Miami chief, Ague-nack-que, who signed a treaty between the English and the Miami in 1748. His mother was a Mohican. Expert ethnologists will tell you that Little Turtle would have inherited a Mohican heritage from his mother that would have disqualified him from ever becoming a chief of the Miami. Nevertheless, that's what happened.

Little Turtle rose to the leadership of his Nation probably because of his obvious talents in leadership. He was a military strategist of the highest order, defeating the much larger forces of Harmar and St. Clair through the use of tactics. After Gen. Anthony Wayne took over the United States forces and reorganized them, Little Turtle advised against confrontation, and when he was overruled, he turned over the leadership of the allied red forces to Bluejacket, who was subsequently defeated at Fallen Timbers.

Little Turtle may have married several times during his life, but one wife was the white woman, Polly Ford, who had previously been married to a trader at Vincennes (see Tanner, p. 20). Polly Ford was among those who left the Indians and lived in Kentucky for awhile, but she missed her red life and returned. Little Turtle's daughters included Wan-man-go-pith (Sweet Breeze), who married William Wells. The sons of Little Turtle were Wah-pl-mon-quah (White Loon), Ma-kak-ta-mon-quah (Black Loon), and Wak-shin-gay.

White Loon's daughter, Town-no-com-quah, Blowing Snow, who took the name Mary E. Taylor. When Mary Taylor came back to Indiana from the Miami reservation to take care of her aged mother, she was described as being "quite a genteel and courteous lady, with an English education."

BLack Loon's son, Coessie, became a chief of the Indiana Miami. Wak-shin-gay was the father of Kil-so-quah (Sunset), who married a Mr. Revarre and also stayed in Indiana until her death.

William Wells and Little Turtle's daughter, Sweet Breeze, have numerous descendants scattered throughout the land. See WELLS.

Ni-nun-de-ku-min, a Miami warrior and a descendant of Little Turtle, married Nancy Ketchum (Au-kee-len-qua), a daughter of the Delaware, Captain Ketchum. They lived near the Eel River in Indiana and moved to Miami County, Kansas. Their children included:

1. Lucy Ketchum (Loa-set-tah-o-quah) who married a cousin, William Riley Ketchum. He was a sergeant in the Civil War, M Company, 6th Kansas Volunteer Cavalry. Their children included Nancy, b. 1849, Joel, b. 1852, Absolom, b. 1856, and Henry Clay Ketchum, b. 1859.
2. Nancy Journeycake (Auh-pa-mun-da-qua) who married Isaac Journeycake, son of Solomon and Sally Journeycake, and they had nine children.

   The eldest, Sally O. Journeycake, married John T. Smith, a white man, and they had five children. Other members of this line married into the Rogers, Randell, Collins, Quinn, McCrary, and Worrell families.

   Another daughter of Issac and Nancy Journeycake, Mary Journeycake, b. 1850, married Dr. R. M. Allen, a physician, and they had nine children.
3. Aup-hee-he-li-qua, another daughter of Ni-nun-de-ku-min and Au-kee-len-qua, married the Miami George Owl. Their children included Sally Owl who married William

Honeywell, a white man. Their children included Ely Moore Honeywell who married an Elnora, Susan Frances Honeywell who married William Dodge, William Honeywell, Enoch Honeywell, and Ada Honeywell who married Charles H. Miles and had twelve children.

Another daughter of George Owl and Auphee-he-li-qua married a Collins. Their son, George Owl Collins married Lucinda Elliot Connor and their children included Ida May who married Clinton L. Goodale, Willie, and George O. Collins.

4. Lo-a-ti-ao-qua, youngest known child of Ni-nun-de-ku-min, married the Rev. James Ketchum, and their children included Nancy Ketchum who married Joseph Armstrong, Mary E. Ketchum who married James D. Henderson, Hester Ann Ketchum who married John Hawkins, Virginia A. Ketchum who married James Yost, and Thomas E. Ketchum who married Belle Thompson.

Anyone interested in this family should get a copy of Ruby Cranor's excellent work on Chief William Anderson and his descendants. This family is elaborated upon in much more detail on pp. 166-168 of her splendid book.

LOGAN – a Mingo name.

The father of Logan, Shickallamy, was a French child that was captured and adopted by the Oneidas when very young. Logan's mother was a Cayuga, and he became identified with Tanacharisson's people, who later became known as the Mingo nation, but were of mixed heritage, mostly Iroquois.

By all accounts, Logan (Tachnechdorus, the spreading branches) was of a peaceable mind. He married a Shawnee, a sister to the wife of Indian trader John Gibson. He was living on the Ohio in 1774. While Logan was away on a trading trip, his wife, children, and other relations (except for John Gibson's infant son) were killed by Jacob Greathouse and a few other drunken white men from Cross Creek. Logan was naturally furious and went on a rampage against all whites. The retaliation for Logan's raid on white settlements began Dunmore's War.

Lord Dunmore sent his interpreter, John Gibson, who was Logan's brother-in-law, to bring Logan in so that peace might be made without further bloodshed. Logan refused to go and his reply was taken down by John Gibson who later said that it was transcribed, word-for-word.

"I appeal to any white man to say if he ever entered Logan's cabin hungry, and he gave him not meat; if ever he came cold and naked, and he clothed him not. During the course of the last long and bloody war, Logan remained in his cabin, an advocate of peace. Such was my love for the whites that...I had even thought to have lived with you, but for the injuries of one man...[who]...in cold blood, and unprovoked, murdered all the relations of Logan, not sparing even my women and children.

"There runs not a drop of my blood in the veins of any living creature. This called on me for revenge. I have sought it. I have killed many. I have fully glutted my vengeance...Logan never felt fear. He will not turn on his heel to save his life. Who is there to morn for Logan? Not one."

The war was waged against the Shawnees, not because they had anything to do with Logan's warriors, but because they held the land that the white Pennsylvanians and Virginians coveted. Cornstalk was able to make a peace before his nation was completely destroyed. Logan lived on after the peace, married again, and had several more children.

In his old age, Logan is supposed to have been a crying drunk. The Rev. Heckewelder referred to him as "a man of superior talents, but of a deep melancholy." One of his nephews is said to have killed him on an order of the tribal elders, more or less to put him out of his misery. But there were children who kept the name and carried it on.

Among the Indians on the 1881 Ontario Census are listed Benjamin Logan, 30, his wife Eliza, also 30, with Agnes, 9, Elizabeth, 4, and Joseph, 2. Another household included Taylor Logan, 71, with Eliza, 65, Lewis, 19, Cornelius, 16, Pauline, 13, and Clarice Logan, 6. Another household included Jacob Logan, 34, with his wife, Rebecca, and their son, Wilson Logan, 9. Also there was Scobie Logan, 23, and his white wife, Isabella, 19; Robert Logan, 32; and Silas Logan, 23. See Prevost, pp. 101-102.

For a discussion of the Logan family of Shawnees, see RENNICK.

LONG – a Wyandot name.

Alexander Long married into the part-Wyandot Zane family. See ZANE.

Thomas Long, possibly a son of Alexander Long, negotiated the purchase of the Wyandot Ohio lands in 1834 on behalf of the Wyandots. The preliminary negotiations produced no sale of lands, perhaps a victory for the Wyandots. See Dwight L. Smith, "An Unsuccessful Negotiation for Removal of the Wyandot Indians from Ohio, 1834," OSA&HQ, vol. 58, #1, pp. 305-324.

Allotted land in 1855 were the Wyandots Irvin P. Long; Ethan A. Long; Issac Z. Long; James M. Long; and Henry C. Long, his wife, Martha, and their daughter, Elizabeth. See KHC, vol. 15, pp. 140-141.

Among the Wyandot guardianship cases heard in 1871 by Ely Parker, Commissioner of Indian Affairs, was the case of Irvin P. Long, who had been guardian for William Long, his brother, Sarah Hicks (then dead), Thomas Hill (who had three daughters), the family of John Williams, and John Squendechter (whose brother, Gibson, had received his money). See JAIFR, vol. VIII, #2, p. 22.

Among the Wyandots on the 1900 Federal Census was James M. Long who lists his father as a white man, his mother as a Wyandot. His wife, Susan Long, was listed as a white woman, born in Pennsylvania, and it says that her father was born in West Virginia. Also on the census is Oscar Long, born in 1825 in Ohio, his father a white man, his mother a Wyandot. His wife, Catherine Long, was a white woman born in Missouri.

Among the Delawares living in Wyandotte County, Kansas, and enumerated on the 1860 and 1870 Federal Census were William Long, age 30, born in Ohio, Catherine Long, 25, Nancy Long, 6, and Charles Long, born Kansas. See Prevost, pp. 9, 83.

LONGTAIL – a Shawnee name.

The Shawnee Longtail family were traditionalists. Longtail was a warrior whose name appears on some treaties and a Longtail was along on the Shawnee expedition to the Florida War.

John Longtail married Rachel McClain at the Shawnee Mission in 1856.

Among the Shawnees on the 1880 census of the Cherokee Cooweescoowee District were Jacob (age 22), Sarah (22), Rosy (7), and Elizabeth Longtail (60). See JAIFR, vol X, #2, p. 28.

An interesting interview with Jake Longtail, transcribed in his own words, was written down by a reporter named James R. Carselowey in the 1930s. Jake Longtail was then eighty-nine years old, having been born on the Kansas reservation in 1848. Longtail bought a farm, and built a comfortable farmhouse for his family. He remembered Bob Ironsides, a storekeeper who married his daughter, Birdie Longtail. Ironsides built the first theater in Vinita, Oklahoma. See SOCC, vol. 1, p. 593, information from Sue Buzzard.

LORIMER, LORAMIE – a Shawnee name.

Louis Lorimer had a trading post on the Saline River. His wife was Shawnee and he had great influence among the Indians. When a troop of Kentuckians destroyed his store, he moved, with some of his Shawnee friends, to the Mississippi River and established the Spanish post at Cape Girardeau. See the MHR, vol. 21, p. 137; v. 23, pp. 137-138. Pierre Drouillard was his brother-in-law and George Drouillard was his nephew.

When Meriwether Lewis was looking for an Indian interpreter/hunter to go on the Lewis and Clark expedition, he called upon Louis Lorimer at Cape Girardeau.

"Lewis found Lorimer at the racetrack, where he was entering several horses. The main contest had just ended as the Virginian arrived and he found the Missourians excitedly settling various betting disputes." Lewis thought that they were acting just like Kentuckians.

Lorimer was supposed to have had children by each of two half-Shawnee wives, and one of his children attended West Point.

LOTTERIDGE, LOTHRIDGE, LAGOTTRIE, LOGGOTHERIE, etc. (variously spelled) – a Mohawk name.

Captain Lotheridge was the equal of Andrew Montour. He led companies of Mohawks in the English interest against the French allies during the French and Indian wars. See the index to the Sir William Johnson

Papers, for many references to his exploits (such as vol. 13, p. 147). He was in the British interest during the Revolutionary War. His family intermarried with the Montours and the Brandts. See also Prevost, pp. 93-94.

Among the students at the Shawnee Mission school in Kansas were Philomene and Rosalie Lagottrie, both Mohawks. A Henry Lagotrie was also a student at the school, listed as a Potawatomi. See Caldwell, p. 188.

LOWRY – a Shawnee/Delaware/Cherokee name.

Lazarus Lowry and his brother James were registered Indian traders as early as 1744. They had great influence among the Indians. The Governor of French Canada authorized a very high price for their scalps to get rid of them.

The Lowry family became one of the major sources of Shawnee and Delaware blood traditions, and they also intermarried with the major Cherokee families.

Among the Cherokees, George Lowry married Nancy, a daughter of Oolutsa (she's come). A brother of Nancy Lowry was Chekawnahler (forget me not). Among Nancy's children were Capt. John Lowry who married Betsy Shorey; Major George Lowry who married Lucy Benge; Jane Lowry who married Taluntiski; Sallie Lowry who married Staydt (Rope); Betsy Lowry who married John Sevier; Nelly Lowry who married Edmond Fallen; and Akey Lowry who married Mr. Burnes.

The family of Major George Lowry and Lucy Benge included James Lowry who married Betsy McLemore; George Lowry who married Betsy Baldridge; Susan Lowry who married Andrew Ross; Lydia Lowry who married Milo Hoyt; Rachel Lowry who married (1st) David Brown and (2nd) Nelson Orr; John Lowry; Anderson Lowry who married Mary Nave;

Anderson Lowry who married Delia Baldridge; and Washington Lowry who married Nancy Gist, daughter of Sequoyah.

The children of Lydia (Lowry) and her husband, Dr. Milo Hoyt, included Dolly Hoyt who married Rev. Nelson Chamberlain; Anna Hoyt who married Rev. Hamilton Balentine; H. Booth Hoyt who married (1st) Ruth Buffington, and (2nd) Elizabeth Candy; Sarah Hoyt who married Richard Hunter; Esther Hoyt who married Monroe Keys; Milo Ard Hoyt who married Harriet Fulsom Washburn; and George Hoyt.

The children of Esther Hoyt and the Rev. James Ward included Darius E. Ward who married (1st) Sarah Ritter, and (2nd) Mary Hester Murphy; Lydia Ann Ward who married William C. Chamberlain; Clara Alice Ward; William W. Ward who married Roxanna Sterner; and Henry J. Ward who married Emma Luckenbach.

The Cherokee genealogy of this family is much elaborated in JAIFR, vol. 1, #3, pp. 43-49, taken from Muriel H. Wright, Springplace: Morovian Mission and the Ward Family of the Cherokee Nation, Gutherie, Oklahoma, c. 1940.

LUMPY – a Wyandot name.

Lump-on-the-head was a Wyandot warrior in the War of 1812. The name was shorted to Lumpy among his descendants.

Among the Wyandots allotted land in 1855 were Theressa Lumpy, 54, Louis Lumpy, 32, and Rebecca Lumpy, 23. Among the Wyandot guardianship cases heard in 1871 by Ely Parker, Commissioner of Indian Affairs, was the case of Lewis Lumpy who was the guardian of Terese G. Washington, his aunt. See JAIFR, vol. VIII, #2, p. 22.

LYNCH or LINCH – a Shawnee name.

Among the Shawnees who settled on the lands of the Cherokee nation by 1869 was Willis Linch. See JAIFR, vol. IV, #2, pp. 100-111.

LYON or LYONS – a Delaware/Wyandot name.

Benjamin Lyon was an Indian trader at Detroit associated with Henry Bostick and Etne. Campion. See Mich. Pio. & Hist. Col., vol. 10., p. 367.

Among the Delawares to ratify a treaty and share in the land on the Sandusky River in Ohio was Thomas Lyon.

Lang says, "Tom Lyons, a Delaware and a friend of Anthony Wayne, who named him Tom Lyons, was a very old and fierce warrior, having lived with his people in Pennsylvania long before they came to Ohio. According to Lang, his wife was "the fairest woman of the Delaware tribe...On making his home at Ft. Ball, he was accustomed to buy trinkets, ribbons, etc. for this woman and to array her in the outfit of a queen. While living in this simple way, two white hunters from Delaware County visited Ft. Ball and finding Lyons in his cabin, murdered him for recreation." See Lang, p. 216.

Two Indians, Jim and Bill Lyons, had huts northeast of Cambridge, Ohio, and were supposed to have been sons of Tom Lyons (according to Wolfe's Stories of Guernsey County, Ohio). Jim Lyons wife was a white woman who had been captured and adopted. She looked "much like an Indian" anyway except for her "light and wavy hair."

Listed on the 1881 Ontario Census and living on the Oneida and Delaware reserve were Lewis Lyon, 20, and Mary Lyon, 21, both born in Ontario and members of the Church of England. See Prevost, p. 114.

McAMMISH – a Shawnee name.

Among the Shawnees who settled on the lands of the Cherokee nation by 1869 were Emma, R. D. sr. and jr., Mary E., Prudence, and Albany McAmmish. See JAIFR, vol. IV, #2, pp. 100-111.

McCARTLE – a Delaware name.

Among the Delawares living in the Cooweescoowee District and appearing on the 1880 Cherokee census were John (age 23), Lizzie (20), and Anna McCartle (2). See JAIFR, vol. X, #2, p. 31.

McCLAIN, McLANE, McLAIN, McLENE – a Shawnee name.

The Shawnee councilor and sub-chief, Henry Clay, was a son of Capt. John Wolf and a grandson of Cornstalk. Henry Clay was educated under the supervision of Indian Agent John Johnston at Upper Piqua, at the expense of the Quaker Friends. Lang, in his History of Seneca County, Ohio, says that Henry Clay "married the daughter of Jeremiah McLain, formerly a member of Congress from the Columbus District." See Lang, p. 210.

Among the Shawnees and Senecas allocated money for the improvements that they had made on their Ohio property were John McLean and Jesse McLene. See Watson, vol. V., pp. 13, 19.

Listed on the 1832 Muster Roll of Shawnee Indians of the Hog Creek and Wapakoneeta bands was the family of Henry Clay which included one female over 55, one male and one female between 25 and 55, and three children under 10, all boys.

Also along was the Shawnee family of James McClain which included one male and one female between 10 and 25, with one male child under 10. See

Roy, pp. 40-41. James McLain married Nancy Daugherty, a daughter of Lewis Daugherty. After the death of James McClain in 1864, Nancy married Tom Bigknife, sr.

But among the children of James and Nancy McLain was Sophia Mclain, whose marriages are a matter of controversy. Her daughter Mary McLane, born 1852, married John Steele in 1869. We know this because of the litigation involving the estate of William Gillis. See GILLIS.

Among the Shawnees who settled on the lands of the Cherokee nation by 1869 were Joseph, John, Henry, Elizabeth, and Rose Anna McLane. See JAIFR, vol. IV, #2, pp. 100-111.

Listed among the Shawnees, Delawares, and Cherokees living in the Cooweescoowee District and appearing on the 1880 Cherokee census was J. B. McLain (listed as a white man, age 38), and living with him were the Cherokees Martha (23), W. H. (10), Mary (8), and Minnie McLain (3). The Shawnees listed were Jane (37) and L. J. McLain (7). See JAIFR, vol. X, #2, p. 32.

Among the Shawnee guardianship cases reviewed by the Commissioner of Indian Affairs in 1871 were the cases of James and Lewis McLane (McClain). Lewis McLane's wards included another Lewis McLane and Elizabeth Thoksemo, among others not named. The younger Lewis McLane seems to have lived with his grandfather, James Mclane, for six or seven years. See JAIFR, vol. VIII, #2, p. 25, 27.

Some of the Shawnee orphans seem to have been adopted by members of the Peoria tribe, with whom many of the Shawnees intermarried. One such was Peter McLane, listed as being 20 years old on the 1889 Peoria Census. Emeline McLane (Chi-lo), age 22, is also listed and might have been his sister. See Valley and Lembcke, p. 247.

Peter McLane is listed on the 1913 Peoria Census,

and his mixed-blood family included his wife, Fannie McLane, a Cayuga, Katie Walker White, Ella Miller Blackfish, John Reathe (husband of his dead sister), Nellie Prather, and Beulah Prather Day.

Edward J. McClain, an Eastern Shawnee, gave an extensive interview in 1937 on the traditions of his people. The interview has been preserved in the Indian Archives of the Oklahoma Historical Society, vol. 6.

Of course, there were other origins of the McClain family name among various tribes. Among these was a Jesse McLain who then resided on his farm in McMinn County, Tennessee in 1835, with his family of five quarterblood Cherokees with one white who had intermarried into the family.

McCLELLAND, McCLELLAN – a name associated with Indian blood traditions.

David McClelland's wife, their two children, and a servant girl were captured by Captain John Peters' war party during Pontiac's War. See "The Captivity of Charles Stuart," in MVHR., vol. XII, #1, p. 60.

Richard Butler saw the older Robert McClelland, an Indian trader, in the company of Pluggy and The Apple Tree in 1775 and noted it in his journal. McClelland was trading at the Indian towns on the Virginia/Pennsylvania frontier at the time.

William Harrod, jr., said that "about 1783, Indians fell upon the families of Robert McClelland and James Archer, who were related and whose families resided in the same cabin about three-fourths of a mile from Ft. Jackson. They came on a foggy morning..." The Indians killed many but a few escaped to tell the story. Some of those reported killed may have been captured to be adopted. One of those could have been the twelve-year-old Robert McClelland who would become one of the most famous scouts of his day.

According to one account in the Draper manuscripts, the youthful Robert McClelland was shortly rescued from captivity by the frontier scout and notorious killer, Samuel Brady. If true, perhaps some of Brady's roughness rubbed off onto McClelland. See Draper 26CC83.

Robert McClelland who married Nancy Pryor, the daughter of John Pryor, August 7th, 1792 in Jefferson County, Kentucky. It was in Jefferson County that McClelland enlisted in William Wells band of spies along with a few others hand-picked by Wells for their abilities, especially the special ability to pass as an Indian among Indians.

Robert McClelland had many skirmishes with the Indians on the Ohio frontier, but the one that haunted him for the rest of his life was the brazen attack on the Delaware camp made by William Wells' band of scouts (see MILLER). McClelland never fully recovered from the wound he received in this fight, and it caused him much pain in later life.

After his service as an Indian spy, Robert McClelland came back to Louisville and settled with his wife near Mann's Lick and Bullitt's Lick, owning taxable property in both southern Jefferson and northern Bullitt counties. His brother-in-law, James Alexander, helped him run a tavern, and McClelland settled down to the business. However, McClelland was never a very good businessman, and he became involved in many suits, some of which were filed away due to his absence.

Some of these suits include interesting testimony, revealing of his fiery temper and hardnosed ways. One of them also reveals that Robert McClelland's wife died in the late fall of 1796. Until we see evidence of another marriage, we will tentatively assume that his children had to be born between 1792 and 1796.

These suits were annoying to Robert McClelland,

and he was a man easily annoyed, a man who really felt uncomfortable in the settlements, a man who yearned for action. And McClelland's life really got complicated after he agreed to become the administrator for the estate of another brother-in-law, Thomas Smith. Smith had borrowed money, sold off his property, and either was killed or deserted, leaving his family and debts behind. Smith's creditors sued McClelland claiming fraud, for it was said that Smith was yet alive, having been seen with the British and Indians in Canada. These suits dragged on for years.

McClelland was usually not there to answer to them, but he reappeared in Louisville a couple of times, perhaps to see his children. The suits were discontinued during his absence and renewed whenever he reappeared.

About 1799, he left his small children in Kentucky with the family of James Pryor, a brother-in-law and one of his partners in a whiskey-trading venture from Louisville to New Orleans. McClelland had then himself accompanied the whiskey cargo to New Orleans. He returned by ship to Philadelphia where he applied for a pension for the shoulder wound he received in the raid against the Delawares.

If a story in Draper's manuscripts is accurate, Robert McClelland must have gone from Philadelphia to Pittsburgh. According to an article that Draper clipped from the Ladies Magazine (published in Pittsburgh in 1836), McClelland conned his way onto the jury that was trying Samuel Brady for the murder of an Indian in 1800. McClelland did this to guarantee acquittal, thus paying Brady back, the article says, as Brady had previously rescued McClelland from captivity among the Indians who had massacred his family. In 1836 there might have been people around who remembered such a trial and the article names Brady's lawyers as James Ross and Alexander Brackenridge.

Perhaps there are other accounts of this around. See Draper 25CC82-83.

McClelland returned to Louisville in 1801 where his notes were overdue and he was pressed for money. Leaving his children with James Pryor, he then absconded and went to live with his brother, William McClelland, and with the Indian traders James and William Hamilton at their trading post in Ohio.

Then came the Louisiana Purchase and the Lewis and Clark Expedition. William Clark considered asking McClelland to come along, couldn't find him, and instead wisely recruited two of McClelland's in-laws, Nathaniel Pryor and Charles Floyd. McClelland shortly followed them west himself.

There are many accounts of Robert McClelland's adventures among the Crows, Blackfoot, and Sioux. They present a consistent picture of the man, looking grizzled and older than his years, quick-tempered and prone to physical violence against all odds.

Once, when he was away from his trading post, a party of Sioux surrounded his store and began to plunder his goods, carrying them off to their village. McClelland returned while they were in the process of doing this. "McClelland burst in...and with blazing eyes, and a voice suffering with rage, demanded an instant return of everything they had taken. Knowing his terrible temper and desperate character of the man, the Indians present hastened to restore their spoils, but by far the greater portion of the goods had already been carried to their village, and the trader had to pocket a loss of some three thousand dollars. Cursing Indians, Spaniards, Frenchmen, and all other damned rascals, as he called them, he fitted up his boats and started down the Missouri, to engage in some business where he could find more honorable competitors." See Tripplitt, pp. 357-369.

Irving saw Robert McClelland in Missouri,

shortly after McClelland's trading expedition had been routed by the Sioux. McClelland was not in a good mood, but Irving thought him "a remarkable man. He had been a partizan under General Wayne in his Indian wars, where he had distinguished himself by his fiery spirit and reckless daring, and marvelous stories are told of his exploits...He was restless, fearless, but of impetuous and sometimes ungovernable temper." See Rust; Carter, p. 228.

Robert McClelland could always escape the Indians, but in 1809 the lawyers caught up with him in St. Louis. He was "in mercy" and in bankruptcy, and an administrator was appointed for him to liquidate his estate for the benefit of his creditors. Later, his children, James, Robert, and John McClelland, are listed in several cases against the estate of James Pryor who had been the guardian of Robert McClelland's children but was then also missing or dead. Some of the suits were dragged out beyond all reason, lasting into the 1830's, but such was the state of law, then and now. Property once deemed worthless became valuable over the years. Heirs of creditors were found and they had lawyers who demanded their share.

He died November 22, 1815 in St. Louis, and was buried on the farm of William Clark there. In 1875, they unearthed an old tombstone there, and found this inscription on it: "To the Memory of Capt. Robert McClelland. This stone is erected by a friend who knew him to be brave, honest, and sincere; an intrepid warrior, whose services deserve perpetual remembrance. A. D. 1816." Historian Harvey Carter thought that William Clark must have put up the marker with his own funds, as McClelland died broke.

See Harvey Carter, "Robert McClelland," pp. 223-228; William Shannon vs Robert McClelland, filed twice as Jefferson County (Ky) Circuit Court cases #4934 and #5042, 1801; William Funk's extr. vs. Robert

McClelland's admr, filed away 1809, and David L. Ward's administrator vs. Robert McClelland's heirs et al, Jefferson County (Ky) Circuit and Old Chancery Court cases #2012, filed away 1824, and #3221, filed away 1828.

The Jefferson County (Ky) Circuit Court case #1959, Daniel Wilson vs. Papers of John Gilly, exor. of James Pryor et al, was not filed away until July, 1827. This case specifically names the brothers and sisters of James Pryor and their heirs, to wit, John B. Gilly and his wife, Jane (Pryor) Gilly, Henry Oldham and Eliza (Pryor) Oldham, his wife, the children of Robert L. Pryor (Jane and Eliza Pryor), and the children of Robert McClelland (James and John McClelland). Did all of these people have the tradition of Indian blood? Yes. If for no other reason, they were all descendants of Nikitti through the Floyds.

Among the Shawnees, Delawares and Cherokees living in the Cooweescoowee District and appearing on the 1880 Cherokee census were C. M. (a white man, age 33), J. L. (a Cherokee woman, age 29), and Cherokee children J. F. (7), M. E. (5), and S. W. McClellan (4); also William (a white man, age 24), Rachel (a Cherokee woman, age 21), and Mary McClellan (listed as Cherokee, age 1). Ella McClellan is also on the census of this district, age and nativity not given. See JAIFR, vol. X, #2, p. 31.

McCORMICK, McCORMACK – a Shawnee name.

John and George McCormick traded with the Indians as early as the 1750s on the Pennsylvania/ Virginia borders.

Alexander McCormick lived among the Indians for some time before the Revolutionary War. He trading with the Indians at Ft. Pitt, then later at the Half King's village at Upper Sandusky.

This Alexander McCormick fell to the Indian

side when hostilities broke out. In the summer of 1780, he rode to Kentucky with the Indians in Byrd's expedition, and assisted in the capture of Ruddle's and Martin's Stations. About 1785, McCormick traded at the Maumee Rapids, married to Elizabeth Turner, an adopted white among the Shawnees. She seems to have been the white Shawnee named McCormick who was captured with some other women and children when Molunthy was killed. The women were taken and held near Danville. Mrs. McCormick was admired by the white settlers for her knowledge of herbal medicines and she is credited with saving the life of a white child there.

Mrs. McCormick and Rachel Kiser, the white wife of Captain Johnny, were asked to stay among the whites, but Mrs. McCormick said, "Do you not love your husband and children? Well, I feel the same way about mine." See Draper 13CC213. Draper interviewed McCormick's son in 1863. See 17S201.

The Indian trader and interpreter, John McCormick, paddled a dugout canoe to the Cherokee town of Tomotley in 1761. He carried Lt. Henry Timberlake and Sgt. Henry Sumpter on their peace mission to the Cherokees. McCormick apparently already was living with a Cherokee woman. In 1777, while talking peace again, "Big Bullet, half-breed son of one McCormick, an interpreter," was peaceably sitting down, mending his moccasins, when a white pioneer took advantage of his preoccupation and shot him. See Alderman, pp. 25, 54.

John McCormick was a member of George Owen's company at Ft. Jefferson, and some of the company were said to have had Indian wives. Tradition says, some of his family became Indian traders in Ohio and Indiana — at least that is what some McCormick descendants have told me. There is an Indian blood tradition among some branches of the family, but additional research needs to be done.

See Draper 17S201; 13CC135-43; Thwaites & Kellogg, Frontier Defense, p. 246. The best work on this family that I have yet seen is by Mrs. Catherine Eagle, "The McCormick Family, First Settlers of Indianapolis," *Indiana Magazine of History*, December, 1925, vol. 21, p. 311.

McCOY – Ginsey McCoy, "a cousin of Jeremiah Payne," was captured at the Pigeon Roast Massacre in southern Indiana during the War of 1812. Later she was discovered by her uncle, Rev. Issac McCoy, living as the wife of "a famed Indian chief." He persuaded her to come back and live among the whites for a while, but she became homesick, and shortly went back to the life to which she had become accustomed. Does anyone know what became of her or to whom she was married?

McCULLOUGH, McCULLY – a Delaware/Wyandot name.

Some of the family were captured and adopted by Delawares including John McCullough who lived among them for nine years at Muskingum. He was one of the "prisoners" forcibly delivered up to General Henry Bouquet in 1764, but he returned and eventually became an Indian trader on the frontiers. See Sipes, p. 474. Richard Butler used him as an interpreter to the Wyandots and Shawnees in 1775.

A grant for 640 acres on the west side of the Sandusky River was made by the Treaty of Miami of the Lake for the use of the seven "quarter-blood Wyandot" children of William McCullough. He had been employed as an interpreter during the War of 1812, was struck by a cannon ball at Ft. Meigs and killed. See Lang, p. 199. There were other McCulloch connections with Ohio's Wyandot families, most of them tracing to Tarhe, the Wyandot Half King usually referred to as the Crane.

Among the Delawares who moved to the Cherokee Nation in 1867 were Thomas, John, Jane, Hilas, Carrie, Lizzie, and Anderson McCollogh (McColloch, McCollough). See Prevost, p. 23.

McDANIEL(S) – a name among many tribes.

Robert McDaniels is on the list of those captured at Ruddle's and Martin's Stations in Kentucky in 1780. Perhaps he had children captured also, as James Trabue, one of those captured there, told later that the Indians sold the adults to the British, but kept the children to be adopted. There were McDaniels living near the Polke and Kinchloe Stations when they were burnt by Shawnees in 1782 and it is possible that some of the family were, along with George Ash, among the 32 people taken prisoner there and later adopted.

One of the Delawares who signed a treaty at Greenville, Ohio, in 1814 pledging not to go to war with the United States was named McDaniel.

Among the "chiefs of the mixed band" of Senecas and Shawnees signing the 1832 Treaty was Jemmy McDaniel. See Watson, pt. 2, p. 67.

Among the Shawnees who settled on the lands of the Cherokee nation by 1869 was John McDaniels. See JAIFR, vol. IV, #2, pp. 100-111.

John Ward, the white son of Bryant Ward, married Catherine McDaniels, "best known in her family as Katie. She was the 17-year-old daughter of a Scotchsman named McDaniel and his fullblood Cherokee wife called Granny Hopper." See Alderman, p. 27.

Watt McDaniel was living with three half-blood Cherokees on his farm in Chickamauga County, Tennessee in 1835.

McDONALD, McDONNELL – a Shawnee name.

Among the Shawnees given money for improvement on their Ohio lands were James McDonald and his wife, and George McDonald. Among the Shawnees signing the 1831 Treaty with the Senecas and Shawnees was James McDonnell who signed with his mark.

McDOUGAL – a Shawnee name.

I'm not yet certain how the name became Shawnee. A man named George McDougal was a young British soldier captured by Indians (at one time a captive of Pontiac). He later became an Indian trader and associated with the British traders at Detroit. The Ottawa were taken with him, and sold him land to live among them.

In the 1790s, a George McDougal was an Indian trader in Indiana and Ohio (as noted in The Andrews Journal; see Knoft), possibly the same man. If so, he quite possibly maintained a Shawnee family.

The Shawnee George McDougal (Squecaw-powee) witnessed several treaties. Henry Harvey wrote that in 1854 Joseph Parks, Blackhoof, and George McDougal (all roughly sixty years of age) were the only chiefs left of "the old stock" of Shawnees except for Letha who was "too infirm to tend to business."

At an 1854 council, there was a discussion of whether the Shawnees should adopt a constitution and white-styled laws. Chief Joseph Parks advocated it, then Blackhoof voiced his approval, and then George McDougal rose and spoke in favor of it, comparing the wandering hunting life with their present style of life patterned after the whites—farming on the reservation.

Harvey was there taking notes, and he wrote that McDougal "was very happy and eloquent, and mixed his comparisons with a good deal of wit. He said he had tried both places — that he liked the ways of the white men much the best; he liked not only the ways of the white people best, but he liked them the best anyhow, and if he knew he would live thirty years longer, that he would have a white wife if he could get one. This caused a great laugh among the Indians." See Harvey, pp. 286-287.

George McDougal was kidding, of course. The Shawnee Steward's book recorded the marriage of George McDougal to Ste-wi-ta-ni-ba on January 2, 1843. However, we do not yet know whether this was George McDougal's second marriage or merely the "christianizing" of an earlier Shawnee marriage.

Among the Shawnees who settled on the lands of the Cherokee nation by 1869 were Allen, Alwina, Fancy, and Polly McDougal. See JAIFR, vol. IV, #2, pp. 100-111.

McGILLIVRAY, McGILVERY, McGILBRAY – a Creek/Cherokee name.

"Of this whole south-eastern portion of the country a characteristic feature was, in the latter part of the eighteenth century, the residence of white traders in every large Indian town...At Fort Toulouse on the Coosa River, established by the French in 1714, Captain Marchand was at one time commander. He was killed there in 1722. He had taken as a wife a Muscogee or Creek maiden of the Clan of the Wind, called the most powerful clan of the Creek Nation. They had a beautiful daughter called Sehoy Marchand."

About 1735, Lachlan McGillivray came from Scotland, established himself in the Carolinas as a trader, and took young Sehoy Marchand — "cheerful in countenance, bewitching in looks, and graceful in form" — as his wife and had by her many children. The most noted of these was named Alexander McGillivray.

After being educated at Charlestown, Alexander McGillivray returned to the Creek Nation where he became a principal chief; he received a British commission during the American Revolution; in 1784, he made a treaty with Spain on behalf of the Creeks and Seminoles, and received a commission from Spain; in 1790, he made his peace with the Americans in New York and took a commission as brigadier-general. He was a wealthy man at the time of his death at Pensacola in 1793.

One of Alexander McGillivray's sisters was Sophia McGillivray who married the trader Benjamin Durant. Another sister married General Le Clerc Milfort, a literate Frenchman who lived among the Muscogees from 1776 to 1796 and later wrote a book about his experiences. Another sibling, a half-sister, married (1st) a British officer named Col. Tate of Fort Toulouse, and (2nd) the Indian trader William Weatherford.

The names McGillivray, Tate, and Weatherford are among the most common to be found in Creek Nation genealogies today.

Robert McGilvery was a half-breed living on the Tombigbee River in 1831. The register showed him having two children under 10 years of age. See Miss. Gen. Exchange, vol. 18, p. 12.

McINTOSH – a common source of the Indian blood tradition.

A white trader named McIntosh was trading at the Creek towns in 1726, and John and Alexander McIntosh were traders living among the Chickasaws as early as 1766.

Lachlan McIntosh, born in Scotland in 1725, came to Georgia in 1736 with his father, John Mohr McIntosh. Roderick and John McIntosh, cousins of John Mohr McIntosh, established a trading headquarters at McIntosh's Bluff, located on the Tombigbee River on land that is now a part of Alabama. Lachlan McIntosh was early on a colonial military leader and diplomat dealing with the Indians, and he especially endeared himself to the Cherokees. He was commissioned a brigadier general in 1776, but after a duel and the death of a political rival, Button Gwinnett, McIntosh was sent to the northern colonies.

Washington directed McIntosh to move through the Indian country with an army to take Detroit. As a prelude to this, he made a peace treaty with the Delawares, enlisting the aid of White Eyes and Killbuck. McIntosh commissioned White Eyes as a lieutenant colonel. Those who followed Capt. Pipe were unwilling to fight with the colonies against the British, despite the best efforts of Killbuck and White Eyes, who was proposing to McIntosh in the council that the Delaware Nation become the fourteenth state.

Archie McIntosh, born at Ft. William, Ontario, Canada in 1834, was the son of a part-Chippewa woman and a Scottish trapper. His father was ambushed on a canoe trip and killed. Sometime after this, his mother took Archie, his three younger brothers and his three younger sisters, to Scotland. Archie attended school for two years in Edinburgh, then returned to Vancouver where he became a clerk for the Hudson's Bay Company. In 1855, he became an army scout, and became associated with General George Crook, for whom he worked in Arizona as a captain of Indian scouts. Thereafter, McIntosh and his company of red scouts were involved in several campaigns, including the 1883 expedition into the Sierra Madre against Nana and Geronimo.

He settled down with his wife, a Chiricahua Apache woman, with whom he had a son, and he bought a ranch at Black Mesquite Springs. He died of cancer in 1902 and was buried near San Carlos. See O'Neal, pp. 164-166.

Donald McIntosh, a half-breed son of a Canadian and an Iroquois woman, was one of Gen. George Armstrong Custer's junior officers at the Little Big

Horn. One story says that the Sioux pulled him from his horse while trying to mount, and smashed his skull with a tomahawk. His mutilated remains were found after the battle and put in a box and for shipment to Arlington. His estate went to his widow. See Connell, pp. 20-21.

McKEE – a Shawnee name.

Thomas McKee was an Indian trader at the Big Island, on the South Branch of the Susquehanna River in 1742. His name is prominent in Indian affairs thereafter. He was a captain in the French and Indian War.

From David Jones Journal: "Wockachalli is Crooked Nose's place. Captain McKee's Indian relatives lived there...Here the people have the best horses in the Nation..."

A son of Thomas McKee by his Shawnee wife was Alexander McKee, who also engaged in the Indian trade. He went to the British side during the Revolution. He was, for a considerable time, in charge of British Indian Affairs. He died of lockjaw, January 13, 1799. See The John Askin Papers, vol. I, 301. Another son of Indian-trader Thomas McKee was James McKee, whose descendants continued to reside in Allegheny County, Pennsylvania — according to Hanna, p. 212.

Alexander McKee, part-Shawnee himself, also married a Shawnee woman and among their children was another Thomas McKee. This is the Thomas McKee who was given land by the Indians at the mouth of the Detroit River in 1785. In 1788, the Ojibwas and Ottawas granted him the lease of Pelee Island, Ontario. In 1794, in Indian dress, he fought in the attack on Fort Recovery against Anthony Wayne's forces. Two years later, he was made a Superintendent of Indian Affairs in Canada. He saw action in the War of 1812, but became increasingly dependant on alcohol. He died in 1814, leaving a wife and several children. His last wife was

Therese Askin, a part-Shawnee daughter of John Askin.

Among the Shawnees in Capt. Joseph Park's company who served in the Florida War was a "William McNee," and possibly McGee or McKee was meant.

Among the Shawnees and Wyandots who sold their Kansas lands was Mary McKee, age 15 in 1855; her entire allotment went to Sarah Kerr. See KHC, vol. 15, p. 169.

Some of the McKees appear to have intermarried with other tribes. Among the Choctaws given land by the Treaty of Dancing Rabbit Creek in 1830 was Alexander McKee.

McKINSEY, McKINZIE – a Shawnee name.

Daniel McKenzies was a member of Capt. William Oldham's Company of Kentuckians on the 1780 expedition against the Shawnees. He is listed on the pay abstract as "prisoner of the Indians." See MRGRC p. 72.

Among the Shawnees and Wyandots who sold their land in Kansas are listed Russell McKenzie (who sold out to Jacob Marshall and William Drake) and Livery B. McKenzie (who sold out to Landon Lyder and William Drake). See KHC, vol. 15, p. 168.

Listed among the Shawnees on the 1900 Federal Census were John A. McKenzie and his wife, Mayme. John McKenzie was a white man, born in North Carolina in 1865. Mayme was a Shawnee born in Kansas in 1874. She said that her mother was a Shawnee, and her father was born in Kentucky.

See also, KINZIE.

McLISH – a Chickasaw/Choctaw name.

John McLish was a half-breed who lived among the Chickasaws. He married one of Saleechee Colbert's daughters. See Miss. Hist. Collections, vol. 8, p. 568.

McNAIR – a Cherokee name.

Among the Shawnees given tracts of land in Ohio by the 1817 Treaty of the Miami of Like Erie was Thacaskka or David McNair. See Harvey, p. 166.

A David McNair was in Capt. Nathan Boone's company in 1812, and was said to have been along with the Shawnees in the Seminole War, but the name does not appear with companies of James Swannuck or Joseph Parks.

A David McNair also became a Cherokee chief and kept a stand at the south end of the portage on the Conasauga River near the present town of Couasauga, Tennessee. A traveler passing through the Cherokee Nation in 1829 came to "Mr. McNair's, a white man who married a Cherokee woman, sister of Mr. Joseph Vann, another Cherokee chief..." See Woodward, p. 155.

Nicholas B. McNair owned the ferry on the Hiawassee River in 1835 with his family of three quarterblood Cherokees.

Living among the Shawnees on the Cherokee Reserve in 1871 were William McNear, Virginia McNear, Nancy Jane McNear, and others of the family. See JAIFR, vol. IV, #2, p. 107.

Among the Shawnees, Delawares, and Cherokees living in the Cooweescoowee District and appearing on the 1880 Cherokee census were John (age 49), Kinney (24), T. B. (27), Rachel (23), Nellie (20), Susie (14), Mary (8), Lee (8) and Oscer (or Oscar) McNair (2). All of the McNairs in this district were listed as Cherokee except for a Columbus McNair (age not given) who probably was a mixed black/Cherokee. See JAIFR, vol. X, #2, p. 33.

McPHERSON – a Seneca/Cherokee name.

The McPherson family history is similar to that of the McNair family.

James McPherson was captured by Indians and adopted and he served as an agent and interpreter. During the years of his "captivity" he worked for the British Indian Department. He married a white woman who had been adopted. McPherson was also adopted and given the name, "Squa-la-ka-ke," meaning "the red-faced man." One of their daughters married Daniel Workman. See MOMV, Logan County, p. 175.

The 1831 treaty with the Senecas and Shawnees specified that James McPherson "at the request of the chiefs of the Senecas and Shawnees...who has lived among them and near them for forty years" be given 320 acres of land. The same number of acres was given to Henry H. McPherson, "an adopted son."

McPherson earlier served the United States at the Ft. Wayne agency in 1814. There is the story of how McPherson and Capt. Johnny teamed up to catch some horse thieves, told in Draper 24S114.

A James McPhearson, then "of Chicamauga, Georgia," took his family of six Cherokees west in 1828. See Baker, p. 36.

Among the Shawnees, Delawares, and Cherokees living in the Cooweescoowee District and appearing on the 1880 Cherokee census were Jack (age 45), Sarah (30), and Ulce McPherson (19), all Cherokees. Also listed are B. F. McPherson (age and nativity not given) and Elmira McPherson a black/Cherokee. See JAIFR, vol. X, #2, p. 33.

MAISONVILLE – a Miami/Shawnee name.

The Maisonville family resided among the Indians at the Ouittan village. Col. George Croghan visited the Ouittan (Wea) settlement in 1765 and noted in his journal: "...they are a mixture of all nations. The principal inhabitants are French intermarried with Indians, and pay little regard to religion or law..." See the 1765 Journal of George Croghan; see Hildreth, p. 112.

Alexis (Alexander) Maisonville was the commander at the Wea town, and he may have had a Miami wife. He was present at several Shawnee and Miami councils in first the French and then in the British interest. Pontiac held him captive. He attended a Shawnee council in 1767. See SWJ, vol. 5, pp. 686-687, 710; vol. 11, pp. 745, 795, 853. Toop Maisonville resided at Tippecanoe (Piconno) in 1790 when he signed a statement certifying the character of Antoine Lasselle. See Quaife, p. 41.

Francois Maisonville was "a creole" who served as "boatmaster" for the British forces in 1778. He may have been part-Miami and he served as a captain of a war party of Ottawas and Miamis in 1779. Col. George Rogers Clark had already taken Vincennes when Maisonville's party came in, and they surrendered to Clark without a shot. Clark ordered them all to be summarily tomahawked. Leonard Helm and some of the other men had no stomach for such butchery, and so Clark angrily said he would do it himself. While they were waiting their turn for execution, Sanscrainte was pulled off the bench and saved by his father, who was with Clark's forces, and Francois Maisonville was pulled off the bench by his sister.

Some of the Indians on the bench sang their death song while they waited. Clark "took a tomahawk, and in cool blood knocked their brains out, dipping his hands in their blood, rubbing it several times on his cheeks, yelping...An Indian chief of the name of Muckeydemonge, of the Ottawa nation, after Colonel Clark had struck the hatchet in his head, with his own hands drew the tomahawk presenting it again to the inhuman butcher, who repeated the stroke...."

Clark yielded to his men's protests and let Sanscrainte live, but Clark ordered his men again to scalp Francois Maisonville, and he was pinioned, halter on his neck, and tied to a gallows. After some of the people came out of the town and cut him down, he was still alive, so some of Clark's men scalped him and, still alive, threw him into the dungeon with British Governor James Hamilton, whom Clark had tried to make the scapegoat of the Revolution, accusing him of buying the scalps of white men.

After Lt. Leonard Helm and several of the other officers of the Illinois regiment voiced their protests over the treatment of these men, Clark let them release Francois Maisonville, but he kept Hamilton as his scapegoat. See Seineke, pp. 104, 144, 315, 320, 350, 355, 482, 546-547. Other collaborating accounts of this exist in Draper's manuscripts.

Afterward, Francois Maisonville resided near the Shawnees and took their side during all disputes. He married the Shawnee woman, Tecumapease, Tecumseh's sister. They resided in New Madrid for many years and raised a large family. She left her husband and went to Quebec. See Ohio Archeology and Historical Society Publications, vol. 25, p. 496.

MALOTT – a Delaware/Potawatomi name.

Some of the Malott family was captured while descending the Ohio River. Catherine Malott was captured by Delawares and adopted. In 1784, she married Simon Girty. She was said to have then been the prettiest woman to appear at Detroit.

Joseph Malott was also adopted and later served as an interpreter. He married Sarah Loulee Vieux, a mixed-blood Potawatomi. Their son, Jerome Malott, married Anna Bertrand, a mixed-blood Potawatomi and the daughter of Joseph H. Bertrand.

Denver Blevins, a white man, married Edna Gay Malott, a part-Potawatomi who descended from the Vieux, Malott, Bertrand, and Navarre families. Their son, Walter Blevins, married Georgia Kanouse. A son of Walter and Georgia, Cory Blevins, applied for tribal membership.

MARSHALL – a Delaware name.

A William Marshall is on the Detroit prisoner list, having been captured in Virginia in June, 1780. See McHenry, p. 24.

At Louisville in 1783, William Marshall and Barnabas Boyle were given money for their services as "spies" for the Illinois regiment at Louisville. These men had been sent as scouts into Indian country, north of the Ohio River. This may have been the same William Marshall who became an Indian trader. For some time, he resided in what is Miami County, Ohio, but after the War of 1812, he engaged in the Indian trade on lands that later became part of Madison County, Indiana. The John Tipton Papers are full of references to him. Marshall was accused of using his influence with the Delaware, Potawatomi, and Miami tribes against the best interests of the United States. It was also said that he sold barrels of whiskey in the Indian Country. See Tipton, III, index.

Moses R. Grinter (formerly of Kentucky), operator of the Delawares' Kansas river ferry, married Anna Marshall, half-Delaware daughter of Indian trader William Marshall. The marriage took place in Wyandotte County, Kansas, January, 1836. See Barry, p. 300.

Among the marriages recorded in Kansas in 1846 was that of the part-Delaware Polly Marshall who married part-Shawnee Henry Tiblow.

Among the Delawares listed on the 1880 Cherokee Nation Census and living in the Cooweecoowee District were W. H. Marshall, age 27, and his family which included Susan, 24, Ida M., 1, and Rosie Marshall, 28. See JAIFR, vol. X, #2, pp. 29-30.

Several members the Marshall family were captured over the duration of the frontier wars and some of their descendants have the Indian blood tradition. When diverse traditions from different parts of the country lead to one common source, I tend to believe in the tradition. For instance, there was Rev. Robert Marshall who was one of the "new lights" (see Draper 15CC25-29) associated with Rev. Arron Tullis, Rev. James Suggett, Rev. William Barbee, Rev. Joseph Coe, and others whose families had red connections. Rev. Robert Marshall's wife may have been the Elizabeth Marshall who lived in the Miami River Valley and whose will was probated April 17, 1834. She mentions her daughter, Sarah; her son-in-laws, William Barbee and Alexander McCullough; and her grandchildren, Martha Vinamon and Elizabeth Dye. The will was witnessed by John Tullis and Hugh McCorkle. Were there part-Indian connections here? That would be my bet.

MATTHEWS – a Seneca/Wyandot name.

Elijah Matthews was captured by the Senecas on Grave Creek. He was later adopted and married among them. See Kent and Deardorff, pp. 303-304. Among the Wyandots who signed the treaty to ratify the peace in 1819 was Matthews (Hawdounwaugh).

MAXWELL – a Wyandot/Shawnee name.

Maxwell family descendants living in Clark County, Ohio, share the Indian blood tradition and at least one of them is a member of the United Remnant band of Shawnees.

"Among the first to brave the dangers of pioneer life was James Maxwell, who was obliged to leave his home in Virginia to avoid prosecution for a murder of which he was subsequently proven innocent. He was a cousin of Col. Zane and it was to the Zane settlement he attempted to reach to find security; but such was not the case, as Zane ordered him to leave at once or he would himself convey him to Berkeley County, Virginia where the crime was said to be committed...."

Later, Ebenezer Zane recommended him to Capt.

Hamtramck as a scout for Fort Steuben. Zane said Maxwell's eye was keen, his step light. See Martzolff, p. 300. Thomas Maxwell of Chester County, Pennsylvania was James Maxwell's father; his mother was William Zane's sister. William Zane's son Issac Zane, sr. was captured when young by Wyandots and married the half-breed daughter of Tarhe, the Crane.

James "Soft-Stepper" Maxwell, his wife, Wild Rose, and their daughter, Sally, all lived for a time in a cabin at Ten Cabin Fort, sometimes called Maxwell's Fort, at what is now Clarksburg, West Virginia. One day they left their infant daughter in the care of Simon Schoolcraft and went to Fort Fincastle near Wheeling. They intended on staying for two days, but there was an alarm of an Indian breaking out, and so they hurried back to their cabin. They found the charred remains of Schoolcraft in the ashes of their cabin. Wild Rose thought that the baby was dead, and cut herself with a scalping knife in her grief.

Maxwell returned to Fort Fincastle and raised a tracking party, but a rain came and washed out the tracks. He became a frontier scout and was employed by Hamtramck and later by General Anthony Wayne. At the treaty of Greenville, Maxwell learned that his daughter, Sally, had not been killed when the cabin was burned, but was carried away and adopted by the Wyandots, by whom she was known as White Water Lily.

Sally Maxwell tried coming back to the whites but she missed her old life and soon went back to the Wyandots. She married a Canadian trader, and later returned to the Ohio Valley and talked with the Rev. Levi Shinn (son of Jonathan Shinn, founder of Shinnston, West Virginia), who recorded her history. A brief time after talking with Shinn, she married Burris Evans who became an early settler of Ohio. See Glenn Lough's Awhile Ago Times, vol. 1, #6, pp. 1-2.

James Maxwell married Hannah Poke in Jefferson County, Ohio, July 9, 1818. The Poke (Polk, Polke, Pogue) family is a major source of the Indian blood tradition in American genealogies.

MERANDA, MORANDA, MIRANDA, MIRANDY – a Shawnee name.

There is an Indian blood tradition among some of the Meranda descendants.

Issac Meranda was first licensed as an Indian trader at Conestoga in 1715. He died in 1732. His daughter married Pennsylvania Governor James Hamilton. See Engle's Notes and Queries, vii, 193.

Issac Miranda's son, George Meranda, was an Indian trader at Allegheny as early as 1736, but probably before that. George Miranda and Peter Chartier were the only two English names on the 1738 petition (in the Pennsylvania Colonial Records) which demanded that no more liquor be brought into Indian Country. See Pennsylvania Colonial Records, vol. IV, p. 88.

Moranda's Son is listed among the Indians who dealt with Indian trader John Owens in his accounts, along with The White Elk, Black Caesar, Bucksenutha and Hopping Anthony.

The Merandas were long associated with the Owens family and some of them accompanied the migration to Bracken County, Kentucky in the late 1790s and later went on to Scott County, Indiana. George Miranda, later of Warren County, Ohio, was a descendant. The family operated the Black Horse Tavern at the site of the old Shawnee town of Piqua.

MILLER – a Shawnee/Delaware/Miami name.

Christopher Miller, the famous scout, was a messenger and interpreter for the Shawnees. In 1782, Miller was one of the boys fishing in a pond near

Louisville when captured along with his brother, Adam Miller. Christopher Miller was adopted by the Shawnees, and Adam Miller by Delawares. See Draper 31J; Harvey, p. 115. Miller's own account later gave the location of their capture as on Wilson's Creek near the present border of Bullitt and Nelson County.

Henry Miller, another brother of Christopher Miller, had also been adopted by Miamis at one time, but returned to Kentucky. After William Wells switched sides and became captain of a band of Anthony Wayne's scouts, he enlisted Henry Miller. They then captured Christopher Miller and persuaded him to change sides. The Millers then became two of the core members of Wells' company, all of whom had to be able to pass for Indians.

One of these scouts, Charles Wells, swore under oath in his pension statement that in 1794 "I again entered the service in a company of spies...called out by Col. [Richard] Butler under the immediate command of Captain William Wells, Lieutenant Robert McClelland, and myself as ensign...started out as a spy expedition with only our company...

"We started from Louisville on the 10th day of July, 1795, with the same officers as before...We crossed the Ohio below the falls and took the nearest route to the Shawnee towns on the Maumee under the guidance of Wells and McClelland who knew the woods...passed three deserted villages...came across three squaws and two Indian boys whom we made prisoners and took to Cincinnati...

"...started out again to the waters of the Maumee and caught two Indian boys. On our return from this trip, we came across five tents full of Indian warriors, supposed to be between 60 and 80 [of them], just as the sun was setting. These tents from my knowledge...were a part of the tents taken by the Indians from St. Clair. They were pitched on a flat ground in the forks of a small stream and we came over the rise back of them and were very close before we discovered them...'

"About the same time, we discovered about thirty Indians rather in our rear coming to the tents...William Wells immediately approached a tent with a bunch of black feathers on it and an Indian came out and held a short conversation with William Wells but what it was I did not know then. When we got clear of the Indians we were informed that the one who talked asked William to light and come in. William replied to him that he had not time, he had a number of skins toward the Ohio and feared that the army of the whites would find and destroy them.

"He started off and we followed. When we had traveled about a mile, someone spoke and said he wished we had fired on the Indians. Without more ado the company lighted. McClellan proposed to go back and give them a fire. William Wells agreed to it. We left our horses and six men [behind] and returned on foot.

"We went up in five parties, and William Wells...approached the same tent as before and stated, as he afterwards told me, that he had returned for provisions to avoid shooting in the woods. In a few moments, the Indian became suspicious, told his men— as I understood — to get their guns, and our fire was made upon them immediately about dusk.

"The Indians returned our fire. I received a flesh wound in the thigh, William Wells had one bone of his right arm broken, McClelland was shot along the shoulder, and four others were slightly wounded. We retreated to our horses, mounted, and travelled all night pursued by the Indians and, on the next morning just as we were finishing crossing the Maumee, some of the Indians reached it. A few words passed between William Wells and them across the river and we continued our retreat and saw no more of them...

"In these last two expeditions as spies, our company was mounted, dressed, and painted as near like the Indians as we could..."

The deposition is signed by Charles Wells, sworn, May 7th, 1833, witnessed by Jabez Horn, a clergyman, Asa Manning, and Carty Wells, all of Mountgomery and St. Charles Counties, Missouri.

Christopher Miller married Mary Walls, a daughter of General George Walls, and the couple retired quietly to Hardin County, Kentucky. Later, in the War of 1812, he commanded a company. Charles A. Wickliffe, a private from Bardstown at the Battle of the Thames, claimed that he identified Tecumseh's dead body from information supplied from Christopher Miller, who knew Tecumseh well, having grown up with him. See Wickliffe, p. 45-49. It is too bad that Miller did not live to be interviewed by Shane or Draper.

Christopher Miller's sons included Christopher Wayne Miller, Isaiah Miller who married a sister of Governor John L. Helm, and James Warren Miller. His daughters were Margaret, Gilly Bethel, Kitty Ann Thomas, Sally Thomas, Elizabeth Moreland, and Maria Walls. Among Christopher Miller's grandchildren were Mary Miller, daughter of Isaiah , and Christopher Isaiah Bethel, daughter of Gilly. Among his great-granddaughters was Mrs. Amanda Miller Harris of LaRue County, Kentucky.

Miller was captured when he was fifteen and he spent eleven years living red. At the age of twenty-six, he might already have had mixed-blood children among the Indians at the time. Possibly. And although there were some members of the Miller family among the Shawnees and Delawares, the Miller surname became essentially a Miami name. Some of them went west, but a large number of them stayed in Indiana and intermarried with the main population.

Among the Delawares listed on the 1900 Census

of Indian Territory were Adam Miller, born 1867, and Mary Miller, born 1850. See Prevost, p. 51.

The proclamation made March 2, 1821, allotting money instead of land to individual Indians by their Commissioner Lewis Cass, essentially involved the Chippewa Nation, but there are names on the list that obviously belong to the Potawatomi and Ottawa and probably intermarried Shawnee and Miami as well. These names include Billy Caldwell and his children, Alexander Robinson and his children, Robert Forsyth "of St. Louis, Missouri," Mrs. Nancy Jamison and child, and Gabriel Godfroy. Also on the list is Margaret Hall, and James, William, David, and Sarah, children of Margaret Hall; and Margaret Ellen Miller, Montgomery Miller, and Finly Miller, grandchildren of Margaret Hall. See JAIFR, vol. XII, #3, 1991.

James Miller, a white businessman, and his Miami wife lived near Peru, Indiana. One of their daughters married a part-Miami named Joseph Winters. Miller and Winters have been two of the most prominent Miami names. See Winger, p. 79.

Joe Miller, an Indian, was living in Louisville in 1858. He stole a hat and was sentenced to serve some time in the workhouse.

Listed on the 1893 Miami Rolls was the family of Thomas Miller which included Louis, John, Esther, and George Woodson Miller.

MILLS – a Shawnee name.

Polly Adams, a Shawnee born in 1807, married the Mr. Dodge who served with the Shawnee Chief John Perry and Capt. Joseph Parks in the Seminole War. Their children included Eliza Jane Dodge (b. 1835, m. Abraham Mills) and Mary (b. circa 1840, m. Alonzo Summers).

After Mr. Dodge died in 1848 in the Shawnee Nation, Kansas, Polly married Mr. Buck, another

Shawnee who had been along on the Florida War adventure. They had at least one daughter, Polly Buck. Polly later became the last wife of the Shawnee subchief, George McDougal.

Abraham Mills was a white rancher; his brand was the double link. The children of Abraham and Eliza Jane (Dodge) Mills included:

1. Sarah Ann (b. 1859, m. 1st William Walton, 2nd Benjamin Rowe).
2. John Andrew Mills (b. 1861, m. Zelda Payton).
3. Frank Harvey Mills (b. 1864, m. Sarah Hunter).
4. Judson Graham Mills (b. 1867).
5. Louisy Alice (b. 1868).
6. Cyrus Bunt Mills (b. 1871, m. Florence Cinderella Bluejacket).
7. Benjamin Abraham Mills (b. 1874, m. Eliza Melcena Ray).
8. Mary Jane (b. 1875, m. Talbert Wheeler).
9. William Edward Mills (b. 1878, m. Mabel Bowers).
10. Samatha Daisy (b. 1881).

The children of Frank and Sarah (Hunter) Mills included William (b. 1890), Loyal Harrison (b. 1893), Auburn (b. 1896). Auburn Mills married 1st Faye Record, and their children included Edwin, Susan Faye, and Nadine Mills. Auburn married 2nd Della York.

The children of Cyrus Bunt and Cinderella (Bluejacket) Mills included Kenneth, David, Theodore, Tessie, Elsie May, Emma, Cyrus, Thomas, Robert, and Cinderella.

The children of Benjamin Abraham and Eliza (Ray) Mills included Waunetta Thelma Mills, born 1907. See SOCC, vol. I, pp. 233, 499-501.

MIRANDEAU – a Potawatomi name. See also MERANDA.

Early Milwaukee Indian trader Jean Baptist Mirandeau was probably of the same basic family as Issac Meranda. Whether he was or not, he took a wife from among the Indians. He had many half-breed children including his daughter Victoire who married Indian trader Joseph Porthier.

The family was associated with the McKinzie (or Kinzie) family. In 1833, John H. McKinzie was the trustee for the treaty funds allotted to the mixed-blood children Thomas Miranda, and for Rosetta, Jane, and Jean Baptiste Miranda. See JAIFR, vol. XII, #3, p. 37.

MITCHELL – a Shawnee name.

Abraham Mitchell was an Indian trader in the Monongahela River region who was living among the Indians in 1764. He was seen with a war party, and it was supposed that he led them in several attacks against frontier settlements. See Glenn Lough's AAT, vol 2, #11, p. 6.

A Capt. Mitchell and his son were both captured by Shawnees in 1788. Ridout speaks of them in his narrative.

Sarah Mitchell was captured in Kentucky in 1790 and spent five years among the Potawatomi. She was delivered up at Wayne's treaty and taken back to Springfield, Kentucky. See the article on Stith Thompson in the Louisville Courier-Journal, August 4, 1946.

MOFFET, MOFFITT, NOFAT, etc. – a Shawnee/ Wyandot name.

Two sons of Robert Moffitt — John, 11, and George, 9 — were out hunting for squirrels when they were captured by Indians. These Indians spoke good English and were not unfriendly. The boys were taken to St. Mary's where they ran a gauntlet, their hair was plucked leaving only scalplocks, and their adopted mothers washed the white out of them in the Miami

River.

After this, they "received the kindest treatment," and they took their place as future warriors of their nation. Over two years later, they fled with the Indians when, in 1782, George Rogers Clark's forces invaded and burnt Piqua. George Moffet was picked up by the militia, and later he was returned to his father. John Moffet continued with the Indians until "ransomed" through the efforts of Conrad Coleman and James Sherlock (see More, p. 98).

George Moffitt (whose Wyandot name was Kiterhoo) first settled in Guernsey County, and then came to Miami County and settled at the south end of Piqua, engaging in the Indian trade and farming. John Moffitt settled west of Piqua where he later died, outliving his brother George by several years.

John Moffitt spent his formative years, from eleven to seventeen, among the Indians. And both brothers, afterwards, chose to live near their Indian relatives. Did they have children who were part-red? Well, that's the tradition.

George Moffitt served as an interpreter at the Fort Wayne agency in 1814 (see Thornbrough, p. 215). He afterwards settled in Guernsey County, Ohio, and engaged in the Indian trade. Many of his descendants are yet in the Miami River valley. George Moffitt's 1831 will named his wife, Mary, and their children who included John, Margaret, Elizabeth, Laura, Catherine, and Jane Brown. He was supposed to have had seven daughters, so no doubt there were other children. See W. H. Beers, History of Miami County, Ohio, Chicago, 1880, pp. 243-245.

Among the Wyandots, there were some individuals who carried the Moffitt surname. This name was sometimes spelled as Mofat and Nofat.

Among the Wyandots on the 1843 Muster Roll were:

1. Nofat's family, consisting of one male 25 to 55, two females 10 to 25, and two males and two females under 10.
2. John Nofat's family, consisting of one male 25 to 55, one female 10 to 25, and four children under 10, three of them female.

In Kansas, the plat showing how the Wyandot land was divided in 1855 shows Susan Mofat receiving the land adjacent to John W. Greyeyes. Shortly thereafter, Susan Nofat married into the Punch family. See KHC, vol. 15, p. 160.

MOLUNTHA, MORUNTHA, MULANTHEE, etc. – a Shawnee name.

Moluntha — the name was spelled a dozen different ways — became a Shawnee chief. He was an advocate of peace, among the least war-like of all the Shawnee chiefs. Historians Joyce G. Williams and Jill E. Farrelly suggested (in their excellent Diplomacy on the Indiana-Ohio Frontier 1783-1791, p. 26n.) that Moluntha's more conciliatory views may have been biased because he was white, and they reference James Alton James.

Although Moluntha was the most pro-peace of Shawnee chiefs and certainly honored the treaty he signed, Benjamin Logan and his Kentuckians invaded Moluntha's town in 1786. The chief was all smiles, the flag of the United States flew over his cabin, and he made peace signs. Hugh McGary (who had led the Kentuckians into the Blue Licks ambush despite Daniel Boone's advice) rode up to the old chief and asked him, "Was you at Blue Licks?" The old chief may have misunderstood him, but nodded an acknowledgement, when McGary said, "Well, Goddamn you, I'll give you Blue Lick pay." He then brained the old chief with his tomahawk and coolly climbed off his horse and took his scalp.

James Alton James, in his *The Life of George Rogers Clark*, says that Moluntha was a white man who had spent years among the Shawnees. I have not yet found where James Alton James got this information, but there is much that I have not yet seen. If he was white, then he must have been with the Shawnees a long, long time.

I have not yet seen anyone — not even the great Allen W. Eckert — come up with a translation of the name. Could it be that Moluntha was an attempt to pronounce his white name? If so, what was his Shawnee name? I'll take a couple of guesses.

First, if the name Moluntha was a Shawnee name, my guess is that it translated as "the civilized man," a concept name not really given to a one word translation. You might think that "civilized" is exclusively a white man's concept, but t'aint so. The Shawnee had their own unwritten value system which recognized the difference between men of words and men of action. Their diplomats and peace chiefs were noted men of words, given to compromise. The war chiefs took over only when all diplomatic formalities had failed.

An early Conestoga chief who served as their ambassador and interpreter was named Capt. Civility. He appears by that name several times in the Pennsylvania Archives prior to the brutal massacre of his peaceful tribe by whites. The Civil surname was "risen up" and continued as a Mingo surname in Ohio. Civil John, his wife, and two sons were among those given money for the property they were forced to leave behind on their Ohio lands. In 1832, Civil John signed the treaty as the leading chief of the mixed band of Lewistown Shawnee/Senecas and his red name was transcribed as "Me-tho-mea." The Civil John family appears to have become the Littlejohn family in Kansas.

Anyway, I've stayed a bit off the track here, but

one other thing should be mentioned about this. Nonhelema was Cornstalk's sister and it was said that she became Moluntha's older wife. She was there when the old chief was murdered. Nonhelema had often served as interpreter, and in more peaceful circumstances, she gave the Shawnee translations of a number of words to Major Ebenezer Denny. He wrote them down in his journal. She told him the Shawnee word for "civil," and he transcribed it as "melooahee."

On the other hand, what if Moluntha, like Joshua Rennick or Francois Godfroy, was a white man adopted as a child, and perhaps to be more accommadating, he used only his white name when dealing with whitemen. If this is true, then what was the common pronunciation of his white name? Moranda, Matheney, Mirandy, Methoney, Marumphey? A lot of possibilities exist. A "J. Mullanphy" was paid a dollar a day for lodging the Lewistown Shawnee/Seneca Indians for 15 days while they were working out the move to Kansas in 1831. The following April, a John Mullanphy was paid for assisting the emigrating Indians. See Watson, vol. V, pt. 1, p. 20; pt. 2, p. 67; and pt. 3, p. 30.

If Moluntha had been white, why wouldn't people notice it?

They would not notice it for the same reason that they took no note of the whiteness of Bluejacket, Wryneck, Big Turtle, and every other white among the Shawnees who dressed, walked, talked, and had the general presence and dignity of Shawnees. Men such as John Ash and Simon Girty dressed as white men and were known as such. But if they had dressed as Indians, they'd have been taken for Indians. William Wells took a whole company of tanned and painted white men through the Shawnee country as spies. When Stephen Ruddle rode to Greenville and announced himself, in English, as Stephen Ruddle, the people with his father thought that he was lying because he looked too Indian. Many, many other examples could be cited. And half-breed Shawnees such as Peter Harper who dressed like white men were taken for white men.

Well, Moluntha dressed as a Shawnee and he probably spoke English with a Shawnee accent.

Since the Shawnees had so much trouble with the "R" sound — usually substituting an "L" for the "R" — perhaps he was kin to George and James Meranda (often pronounced Merana or Mirandy), who are among the Indian traders whose descendants carry an Indian blood tradition. George Meranda lived so long among the Shawnees that he must have had a family among them, and a "Moranda's son" who was with the Indians and dealt with trader John Owens in 1756. James Meranda lived on the south branch of Ten Mile Creek near the Owens and McClellands and may have had some of his family captured and adopted. Just a wild guess here, a shot in the dark — this is still a mystery to me. If you know how Moluntha may have been white, please send me the information with your sources. I crave only light.

MONOQUE, MONAGUE, MENOUCOU, etc. – a Wyandot name.

Monocue was a preacher at the Wyandot mission in Ohio prior to War of 1812. He is described as "a man of great eloquence, a cheerful and ready worker." The histories of Wyandot County, Ohio carry a wood engraving of his likeness which shows him as a handsome, intelligent-looking man.

Among the Indians who signed a treaty at Greenville, Ohio, in 1814 pledging not to go to war with the United States was Menoucou, a Wyandot.

Among the Wyandots who signed the ratification of the peace treaty in 1819 was Thomas Manocue.

That Thomas Monocue was a literate man is shown by the following letter that he wrote in 1830 from Upper Sandusky, Ohio, to the Rev. J. B. Finley:

"One of our young men was killed by another about two or three weeks ago. The murdered was John Barnet's half-brother, the murderer, Soo-de-nooks, the Black Chief's son. The sentence of the chiefs was the perpetual banishment of the murderer and the confiscation of all his property. When the sentence was made known to the nation, there was a general dissatisfaction, and the sentence of the chiefs was set aside by the nation. On Thursday morning, about daylight, he was arrested and brought before the nation assembled, and his case was tried by all of the men (that vote) over the age of twenty-one, whether he should live or die. The votes were counted, and there were 112 in favor of his death, and twelve in favor of his living. Sentence of death was accordingly passed against him..."

Monocue said that a firing squad of six men was chosen from among the Wyandots, including Francis Cotter, Lump-on-the-head, and Silas Armstrong, and on the second Friday the convicted murderer was shot. "The execution was conducted in Indian military style; and we hope it will be a great warning to others, and be a means of preventing such crimes hereafter." See HWC, pp. 295-296.

MONTOUR – a Mohawk name.

Madame Montour, as she was called, was the grandmother of the notorious Queen Esther Montour. Born about 1684, Madame Montour was the daughter of a frenchman named Montour and an Indian woman. She was captured and adopted by the Iroquois (probably Mohawk) in childhood, she grew up Iroquois and married an Oneida chief named Robert Hunter or Carondowanna (Big Tree). Madame Montour was active in tribal affairs and sometimes served as interpreter.

Madame Montour's husband, Big Tree, was slain in a battle with the Catawbas, and John and Thomas Penn sent her a message of sympathy upon learning of his death. Among their children were French Margarette, Henry, and Andrew Montour. All three served Pennsylvania as guides and interpreters at various times.

Andrew Montour (Sattelihu) was a frontier scout (a la James Fennimore Cooper's Hawkeye) and he commanded a company of Indians and mix-bloods during the Beaver wars and during Pontiac's War. Usually, he was on the side of the English, at least when it coincided with his own best interests.

Andrew Montour seems to have been an excellent man, not without a sense of humor. He may also have liked his liquor. At a serious council, the Beaver asked George Croghan to renew the sale of rum to the Indians, inasmuch as hostilities had ceased and that the Delawares ought to be able to purchase it again, as "they loved it." Montour, who had been interpreting, broke the formalities and spoke up, saying that he loved it too, and "he thanked ye Beaver King for his speech, which made ye Indians laugh so hearty that some of ye young men could hardly stop." See "James Kenny's Journal 1758-1759," Pa. Mag. of Biog. & Hist., vol. 37, p. 429.

One of the Montour's — Schaaf says Andrew Montour — killed Silverheels in 1770. John Montour, "half-white, half-Indian," attended a council in 1777 at Ft. Pitt along with Cornstalk, the McKees, White Eyes, the White Mingo, Kayashuta, and Logan; and John Montour was active in the intrigues of 1778; See Seineke, p. 13, 197.

The Montours have intermarried with other tribes and the name is now fairly common. Among the Delawares who signed a treaty at Greenville, Ohio, in 1814 pledging not to go to war with the United States was Montgomery Montawe (Montour). Among the Delawares who signed the 1819 treaty at the Miami was Billy Montour (Hawdoronwatistie). Among the Shawnees and Wyandots who sold their Kansas lands was Mary Monture. See KHC, vol. 15, p. 169.

Gilbert C. Monture, a Mohawk and a direct descendent of Joseph Brandt, was "the son of a sailor turned hard luck farmer," and the family had to struggle to survive. Nonetheless, Monture persevered and made it to college where his studies were interrupted by World War I. Although he enlisted as a gunner, he later became a commissioned officer in the Royal Canadian Engineers. After the war, he became one of the foremost authorities in mining and metallurgy and had an illustrious career, working for NATO and the United Nations and traveling the world. He married Elva Leona Penwardem of Cobourg, Ontario, and their children included Barbara Ann (Mrs. A. E. Malloch). See Gridley, pp. 101-103.

Art Montour, who is associated with the Mohawk Warrior Society, was a principal player in the violence that shook the Mohawk Nation in 1989. Rick Hornung, who wrote an excellent account of "the Mohawk Civil War," says that Montour prefers his tribal name, Kakwirakeron, meaning "many branches on the ground." Proud of his heritage, Montour rejected the white-styled governmental regulation of the Six Nations. He advocated a return to the long-house traditional government, with the Iroquois leaders enforcing tribal laws with their own police.

MUDEATER – a Seneca/Wyandot name.

The first Mud Eater of whom I find record is Gaustarax (Oscotax, Austerex, etc.), a Seneca, for years the chief of the Genesee River band. He signed the treaty selling the Susquehanna lands to Pennsylvania but later, perhaps feeling duped and deceived, he bitterly opposed the white settlements as they moved west thereafter. One source says that it was Gaustarax who led the red forces against General Henry Bouquet at the Battle of Bushy Run. Another contemporary source compared the influence of Gaustarax with that of Pontiac.

In 1765, William Johnson wrote that "Gaustarax, one of the Seneca hostages now here, is not only the chief of that nation, but may be considered as the most leading man of any...I have accounts of his having very great influence as far as the Illinois...."

I think that Gaustarax was perhaps the first Wyandot Half King, a product of a Seneca/Huron mating. At another council, an Onondaga chief told Johnson "that the nephew of the chief man of the Hurons named Aghstahregck [Gaustarax] being killed in the battle at Niagara in 1759, the Hurons had last winter sent a party towards Virginia to revenge his death" with some Shawnees.

The Mud Eater name may have been associated with the Mud Turtle Clan. And the name evoked a legend; it was "a concept name," a name to be "risen up" after the death of Gaustarax, possibly being bestowed on a newborn nephew or on a white adoptee to replace the fallen chief. A returned captive told of "a son of Gaastrix" being with James Sherlock and the hostile Senecas and Delawares in 1764. See SWJ, vol. 3, p. 699; vol. 4, p. 496, 748.

Among the Indians whose names appear on the ledger of Indian-traders Richard and Samuel McClure in the early 1800's were General Mud Eater and his son, Young Mud Eater. The McClures characterized General Mud Eater as "one of the greatest warriors in the Wyandot Nation" and they noted that the Mudeaters had become extension farmers. See Lewis, p. 239.

"The Walker, Hicks, Zane, Armstrong, and Mudeater families were all founded by captives who were adopted into the tribe." See "Methodist Missions Among the Indians in Kansas," Kansas Historical Collections, vol. 9, p. 213.

Among the guardianship cases reviewed by the Commissioner of Indian Affairs in 1871 was the case of Matthew Mudeater, a Wyandot, guardian for the Cherloes, Coons, John Whitewing, Jacob Hooper, among others. See JAIFR, vol. VIII, #2, p. 17. Chief Matthew Mudeater was a distinguished, intelligent-looking individual. For his picture, see Tooker, p. 404.

Listed among the Wyandots in 1880 was the family of Benjamin Mudeater (age 52), including Duane Mudeater (18), Gertrude Mudeater Wadsworth (18), and a Mudeater child (age 7) whose name is not given. Also listed among the Mudeaters are Alfred (age 48) and Julia (age 38), living with Irvine (53) and Julia Mudeater (7).

Among the Wyandots listed on the 1900 Federal Census of Indian Territory were Alfred Mudeater, born 1853 in Kansas. His father was born in Canada, and his mother was born in Ohio. His wife, Julia Mudeater, was also a Wyandot. His sister-in-law, Lena E. Robitaille, also lived in the household.

Also listed was Benjamin Mudeater, born in Kansas in 1851, his father born in Ohio among the Wyandots. His wife, Sidney Mudeater, was a white woman whose father was born in Virginia. See Prevost, p. 83.

NAVARRE– a Potawatomi name.

Peter Navarre was an early settler of Michigan who married a Potawatomi woman. He was an Indian trader, an agent of the American Fur Company in 1820, and the Draper manuscripts contain some of his lively recollections about those with whom he dealt. He and his family lived for some time in St. Joseph County, Indiana.

NEWCOMB, NEWCOME – a Delaware name.

Among those Delawares who joined the Cherokee Nation in 1867 was Thomas Newcomb, age 44, born in Kansas. His father was a Stockbridge (Mohican), born in New York. His mother was a Delaware. He was also known as Hamilton Newcomb. Also listed is Mary Newcomb Nairn, who was probably his sister. Mary had married Dr. William Nairn. See Prevost, p. 38.

Joseph Newcomb, age 19, a Delaware, is listed on the 1880 Cherokee Nation census as living in the Saline District. See JAIFR, vol. VI, #2, p. 33.

NEWMAN – a Delaware name.

John Newman was a Delaware "born in Virginia about 1845," and he died in Indiana in 1939. When he came to Indiana, he married Jane Bunday, the widow of Coon Bonday (Bundy), a part-Miami. She was a cousin to the Miami chief, Me-shin-go-me-sia. By her first husband, she already had three children whose names were George, William, and Mary Bunday. By John Newman, she had Benjamin, Martha, Eliza, and Walter Newman. Many of their descendants live in Indiana today. See Winger, pp. 64-65.

NICHOLS, NICKELS, or NICHOLAS – an Oneida/Mingo/Delaware/Shawnee name.

"Big Nichols of Oneida" sent two belts of wampum through the Six Nations to the Senecas urging a continuation of Pontiac's War. He was said to be in league with the Seneca renegade, Cut the Pumpkin (Squash Cutter), the ring leader of the irreconcilables in 1764. Cut the Pumpkin surrendered, they gave him blankets from the small pox hospital, and he shortly died. But I have not seen where Big Nichols surrendered. Perhaps he went to the Ohio country with the White Mingo. See SWJ Papers, vol. 11, p. 75.

Perhaps, too, like several Oneidas, Senecas, and Cayugas, he became associated with John Logan's Mingo band. A Nickels lived among the remnants of Logan's tribe in Seneca County, Ohio. Lang said, "Billy Dowdee, known as Capt. Billy, was a fellow scalper of old Tom Lyons, but an extra good Indian after the War of 1812. His son, Tom, and his son-in-law, Nickels, were two of the worst characters in the Wyandot country, the peers of Pumpkin of the Senecas. Nickels was killed by one of the settlers of Wyandot county, much to the satisfaction of his father-in-law." See Lang, pp. 216-217.

Well, perhaps Nickels had children, or perhaps his name was just "risen up." It seems clear that the Delaware whom came to be known as Big Nigger was actually named Big Nichols. He was one of the Delaware free hunters, but I believe that he was possibly Delaware, part Iroquois and part black.

Ruxton said: "Amongst the hunters on the upper Arkansas were four Delaware Indians, the remnant of a band who had been trapping for several seasons in the mountains and many of them had been killed by hostile Indians, or in warfare with the Apaches while in the employ of the states of New Mexico and Chihuahua. Their names were Jim Dickie, Jim Swannick,

Little Beaver, and Big Nigger. The last had married a squaw from the Taos Pueblo and happening to be in New Mexico with his spouse at the time of the late rising against the Americans, he very naturally took part with the people by whom he had been adopted. In the attack on the Indian Pueblo, it was said that Big Nigger particularly distinguished himself, calling by name to several mountain men who were amongst the attacking party and inviting them near enough to `throw them in their tracks....'

It was said "that the Delaware killed nearly all who fell on the side of the Americans, his squaw loading his rifle and encouraging him in the fight. By some means or another he escaped after the capture of the Pueblo."

In Henry L. Carter's excellent "Jim Swanock and the Delaware Hunters," he says the core of Jim Swannock's brave band of roving free hunters consisted of Little Beaver, Jim Dickey, and Big Nigger These men refused to be tied down by reservation life. Because of their savy and love of freedom, they earned the respect and admiration of all the trappers, the soldiers, and the other tribes with whom they had contact.

Big Nichols (whom the traders referred to as Big Nigger) probably was born in 1823 in Ohio. He probably trapped and traded as widely as James Swannock, which means he went from the lands of the Puebloes to the land of the Blackfeet and Nez Perce and all points in-between.

Carter says, " 'Big Nigger' appears as an entry in John Brown's account book under date of December 28, 1846. Apparently the Delawares did some trading at Brown's post on Greenhorn Creek. From here Big Nigger went to Taos. where he was reported to have a wife among the women of Taos Pueblo. When he arrived there the Taos Rebellion against American occupation of New Mexico was already being fomented and when it broke out on January 20, 1847, he threw in his lot with his wife's people. On February 3, the American forces under Colonel Sterling Price and a volunteer company of Mountain Men under Ceran St. Vrain attacked Taos but were repulsed, with the loss of Captain Burgwin who led the attack. Big Nigger was a conspicuous leader among the rebels. Next day, when the attack was renewed, Big Nigger was one of those who stubbornly defended themselves in the adobe church. He was finally killed in a back room of the church to which he had retreated for his last heroic but unavailing stand against overwhelming odds.

"So spectacular was the fight he put up that the legend arose that he had escaped to the Wet Mountain Valley, a favorite hunting ground of the Delaware trappers, where he was said to have lived as an outlaw. There is no reason to believe this tale but its existence is a tribute to a valiant fighter, who died after such desperate resistance that people were reluctant to believe that he was gone."

Carter says in a footnote, "For two contemporary accounts of Big Nigger's outstanding part in this battle, see George F. Ruxton, Adventures in Mexico and the Rocky Mountains...Garrard visited the church after it was stormed and says that Big Nigger's body had thirty bullets in it. Garrard is uniformly more trustworthy than Ruxton and there is not the slightest reason to distrust his account. If Big Nigger had survived it seems likely that his name would have appeared in Barclay's diary after this date. It does not, although the other Delaware hunters continue to be mentioned. However, Ruxton's statement that, during the fight, Big Nigger called by name to the Mountain Men whom he knew, daring them to come near enough for him to shoot them in their tracks has the ring of truth."

Well, after reading this, I thought it possible that Big Nichols escaped. The reason he no longer appeared in the trader's logbooks around Tao was, it seemed to me, that he went back to live in the Delaware Reservation in Kansas.

Sometime after I finished the above, historian Rodney Staab sent me yet another version of the Big Nichols story. It is, I think, an interesting account — a remarkable lesson in history.

It seems to me now, barring further revelations, that we have the truth about Big Nichols. Here is the story:

Capt. James Swannuck left home with three other free hunters in 1844 to trap in the mountains around Taos. The others in his band were, as Carter pointed out, Jim Dickie, Little Beaver, and Big Nichols, whom the traders referred to as "Big Nigger," and whose Delaware name was En-di-ond, "Where-he-was-seen."

In February or March of 1847, they were trapping in the mountains about two days travel from Taos. Big Nichols told the other trappers that he was making a trip into Taos to get some bread-stuff and whiskey. When he arrived at Taos, he stopped at the house of a Pueblo and was invited inside. A crowd of Pueblos came into the house and demanded to know why Big Nichols was there. Big Nichols, who spoke a little spanish and "tolerably good English," explained his purpose, but the Pueblos were rebelling against the authorities of the United States, and accused Big Nichols of being a spy.

They stripped Big Nichols of his guns and knives, took him to an adobe house, and put him under guard. After keeping him there a few days, they came and told him that they had already fought the whites one time, and that the whites were on their way to the town to fight them again. They offered him his life if he would join them in the upcoming battle. Big Nichols agreed to fight, and the guard brought him his gun.

Soon after, the white troops came in sight, and

Big Nichols kept his word and fought with the Puebloes until the whites stormed the church, and then Big Nichols and the Puebloes concealed themselves in the adobe buildings.

The Puebloes then decided to give up and make peace, but they did not know how to talk to the whites. Big Nichols told them if they made a white flag and walked out under it, the whites would not shoot them. They sent two women out with the flag first, and the men followed. Big Nichols stayed behind, hidden in the upper story of a large house.

In the lower story of the house that Big Nichols was hiding in, there was a big whiskey barrel where the white men came every day to drink, and Big Nichols observed their coming and going. His thirst got the best of him at last, and he asked for a drink. Two white men told him to come on down and get some whiskey. He came down. The white men said, "You are no Pueblo. Who are you?" He told them, and they informed their officers of his presence.

His old Pueblo guard came to Big Nichols, warning him to make his escape as the officers had been overheard talking about him, that they were planning on doing "something bad to him." The guard brought Big Nichols his gun and he escaped in the night.

Big Nichols rode his horse hard, two days and two nights. He found the other Delawares, and told them what had happened. They gave him some extra gun powder and advised him to go back to the Delaware reservation. So Big Nichols started home.

After he got over the mountains and near the road, he fell in with a band of Cheyennes whose camp was adjacent to that of a Commanche village. The Cheyenne treated him as a friend and gave him plenty to eat. Big Nichols stayed among them for several weeks, letting his horse recover.

A few days before Big Nichols was to continue his journey home, some Spanish traders came with corn flour and goods to trade with the Cheyennes and Commanches. They called a council and invited Big Nichols to attend. When the council convened, the Spanish traders told the chiefs that they wanted them to kill every white American they could find and to take and destroy everything they had. The traders detailed the battles that had taken place between the Puebloes and the white Americans, and told them that there was one remarkable Delaware among the Pueblo at the battle and that he had killed thirty white Americans himself. The Cheyennes laughed and said maybe this is the same man who is now with us.

In a few days, a Mexican captain came and called the Cheyennes and Commanches to council again, but this time the Cheyennes would not permit Big Nichols to attend, possibly for his own safety. When he left, the Cheyennes told him of an Arapaho camp, and advised him to call on them on his way home, where he would be welcomed. After riding some time, Big Nichols rode into the Arapaho camp. As the Cheyennes had said, they were friendly and treated him well, and so he lingered there, letting his horse graze and recuperate a few days.

After starting again for the Delaware reservation, he came upon some Cheyennes and Commanches who were preparing for war upon the white Americans. They detained him, as they were afraid he would warn them of their plans. But finally they let him go and he returned to the Delawares and related this story to the chiefs, who related it to their Indian agent, Richard W. Cummins, who wrote an account of it to Major Thomas H. Harvey, the Superintendent of Indian Affairs at St. Louis.

See William A. Goff, "What Happened to En-Di-Ond?", Westport (Mo.) Historical Quarterly, vol. 10,

March, 1975, pp. 109-116; Harvey L. Carter, The Mountain Men and the Fur Trade of the Far West, ed. LeRoy R. Hafen, Arthur H. Clark, Glendale, California, 1972, vol. VII, "Jim Swannock," p. 297.

Big Nichols (Big Nigger) became one of the councilors to Chief Neconhecond of the wolf clan of the Delawares along with John Sarcoxie, Jim Simond, Big Raccoon, and George Washington.

In 1860, disgusted with their Kansas reservation, the leading Delawares, including Big Nichols, signed a letter to the Cherokees requesting to buy land from them or to join their nation and settle among them. The Cherokees agreed, and accordingly Big Nichols and his family moved to the Cooweescoowee District of the Cherokee Nation around 1867.

"Big Nigger or Big Nichols" appears on the non-dated list of Delawares appearing in the JAIFR, vol. VI, #1, p. 51. A Big Nichols appears on the 1867 list of Delawares admitted to Cherokee citizenship. A John Nichols appears on a list of schoolboys at the Delaware Baptist Mission School.

Weslager's The Delaware Indians contains pictures of the Delaware leaders including John Sarcoxie, Colonel Jackson, Big Nichols, and others. In one of the pictures (p. 409) is a Willie Nicholas who, I suspect, is Willie Nichols, Big Nichol's son.

See Carter, pp. 295-298; Weslager, pp. 408-409, 511.

A William N. Nicholas (age 34) is among the Delawares in 1867. See Prevost, p. 38. Among the Delawares living in the Cooweescoowee District and appearing on the 1880 Cherokee census was Big Nichols (age 57) and his family which included Nancy (55), and Sarah Nichols (18). See JAIFR, vol. X, #2, p. 37.

Of course, Big Nichols wife may have been Shawnee. A William Nichols appears on the 1900 census, listed as a Shawnee born in 1863 in Kansas. His mother was born in Kansas, but his father was born in Ohio. Mary Nichols, his wife, was born Kansas, and she and Willie P. Stand (William Nichols' step-son) are also listed as Shawnees. See Prevost, p. 73.

NICHOLSON or NICHOLAS – a Seneca name.

Joseph and Thomas Nicholson, brothers, were among the white people delivered up to Bouquet in 1764 and like the Carpenters, Owens's, and others, they both became hunters, guides and served as interpreters.

Joseph Nicholson had been adopted by the Senecas; he was one of George Washington's guides and interpreters during his 1770 trip down the Ohio.

In 1772, the Rev. David Jones went to the Pickaway town by himself, a bit uneasy about being alone and not speaking Shawnee, "but my anxiety was soon removed by seeing Mr. Nicholas, with whom I was acquainted at Ft. Pitt. He received me very kindly, and entertained me with such refreshments as the situation afforded." See Jones, p. 266.

During Dunmore's War in 1774, Joseph Nicholson and David Owens were the guides for Major Angus McDonald's expedition.

The whites "attacked the Upper Shawnee Town, destroyed their corn fields, burnt their cabins, took three scalps, and made one prisoner." They then went to Wapatomica where they had a skirmish with some Indians, killed two, one of them a Delaware. The Indians fled into the Snakes' Town; the whites followed, stopping on the opposite side of the river from the town.

Joseph Nicholson called to the Indians that he wanted to talk, that he belonged to the Six Nations. The Indians called back, asking for Simon Girty, but Nicholson told them that Girty was at Ft. Pitt. The Indians then sent out four Indians over for a council and Major McDonald ordered his men not to molest them. It appears that the truce was broken by the whites, one of whom fired across the river and killed an Indian while the council was taking place.

Major McDonald ordered them to go get two white women who were among them and bring them back; however, none of them returned but one, an Onondaga, and without the women.

The whites then attacked the town, destroyed all the corn left standing and all the stores. See Thwaites, Dunmore's War, p. 152-155. Draper 3D5-11.

Thomas Nicholson also served as a guide in Dunmore's War in 1774 and in Crawford's disastrous expedition in 1782. He later was said to have resided in Pittsburgh. After Lewis Wetzel murdered White Eyes, Thomas Nicholson was appointed to inventory the chief's estate.

Joseph Nicholson, then of Pittsburgh, served as an interpreter for General Anthony Wayne.

A Thomas Nicholson was the name of an early settler of Guernsey County, Ohio among such other names as George Moffitt, James Sharlock, John Leith, and others who possibly had Indian connections.

See Williams, p. 393; George Washington's Journal, Pennsylvania Archives, Series 2, vol. XIV, p. 705; Thwaites and Kellogg's Dunmore's War, p. 13-14.

NIPP – a Shawnee name.

Among the Shawnees who settled on the lands of the Cherokee nation by 1869 were Joseph sr., Joseph jr., Emile, and Franklin Nipp. See JAIFR, vol. IV, #2, pp. 100-111.

NORTHRUP, NORTHROP, NORTHCUT, etc. – a Wyandot name.

Northrop was a white Indian trader who married a Wyandot. Among the Wyandots allotted land in

Kansas in 1855 were Hiram M., Margaret, Milton, Andrew, Thomas, and McHenry Northrup.

Among the Wyandot guardianship cases reviewed by the Commissioner of Indian Affairs in 1871 was the case of H. M. Northrup, an "intermarried citizen," then living in New York City.

Northrup's wards included Abraham Arms, Abraham Williams, John H. Standingstone, Sarah J. Washington, John Bigtree, James Menture (Montour), Amos Cotter (J. H. Cotter was a brother), Mary S. Williams, Sarah and Mary Collier, William and Henry Coon (children of Sarah Coon), and Eli, Leslie, and William Zane.

Northrup was related to Arms, as well as to his ward Charlotte Clarke who was then (in 1871) living with her husband near Lafayette, Indiana. See JAIFR, vol. VIII,#2, p. 17.

NORTON – a Cherokee/Wyandot name.

John Norton was a son of a British Army officer and a Cherokee woman. He spent his early years among the Iroquois, but was sent to England to receive a formal education. He became a highly literate man, and although I have not yet seen his journal, historian Bil Gilbert says that it reflects his quick mind and sense of irony.

In the 1790s, he was in Ohio country where he made friends with some of the Shawnees and sided with them against General Anthony Wayne's forces. His jounral of 1810 concerns observations on Tecumseh and Stephen Ruddle, who was then trying to convert the Shawnee to Christianity. See Gilbert, pp. 252-253, 281.

Among the Wyandots allotted land in Kansas in 1855 were Henry C. and Hannah Norton.

NUGENT – a Wyandot name.

A Nugent family moved to southern Indiana territory and engaged in the Indian trade there. One of the Nugent women was supposedly mistress to the notorious Peter Smith for awhile. One of the Nugent men married Rachel Williams, a daughter of the part-Wyandot Issac Williams and was allotted land by the treaty in Ohio in 1816. See Prevost, p. 2.

OWENS – a Seneca/Shawnee/Delaware name.

John Owens was one of the first Indian traders to establish a trading post west of the Allegheny Mountains. His trading post appears on the earliest maps of the Monongahela area.

He or his son, John Owens jr., served as a guide for Gen. Forbes and Gen. Bouquet during their military campaigns in the area. For the duration of Pontiac's War, he moved his trading headquarters to Ft. Pitt. In the 1760s, James Kenny noted in his journal that John Owens arrived at his trading post with a company of Shawnees.

John Owens had an Indian wife. She was a daughter of the chief Tanacharisson. Variously spelled, his name was supposed to mean "this side of the sky." The man was a Seneca, and he became chief of all the western Iroquois in the Ohio lands. The English called him "the Half King."

Both the French and the English vied for the Half King's allegiance; but despite the man's weakness for French brandy, this chief remained as true to the English as the eastern Iroquois. Joncaire, the French ambassador, referred to him as "hardheaded" and "more English than the English." The French commander ordered that the Half King be killed in such a way that the French would not be implicated in the murder.

Tanacharisson was noted for his diplomacy, although the he was sometimes reported as being too drunk to attend council. He could be an eloquent speaker. He is supposed to have said to George Washington, "The English claim all the land on one side of the Ohio; the French claim all the land on the other side. Where lies the Indians' land?"

Some accounts say that it was the Half King who

tomahawked the French ambassador Jumonville in a skirmish that sparked the opening of the French and Indian War. The French blamed George Washington for "the assassination of Jumonville."

According to a report brought by the Indian trader John Davidson to Conrad Weiser, "Col. Washington and the Half King differed much in judgement, and on the Colonel's refusing to take his advice, the Indians separated from the English. After which the Indians discovered the French in a hollow and hid themselves, lying on their bellies behind a hill. Afterwards, they discovered Col. Washington on the opposite side of the hollow in the gray of the morning, and when the English came out of their cover and closed with the French, they [the Indians] killed [some of] them with their tomahawks, on which the [remainder of the] French surrendered."

George Washington, then a young man, underestimated both the loyalty and the tactical sense of the Half King, and probably this was the cause of his defeat later at Ft. Necessity. The old European style of meeting the enemy face-to-face in lined ranks did not appeal to the Indians. Many deserted the Half King and the English after this defeat of the larger English force by a token force of French and Indians.

In September, 1754, Conrad Weiser reported in his journal that "Tanacharisson, otherwise known as the Half King, complained very much of the behavior of Colonel Washington to him, tho' in a very moderate way, saying that he was a good-natured man but had no experience, and saying that he took upon himself to command the Indians as slaves, and would have them every day upon the Out Scout and attack the enemy by themselves, and that he would by no means take advice from the Indians; that he lay at one place from one full moon to the other and made no fortifications at all but that little thing upon the Meadow [Ft. Necessity] where he thought the French would come up to him in the open field; that had he taken the Half King's advice and made such fortifications as that Half King advised him to make, he would have certainly beat the French off; that the French acted as Great Cowards but the English acted as Fools in that engagement; that he (the Half King) had carried off his wife and children as did other Indians before the battle began, because Colonel Washington would never listen to them, but was always driving them on to fight be his directions."

The Half King signed a treaty at Aughwick shortly thereafter. Conrad Weiser reports that the white people present were the Indian traders Andrew Montour, Peter Sheffer, George Croghan, Hugh Crawford, Thomas Simpson, and John Owens. A fortification was built there that they named Ft. Shirley, at the end of Owens Hill. This is where Queen Alliquipa and some of the other "friendly Indians" came to spend their last days. John Owens owned the land and it was later mentioned specifically the will of John Owens jr.

Within a month after the conference at Aughwick, on October 4th, 1754, the Half King died.

The Indians blamed the French for his death "by bewitching him, as they had a Conjurer to inquire into the cause [of his illness] a few days before he died, and it is his opinion, together with his relations, that the French have been the cause of the great man's death" It was generally assumed by the colonists that the Half King had been poisoned, perhaps with rotgut whiskey.

After Washington's defeat and the death of the Half King, the Shawnees and Delawares totally went over to the French side, along with most of the western Iroquois. Monacatoocha, possibly the son of Tanacharisson's sister, became known as the new Half King and he was able to persuade some of the Indians to fight on the English side during Braddock's campaign in 1755. But when Braddock insulted the Indians, all of them ran off except Monacatoocha, Silver Heels, Old Belt, Hendrick, Kanuksusy, Johnny (Tanacharisson's son), White Thunder, and possibly the White Mingo. And then when Braddock hardheadedly used the same tactics as Washington, he was defeated by a much smaller French and Indian force. George Croghan later said, "But I am yet of the opinion that if we had fifty Indians instead of eight, we might have prevented...our unhappy defeat." And the defeat had consequences. The Indians who had previously been loyal or neutral despaired, and many went to the other side.

Monacatoocha (the Sky) was discredited among the Indians after Braddock's defeat, and like Silverheels and Johnny, he served as an express rider and messenger. Eventually, he went to Ohio with the other Mingoes, but not as a chief. Tanacharisson's son Johnny was "very much disgusted" at his not being more particularly noticed and rewarded for his services as a scout and an express rider. The two leading chiefs of the western branch of the Iroquois nations were the Old Belt and the White Mingo, but they could not agree upon a successor to the title of "Half King." The Delawares and Shawnees, who formerly had been guided by their "uncles" the Iroquois, rejected all former alliances. The White Mingo was rumored to be taking his band across the Ohio to join the French.

On July 22nd, 1756, commissary James Young wrote from Carlisle that "Last Monday two Indian squaws that were at Fort Shirley went off with one of our men, a fellow that had formerly been an Indian trader; the squaws are the daughters of the Half King that was killed last winter. I fear that fellow may be of bad consequence, as he knows our situation well."

Another letter of the day, quoted by Benjamin Franklin's Pennsylvania Gazette, stated that "the Indian wife of John Owen and another Indian woman have left Fort Shirley, and it is imagined are gone to the Ohio with one McLure, a soldier, who has deserted."

Things looked bleak for the English until General Henry Bouquet took command, and then the tide was turned. For the duration of the war, most of the Indian traders resorted to working for the army, either as soldiers, in the commissary, or as interpreters or guides. In July of 1761, the French were having difficulty supplying the Indians and some of them began to sue for peace. One band of Indians sent a message to Pennsylvania Governor James Hamilton requesting a council; the note was composed by "the King of the Six Nations," but written and signed by David Owens.

This David Owens was the son of John Owens, the Indian trader. David Owens was living red, just one of the many white renegades, half-breeds, and runaway servants among them. "John Owens' son" appears as an entry in the Indian trader account books along with other whites living red including Meranda's son, Indian Davis, Phillip Phillips, James Sherlock, Bill Hickman, and others.

On March 26th, 1764, James McCallister wrote that a war party that had ravaged the Pennsylvania frontier the previous week. On the preceding Tuesday, "came a lad to my post at the fort with an account that the Indians had surrounded the house of one Adam Simms...we ran to the place being five miles distant and found the house in flames and the enemy fled...this being near night, dark and raining...we could not march in quest of the enemy 'ill next morning...before day we discovered the house of John Stuart in flames...'"

McCallister was joined by the companies of Capt. William Piper and Capt. Brady, and together "...when we had light we took the tracks of the enemy and pursued toward the Path Valley — nigh which we met some people fleeing who informed us the enemy was gone past that place, and burnt a barn belonging to one

Walker...at our return we found there James McCammons house in flames [set fire by a portion of the war party who remained white the main body went on with the prisoners who included the wife of John Davis and one child, two of John Mitchell's children and a son of Adam Simms, all of whom]...may be preserved to enlarge the savage tribes..."

The Indians were followed "to Sidling hill and...by their dividing into small parties and keeping on the hard and stony ledges" the trail was lost and the pursuit ended. McCallister also reported the account of a man sent from Littleton to Aughwick to give notice of the Indian alarm. He alerted them of the danger, and on the trip back, they camped at the Black Log. In the middle of the night, the messenger awoke suddenly in the middle of the night to find the Indians tomahawking his companions. "He says he saw an Indian strike old John Owens, heard a great uproar, but as he was at the remotest part of their encampment, he made his escape."

Perhaps David Owens, living among the Delawares, received word that his father had been scalped, or perhaps he even saw his father's scalp and recognized it as such. If so, my guess is, it must have had a profound effect upon him. The following month, in the latter part of April, 1764, David Owens appeared in Philadelphia with five scalps. Governor John Penn gave him a traveling pass and sent him to Bouquet with a sealed letter which identified Owens as a man who "was not much to be trusted." Penn wrote, "Owens takes five scalps with him, of which he will tell his own story."

Sir William Johnson wrote Governor Penn on June 18th that "David Owens was a corporeal in Capt. McClean's Company, and lay once in garrison at my house. He deserted several times, as I am informed, and went to live among the Delawares and Shawnees with whose language he was acquainted, his father having been long a trader amongst them. The circumstances relating to his leaving the Indians have been told me by several Indians — that he went out hunting with his Indian wife and several of her relations, most of whom, with his wife, he killed and scalped while they slept. As he was always much attached to the Indians, I fancy he began to fear he was unsafe amongst them, and killed them rather to make his peace with the English than from any dislike either to them or their principles." Another letter to Sir William Johnson identified two of his Munsee Delaware brothers-in-law (possibly the Night Walker and Dead Knocker) whom he killed while they slept.

Robert Robinson, who had been captured by the Indians, later told the following story: "At this time, Bouquet went down the Ohio seventy-five miles below Ft. Pitt, and sent one David Owens, who had been married to an Indian woman, and had by her three children, when, taking a thought that he would advance himself, killed and scalped his wife and children and brought their scalps to Philadelphia. He received no reward, only was made ambassador between General Bouquet and the Indians.

"When Owens was sent to let the Indians know they might have peace, they made a prisoner of him for the murder he had committed, two of his wife's brothers being there. Owens gave them to know, if they killed him they would never have peace. The Indians held council three days upon him. The then let him go, and came up themselves, agreeable to the invitation which was sent to them, and agreed to give up the prisoners. So ended that campaign."

Robinson's account differs from the official account which appears in the Pennsylvania Colonial Records, vol. IX, p. 222-223. In this account, dated November 6th, 1764, Bouquet sent Owens and Turtle

Heart to the Shawnees to find out if they were coming to surrender. Owens returned the next day and said that the Shawnees would arrive with their prisoners on the ninth.

Beaver, chief of the Delawares, requested that an interpreter be sent with Killbuck and the other Delaware deputies to Ft. Pitt to negotiate terms of peace.

General Bouquet told him to name the one he wanted.

Beaver replied, "As Owens speaks our language so well and is accustomed to the woods, we should be glad if he could accompany them."

"They shall have them," Bouquet promised.

It was a part of the truce agreement that the tribes would submit hostages that would be held until all whites, whether adopted or not, and all deserters, French, and blacks among the Indians could be rounded up and handed over.

Most, if not all, of the Delaware hostages were whites who had been adopted into the tribe. They were Mondeaticker (William Davis), Mendies or Noondias (Andrew Trump), Simon Girty, and Steel.

Early in 1765, General Thomas Gage wrote to Sir William Johnson concerning the Delaware hostages: "The Indians have used the same delays in coming to Ft. Pitt as they have to you...There seems to be something hatching amongst them. Two of the Delaware hostages desired on some account to go to Fort Bedford, who have been no more heard of. It was apprehended they had been killed, but it is said from Ft. Pitt that they went home, having been terrified by Owens the interpreter, who is now with you. This fellow, it seems, in a drunken frolic, acquainted the hostages that we intend to murder them."

The Shawnee hostages were Red Hawk, Cornstalk, Wakeeampa, Ewickunwee, and Neighthakeina.

On December 19th, 1764, Samuel Wharton wrote Benjamin Franklin, "I am sorry to inform you that the Shawnee hostages have run off from Ft. Pitt...What renders the defection of the Shawnees the more alarming is, that Bouquet sent some Canada Indians [Iroquois] with one Owens (the person who appeared before the Commissioners and claimed the reward for scalping so many Indians) to invite the hostages to return to Fort Pitt, when unfortunately some difference arose between one of them and this Owens, who immediately took up his rifle and shot him dead upon the spot..."

You might think that this would create a lasting feud between David Owens and the Shawnees and Delawares. But he continued to be associated with them, living amongst them and serving as interpreter. White Eyes and Killbuck spoke well of him and recommended him as an interpreter. If they forgave him, his reputation was not good among white Americans.

David Owens afterwards was Rev. David Jones interpreter in 1772 and the next year was a scout for the whites in Dunmore's War. Owens commanded a company under Major Agnus McDonald. In Philadelphia in 1775, David Owens was arrested and jailed "on suspicion of enlisting Negroes," it being illegal to arm blacks, or reds who looked like blacks, even in times of war. And the Revolution was brewing. David Owens was shortly afterwards a captain of militia in the Revolution, but lost his command to William Harrod, perhaps due to the lingering shade of his reputation. A group of his men petitioned to have him reinstated as their commander, but this did not happen.

Owens was George Rogers Clark's interpreter and guided him on his first trip down the Ohio River. Later he accompanied Clark's army from the falls, and when Ft. Jefferson (and the adjacent town of Clarksville) was built at the junction of the Ohio and Mississippi

Rivers, he went there with his half-brother George Owens as well as some other members of the family.

Leckey says that George Owens probably lived with David near Ft. Jackson on Ten Mile Creek, and one account tells of him killing two Indians who had chased Corbus Lincecum into the fort. George Owens commanded a company of forty-four men in defense of Ft. Jefferson. Magee, in her excellent history of the fort (p. 30), says "another tradition that is often told in the Purchase area is that a number of soldiers at Fort Jefferson married Indian maidens."

English says of the Battle of Fort Jefferson, that "finally the Indians made a desperate night assault on the fort, but were entrapped into a position within reach of the musket balls. This had been planted by Captain George Owens in a place unsuspected by the Indians, and was fired when they were crowded together in close range of the gun. The carnage was terrific, and the survivors withdrew in hot haste...'

"Captain George Owens, a native of Pennsylvania, and the chief actor in this slaughter of the Indians, came to a sad end a few years later, and the savages had a terrible revenge. They captured him near the falls of the Ohio, in what is now Indiana, as he was hunting, or attempting to pass between the falls and Vincennes, and, after torturing him in the most frightful manner, finally burned him to death at the stake at or near the Wea towns...

"It is said he himself had some Indian blood in his veins. His descendants settled in Scott County, Indiana. The author knew them intimately, and when a young man heard Captain Owens' sons, George and Thomas, then old men, speak of these events.

"Abednego Owens, who died in Scott county in 1894 at an advanced age, and Thomas Owens, who moved to Texas many years before that, were grandsons of this historic Captain George Owens, and there were other grandchildren whose names are not remembered."

A letter of George Rogers Clark notes that George Owens was burnt at the Wea towns in 1789. Up until that time both George and David Owens continued to serve in the capacity of interpreters, scouts, and express riders. Bland Ballard told the Rev. John Shane that these men were half-brothers, and he should have known. James Ballard's pension statement lists service in George Owens company of Indian spies in 1782 before Ballard was at Floyd's Defeat.

George Owens's brother, John Owens jr., had inherited the land at Aughwick (old Ft. Shirley which had been built at the foot of Owens Hill) and other tracts of land elsewhere, but he was living near present Waynesburg in 1781. In the spring of that year, he was out making maple sugar with some of his neighbors and their sons, and they were waylaid by Indians. John Owens was among those killed. There are several specific accounts, each one different, but as I write this, the best evidence suggests that Capt. Pipe commanded the war party.

It was John Owens jr. that James Kenny saw among the Shawnees, and Kenny recorded their conversation. The will of John Owens, jr. was probated April 6, 1781. He mentions his aged mother and names as his heirs his wife Susannah (Hannah) and sons David and John. There were then guardians appointed for his minor children and the records of Bracken County, Kentucky, show that there were others who went back to Washington County to share in the final settlement of his estate. His children included David, John, Vincent, George, Mary, James, Sarah, Judith, and Hannah. Sarah married Richard Gragston and Hannah married Thomas Broshears.

David Owens continued to serve as a messenger and interpreter at Clasksville, Indiana, where he died of natural causes near the turn of the century. Some believe that he married a sister of the Rev. David Jones, and it appears that he had at least two sons and perhaps some daughters as well. Most of the family of the old Indian trader's son, John Owens jr., went to Bracken County, Kentucky for a while, and then some of them went on to Scott County, Indiana where they joined the families of George and David Owens.

Hannah Owens, one of the younger daughters of John Owens, jr., married Thomas Broshears who served in the Revolution at Ft. Jackson on Ten Mile Creek in Pennsylvania, and later became a tavern-keeper at Augusta, Kentucky. After arriving in Bracken County, Kentucky, Thomas Broshears gave his power of attorney to his brother-in-law, James Owens to recover anything "which may be due...from the estate of John Owens," in right of his wife, Hannah, a final settlement of the estate being due when the children reached maturity.

The children of Thomas and Hannah (Owens) Broshears included:

1. William Broshears, b. 1797.
2. Judith Susan Broshears, b. 1802, who m. Clement Bradshaw.
3. Sarah (Sally) Broshears, b. in 1803, who m. James Owens, apparently her cousin.
4. Owens Broshears, b. 1804.
2. Nancy Broshears, who m. Joseph Lord.
3. Elizabeth Broshears, who married John Meranda who also may have had Indian blood.
6. George Washington Broshears who m. Susanna Craig.

The children of Clement and Judith Susan (Broshears) Bradshaw included:

1. Hannah Bradshaw who m. William Augustus Howe.
2. John Bradshaw.

3. William Augustus Bradshaw
4. Amanda Jane Bradshaw
5. Elizabeth S Bradshaw who m. William Beeker in 1839.
6. Sarah C. Bradshaw.

The James Owens who married Sarah (Sally) Broshears moved to Jackson County, Indiana, and their children included David R. Owens (1808-1877) who married Sarah Blount in 1828. The children of David and Sarah Owens included David L. Owens, b. 1849.

Some of the Owens family with their relations—Broshears, Bradshaws, Merandas, and others—later moved to Ohio and some, including Owens Broshears, John Owens Meranda, and Thomas Broshears, also later moved to Scott County, Indiana. Their descendants have spread across the country, taking the Indian blood tradition along with them.

Thomas Owens, who served in the War of 1812, was among those who moved to Scott County, Indiana. One of his sons, Abednago Owens is mentioned above. One of Abednago's sons was Andrew J. Owens (b. 1838). He married Sarah E. Jackson, daughter of John L. Jackson, in Ripley County, Indiana. Their children included Andrew, William, Jesse, Sarah, John M., A. C., Emmet, Lena R., Perarl, and Iva Owens.

For sources, see Owens.

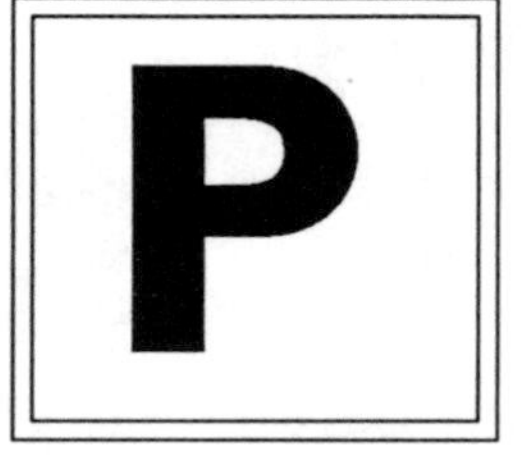

PARKS – a Shawnee name.

On the Ohio frontier, Nancy Parks, and perhaps others of her family, were captured by Indians. See Thompson, *History of Brown County, Ohio*, p. 74.

There was a Parks family of Indian traders in southern Indiana in the early 1800s, and also a William Parks who was an Indian trader at Detroit.

Joseph Parks was educated in the home of General Lewis Cass. Cass knew him well. Sometime after Joseph Parks had gone west with the Shawnees, he came back to Washington, D. C., as interpreter, along with a delegation of his tribe. One day the Shawnees set in the gallery to view a legislative body at work. From the floor, Gen. Cass delivered a speech in which he referred to Parks "as a white man who had been captured and raised by his adopted people," and pointed him out in the gallery as well as a son of Blackhoof and a son of Captain Tommy (meaning Spybuck).See Draper 3YY49 which contains "Witherell's Reminiscences."

Among the Shawnees given tracts of land in Ohio by the 1817 Treaty of the Miami of Like Erie was Lawnoetucha or Billy Parks and Joseph Parks. See Harvey, pp. 167-168.

"At the request of the chiefs, there is granted to Joseph Parks, a quarter blood Shawnee, one section of land to include his present improvements at the old town near Wapaghkonnetta, in consideration of his constant friendship and many valuable services." The services included being interpreter at the treaty for which this was Article XIII.

William Parks was a farmer among the Shawnees and Joseph Parks became the interpreter for the tribe and he led them west and eventually became head chief. See Harvey, pp. 226, 246, 281-282.

Joseph Parks (under Chief John Perry) was a leader of a company of Delaware and Shawnee scouts who went to Florida to assist Zachary Taylor against the Seminoles. William Parks was also in the company.

After the death of Chief Francis, Joseph Parks became the first Shawnee chief elected by popular vote in a white-styled election.

The Shawnee Charles Tucker told Draper that Capt. Joseph Parks' Shawnee name was Pa-sah-tah-kah-ka (he who runs against something). See Draper 23S175.

According to Caldwell, Joseph Parks was a remarkably large and athletic man. He died April 3rd, 1859.

Among the Shawnee guardianship cases heard in 1871 by Ely Parker, Commissioner of Indian Affairs, was the case of Joseph Parks, deceased, to divide up money and land from his estate. One daughter was living in the Cherokee Nation. A granddaughter married a man named Swatzell and lived in Wyandotte County, Kansas, near Westport, Missouri. Another granddaughter was the wife of Joseph Kilpatrick (or Fitzpatrick). Parks left land in Johnson County, Kansas. See JAIFR, vol. VIII, #2, p. 25.

When Draper passed through the Shawnee reservation in 1868, he interviewed a granddaughter of Capt. Joseph Parks whom he identified as Mrs. Rebecca Rogers Fitzpatrick, the daughter of Sally Parks Rogers. Her sister was Catherine Rogers Swatzell. See Draper 23S206.

Among the Shawnees living among on the Cherokee Reserve in 1871 were Joseph, John, and Mary Parks. See JAIFR, vol. IV, #2, p. 107.

Among the Delawares, Shawnees, and Cherokees living in the Cooweescoowee District of the Cherokee Nation were eleven members of the Parks family, as they appeared on the 1880 census. They were J. B. (age

34), Caroline (33), John (18), Mary (16), J. F. (7), George (6), James (4), and D. W. B. Parks (10 months), all listed as Delawares. Samuel (30), Clara (22), and S. P. Parks (19) were listed as Cherokees. See JAIFR, vol. X, #3, p. 8.

PARIS or PARISH – a Shawnee/Cherokee name.

Robert Paris was among the Indian traders at Ft. Pitt in 1761. Robert and Richard Paris are frequently referred to in the colonial documents. According to the Pa. Mag. of Hist. & Biog., vol 2, p. 471: In 1757, Paris brought a number of Cherokee and Catawba Indians to Pennsylvania.

Parish was a Kickapoo chief who had a village at what became Parish Grove near Earl Park, Benton County, Indiana. See Allison, p. 290.

Among the Cherokees on the original tribal roll was Robert Parris who was residing on the Chatahoochee River at the time. In 1819, George Parris of Georgia was added to the Cherokee rolls.

Among the Shawnees who settled on the lands of the Cherokee nation by 1869 were Issac, Virginia, Aeerith, Penola, Oren, Nancy J., Catterson, George, Georgiana, and Mary E. Parrish. See JAIFR, vol. IV, #2, pp. 100-111.

Virginia Parish, a Shawnee, married George S. Ford, a white man, in the Cherokee nation on October 10, 1881.

Among the Shawnees listed on the 1900 Federal Census of Indian Territory was Samuel Parish, born 1869 in Kansas. Her father was a white man, his mother a Shawnee. His wife, Adda Parish, was listed as a Shawnee born in 1875. Both of her parents were Shawnees born in Kentucky. See Prevost, p. 73.

PASCHAL or PASKELL – a Shawnee/Delaware/Peoria name.

Among the students attending the Ft. Leavenworth Shawnee Indian School in 1841 was John

Paschal, a Peoria.

Among the Shawnees who settled on the lands of the Cherokee nation by 1869 was "the Widow Pashal." See JAIFR, vol. IV, #2, pp. 100-111.

Among the Delawares living in the Cooweescoowee District and appearing on the 1880 Cherokee census were John Paskell, 38, and Lizzie Paskell, 30. See JAIFR, vol. X, #3, p. 8.

PATTERSON – a Mohawk/Delaware name.

Michael Patterson was captured in Virginia in 1756 and was among the captives delivered up to Bouquet in 1764.

David Patterson was a Mohawk and principle chief under Joseph Brant in 1794. See American State Papers, Indian Affairs, vol. 1, p. 529.

William Patterson was on the preliminary list of people killed by the Indians in Pontiac's War, being taken at Cross Creek by White Eyes' cousin. However, some on the list, such as John Gibson, were taken prisoner by White Eyes and held under protective custody until after the war. This seems to have been the case with William Patterson.

This was probably the same William Patterson who was a Delaware (or possibly an adopted-white or half-breed) living at the Moravian Mission on White River in Indiana. He may have been the same man as Capt. Patterson, a Delaware chief whose sister became the second wife of half-white Chief William Anderson. At the death of Chief Anderson, William Patterson (Me-shaw-quo-wha) became chief of the Delaware Nation. See Cranor, pp. 4, 11, 13, 14, 19, 39, 40.

PATTEN, PATTON – a Shawnee/Delaware name.

For one reason or another, the Patton/Patten surnames often carry with them a tradition of Indian blood.

A James Patton was a Pennsylvania Indian trader, captured during the French and Indian War but ordered released by Tanacharisson at a council at Logstown. He seems to have continued in the Indian trade.

A James Patten, captured about 1791 on the Muskingum, spent four years among the Shawnees and Delawares and was delivered up in 1795. See Knoft, p. 67.

PAYNE – a Shawnee name.

Among the Shawnees who settled on the lands of the Cherokee nation by 1869 were Henry and Mary Payne. See JAIFR, vol. IV, #2, pp. 100-111.

PEACOCK – a Seneca/Wyandot name.

Among the Wyandots allotted land in Kansas in 1855 were George, Granville, Boyd, Sarah, Rosannah, Moses (age 41), Daniel (age 38), James (age 18), and Samuel Peacock.

Among the Wyandots who sold their land in Kansas was Issac Peacock, jr. See KHC, vol. 15, pp. 122, 169.

Moses Peacock died in 1857 or 1858, his heirs including his sister, Mary Kayrahoo, and the children of his brother, Matthew Peacock, who were named as Amelia Browning (Charlow), Elizabeth Peacock, Mary Bearskin (wife of Peter Bearskin), Rebecca Hicks (wife of James Hicks), and George and Issac Peacock.

Margaret B. Peacock died in 1859 and named as her heirs her father, Dr. Whitetree, but mentioned also her half-brother, Thomas Monacue.

PECAN – a Shawnee name.

Among the Shawnees who appeared on the 1880 Cherokee census of the Cooweescoowee District were John (age 30), Nancy (25), and Lizzie Pecan (10). See

JAIFR, vol. X, #3, p. 9.

PEEPYS – a Delaware name.

Joseph Peepys was an adopted Delaware who traveled with the Night Walker's band of Indians in 1761. His wife's name was Hannah. He often served as a messenger and interpreter.

He spoke for the Night Walker at a Council on August 8, 1861, he spoke in front of Pennsylvania Governor James Hamilton and others:

"...Years ago, our Brother, General [Sir William] Johnson, moved the Council Fire from Albany to his own house, where he said to us: 'I am one-half Indian and one-half English'...he had kindled the Fire ...he took up a tomahawk, gave it to them, and told them that he was going to war against the French, and desired them to join with him, and promised them, that after the French were all conquered, trade should be made open and free to them, and all kinds of goods should become more cheap, and that furs and skins should bear a good price...as General Johnson has not performed his promise to us, we see death coming upon us, and the God above knows that he has wronged us..."

Joseph Peepys was a Monravian convert, and when Rev. David Jones, a Baptist, went to Killbuck's Town in 1773, he would not employ Peepys as interpreter. The two men did not agree on Christian ideology and Killbuck told him that Joseph would not interpret his words correctly but would instead preach from his own heart. Jones wrote in his journal that the Monravians "taught their Indians to disregard others" and he lamented the absence of his other interpreter, David Owens, who had gone to the Wabash with White Eyes.

PELTIER – a Miami/Potawatomi/Osage/Sioux name.

A James Peltier was with Byrd's expedition against Ruddle's Station in Kentucky in 1780.

James Peltier was an interpreter at the Ft. Wayne Agency in 1814; he had taken a wife among the Miamis.

Joseph Peltier was present during the siege of Chicago, an Indian trader. His wife was Victoire Mirandeau, one of the half-breed daughters of Indian trader Jean Baptist Mirandeau of Milwaukee.

The Peltier family was prominent in Peter Matthiessen's tale of Indian/FBI confrontations, In the Spirit of Crazy Horse. Leonard Peltier and Robert Robideau were principle players in the events chronicled by book. Leonard Peltier was the son of Leo and Alvina (Robideau) Peltier. According to the book, Leonard Peltier said that his maternal grandmother was "full-blooded Sioux" and that his father was "three-quarters Objibwa, one-quarter French." "Free Leonard Peltier!" has become an AIM battle cry.

PERRY – a Shawnee name.

John Perry was one of Johnny Logan's band of Shawnee scouts during the War of 1812. He may have been in the shootout with the Potawatomis when Johnny Logan was killed. After Capt. Chieska took command of the scout band, John Perry continued to serve the United States.

Among the Shawnees given tracts of land in Ohio by the 1817 Treaty of the Miami of Like Erie were John Perry (Lollaway) and William Perry (Kayketchheka). See Harvey, pp. 166-167.

William Perry, the first sub-chief, preceded Chief John Perry to Kansas, arriving there in 1828 in the company of Cornstalk (Nern-pe-nes-he-quah, see under CORNSTALK) and the Prophet. See Barry, p. 153, who quotes Rev. Issac McCoy.

Peter Pitchlynn, the mixed-blood Choctaw, also

noted in his diary that the Choctaws, who were traveling west, were visited by Perry, Cornstalk, and the Prophet in November, 1828:

"Perry is a stoutly built personage having a very determined countenance. His dress was simple, consisting of a hunting shirt, cotton leggings, and moccasins of dressed deer skins, handkerchief round his head. The Cornstalk is taller than the Prophet or Perry and of a more serious cast...

"Perry first rose and spoke for some length of time. He was glad, he said, that we did not pass his nation as strangers...He then spoke some time of the former interviews they had with our forefathers, and that it seemed the Great Spirit had ordered it so that we should meet again and take each other by the hand. After he had ended his speech, he presented to each of the delegations white beads and tobacco as a renewer of our old friendship." See Pitchlynn, pp. 66-67.

In 1832, about half of the main body of Ohio Shawnees from the Hog Creek and Wapakonetta bands arrived in Kansas. About half dropped out along the way, but many of these came to Kansas the following year.

On the 1832 Muster Roll of Shawnees, Chief John Perry is listed with a family of six: one male and one female 25-50, one female 10-25, and three boys under 10 years of age. See Roy, p. 40.

John Perry was the head chief of the Shawnee delegation to Washington along with Clearwater (Wayweleapy), Blackhoof (Quasky), Spybuck, and their interpreters Frances Duchequate and Joseph Parks. See Harvey, pp. 188, 208.

Chief John Perry and Capt. Joseph Parks led a company of Shawnees in the Florida War against the Seminoles. They talked Chief Alligator's band into surrendering, but after the Seminole leaders were betrayed by the whites and hostilities were resumed, the

Shawnees refused to fight. They were never paid for their service in the war. There is more discussion of the Shawnee participation in the conflict elsewhere in this work.

The treaty of 1833 was signed by John Perry as first chief, William Perry as 2nd chief, then Clearwater, then Cornstalk. One missionary noted that in 1835 John Perry and William Perry were co-principal chiefs of this band, with Capt. Blackfeather, Little Fox, Henry Clay, and Letho as their sub-chiefs and councilors, Marston G. Clark as their agent, Charles Chene (son of Anthony Shane) as their interpreter, and L. Jones as their blacksmith. See Caldwell, p. 19. By 1844, both William Perry and Clearwater were dead or had left Kansas, as their names do not appear on the treaty signed by John Perry that year.

And on November 16, 1845, John Perry died, "quite an old man," at his home on the Shawnee reserve. "I once stayed all night with the old chief and he gave me the best he had for supper and at bed time he and his wife gave up their only bed and told me to sleep in it, they would take their blankets and sleep on the floor. As the night was quite cold and I had but one blanket with me, I accepted their offer...." See Hamilton's Journal, Barry, p. 251, 566.

In the 1850s, Thomas Perry was among the Shawnees allotted reserve lands. See KHC, vol. 15, p. 178.

Among the Shawnees who settled on the lands of the Cherokee nation by 1869 were James, Nancy, and Emma Perry. See JAIFR, vol. IV, #2, pp. 100-111.

Among the Shawnees who appeared on the 1880 Cherokee census of the Cooweescoowee District were James (age 38), Mariah (36), Frank (19), Emma (15), John (age not given), Samuel (age not given), and William Perry (23). All are listed as Shawnees except William who is listed as a Delaware. See JAIFR, vol. X, #3, p. 9.

The mixed-blood Delaware John Secondine, son of James Secondine, took a mixed-blood Shawnee girl, Emma Perry, as his second wife, and among their children were Victoria (b. 1887), Tecumpsi (b. 1891), Delaware (b. 1893), Anna E. (b. 1895), Clarence (b. 1898), and John (b. 1905). Victoria Perry Secondine married James A. Nolan, jr. and Anna E. Perry Secondine married Raymond Longbone.

Fillmore Secondine, a son of John Secondine of mixed heritage, grew up with Thomas Secondine and became the father of Polly Secondine by his second wife, Betsy Jackson Secondine. Polly married Willson Perry and continued the Perry surname thru sons Adam and William Perry. See Cranor, pp. 50-54.

In 1937, the Shawnee Sam Perry gave information to the Oklahoma Historical Society on Shawnee customs, and he is quoted several times by James H. Howard in his excellent Shawnee!, a book on the Shawnee cultural background.

Kirt Rosell (Lawaagaw), the current (1993) sub-chief of the United Remnant Band of Ohio Shawnees, is also a Perry descendant.

PERTHUIS – a Delaware name.

Joseph Perthuis was an Indian interpreter in the service of Sir William Johnson in th 1760's. He may have been a refugee from the French. See New York Colonial Documents, vol. VII, p. 718; vol. VIII, p. 38.

Perthuis worked for Capt. James Maxwell, an esteemed friend of Sir William Johnson. Maxwell commanded the fort at Green Bay in 1765, and Perthuis found him too harsh a taskmaster and wanted a transfer to Niagara. See SWJ, vol. 8, p. 212.

PETERS – a Delaware name.

In February, 1757, six children of Jacob Peters were captured by Indians. John Peters (Tollema), sometimes called Indian Peters or Capt. Peters, was living among the Delawares as early as 1757. He served as an interpreter and often signed treaties. Some of these treaties appear in the Pennsylvania Archives.

James Kenny, the Quaker trader of Ft. Pitt, wrote of Indian talked of Indian Peters as being friendly, as living opposite Redstone and he came up on them while Indian Peters and "a white man" were ploughing a cornfield together. "I informed them of ye Indians breaking out again which put them in great fear. Got breakfast at Indian Peters' house and they talked that he and his family would come down in ye country amongst his wife's relations, [she] being a white woman." See Kenny, PMOB&H, vol. 37, p. 199.

Indian trader Patrick Mullen's ledger shows that he was "robbed by John Peters of 134 bucks & 1 doe." See Bailey, p. 52.

Among the Delawares who surrendered to General Henry Bouquet and signed the treaty were Capt. N. Jacobs, Capt. Pipe, Capt. Johnny, Thomas Hickman, Simon Girty, and John Peters. See Pennsylvania Colonial Records, vol. 9, p. 256.

Among the Delawares who appeared on the 1880 Cherokee census of the Cooweescoowee District were John (age 41), Mary (30), and Henry Peter (2). See JAIFR, vol. X, #3, p. 9.

Among the households containing mixed-blood Munsey Delawares on the 1881 Census of Ontario Canada were:

1. Abient Peters, 23, his wife Annie, 18, and a one-year-old daughter, Alice.
2. Nelles Peters, 25.
3. Wesley Peters, 27.
4. William Peters, 48, his wife Elizabeth, living with Johnston Peters, 18, (probably a son), and Lucy A. Peters, age 9.
5. John Peters, 77, with his wife Eunice, 71, and

living in the same household was Caroline Logan, age 18.

6. John Peters, jr., 42, with Mary J., 23, Elvinia, 16, Petter, 12, Henry, 7, Lucy, 5, Archie, and Gurtie Peters, one month.

See Prevost, pp. 103, 122.

PETTIT – a Cherokee name.

In 1796, President George Washington sent Benjamin Hawkins to be a temporary Indian agent. Hawkins "encountered mixed bloods in practically all Cherokee settlements...By 1796, the Doughertys, Galpins, and Adairs from Ireland had married Cherokees and had mixed-blood families. The Rosses, Vanns, and McIntoshes were of Scottish origin. The Waffords and other intermarried whites were originally from the Georgia and Carolina colonies. At one settlement Hawkins met Thomas Pettit's halfblood wife and quarterblood daughter and described Pettit's daughter as having white-styled hair "and a beautiful rosy complexion." See Woodward, p. 120.

PHEASANT – a Shawnee/Delaware name.

Chief Pheasant (Kawcowatchety, Cawcawachety, etc.) was one of the most important chiefs in recorded Shawnee history. He negotiated the move to the Wyoming lands (in present Pennsylvania). Under his leadership, the Shawnee population expanded, in large part through the adoption of outsiders, and their reputation was established as a powerful nation, in trade or in war.

When the Pheasant died, one of his nephews, Hard Striker (Paxinosa, Pucksenutha, etc.) became the chief of the Wyoming Shawnee. The name of the great Chief Pheasant was "risen up," and bestowed upon a white captive. At the close of Pontiac's War, when General Henry Bouquet demanded that all whites be delivered up even if they had to be bound, some of the returned "captives" either did not remember their white names or refused to give their white names. On the list of captives are such names as Sour Plums and Crooked Legs. But also listed was Cawacawache, the Pheasant.

The Pheasant was listed on the account books of some of the Ohio Company traders, who gave him credit. It's possible that he gave himself up, as a sacrifice to obtain peace for his people. Perhaps he was married to another white captive, and perhaps he was the Indian who was seen, at great risk to his own life, running alongside the whites who were guarding a white woman, taking her forcibly back to her white family in the east.

The Pheasant, like most of the others returned at this treaty, found his way back to the Shawnee towns. See the Sir William Johnson Papers 1764-1765, p. 485. Cawacawache is returned captive #24 on the list. "Cockawatchy's nephew, the Pheasant" and Joseph Nicholson accompanied George Washington on his 1770 tour of the Ohio County. He may have been Nathaniel Carpenter or one of the others known to be living among the Shawnees at this time, but the research on this is not concluded.

Among the Delawares on the 1881 Census of the Ontario Reserve were:

1. James Pheasant, 24, living with Jacob John, 70, Betsy Jacobs, 26, and Frederick Jacobs, 4.
2. Joseph Pheasant, 48, and his family which included Betsy, 42, Alexander, 18, Monroe, 12, and Isabella, 13.

See Prevost, p. 122.

PHILLIPS – a Delaware/Shawnee/Osage name.

Some of the Phillips family were captured during the French and Indian War and also during Pontiac's War.

Phillip Phillips was among the Indians dealt with by the traders of the Ohio Company as early as 1756. During Pontiac's War, he was with the Shawnees and Wyandots. Capt. William Trent wrote that "the low Dutchman's name that was with the party that robbed our people is Phillip Phillips. His mother lives near Col. Johnson's. He was taken by the French Indians about six years ago." Trent said that Phillips intended to go see his mother during the summer and suggested setting a trap to apprehend him. See Hanna, pp. 230-231.

A Phillip Phillips later appears as an Indian trader at Ft. Pitt, likely the same man, and a Phillip Phillips was an interpreter at the Treaty of Ft. Stanwix in 1768. Was this man of the same family as the Phillip Phillips who came to Kentucky about the same time as David Owens, Benjamin Linn, and William Butler and who appears in the early records of Jefferson, Nelson, and Hardin counties?

In McClure's history of Hardin County, Kentucky, on the same page, there are biographical sketches of John Severns and Phillip Phillips. Reading their sketches, we would think that both were too respectable and highfaluting to have ever been "white Indians." But we know that John Severns (or Soverigns) was an adopted red, and another adopted red whose sketch appears in the same book, Christopher Miller, became respectable enough to represent the county in the state legislature. See McClure, p. 183.

A John Phillips signed the treaty at Lancaster, Pennsylvania in 1762 as part of Teedeyskung's Delawares.

See American State Papers, vol. 5., p. 196: "Capt. Peter, a Munsee [Delaware], and one called Jacob Phillips, who both talk English. Phillips is well known at Detroit as a Delaware."

Draper heard stories about one of these, called

Indian Phillips, and some of his inquiries about him were answered in volume 23S. People said that they took him for a white man when first meeting him. He possessed a fearsome demeanor, but some said that he was a nice, peaceable fellow. See Draper 23S238, for instance.

John Mack Faragher, whose recent biography of Daniel Boone is the best ever, says that when "Boone removed to Missouri there was a small village of Indians across the river from Saint Charles, where the western St. Louis suburb of Bridgeton now lies. There he encountered a number of friends from his days as a captive, Delawares and Shawnees from the town of Chillicothe on the Little Miami who had emigrated during the 1780's, including a number of former American captives who had chosen to remain and had raised Indian families, like Joseph Jackson, a former salt maker, Charles 'Indian' Phillips, and Jimmy Rogers, now the village chief."

Charles Phillips, "a Shawnee who lived with his Osage wife in Charette, one of a number of mixed families there," was an expert hunter, and Boone took him along on his Missouri hunts. See Faragher, pp. 313-314.

Among the Osages listed on the 1908 roll were William Phillips, listed as 1/4 blood, born in 1870, and his children Angeline M. Phillips Allen, b. 1893, Iva M. Phillips Gardner, b. 1895, and James W. Phillips, b. 1897. The children are listed as 1/8 bloods. See JAIFR, vol. 10, #4, p. 47.

PIGGOTT – a Cherokee name.

Capt. James Piggott headed the land company which settled the town next to Fort Jefferson in 1780. Magee, in her excellent work on Ft. Jefferson, says that there is a tradition that some of the men there had Indian wives. And historian Carl Baldwin thinks that

Piggott's last wife was Cherokee.

Capt. Piggott's wife was among those who died during the siege.

He then took up with Frances Bellew, of Cherokee descent, who had been abandoned by her husband, an Indian trader associated with James Sevier. She merged her family of four Bellew children (Timothy, Agnes, Frances, and Margaret) with Piggott's three and the couple had nine more children, Baldwin says, before Piggott died about 1799.

See Carl Bladwin, "James Piggott," Illinois State Genealogical Society Quarterly, vol. VIII, #4, pp. 177-183, Dec., 1976.

PILCHER – an Omaha name.

Fielding Pilcher was a member of William Wells band of scouts, some of whom had Indian connections.

Joshua Pilcher was in Kentucky in the 1820's, moved west, and became an Indian trader associating with John Dougherty, William and Marston G. Clark. He succeeded William Clark as Superintendent of Indian Affairs in St. Louis. Unlike most of the Indian traders who later became politically powerful, he openly acknowledged his son by an Omaha woman.

Joshua Pilcher's grandson, William W. H. Pilcher (Little Elk) was raised on the Omaha reservation but left to become an entrepreneur. He was highly successful as an accountant and held several business positions including that of president of the Whittier Insurance Agents. He also was active in promoting Indian affairs and was a member of the Republican Party's American Indian Political Advisory Committee.

William W. H. Pilcher married Nellie Esther Gray of Shelbyville, Indiana, and their children included Jean (Mrs. Carl Dearborn) and Susanna (Mrs. Alphonse Coppula). See Gridley, pp. 103-104.

PIPE – a Delaware/Wyandot name.

Two of the white families on the Pennsylvania frontier carried the surnames Pipes and Piper. Some of these may have been captured very early. Also during the William Crawford's expedition, there was a Joseph Pipes along. Pipes was captured, taken to the Shawnee towns, and spent four years among them. See Brown, p. 332.

The original Capt. Pipe was Custaloga's nephew. One account says that Capt. Pipe Sr. may have been killed on Pipe Creek in 1774 by Michael Cresap. See the letter of Michael Cresap jr. in Draper Mss. 7J4.

Capt. Pipe's sister married Roundhead, the Wyandot war chief, and had several children. His sister and the children were massacred by white militia upon what later became known as Capt. Pipe's Hill. These murderers escaped, but their commander, Col. William Crawford, was captured and brought into the camp. Even before this, Capt. Pipe leaned toward the British and opposed the pro-American policies of White Eyes and Killbuck, but he was not for all out war until after his family had been decimated by Crawford's militia.

Still, Colonel William Crawford would not have been killed if he had let Simon Girty help him. Instead, he thought he would escape by giving the Delawares a speech, by persuading them that he was on their side. He insisted that Girty interpret his speech word for word before the council, and he began by detailing the atrocities committed against the Indians which he had actively sought to stop. But the mention of these wrongs against the Delawares only evoked rage in those listening, and finally Capt. Pipe could take no more, and in a flurry he cut Crawford's ears off. Then, "since the meat was spoiled," they decided to burn him.

Thereafter Capt. Pipe was said to have led many war parties against the frontier settlements.

The son of the Capt. Pipe who burned Crawford was also called Capt. Pipe. He had a Delaware Indian village at the north of Brokensword Creek in Ohio in 1816. He migrated west and died at the mouth of the Kansas River. See Draper 11YY31-33.

John Pipe was one of the Delawares who served under Capt. Swannuck in the Florida War in 1837. He also may have married a Wyandot. Living among the Delawares, Wyandots, and Shawnees in Kansas in 1855 were John Pipe, 31, and Thomas Pipe, 35. See KHC, vol. XVI, p. 754. Among the Wyandots allotted land in Kansas in 1855 were the families of John and Thomas Pipe. John Pipe's family included Mary, Maria, and Winfield Pipe. Thomas Pipe's family included Margaret, Mary, and Hannah Pipe.

PITCHER– a Shawnee name.

Among the Shawnees who settled on the lands of the Cherokee nation by 1869 were John, George, Horace, and Jane Pitcher. See JAIFR, vol. IV, #2, pp. 100-111.

Among the Shawnees on the 1900 Census of Indian Territory was Luis Pitcher, a widow, born in Missouri in 1873. Her father was a white man, her mother a Shawnee. Her children were Viola, 8, George, 6, Perl E., 4, Charles, 2, and Harris G. Pitcher, three-months old. Peyton M. Parks was listed as her brother (possibly a step-brother or brother-in-law). F. P. Bannamun is listed as her uncle. See Prevost, p. 73.

POLK or POLKE – a Shawnee/Potawatomi name.

Charles Poke was one of the earliest settlers west of the Allegheny Mountains. He long associated with the Indians, and probably did have an Indian wife. Glenn Lough and other frontier historians have much to say about him, but there is probably more on him than I have yet seen.

Several members of the Polke family were captured at Polke's Station (or Kinchloe's Station or the Burnt Station) in Nelson County, Kentucky in 1782. Charles Polk (Poke, Polke, etc.) was captured by Shawnees that year but was only among them a few months.

William Polke, another member of the family, was one of the four children of Mrs. Polke who was captured by Shawnees in the attack on Polke's Station in what is now Nelson County, Kentucky. William Polke later served as an interpreter and guide during the War of 1812. He and his family later resided in Knox County, Indiana. William Polke served as interpreter for the Baptist missionary Issac McCoy who married his sister, an adopted Shawnee. See Ky. Pio. & Gen. Rec., vol. 7, 1986, p. 93-94.

Robert Polke opened a trading post among the Potawatomi (on Pottawatomie Creek, where present Lane, Kansas is today). His oldest son, Thomas W. Polke (about 23 in 1838) probably was associated with the trading house from the beginning, and his second son, John W. Polke later became a trader and married Sarah Ann Chick. Several members of the family intermarried with the Potawatomi tribe. See Barry, pp. 283, 321, 341, 425, 479.

POPE – a Shawnee name.

In 1785, Col. William Pope near Louisville, Kentucky, employed a private teacher to instruct his children along with the children of the near neighbors. One day in February, 1785, the Linn brothers, William and Asachel, Abram Pope and three other boys (ages 9 thru 11) went into the woods to hunt. It was at this time that they were captured by Indians. They were held at the Indian towns until mid-fall.

Among the Shawnee and Delaware, the last part of fall [Indian summer] was the customary time for expeditions and adventures. These activities engaged almost all of the young men, and they would leave the old men, women, and children behind in the village.

According to Walter W. Spooner, it was at this time that the Linn brothers plotted their escape. They were taken fishing by an old man and his wife. "This trip would require several days and nights away from the town. And it was during this while that the boys made their escape, after killing their Indian guards in the night while they were sleeping."

Spooner says that Abram Pope remained behind, and "it was afterwards ascertained that he grew to manhood among the Indians, married the sister of a noted chief, and became so attached to the life of a savage that he had no desire to return to civilized society."

See Walter W. Spooner, *The Backwoodsman*, and *Pioneers in the Settlement of America*. Also, Glenn Lough's AAT, vol. 3, #10, p. 7. The Popes — like the Rennicks, Carters, and many other families — must have tried to persuade their stray son to return, but most adopted reds, given the choice, chose the free red life to the constrictions of white civilization. It would not surprise me to learn that Nathaniel Carter and Abram Pope were actually General Mudeater and the Tame Hawk (Kikipelathy).

The Abram Pope story seems essentially true. The three or four other boys captured with the Linns and Abram Pope also stayed behind and some of their stories are better known. The list of adopted whites and mixed-blood sons of Indian traders living red is a long, long list. There must have been many others of whom we are not aware, or at least, only vaguely aware.

Jerry L. Hawk Pope (Tukemas) is the current chief of the United Remnant Band of the Shawnee Nation in their traditional lands. In 1984, the Remnant

Shawnees published a pamphlet in which Chief Hawk Pope wrote:

"...1856 saw the first use of the name Remnant Shawnee under Chief Two Hawk/Elijah Pope...My grandfather and chief of the Shawnee Nation, United Remnant Band, was Reva C. Pope, born 1889. At the time of his death in 1959, there were a total of 52 people still in the area of the original central Indiana community, Blue River...

"In the years after my grandfather's death, I and a few of the others worked to search for and to regroup the persons of Shawnee descent in the tri-state area. In September of 1971, I was elected to the position of principal chief of my people and have served as such for thirteen years now — 1984."

Of the history of his band, Chief Hawk Pope wrote that "most of what was left of the Kispotaka and Piqua [divisions of the Shawnee Nation] took white-sounding names and homesteaded land in such places as central Indiana and S. Ohio. These are our grandfathers and grandmothers. Two years before, the Shawnee on the Ohio reservations were forced to remove west to Kansas...the main body of this group was left to make their own way west and many of them dropped out as they passed near the homes of relatives..."

This seems to be exactly what happened. William Perry, Cornstalk (Nern-pe-nes-he-quah), and the Prophet went to Kansas in 1828 and secured village sites. But most Shawnees were reluctant to leave Ohio. In 1832, Joseph Parks and Chief John Perry guided the migration of Shawnees from Ohio, arriving there with about half of the nation. The Shawnees at first liked their new lands and the word must have gotten back to those left behind.

The following year, Joseph Parks brought some more of the remnant Shawnees west. They left Ohio in June, 1831, and traveled overland by way of St. Louis.

"Originally the emigrating party numbered more than 80, but Parks reported that two had died on the way, one family (Barnett's brother) turned back, three went over to the Delawares, and one family did not leave Ohio. Leading men in this band of Shawnees were: Little Fox, George Williams, Quilina, and Peculse-coe." See Barry, p. 243, who quotes Joseph Parks' diary.

When Draper visited the Shawnees in Kansas he wanted information on Tecumseh, and so he asked to speak to members of the Kishpoko division whose families had been at Tecumseh's side during the war. He was told that, except for She-me-ne-to (the Great Snake) and a couple of others, none of the Kishpoko division were living in Kansas. Draper surmised (and other historians have taken it from Draper) that the Kishpoko division was apparently almost extinct because they had been decimated by the war. Partly true — but there were others who were living quietly in Ohio, Indiana, and Kentucky.

If Abram Pope was known to have lived as a Shawnee, what was his adopted name? By whom was he adopted? What happened to him?

As of this writing, I have yet not heard directly from Jerry Pope, but the tradition seems to have found its way into print in James Alexander Thom's historical novel, *Panther in the Sky,* one of the better renditions of Tecumseh's story.

POWHATAN – a Powhatan name.

The name of the chief is the name that the colonists gave to the entire tribe. He was certainly one of the founding fathers of American Indian genealogy. He was a real person, of course. No fairy tale. His daughter, Pocahontas "saved" Captain John Smith, but she married John Rolfe and went to England. Their son, Thomas Rolfe, returned to Virginia and founded an ancestral line that continues today, and descendants are scattered like maple leaves through the autumn woods.

Rivaling the Pocahontas legacy in the number of descendants was another daughter of Powhatan's through her only daughter, Nicketti.

"Thomas Hughes lived some time in tide-water Virginia, and later ran away to the mountains and lived with the Indians. He married Nicketti, granddaughter of Powhatan (a daughter of a younger sister of Pocahontas) and by her fathered a number of children. One daughter, Elizabeth, married Nathaniel Davis and descendants of this marriage became the ancestors of many important pioneer Virginia families. A daughter of Nathaniel an Elizabeth, Mary, married Samuel Burks; a granddaughter married Abraham Vanable, Jr.; another became the wife of William Floyd; another, Elizabeth, married Capt. Cabell. A son of Nathaniel and Elizabeth, Robert, is given as a forefather of Jefferson Davis. Another son, Nathaniel, was the ancestor of William "Powder maker" Davis, who lived with the Indians for many years." See Glenn Lough's AAT, vol. 2, #6, p. 6. Also see Kegley's *Virginia Frontier*, p. 23-24.

Lough says that Thomas Hughes who married Niketti was the ancestor of Thomas Hughes on the Monongahela River area, ancestor of the Indian fighters Elias and Jesse Hughes.

POWLES, POWLESS – a Mohawk name.

Margaret Brant, a daughter of the mixed-blood Mohawk chief, Joseph Brant, married a Mr. Powless, and the name became common among the Mohawks and intermarried tribes. Some of them lived white-styled lives and lived in New York, Pennsylvania, and Ohio. See Draper 13F32.

Among the Senecas allotted money for their Ohio lands were Powis Brandt, Oneida Bowlus and

Dennis Bowlus. I suspect the Bowlus's may have been members of the Powless family. See Watson, vol. V, pt. 3, p. 11.

A Henry Powless signed the 1832 Treaty with the Brothertown and Munsey Delawares as a representative of the Six Nations. See Watson, vol. V., pt. 13, p. 73.

The 1881 Ontario Census showing the Oneida and Delaware reserve listed Baptist Powless, age 24, a Baptist, with Sara Powless, age 20, and with Leizer Ninham, adopted. Also listed was Peter Powlen (or Powles), age 59, with Louisa, 25, Joseph, 16, Amos, 12, and Jacob, 5. See Prevost, p. 115.

A Henry Powless, listed as an Onondaga, was among those killed at Tarawa fighting for the United States in World War II. See JAIFR, vol. XI, #1, p. 27.

PRICKET – a Wyandot name.

"Josiah Prickett settled on the north side of Stonelick...in the spring of 1801. He was a native of Virginia and came to Geraul's Station in company with his parents in 1791. In 1792, his youngest brother, Richard Pricket, was stolen by the Indians while he was hunting the cows a short distance from the station. He never returned to the whites, having married an Indian woman and raised a large family. In the war of 1812, he was an interpreter for the Wyandots, by whom he had been adopted. He died at an advanced age, in 1847, and was the wealthiest man on the reservation." See the Louis H. Everts, *The History of Clermont County, Ohio*, p. 520.

Richard Pricket was paid for being an Indian interpreter at Green Bay in 1820. See American State Papers, Indian Affairs, vol. 2, p. 444.

PRIOR, PRYOR – an Osage name.

Nathaniel Pryor had Indian blood. His mother was a sister of Col. John Floyd, hence he was a direct descendant of Powhatan through Nikitti. The noted scout, Robert McClelland, married Nathaniel Pryor's sister.

Nathaniel Pryor's father, John Pryor, may have had Indian blood also. He was a part of the militia at Ft. Randolph when it was besieged by Black Fish and his Shawnees. Blackfish detailed a token force to keep the garrison hemmed in while the main body of reds broke up into war parties and set out to harass the single farms and smaller frontier settlements. Phil Hammon and John Pryor, dressed to look like Indian runners, slipped out of the fort, overtook a war party, and slipped through their ranks to warn the settlements in their path. See the Huntsville, Alabama, *Southern Advocate*, July 10, 1830, which was reprinted in *Revolutionary Soldiers in Alabama*, p. 324.

John Pryor later came to Kentucky, and according to Burnett's *History of the Northwest*, the Indians killed John Pryor on Salt River. Harvey's *The Shawnee Indians*, reprinted the deposition of two Shawnee warriors, taken in 1794. "...[that a war party of Shawnees]...had stolen about fifty horses from the Kentuckians on Salt River during the spring and summer...that they only killed one man and took no prisoners...that the man was killed by a white interpreter whose name is Kiddle." If the Shawnees could have pronounced the "R," they might have identified this man as Ruddle, and probably Stephen Ruddle. See Burnett; Harvey, pp. 112-113.

Nathaniel Pryor was one of the more active men on the Lewis and Clark expedition. But it was when he left the expedition that his life took a violent turn. He and his Osage companions were attacked by the Sioux. During the War of 1812, he rode on a spying mission against the Shawnees and narrowly escaped with his life, protected by some Sac and Fox women. Later, he married an Osage and ran a trading post and dealt mostly with that tribe. It was been said that "all of his children were given Indian names."

Surely they were, but also they carried on the Pryor name. Mary Jane Pryor, an Osage, married Francis Michel (St. Michel) in 1841 and their first daughter was named Pelagie Michel. As late as 1908, the Osage roll included Martha Pryor Oberly, b. 1883, Mary June Pryor, b. 1894, William Pryor, b. 1876, Mary Pryor Blaine, b. 1873, John Pryor, b. 1903, Louis Pryor, b. 1879, Andrew Pryor, b. 1906, and Antwine Pryor, b. 1881. See Barry, pp. 139-140; JAIFR, vol. X, #1, p. 5-28.

PROPHET, PROFFIT, PROPPET, etc. – a Shawnee name.

Tecumseh's most famous brother was Lalawethika (the rattler, or he who makes a loud noise). He became a Shawnee councilor, a mixture of holy man and psychiatrist and not unlike any in every human culture — part magician, part doctor, part fraud.

As a youth, Lalawethika was seduced and corrupted by the white man's ways and he became a drunkard. But after a few years he started to fall into trances and have visions. He was, in a manner of speaking, born again. He became Tenskkwatawa (the open door), and was commonly called the Prophet.

On occasion, the Prophet had lengthy conversations with the Great Spirit who told him that the Indians must forswear white ways and return to the traditional ways. They must love one another, and youth must listen to the traditional wisdom of the elders of their tribe. All substance coming from white culture must be refused, especially the alcohol. They should no longer dress as white people, but they must return to wearing skins and to eating native animals and plants obtained and prepared in the traditional manner.

The Prophet objected to all buying and selling of property, saying that there must be a return to the traditional holy way, where the land was held by the Great Spirit for his red children to live and hunt on in common. Once the people returned to the holy way, the Great Spirit told Tenskkwatawa, the whites would be driven off, the animals would return to the hunting grounds, the corn would grow in the fields, and things would be right again.

These ideas weren't all bad, and they caught on. The Prophet gave his people hope again. While his ideas made some white frontiersmen nervous, they struck a cord in the hearts of many red people whose culture, after the Treaty of Greenville, was disintegrating rapidly.

The Prophet was an intuitive man of words who was able to inspire people with his ideas. His brother, Tecumseh, was a handsome, bold, decisive man of action. Together, they initiated, fought for, and lost their chance to create a separate Indian nation on the American continent.

After Tecumseh's death, the Prophet resided in Canada until 1824 when he moved to Michigan with Tecumseh's family and some of the other Shawnees. In 1826, he moved to Wapakonetta, Ohio, with Pachetha, a son of Tecumseh.

The following year, it is said, the Prophet went west to the Missouri River. He was in what is now Kansas in 1828 where, in company with William Perry and Young Cornstalk, he visited the Choctaws. See Pitchlynn, pp. 67-68.

The Prophet died in Kansas in 1837. He was not handsome, but his wives were said to have been beautiful, perhaps attracted to him by his notoriety. One of his wives was said to have been a Cherokee. By his wives, he had at least one son, John Prophet, and three daughters.

From information obtained from Mrs. Deere, the wife of Robert Deere, a son of Echo Harjo, principle

Creek chief of the Little River Tallessee Town: Robert Deere, then a youth, was present when his father, Echo Harjo, Micco Hatkee, and some others greeted John Prophet and some other Shawnees who had come into the camp. See Draper 1YY8.

Among the Shawnees who went with Capt. Joseph Parks and served in the Florida War was "Young Prophet," most likely John Prophet.

John Prophet married a mixed-blood daughter of Spybuck. Spybuck, who people usually took for a white man, was the son of Capt. Chieska and his half-breed wife, possibly a daughter of Richard Butler by a daughter or sister of the old Cornstalk.

Among the Shawnees who settled on the lands of the Cherokee nation by 1869 were Jane, Anna, William, and Nahnahhahpewase Prophet. See JAIFR, vol. IV, #2, pp. 100-111.

Among the Shawnees who appeared on the 1880 Cherokee census of the Cooweescoowee District were James (age 45), Mary (25), Susan (18), Jacob (8), Sam (6), Minnie (3), Margaret (2), and Peggy Prophet (1). See JAIFR, vol. X, #3, p. 9.

Some of the Shawnee orphans seem to have been adopted by members of the Peoria tribe, with whom many of the Shawnees intermarried. Once such was Dick Prophet, listed as being 17 years old on the 1889 Peoria Census. See Valley and Lembcke, p. 251. Dick Prophet died a Peoria in 1915, leaving mixed-blood heirs who included Molinda Harvey, Ed Stand, Joe Hill, Katie Billet, Lucinda Brown, Annie Brown, Grant Lenno, Perry Bigjohn, James Parks, and Nancy Sky (nee Prophet).

PUMPKIN or PUNKIN – a Delaware/Shawnee name.

Cut the Pumpkin (Squashcutter, Yaghkapoose) was the main Delaware warchief of the Chenusso Delaware/Seneca band during the late stages of Pontiac's

War. Returned captives spoke of Yaghkapoose as the main mischief-maker, and Sir William Johnson put a bounty on his scalp. No one collected the reward, after Johnson demanded that Cut the Pumpkin be delivered up as terms of the Shawnee/Delaware peace, Killbuck summoned him. Then with David Owens interpreting, Cut the Pumpkin agreed to the terms of the peace, affixing his mark to the treaty. He kept as a hostage, was personally given blankets from the smallpox hospitol, and he shortly died. See SWJ, vol. 4, pp. 336, 772; vol. 11, pp. 704-708, 800, 821.

The Pumpkin lived among the mixed-mingo band in Seneca County, Ohio during the early 1800's. Lang said that he was an irreconcilable, a bad actor.

In the 1850s, a missionary observed that the Shawnee Pumpkin family was at least half-white, perhaps more. Among the Shawnees who settled on the lands of the Cherokee nation by 1869 were John and Elizabeth Punkin. See JAIFR, vol. IV, #2, pp. 100-111. John Pumpkin was associated with the Shawnee Mission.

Among the Delawares, Shawnees, and Cherokees living in the Cooweescoowee District and appearing on the 1880 Cherokee census were Jim and Sallie Pumpkin, listed as Cherokees. Listed as Delawares were Jane James Pumpkin and Mary James Pumpkin. See JAIFR, vol. X, #3, p. 10.

John Pumpkin of this family was a mixed-blood Shawnee, and his wife, Nancy, was French. One of their daughters, Louisa, married George Washington Franklin, a white man who had been born in Illinois in 1836. Their sons included Francis, John, and Alex Franklin. See FRANKLIN.

PUNCH – a Mingo/Wyandot name.

The Bunt, an important Onondaga chief, sent seven of his men to Sir William Johnson who outfitted them as a war party on "a fine fall morning" in 1759. Johnson wrote, "I ordered a whale bone for them, and everything necessary. Gave a silver gorget to Bunt's grandson, who was appointed their leader. His name is Punch."

This man, Punch, the Bunt's grandson, "was some time ago in company with some Shawnees who took two horses loaded with skins...to trade at Ft. Pitt. When they were met with and robbed by some of the English." See SWJ, vol. 3, p. 699;v. 13, p. 145.

Some of his family seems to have carried on the Punch name, or at least the name was "risen up" later among both the eastern Iroquois in New York and their relatives with the western Mingo and Wyandot bands.

The Crane (Tarhe or Tarhee), chief of the Wyandots, broke with Roundhead's band after the defeat at Tippecanoe and refused to make war on the United States. After Roundhead gave some speeches amongst the Wyandots urging war, the Crane used his influence with the Wyandot Council to have them recognize George Punch as war chief in lieu of Roundhead. Allan W. Eckert (Tecumseh, p. 572) has it that Roundhead was replaced "with a puppet chief named George Punch." No doubt Tecumseh would have looked at it this way. But one man's puppet is another man's inspired leader.

George Punch was probably the "Tayauendottoontraw," Spliced Arrow, that had earlier, in 1791, accompanied Grey Eyes on his mission to the Creeks, Cherokees, and other southern tribes in an effort to meld an alliance with them against the forces of General Anthony Wayne.

George Punch and the Crane who were able to put an end to the Prophet's witchcraft executions among the Wyandots, and George Punch was among the those who signed a treaty at Greenville, Ohio, in 1814, pledging not to go to war with the United States. His name was then given as Punch, his Wyandot name transcribed as Teanduttasooh. And George Punch was listed as signing the treaty of ratification in 1819 when his Wyandot name was transcribed as Tawyoudantansan.

On the 1843 Wyandot Census is listed George Punch Sr.'s family, consisting of one male over 55, one female over 55, one female between 25 and 55, one female between 10 and 25, and five children under 10, four of them boys. George Punch jr.'s family, consisted of one male 25 to 55, and two males under 10. At the time they arrived in Kansas, it was said, there was not a member of the Wyandot nation more than 1/4 Wyandot. People took them for white at first glance.

Among the Wyandots allotted land in Kansas in 1855 were Margaret, Thomas, Margaret (the younger), and Elliot Punch. Among the Wyandots who sold their land in Kansas was Margaret B. Punch (age 40), Eliza Punch (20), and John Punch (21).

Eliza Punch died in 1861 and left as her heirs, her cousins, John Punch, the son of John Kayrahoo (Carrymau, Carahoo, etc.), Thomas Punch jr. and his sister, also Eliza and George Punch, and her uncles Thomas and John Punch. See KHC, vol. 15, p. 160.

The Punch family of Wyandots seems intermarried with whites as well as the both the Senecas and the Shawnees. Some of them went back to Ohio, and some of them went back to New York.

PURCELL or PURSLEY – a Shawnee name.

The Kentucky family went by both names, and the alternate spelling appears sometimes on the same court case in the Nelson County records.

A man called Pursley was known to have been captured in Kentucky in 1780 at Ruddles' Station. See Lafferty, p. 33.

Among the Shawnees who settled on the lands

of the Cherokee nation by 1869 were R. W., Harriet, William W., Sarah E., Charles H., Ida Alice, S. Lincoln, and John Wesley Purcell. See JAIFR, vol. IV, #2, pp. 100-111.

Among the Shawnees living in the Cooweescoowee District and appearing on the 1880 Cherokee census were Josh B. Purcell, listed as a white man, (age 50) and his family, listed as Shawnees, included Charles (19), Alice (16), Westley (14), and Lincoln Purcell. See JAIFR, vol. X, #3, p. 10.

QUICK – a Delaware/Shawnee name.

A named named Quick was captured by the Shawnees under Blackhoof (who was also called Blackfoot), with his wife and children.

"Before I came here, one Quick had settled at the mouth of this river just above the bottom. One morning his wife went out to bring in a little something to put in the fire...and Blackfoot [Draper says Blackfish on the side, but it was actually Blackhoof that was sometimes referred to as Blackfoot by Kentuckians] stepped up and said, how-dy-do?

"He didn't offer to trouble her, and she went into the house and told them the Indians were out of doors. They flew to their guns and were going to make a defense, but Blackfoot — who had come up — told them they might as well surrender for there were too for them...Quick concluded to do so and opened the door. Blackfoot came in and shook hands with them all around.

"After they had been there about 3 hours, Kennedy brought a black man and came to see Quick. When the Indians saw him coming, they slipped out and surrounded them. Blackfoot told Kennedy he must go with them. Kennedy said he be damned if he would. Blackfoot told him he might as well go along peaceably and they wouldn't hurt him. Kennedy then told the negro to go home and tell his mistress what had happened. But he must go too, said Blackfoot.

"Kennedy said he be damned if he should. Blackfoot said he wanted him too. Kennedy then drew his sword and aimed to strike Blackfoot when one of Blackfoot's men shot him dead.

"Blackfoot asked Quick if he had any horses. He said two. They were out in the meadow. He told him to go and get them, he could catch them better than they could and if he ran off, they would kill his wife and children. If he came back, they would treat him well. Quick went and got the horses and they then put his women and children across the river in a pirogue and swam the horses.

"I saw him afterwards. He came back on a visit. Said it was the best swap he ever made in his life..." This is as told to the Rev. John D. Shane by Capt. John Dyal who came to Kentucky with George Rogers Clark in 1781 and subsequently served in several campaigns against the Indians including the commanding of a company under Harmar. See Draper Mss. 13CC2326-237.

In Canada some time later, the man changed sides and went over to the British. I do not yet know what happened to his children, but some of them may have been scattered and adopted into the tribes. A Mrs. Quick was seen among the Indians by William Smalley in 1792. See Paul C. Wilson, *A Forgotten Mission to the Indians: William Smalley's Adventures Among the Delaware Indians of Ohio in 1792*, Galvenston, Texas, 1965.

A John Quick (or Quake) appears on the treaty with the Delawares in 1818. This is the same man who name appears as John Quick on the 1829 treaty as Jonny Quick. He may have been an adopted son of Chief William Anderson as his name appears on the latter treaty directly under Pooshies and Capt. Swarnock, with whom he must have closely associated. Chief Anderson sent him on a mission in 1830 to scout out the lands in Kansas and Johnny Quick must have died shortly after his return as money was allotted by Pierre Menard to Anthony Shane for "the funeral expenses of J. Quick" in December, 1831. See Watson, vol. V., pt. 13, p. 58, 64, 66. See Barry, p. 176-178.

The Quick surname hung on among the Delawares, Shawnees, and Peorias at least into the current century.

I found a letter in the Quick family file at the Kentucky Historical Society in Frankfort from Mrs. Patricia M. Smith of Detroit, Michigan. In 1972, over twenty years ago now, she wrote asking for information concerning Joseph Quick's family, saying that he was the son of John Alexander Quick and his wife Mary, and that Joseph Quick's brothers and sisters seem to have included Solomon, Benjamin, Cornelius, Elijah, John, Alexander, David, Sarah, Elizabeth, Mary, and Polly. And she quotes the Commemorative Biographical Record, County of Essex, Ontario, Canada, p. 48: "Joseph Quick was born in Kentucky, about one mile from Cincinnati, Ohio. He was the eldest of the family, and with his sisters, was captured by the Indians. While two of his sisters were brought back, he was kept thirteen years before released through the agency of Col. Elliott of Amherstburg. He followed his parents to Canada, and after his father's death, he carried on the clearing of the farm and homestead, a tract of 200 acres in Lot 8 of the Gore, Harrow, Ontario, given his father by the Government as a regard for his loyalty. Joseph Quick died of typhoid fever...Aug. 29, 1845, aged seventy-six...."

Joseph Quick had married Susan Munger by whom he had twelve children. She died Jan. 16, 1849. I'm wondering if this was the same Munger family as married into the family of Simon Girty. Some of the Mungers were captured at Ruddles Station in Kentucky in 1780. See Lafferty.

RANDALL or RANDLE – a Shawnee name.

William P. Randle, age 46, was listed as a Shawnee on the 1900 census of Indian Territory. He said that his father was born in Kentucky and that his mother, who was a Shawnee, was born in Ohio. See Prevost, p. 74.

Among the Shawnees who settled on the lands of the Cherokee nation by 1869 were Eliza, Mary, Julia, and William P. Randall. See JAIFR, vol. IV, #2, pp. 100-111.

RANKEN, RANKIN – a Wyandot name.

Tom Rankin was captured as a youth on the Pennsylvania frontier. He was adopted and raised by Indians. See Draper 17S46.

James Rankin, sr., was an Indian trader in the Ohio lands and at Detroit. He married Yau-a-tau-rant, a Wyandot woman, with whom he had several children.

The 1785 deposition of James Rankin is in Draper 14S195-201. In it, he related the conditions at the Indian towns, the grievances of the Indian Nations. Mentioned in the deposition were James Sherlock, John Harry, Issac Williams, Simon Girty, Robert Surphlet, Joseph Soverigns, the Wyandot Half King, and several others.

A James Rankin, a Wyandot, was elected to the Board of Chiefs in 1851. A Samuel Rankin voted in the Wyandot election of 1852. See Barry, p. 1029, 1129.

A James Rankin, jr. is listed on the 1900 census in Indian Territory, Oklahoma. The younger James Rankin seems to have lived among the Choctaws and Chickasaws after arriving in Kansas.

Elizabeth Rankin, a half-breed daughter of James Rankin, married William Walker, a white man who had been captured by the Delaware in 1781, and was transferred to Chief Adam Brown of the Wyandots and adopted.

One of the children of James Rankin, sr., seems to have been Samuel Rankin, also known as Te-zhareliah and commonly called Jack Brandy, lived in the Wyandot Brownstown (Michigan) settlement, then moved to the Wyandot town at Sandusky.

Sam Rankin was known as Jack Brandy, and during the War of 1812 when he was a captain under Roundhead (Stiahta), who was killed in action in the fall of 1813. The loss of Roundhead was a shattering blow to Tecumseh's small army of reds, for as historian Bil Gilbert points out, Roundhead was to Tecumseh as Stonewall Jackson was to Robert E. Lee. It was Sam Rankin and Roundhead who helped Tecumseh put a stop to the Potawatomi killing of white prisoners after the battle at River Raison. Rankin commanded a party of about twenty Wyandots and captured General William Winchester and the white scout, James Knaggs. Arriving at the scene of the River Raison killings, he reportedly went into a burning cabin and dragged out a Kentuckian named John Green, saving his life.

Like many of the Wyandots who went west to Kansas, some returned to Ohio to the lands and relatives they had left behind. Some stayed in Kansas. Sam Rankin himself seems to have returned to Ohio.

General Hunt saw Sam Rankin in the latter part of 1835. When he was on his way to Columbus to serve in the State Senate, his stage drove through the Wyandot village. "Hunt noticed a decrepit old Indian hobbling along, as best he could, on crutches. Hunt asked where he lived. He said about two miles ahead on the road. He was then invited to get into the stage and ride; and as Gen. Hunt was helping him in, asked him, `Are you not Jack Brandy?.' `Yes, me Jack Brandy.' Then Gen. Hunt related to his fellow passengers the anecdotes about Jack..."

Rankin was did not recognize Hunt until he told the tale of how Jack Brandy had once tracked down the thief who made off with Henry Jackson Hunt's horse, a prize dapple grey later which Hunt later sold to the British General Henry Procter, the one he made his retreat on at the Battle of the Thames. After concluding this story, Rankin "archly and triumphantly exclaimed, `Ah, me know you now — you a Hunt — brodder of Harry Hunt.' As the now-aged warrior alighted from the stage, crippled." See Prevost, p. 87-88; NOQ, (1933), v. 5. in which is printed Draper's field notes, p. 41-143.

Among the Wyandot guardianship cases reviewed by the Commissioner of Indian Affairs in 1871 was the case of Elizabeth Rankin, guardian of Jacob B. Hill. Elizabeth was then living Brantford, Brand County, Province of Ontario, Canada, having moved there in 1858. See JAIFR, vol. VIII, #2, p. 20.

REED or REID – a Shawnee/Ottawa/Cherokee name.

Among the students attending the Ft. Leavenworth Shawnee Indian School in 1849 was Thaxter Reed, an Ottawa.

Capt. Reed (Wacasesaka), a Shawnee, lived among the Lower Cherokees for several years and may have had a wife among them. After the Treaty of Greeneville, General Anthony Wayne used Capt. Reed as an intermediary to persuade the militant Cherokees who resided among the Ohio Shawnees to to leave them. See Tanner, p. 100.

Among the marriages recorded in Kansas in 1845 was that of the part-Shawnee John Reed to Lyona, his wife.

Among the Shawnees, Cherokees, Delawares, and adoptees living in the Cooweescoowee District of the Cherokee Nation in 1880 were Emeline (age 46), Andy, (27), and David Reed (24), all Cherokees. See JAIFR, vol. 10, #3, p. 11.

RENNICK, WRYNECK, RENICK, RYENECK – a Shawnee name.

In 1779-80, Wryneck was referred to as "principal warrior and chief of the Pickowee tribe of the Shawanese Nation." He was actually Joshua Rennick, a white man. He married Tecumpease, Tecumseh's sister, and was the father of the Shawnee scouts, James and John Logan.

You won't find any mention of Wryneck in Allan W. Eckert's books including Johnny Logan and his greatest work, *A Sorrow in Our Heart: The Life of Tecumseh.* He says in a footnote (...Tecumseh, page 697) that "in twenty-five years of research," he finds no evidence for the Joshua Rennick story except "a brief comment in a letter written in September 1845 to historian Lyman Draper (see Draper Manuscripts DD-YY-1/44), in which one Robert Remick (also spelled once as Renick) states the tradition that his father, Joshua, married Tecumseh's elder sister, Tecumapese, and that Joshua Remick was the father of Spemica Lawba." Eckert, an expert on historical fact, says he considers the entire Rennick story "a fabrication."

It frankly amazes me that Allan Eckert could accept the story of Bluejacket/Van Swearington in its entirety while rejecting completely the more highly plausible story of Wryneck/Rennick. Nor does Eckert consider the Richard Sparks story valid. It should also be noted that there is no mention, in any of his works published thus far, of David and George Owens, George Ash, Peter Harper, Phillip Phillips, Joseph Soverigns, James Sherlock, and many, many others in this work. This should just remind you again that nobody knows everything. Take your own look at things. Weigh the evidence yourself.

Someone whose first language was Shawnee usually had trouble with the "R" sound, but Wryneck himself, whose first language was English, did not have that trouble.

A letter to the Filson Club, sent by Russell Johnston over forty years ago, contains much accurate information of the Renicks. "By now I have a fairly extensive genealogy of most of the branches of the Renick family, but not too much about Henry Renick's connection with the others. It seems to me that there were two brothers, George Renick and Thomas Renick, who came to Pennsylvania about 1720 from Enniskillen, Northern Ireland. George's children removed from the vicinity of Paxtang or Derry, Lancaster Co, Pa, about 1740 to Augusta County, Va. One son of George was Robert who was Captain of Augusta County Militia and is said to have been wounded at Braddock's defeat in 1756. He was killed by a raiding party of Indians in 1757 and his family taken captives. They were returned under the provisions of Bouquet's treaty about 1764 — except for one son, Joshua, who refused to leave the Indians and, according to family tradition, raised in the family of Tecumseh and became a chief...one of his sons is said to have been Logan...."

In July, 1757, Robert Rennick was killed by Indians at the forks of the James River, and as seen from the prisoner lists (in The Sir William Johnson Papers and The Virginia Historical Magazine), Mrs. Rennick and their seven children were made prisoners. Later, an Indian named Ryeneck appears among the Indians who dealt with the Ohio Company Indian traders. Among the captives delivered up to Bouquet in 1764 were listed a Peggy Reyneck and a "Nansey Raneck, her sister. and four brothers." See Hanna, II, 388.

Wryneck was one of the Shawnees invited to a council in 1775. Capt. James Wood noted in his journal that "The Cornstalk, Nimwha, Wryneck, Blue Jacket, Silver Heels, and about fifteen other Shawnee arrived; they immediately got drunk and continued in that situation for two days." See Thwaites, Rev. on the

Upper Ohio, p. 41.

The Mingoes referred specifically to Nimwha and Wryneck as the Big Knife chiefs, Cornstalk explained told a council, "because we are determined to hold fast our friendship." The Mingoes threatened to come into the Shawnee camp and "to tie and carry off Nimwha and Wryneck." See Schaaf, p. 190.

See Draper Mss. 15S37; Wryneck resided at the Pickaway Town (Piqua); but apparently, he traveled to the Wabash where he made a peace with George Rogers Clark in 1778, according to Draper Mss. 1H17.

In January, 1779, Wryneck (Aquilsia) was at an English council representing the Shawnees of Piqua. Present were Capt. Alexander McKee, Lt. William Caldwell, Matthew Elliot, Simon Girty, George Girty, James Girty, Simon Surphet, the Raven (the Overhill Cherokee chief), the Weed (an Iroquois chief), and River Bottom (a Mingo). His speech reflected the sentiments expressed by the others present, agreeing to take up the rusty hatchet in defense of their lands against the encroaching Big Knife (Kentuckians and Virginians). See Seineke, p. 416.

The tradition says that Wryneck married Tecumapease, Tecumseh's sister, who we know also was married, at different times, to Francois Maisonville and Wasegoboah. Eckert (in ...Tecumseh) also has multiple marriages for Tecumapease but instead of Wryneck, he shows her marrying a warrior he calls Chaquiweshe. Well, compare the name for Wryneck as given in the English transcription of the 1779 council. Wryneck was not a Shawnee name; Aquilsia was his Shawnee name. And Aquilsia was the same man as Eckert's Chaquiweshe, sort of — he was a white man whose white name was Joshua Rennick.

See Draper 21V131: After the storm of the Revolutionary War had measurably subsided, as it did for awhile, Joshua Rennick, accompanied by an Indian named The Racer, united with his white connections in Greenbriar County. His brother, William, tried to evangelize him, to make him stay with the whites, but Joshua Rennick was "thoroughly imbibed with the Indian dread of restraint," and he would not stay among them.

There is the story of how he managed to escape the traps that were set for him, and of how glad he was to return to his people, the Shawnees living on the Wabash. Draper says, "...he was a free man again and soon returned to his people in the Indian Country but died a year or two afterwards, about 1784, when his youngest son James was perhaps ten years of age. His oldest son, John, was some two years older."

According to Draper Mss. 4CC117-119, Wryneck was the father of the Shawnee scout, Lawba or James Logan. For a speech of Wryneck, see Mich. Pio. & Hist. Col., vol. 20, p. 181; also vol. 10, p. 463.

See Draper 11S210-214: Chieska's notice of the death of Wryneck ("our Great Chief Rynack") was in the message to the Ft. Nelson; David Owens carried a message back from Col. George Walls to the Indian towns expressing sorrow for "the loss of your great chief Wryneck." These messages are also in The Calendar of Virginia State Papers (March 2nd, 1784, p. 565).

James Logan (Lawba) was the part-white son of Wryneck (and the adopted son of Moluntha), captured by Benjamin Logan when Moluntha was killed. Lawba picked up the name, James or John Logan, by which he became famous as a frontier scout. Was there one Logan or two? Were James and Johnny Logan the same man? I'd like to think that Eckert had already looked closely at this, but if he can miss the Wryneck story he could miss other things on this too. The Shawnees that Draper interviewed in Kansas all referred to Eckert's Johnny Logan as James or Jim Logan. Someone besides

Eckert needs to take the time to sort out all of the references to James or Johnny Logan and get this straight.

James Logan and Bluebird (a beautiful Shawnee girl who had been captured when young and raised by John Hardin's family) were returned to the Indians in the prisoner exchange of 1787. Logan and Bluebird fell in love, married, and their descendants kept the Logan surname.

As the leader of a company of scouts, James Logan engaged in several skirmishes, always on the side of the United States. He was killed in a shootout with some Potawatomis in January, 1813. See Quisenberry, pp. 48-49. The children of the late Shawnee chief, Captain James Logan, were given land in the 1817 treaty held at the Miami Rapids. John Johnston said that James Logan wanted his children raised with the whites, but that his wife would not permit it.

A man with the unlikely name of Scattergood Treas traveled through Indiana in 1821 and saw Anthony Shane, who ran the ferry at Shane's Crossing, and there he talked with Captain John Logan (James Logan's son or brother?) and his son, Walk-by-the-side-of-the-water (James Logan). Treas thought that Captain John Logan was then "a fat, butcher-like man," but that his son was "the most perfect specimen of male beauty I ever saw." He also described the Shawnee town of Wapakonetta as "a town of considerable size, with a street a mile long," and a number of white traders, a grist mill, a saw mill, and a school to be opened." See Rave.

Among the marriages solemnized in Kansas in 1843 was the that of James Logan and his wife, Cowapease. This Shawnee Logan family intermarried with the Chouteau family and other tribes including the Osage, Peorias, and Senecas.

Among the Shawnees on the 1880 census of the

Cherokee Cooweescoowee District was Nancy Login (Logan), age 40. See JAIFR, vol X, #2, p. 28. Among the Senecas on the 1881 Census (Quapaw Agency) were the households of Widow Logan, 55, James Logan, 31, and John Logan, 28. John Logan's family included his wife, Mary, 28, their daughter, Julia Logan, 9, and their son, Thompson Logan, ten months.

RICHARDVILLE – a Miami name.

John B. Richardville (Pe-che-wa, Wild Cat) succeeded Little Turtle as chief of the Miami Nation. He was the son of a french trader and his mother was a sister of Little Turtle. Richardville's father was an Indian trader with a store at Ft. Wayne. His father's brother ran a trading post at Vincennes.

He looked like a half-breed, some thought. His skin was blotched with some red, some white. He had light blue eyes. However, everyone who knew him thought that John B. Richardville conducted himself more like a cultured frenchman than an Indian chief. He was in a few battles, including St. Clair's Defeat, and he said that the action was so thick in the creek in front of him that you could step across to the other side on the dead bodies. The war mellowed him, as wars tend to do, and he became a diplomatic advocate of lasting peace.

"William G. Ewing — a brother of Colonel George Ewing — had some difficulty with a Mr. Berthelette [Brollioutte], another Indian trader, who was an intimate friend of Chief Richardville. Berthelette became very much incensed and went to see the chief about the matter."

I want your pistols, he said to the chief.

"Oui, oui; what for you want my pistol, Mr. Bar-te-lette?"

I want to kill Bill Ewing.

"Ah, oui, you shall have my pistol, Mr. Bar-te-lette; but come in and eat some dinner with me."

After dinner was over, Bertelette became restless, but the chief said no more about the pistols, so Bertelette finally pressed him. "Chief, now for the pistols."

"Ah, oui, I get you dem pistol." The chief retired a few minutes and came back with two bottles of wine. "Here, Mr. Bar-te-lette, my pistols," — handing him the two bottles of wine — "but take care now, you shoot yourself."

John B. Richardville ran a trading post at Ft. Wayne and later on the Wabash. His family remained at home on the St. Mary's, and on the Wabash, Madame Margaret La Folio [Follette?], a beautiful and gracious french lady, was his housekeeper for many years.

He died on St. Mary's, August 13, 1841. He had several sons who carried on the Richardville name. He was given a Catholic funeral, and his three daughters, La Blonde, Catherine, and Sarah erected a monument over his final resting place. See Stephens, pp. 28-29.

Many of the Richardville descendants can be found in the Indiana county records, especially the Knox County Records where the genealogist can easily trace the Richardville connections to the Donovan and Godare families, among many others.

RIDDLE (see also Ruddle) – "Captain John Riddle was born in Mississippi in 1809. He was the descendant of a Virginian who had married a full-blood Choctaw woman and settled in the Nation at an early day. Their daughter, Mary, reported to have been a very beautiful girl, married John Walker, also a Virginian. They in turn were the ancestors of Governor Tandy Walker, of Skullyville, who was therefore a relative of Captain John Riddle.'

"In 1831, the Riddles and the Walkers lived in the Northeastern (Mosholatubbi's) District of the nation east of the Mississippi River, on the highway a few miles from Demopolis, Alabama."

Captain John Riddle had attended Kentucky's Choctaw Academy when young and he became one of the most prominent leaders of his nation. His son, George Riddle, established Riddle's Station east of present Lutie, Oklahoma.

RIDOUT – an adopted Shawnee.

Thomas Ridout was captured near Limestone while enroute to Louisville in 1788. He wrote an interesting narrative of his capture by the Shawnees.

"...A white man, about twenty-two years of age, who had been taken prisoner when a lad and had been adopted, and was now a chief among the Shawnees, stood up and said to me in English, 'Don't be afraid, sir, you are in no danger, but are given to a good man, a chief of the Shawnees who will not hurt you; but after some time will take you to Detroit, where you may ransom yourself. Come and take your breakfast.'"

On the way to the Indian town, he saw that the party consisted of about ninety Shawnees, twelve Cherokees, and seven prisoners. While the Shawnees took time out to celebrate a feast, the Cherokees were assigned to guard and protect the prisoners.

Ridout gives a good account of life at the Shawnee hunting camp. After they had collected their pelts, they travelled to Detroit to trade. Along the way he encountered many interesting characters, including Simon Girty, George Ironside, The Great Snake, Black Fish, Blue Jacket, and others of note.

He was protected by Mr. Parkes [Parks] of the Miami and Mr. Sharp. With the help of Kakinathucca, who had adopted him, he obtained his release. He was well treated, and speaks highly of his captors, especially Kakinathucca.

Kakinathucca's wife was Metsigemewa. "About forty years old and rather corpulent." Ridout said of her, "...though her look was savage, her heart was naturally kind and tender." Kakinathucca's daughter was "about eighteen years of age, called Altowesa, of a very agreeable form and manners." She did not live with her father, according to Shawnee custom, lived with other relations. Kakinathucca's extended family also included a black man called Boatswain (or Boosini).

According to Ridout, Kakinathucca "had a principal share in the defeat of the American Army under St. Clair three or four years after this period."

Ridout says that Kakinathucca was "of the most mild and intelligent countenance. I never once saw him out of himself, and as soon as he arose, which was early, he began to sing." Ridout did not want to stay with the Indians, and Kakinathucca obtained his release.

Ridout says,"In the year 1799 my friend Kakinathucca, accompanied by three more Shawnee chiefs, came to pay me a visit at my house in York town (Toronto). He regarded myself and family with peculiar pleasure, and my wife and children contemplated with great satisfaction the noble and good qualities of this noble Indian. He died about the year 1806 under the hospitable care of Matthew Elliot..." See Ridout.

See "An Account of My Capture by the Shawnee Indians," reprinted in the WPHM, vol. 12, January, 1929.

ROBIDEAU, ROBIDIOUX, ROBIDOS – a Miami/Osage/Sioux name.

Henry Hays saw the French-Indian trader Robidos at the Glaize in 1789 along with James Sherlock, George Girty, and others. A Robidoes appears on the Miami payroll appearing in the Tipton Papers and the name became associated with many tribes who associated with the Miami. The Robidoux brothers, of the same basic family, operated a trading post out of St.

Joseph. The name became fairly common among several tribes.

Members of the Robideau family, Lakota Sioux, were prominent in Peter Matthiessen's chronicle of red\white confrontations in the 1970's, In the Spirit of Crazy Horse.

ROGERS or RODGERS – a Shawnee name.

Several members of the Rogers family were captured and adopted by Shawnees during the Beaver Wars and Pontiac's War. Among those captured in Virginia and given up in 1762 at Lancaster, Pennsylvania were Richard, Esther, and Jacob Rogers. See Minutes of the Provincial Council of Pennsylvania, p. 728.

When General George Rogers Clark attacked the Shawnee town of Piqua (Pickaway) in August of 1780, there were members of his family living among them, and at least one of them, a nephew, was at Piqua at the time. We know of this nephew, Joseph Rogers, because he reportedly ran out of the village toward Clark's men and was shot "by mistake." Wounded and dying, he identified himself and asked to speak to Clark, who refused to go see him.

Silverheels was among those Shawnees who fled Piqua and he reported to the British that Rogers was missing when he came away but that the Indians "harbour too good an opinion of him to think he is deserted..." See Seineke, p. 453.

Also living among the Shawnee was Henry Rogers, who had been adopted by Blackfish, but was probably living at another village. Henry Rogers' half-breed children included Lewis Rogers, William Rogers, Polly Rogers, and Graham Rogers.

About the year 1824, Mackinaw Beauchemie [Buschman], an adopted Potawatomi, married the Shawnee Polly Rogers, daughter of Henry Rogers, son-in-law of Blackfish. Their children included Annie (who married N. T. Shaler) and Julia Ann (who married Thomas Nesbit Stinson), Alexander, William, and Martha Boshman and possibly others.

Lewis Rogers, "a white chief of a band of Shawnees and Delawares on the upper Meramec," appealed to Meriwether Lewis for assistance after being threatened by Osage horse thieves. This was after the Lewis & Clark expedition. See Dillon, p. 291.

A Lewis Rogers was head of a holdhold among the Cherokees in Arkansas in 1828.

Graham Rogers was a carpenter for the Shawnees according to Caldwell, p. 22.

In 1851, there was a simmering dispute among the Shawnees. The dispute was the usual political one pitting the traditional tribal elders against the white-styled progressives, the conservatives vs. the liberals. The traditionalists included Blackhoof and George Bluejacket and the modernists included the Rev. Charles Bluejacket and Graham Rogers. The specific issue at hand in 1851 was whether the Shawnee council chief should be passed nephew to nephew in the traditional way or else elected by popular vote of the entire tribe, white-fashion.

When Chief John Perry died, he was succeeded by James Francis, the son of his sister, the last traditional hereditary chief. Thereafter, the chief was elected. In 1851, Joseph Parks was voted in as head chief and Graham Rogers as second chief. When Parks died in 1859, Graham Rogers became head chief.

In 1860, Paschal Fish and William Rogers were the principal chiefs of the Fish or Jackson band of Shawnees, with Charles Fish, Charles Tucker, George Daughtery, Charles Tooley, and Jackson Rogers, subchiefs and councilors. See Caldwell, p. 105.

The Shawnee Steward's book records several marriages included that of Lewis Rogers to Miria, William Rogers to Mary Gillis, Wilson Rogers to Polly

Samuels, all in 1843; then Benjamin Rogers to Jane Luckett in 1844, Rachel Rogers to William Donaldson in 1845, and Jane Rogers to Issac Parish in 1848. The Steward's book names Lewis Rogers as one of the "exhorters" of the church in 1839, William Rogers as a councilor, and Henry Rogers as a steward.

Lewis Henry Morgan, an ethnologist researching Shawnee customs, visited Graham and Anna Rogers. Graham had married Anna Carpenter, a daughter of Kotsey (Koh-che-qua) and Morgan said of her, "She is a half-breed, was educated at the Quaker Mission school, and is in every respect a bright, intelligent, and even beautiful woman...Their house is a fine one, and well furnished and as neat as a pin..."

The Shawnees furnished a company of men to the Thirteenth Regiment of the Kansas Militia during the Civil War, on the Union side. Graham Rogers was elected captain, Jackson Rogers first lieutenant, and Charles Bluejacket second lieutenant. After the war, Graham Rogers was again elected head chief.

The children of Graham and Anna Carpenter Rogers included daughters Cenith and Rachel and sons Richard and Stephen.

Cary Rodgers died in 1866 and left as heirs John Hat and George Spybuck who were his grandfathers and Mary Coon who was his cousin. See Kan. Hist. Col., vol. 15, p. 161.

Among the Shawnees who settled on the lands of the Cherokee nation by 1869 were Nancy B., David, Sally, John H., Aeenith, Rachel, Simpson, Eli, Serene, Samuel, Polly, Jackson, Soapqua, Henry, Mary, and Graham Rogers. See JAIFR, vol. IV, #2, pp. 100-111.

In 1871, Graham Rogers was listed as "late principal chief of the Shawnee Tribe" when 772 Shawnees officially joined the Cherokees on the Cherokee Reserve lands. The agreement was signed by Charles Tucker as "late assistant Shawnee chief," and by W. L. G. Miller as the tribal secretary. On behalf of the Cherokees, it was signed by Lewis Downing, "principal chief of the Cherokee Nation."

Among the Shawnee guardianship cases reviewed by the Commissioner of Indian Affairs in 1871 were the cases of William, Jackson, Graham, and Wilson Rogers. The wards of these men are not listed. The wife of Wilson Rogers was "a cousin to Cornatzer's wife." See JAIFR, vol. VIII, #2, p. 28.

ROSS – a Shawnee name.

Jacob White told Draper that in 1778, "Lt. Parks of John Gibson's regiment and David Ross, a spy (a former prisoner with the Indians) generally called by his Dutch friends Tavernor Ross...were both killed by Indians."

As others have noted, apparently White was wrong about the death of Ross, because pioneer Samuel Murphy told Draper that he knew Ross well, that Ross had been captured and adopted during the French & Indian War, that he was twenty years with the Indians, that he fought on the Indian side at the Battle of Pt. Pleasant, that after Dunmore's War, he returned to live among the whites and settled in Butler County, Pennsylvania. See Draper Mss. 3S5-17. 3S320-23 and 3S9, 5S7-9.

RUDDLE or RIDDLE – a Shawnee name.

Several members of Issac Ruddle's family, including at least two sons — twelve-year-old Stephen and six-year-old Abram — were captured at Martin's and Ruddle's Station (on Licking Creek, Kentucky) and were given to the Shawnees. Both boys grew up to be major hunters and councilors among the Indians. The Ruddles fought on the red side at Harmer's Defeat and at St. Clair's Defeat. And both married Indian women.

But after the Battle of Fallen Timbers, according to Daniel Trabue's first-hand account (edited a little to correct the spelling): "General Wayne did hire some of the first Indians that came to the treaty to go to other towns and get the Indians to come to the treaty...

"...A number of men and women that came to this treaty that had been taken when children did look like Indians...we saw an Indian a-riding up towards the fort, and when he got in about 200 yards, he halted. Capt. McColester beckoned to him and told him to advance. He came up some nigher and stopped. Capt. McColester went out to meet him and I went with him. We took no arms with us, and this Indian told us he was a chief and he was willing to talk a little about this treaty. He could speak broken English.

"When he told us what nation he belonged to, Capt. McColester asked him if he knew Stephen Riddle and Abram Riddle. He said he did. Capt. McColester then told this Indian that the father of the Riddles was then at Greenville and wanted very much to see his children, and that he (old Capt. Riddle) had given many presents to other Indians to go with presents to his children and persuade them to come in.

"Capt. McColester invited this Indian when he first came up to alight and come into the fort. Drink some whiskey. He refused and after talking some time and asking him more particular about the Riddles, he said, `Me,' and striking his hand on his breast said, `Me Stephen Liddle.

"The Capt. and immediately shook hands with him and told him we was mighty glad, we was mighty well acquainted with his father..."

At first, Trabue suspected that the man was an imposter as he looked like a full-blooded Indian. But later he found that all the whites among the Indians looked like full-bloods. Stephen Ruddle rode in on horseback with his Shawnee wife, his brother Abram, and Abram's adopted brother. Trabue thought none of them could speak English, except for Stephen, and his was broken.

They took them to Capt. Issac Ruddle and introduced them.

"Immediately old Ruddle cried out aloud and fell down on the floor, crying and bewailing his condition. Said he, `My children are Indians!'

"Stephen took hold of his father and said, 'Holt your heart, fater. Hold your heart, fater.'

"These Indians, the white women, and some of the soldiers all cried and several cried aloud. Old Capt. Ruddle continued some time crying. Whenever he would look at his children he would renew his crying..."

But the next day, Issac Ruddle tried to get his sons to dress as white men and to get them to come home with him. Abram agreed to go, but Stephen refused to go unless he could take his Shawnee wife. Old Issac Ruddle took Trabue aside after two or three days and asked him to persuade Stephen to "quit his old squah and go home with him."

"I talked to him about it. Stephen said he would not give up his squaw. He was willing to go home with his father but he would take her with him. He would not give her up for any woman in the world."

Stephen Ruddle's wife was too dark for Trabue's taste, but he noted that she was a remarkable woman. He says, that one night at Greenville, Stephen Ruddle's horses ran away with the horses of the other Indians. Trabue asked Stephen if he was going to hunt them, and the reply was that, no, his wife had gone after them. "Who went with her?" Trabue wanted to know. No one, he was told. She was capable of tracking the horses by herself.

Trabue notes that "She was gone two or three days and brought all their horses (5 in number) and she by herself. She found the horses at a distance of 40 miles. I then thought she was worth all the rest of her company together...I saw many such circumstances of the kind."

The account given here is from pp. 140-143 of The Narrative of David Trabue, edited by Chester Raymond Young to whom we are indebted. Another similar first-hand account of the meeting is in Draper Mss. 32S453.

Stephen Ruddle came back to the whites and took up the safest profession among Indians trying to live white, becoming a Baptist preacher, proclaiming himself saved, and traveling across Ohio, Kentucky, Indiana, Illinois, and Missouri. He died in Illinois in 1845. His son, by a later white wife, was supposed to have been John M. Ruddle, represented Adams County in the Illinois House of Representatives, 1846-1848.

Abram Ruddle was taken younger and clung harder to his Indian ways than Stephan did. He served as a scout and an interpreter for several years, then he and his wife Mary (Culp) went to New Madrid, Missouri. About 1812, they moved to Batesville, Arkansas where they lived until Abraham Ruddle died in 1857. His children included Abraham, Daniel, America Ann Caldwell, Sally Criswell, Elizabeth Shannon, and Esther Harris. See Barb, p. 20.

Some of the Ruddle family continued to associate with the Shawnees. Captain Issac Ruddle's will, probated in Bourbon County in 1812, mentions sons Stephen, Abraham, George, Issac jr., Cornelius, and daughters Elizabeth Mulharen and Margaret Dewitt, and several grandchildren. Some of the family had moved to southern Indiana and were engaged in Indian trading until the War of 1812.

Some of the family seems to have married into families with Shawnee names. George and his wife Theodosia (Linn) Ruddle (also taken at Ruddles Station as a child and adopted), then of New Madrid, sold their Bourbon County, Kentucky property. One George Ruddle married Clorinda (Clarinda) Gore and among their children was Ambrose Gore Ruddle who married into the Lair (Lail) family.

According to historian William E. Connelley, "A daughter of Issac Ruddle [Sarah] was carried away captive when the station was destroyed and remained among the Shawnee for a number of years. Later she married a man named [Thomas] Davis and settled at Fayette, Missouri. Her daughter married Rev. Thomas Johnson, a Methodist preacher, who founded the old Shawnee Mission in what is now Johnson County, Kansas. When she came to live with her daughter she found many Shawnees she had known in Ohio when in captivity. They were much attached to her before she was rescued and they were greatly pleased to have her with them there. She knew the Shawnee language as well as she knew her own and the Shawnees spent hours and hours talking to her about old times." See Lafferty, pp. 313-318.

This was Sarah (Ruddle) Davis Johnson. Kansas artist Charles Goslin, an adopted Shawnee, discovered Sarah T. Johnson's Holy Bible along with a hymnal, the hymns translated into Shawnee, possibly by Sarah Johnson herself. At his own expense, he had some copies of the hymnal reproduced and he was kind enough to give me a copy. Goslin is an excellent man, and I appreciate his timely assistance.

Among the Shawnees, Cherokees, and Delawares who had been given permission to join the Oklahoma Cherokees and were living in the Cooweescoowee District in 1880 were Joseph Ruddles (age 55), listed as an adopted white man, J. F. (age 24), probably a daughter, J. L. (23), C. B. (22), probably sons, and Mary E. (16), Emma (13), Augustus (11), Oliver (9), Nora (3), Cynthia (46), Charles R. (22), and William (3). All of the children are listed as native Cherokees except William who was an adopted black/Cherokee. See JAIFR, vol. 10, #3, p. 15.

ROBITAILLE, ROBITAIL, etc. – a Wyandot name.

"Robert Robitaille, an engaging French-Canadian of good family, also is known to have lived in Zane's Town, possibly as early as 1793 or 1794, bringing with him from Montreal a stock of goods with which he set up a trading post with the Wyandot Indians." He was in Ohio "when the first settlers arrived, and he had married Elizabeth Zane previous to 1800, while at the time of his removal to the Ludlow district south of Bellefontaine, they had two sons." See MMV, p. 175. His descendants can trace their lineage back to Tarhe, the Wyandot Half King.

As with the Zane, Ranken, Hicks, Peacock, Punch, Barbee, Tulli, and Clark families, among many others, some of the part-Wyandot descendants of Robert Robitalle stayed in Ohio, and some went west. Some later came back to Ohio and their descendants have carried the Indian blood tradition to Kentucky, to Indiana, and eventually to all points of the compass.

The 1850 Jackson County, Missouri, census listed Robert Robitaille (a merchant, age 46), with children Robert W., 12, Rosalie, 10, Elizabeth, 8, James, 4, and Mary A., 2. Robert Robitaille became the first postmaster at Union Town trading post. He traded with the Wyandot and Potawatomi Nations, among others. See Barry, pp. 880, 949, 985-986, 1025.

On the 1855 Wyandot census, a family is listed which included Robert Robitaille, age 50, Robert Wolford Robitaille, 17, Rosalie Robitaille, 15, Elizabeth Robitaille, 13, James Robitaille, 10, and Mary Ann Robitaille, 7. See KHC, vol. 15, p. 115.

Among the Wyandot guardianship cases reviewed by the Commissioner of Indian Affairs in 1871 was that of Robert Robitaille, guardian for the children of both Elizabeth Peacock and James Bearskin. George and Joseph Bearskin were his wards. See JAIFR, vol. VIII, #2, p. 21.

Among the Wyandots listed on the 1900 Federal Census of Indian Territory were Charles, Frank, and Lena E. Robitaille. Lena was Frank's sister; their father was born in Canada, their mother in Ohio. Lena Robitaille lived in the household of Alfred Mudeater, her brother-in-law, and his wife Julia Mudeater. Charles Robitaille lived in the household of his brother-in-law, Robert Schiffhauer and his wife, Azilda. Robert Schiffhauer's father was a German-American, his mother was a Seneca, and his wife a Wyandot. See Prevost, p. 84.

SAMPSON – a Shawnee name.

Listed as living among the Shawnees, Wyandots, and Delawares in the Ohio Company papers from 1856 were Sampson, Sampson's brother, and Sampson's son. See Bailey.

G. S. Sampson — a justice of the peace of Crawford County, Ohio — signed the 1832 Treaty with the Wyandots. See Watson, pt. 4, p. 47.

Among the Shawnees allotted funds for improvements upon their Ohio property that they were forced to leave behind in 1833 was Sampson who was paid $31. See Watson, pt. 3, p. 15.

Listed on the Muster Roll of Shawnee Indians of the Hog Creek and Wapakonetta bands was the Sampson family which included two males between 25 and 55, one female between 10 and 25, and three children under 10, two of them girls. See Roy, p. 43.

SANDERS or SAUNDERS – a Shawnee/Cherokee name.

A young man of the Sanders family was some distance from the fort when the Shawnees came to Boonesboro. Later, after the Indians were gone, a search party was sent out, but no trace of Sanders was found.

The John Sanders who was among the original settlers of Louisville certainly had lived among the Indians for a while, either as a captive or voluntarily. He occasionally served as a guide and an interpreter. Primarily, though, he was an Indian trader and an independent long hunter, supplying the settlements with meat during hard times. I have met Sanders descendants who claim an Indian blood tradition and think that they descend from this man.

John Sanders was with a party of hunters, including John Duff, when George Roger Clark launched his attack against Kaskakia. Clark impressed them into service as guides, but he did not trust them. Sanders had some tense moments on the trip, because some of Clark's men suspected that he was getting them lost — on purpose. He led them to Kaskakia, however, and was rewarded for his service.

John Sanders was a renown hunter, and he is noted in the Thruston papers and elsewhere for supplying the early Kentucky settlements with meat. He was the the trading partner of William Grills when they left Louisville for their hunting camp and were never heard of again, supposedly killed by Indians on Eighteen-mile island circa 1785. See Draper Mss. 13J33-36...

Among the Indians doing business at McClure's trading post (1804-1810) was "the Shawnee James Sanders" along with other notables including Captain Johnny, General Mudeater, John Battise, and Chieska.

Among the Shawnees given tracts of land in Ohio by the 1817 Treaty of the Miami of Like Erie was "Tapea or Sanders." See Harvey, p. 166.

In June, 1853, Capt. John W. Gunnison's expedition passed through the Shawnee reservation, stopped at Thomas Stinson's trading post, and hired three "Delaware Indians (John Moses, guide; Wahhone, hunter; James Sanders, interpreter)." See Barry, p. 1168.

Among the Shawnees living in the Cooweescoowee District as listed on the 1880 Cherokee census were Ann Sanders (age 25) and Minnie Sanders (age 9). See JAIFR, vol. X, #3, p. 17.

The Saunders family also has an Indian blood tradition. Joseph Saunders was also a scout, and George Rogers Clark wrote that he considered him one of the most dependable. Even after Matthew Elliot's threat to have him killed, Saunders served as an express rider through the Indian territory. See Draper 11J123 for Saunders' deposition concerning the hostility of the

Indians. Also see Draper 1W185 and 14S216-219.

James Saunders (or Sanders) was among the Shawnees allotted land at Wapakonetta. See Prevost, p. 2.

Samuel Saunders (or Sanders) was a Shawnee interpreter for Tecumseh. See Sugden, p. 55. Samuel Sanders was an indentured servant who came from England to Virginia about 1760. From there he went to Kentucky and was captured by Shawnees, possibly at Boonesboro, and adopted. His daughter married Adam Brown, jr., who was part-Wyandot. One of their daughter was Quindaro Nancy Brown who married Alberie (or Albelard) Gutherie who was later a Congressman. See Prevost, p. 87.

SARRAFRASS or SARRSHAFS – a Wyandot name.

There were two households on the 1843 Muster Roll of Wyandots from Sandusky, Ohio. One Sarrahafs family consisted of a male over 25, a male between 10 and 25, and a female between 10 and 25. The other Sarrahafs family consisted of two males over 55, one male and one female 25 to 55, and one male under 10.

Also on the 1843 Wyandot Muster Roll was the John Sarrahafs family, consisting of one male 25 to 55, one female 10 to 25, and one male under 10.

SARXOXIE – a Delaware name.

Anderson Sarcoxie, a son of old Chief William Anderson, and John Connor, principal chiefs of the Delaware in 1861, issued a resolution calling on all the tribes in the region to stand by the Union. They sent fifty mounted warriors into the northern army. See Hoig, p. 139.

Among the Delawares living in the Cooweescoowee District and appearing on the 1880 Cherokee census were Elizabeth (age 27), Henry (15), Reuben (5), John (59), Lizzie (44), Henry (9), William

(38), Lizzie (16), Nancy (16), Jeff (14), and Anderson Sarcoxie (9). See JAIFR, vol. X, #3, p. 16.

SCARRETT – a Shawnee name.

Among the Shawnees who settled on the lands of the Cherokee nation by 1869 was Edward Scarrett. See JAIFR, vol. IV, #2, pp. 100-111.

SCOTT – a Shawnee/Seneca name.

Daniel Trabue wrote that when his brother, James, was taken prisoner at Ruddles Station in 1780, he had a slave, "a very likely young negro woman," captured by the Indians. "I heard where she was but could not get any Indians to fetch her. General Wayne told them they must fetch her and all the rest of the prisoners to this treaty. This negro woman had at that time 2 or 3 children. Her name was Selah. She was at, as I understood, near the mouth of St. Duskey but some of the Indians denied it. It was stated that a half-breed Indian by the name of Joe Scott had her as his servant. The Indians did not bring in all the prisoners." See Chester Raymond Young, p. 142.

SECONDINE, SAGUNDAI, or SECONDEYE – a Delaware /Shawnee name.

A white boy found by a Delaware war party was adopted by James Secondine. The boy grew up Delaware and took the name Thomas Secondine. He later married Jane Hill, the part-Delaware daughter of the White/Delaware free hunter Tom Hill (who had also been adopted as a child).

The first Secondine was a son of Chief William Anderson, and mentioned as such in a letter of the old chief shortly before his death. Along with James Swannuck, Crane, Big Nichols, and others, James Secondine became famous as a free Delaware hunter, roaming the west and occasionally hiring out for scout duty with Capt. James Fremont and others of note. James Secondine became affiliated with the Texas Delawares along with John Shaw, Jack Harry, and James Connors. About 1811, James Secondine married Nancy Washington Hill, a Wyandot. She had previously been married to Tom Hill and already had a child, named Sally Hill.

James Secondine and the other Texas Delawares served with Sam Houston in Texas. Later, Secondine saved the life of Kit Carson by jumping off his horse and striking down a Klamath man who was about to assassinate him.

The children of James Secondine included:

1. Filmore Secondine who married Rachel Logan, a daughter of Nancy Conner, wife of John Conner. Their children included Wilson, Rosa, Issac, and Anna Secondine. Later, Filmore Secondine also had two children by Betsy Jackson. He later married a Shawnee woman, Lucy Dick, by whom he had four more children. Still later, he married Jane Partridge and had Filmore W. Secondine and Esther Secondine who married a Moore and then a Sims and had eight children. Small wonder that the Secondine family has so many descendants around.
2. Thomas Secondine (adopted) who married Jane Hill, daughter of the adopted Delaware scout Thomas Hill. Thomas and Jane Secondine's children included Anna, Lizzy, Joseph, Anderson W., Lilly, Silas, Lucinda, Katie and Jacob. Thomas then married Malinda Harvey and had two more children by her. Lizzy married into the Marshall, James, Longtail, and Dillon families and had several children.
3. Mary C. Secondine, born 1847, in Kansas,

who married Charles Armstrong by whom she had Solomon F. Armstrong. She then married Thompson Smith and had two children. She later married Stephen Bezion (1858-1907), an educated man who played a major role in Delaware affairs after they joined the Cherokee nation. Solomon F. Armstrong became a renown cowboy when he was nineteen, married a white girl named Minnie May and their children included Myrtle R. Armstrong who married Mattox and Ruby D. Armstrong who married Reuben Sarcoxie.

4. John Secondine (b. 1850) who married Mary Jane Martin; then he married Julia Ann Ketchum; then he married a Shawnee girl, Emma Perry. He had Nancy, Laura, and Susanna by his first wife; and by Emma, his Shawnee wife, he had Victoria, Tecumpsi, Delaware, Anna E., Clarence, and John.
5. Matilda Secondine who married Jefferson Zane (1844-1912). Their children included Mary, Willie, Arizona, Maggie, Mina D., Ethel, and Minbnie Zane.
6. Simon Secondine who married Ruth Lyons.

For a much more elaborate account of this family, see Cranor.

Among the Delawares living in the Cooweescoowee District and appearing on the 1880 Cherokee census were Tom (age 40), Jane (36), Lizzie (15), Joseph (12), Anderson (10), Jacob (4), Silas (3), Lucinda (2), Simon (25), Polly (16), Jane (24), Rosie (11), Issac (6), Anna (3), Rosie (3), Charlie (7 months), and Alvin Secondine (38). See JAIFR, vol. X, #3, pp. 17-18.

Eva Secondine, a Shawnee, is mentioned in *Shawnee!*, a book on tribal customs and ceremonials. See Howard, pp. 160, 254, 293-294.

SHANE, CHENE, CHAINE, etc. – an Ottawa/ Shawnee name.

Isadore Cheine was a French Indian trader. In 1777, he was with Blackfish of the Shawnees and helped to plot the attack on Boonesboro. His son by his Ottawa wife was called Anthony Shane, who lived among the Shawnee and became one of the most important scouts for the United States in the War of 1812.

McAfee, in his recollections of the war, tells of "their trusty guide," Anthony Shane, of how Shane was at the River Raison and had seen Capt. Joseph Simpson fall. He led McAfee to the site later and pointed out the exact spot to him. They all thought he had been killed there, but Shane somehow escaped. Or did Tecumseh let him go? See the interview with Nathan Reid in Draper 10NN.

Anthony Shane served as interpreter for the Ft. Wayne agency after the war, and it is from his recollections (found in the Draper and Shane papers) that we have most of our information on Tecumseh.

Both Anthony Shane and his father were large men. The elder Shane died June 29, 1793 according to one of his granddaughters. See Draper Ms. 4J145.

Anthony Shane's Shawnee wife was named Lawnatese or Launateshe, from the same clan as Tecumseh. His brother, Joseph Shane or Dushane, lived among the Shawnees at Lewistown and appears to have married a Seneca there. Charles Shane or Chein, son of Anthony Shane, attended Richard M. Johnson's Choctaw Academy in Kentucky in the 1830's.

In 1838, Charles Shane was serving as an interpreter for the Shawnees when he joined Capt. Joseph Parks Company and went to Florida where he served in the Seminole War. Joseph Deshane is on the muster roll, but Charles is not. However, Caldwell says that they were forced to use a different interpreter at the mission, as Chein was called to the Florida War. See

Caldwell, p. 25.

Mary Shane was among the Shawnees allotted land on the Shawnee reserve in the 1850's. See KHC, vol. 15, p. 179.

Among the Shawnees who resided on the Cherokee Reserve in 1871 were John and Phoebe Shane. See JAIFR, vol. IV, #2, p. 108.

SHAPP or SNAPP – a Miami name.

Shap-peer-a-maw, abbreviated by the whites as Shappeen, died at his village east of Roanoke, Indiana. His son, who was well-educated, went west with some of his tribe. See Draper 1YY117-118.

Shappstown was the name of a Miami village in Indiana.

Listed among the Miami in 1880 Census were Mary Shapp (Pu-quish-e-mo-quah, sun-setting), age 20, and her ward Elizabeth Davis, age 9.

Listed on the 1893 Miami Payroll were Peter, Mary, and Susan Shapp.

On the 1895 Miami Payroll are listed Joseph, Charles, John, Walter, and Suzette Shapp.

SHARP – a Mingo name.

According to family tradition, Indians raided the Sharp homestead while Abraham and his nephew Solomon Sharp, the only adult males of the household, were away on a scouting expedition. The cabin was burned and Rebecca Armstrong Sharp, wife of Abraham, and their three older children — Catherine, Mary, and William — were captured. Another child, Priscella (born 1785), escaped by hiding in the well.

Attempts were made to obtain their release, and the Indians demanded their ransom in horses. Some horses were collected, but only enough to ransom Rebecca and Catherine. The other children, Mary and John or William, were adopted at the Indian towns.

After several years, they were "rescued" by a party of white men who burned the village. Returning to Kentucky, the men stopped at Corn Island to spend the night. During the night, Mary escaped from her "rescuers" and returned to the Indians where she married a chief. Her brother, John or William Sharp, also wanted to return to the Indians and "had to be watched."

According to Draper 11YY11, a Miss Sharp was taken prisoner when a child and adopted; "she grew up pretty and became the wife of the Crane."

In 1788, Ridout noted that a Mr. Sharpe was one of the English traders who lived at Fort Miami. See Ridout, p. 28.

SHAW or SHAWNEE – a Delaware/Shawnee/Cherokee name.

John Shaw, a white man, was a scout and express rider for the Fort Wayne agency in 1813 along with John Flinn and Abraham Ash. See Thornbrough, index. John Shaw or his sons may have had their red connections. Men alternately carrying the names and John Shaw and John Shawnee were associated with the tribe over a long time in Ohio, Indiana, Kansas, Texas, and Oklahoma.

"During late March, Van Dorn had sent a requisition to Capt. S. P. Ross, agent for the Brazos Reservation, requesting a body of friendly Indian scouts and trailers. Fifty-eight, including Wacos, Caddos, Kichis, Tonkawas, Delawares, Shawnees, and others arrived on April 27 [1859]. They were led by a Delaware the whites called Jack Harry and another Indian called Shawnee Jim. The latter, a veteran of the Texas Revolution, was a man of considerable intelligence and spoke excellent English." Chalfant, p. 51. Shawnee Jim was James Shawnee and also Jim Shaw, apparently.

A Jim Shaw, his wife Nancy, and their two daughters appear with the families of Joe Harry, George

Williams and others on a list of Texas Delawares, some of whom had Shawnee connections. See Staab, A List of Delawares...

Jim Shaw and Jack Harry were scouts working with Jesse Chisholm on the Texas frontier. See Hoig, pp. 54-55.

Among the Delawares who served in Company M. of the 6th Kansas Volunteer Cavalry in 1864 was John Shawnee. See Weslager, p. 514.

Among the Delawares, Shawnees, and Cherokees living in the Cooweescoowee District and appearing on the 1880 Cherokee census were John Shawnee (33) and his family which included Julie (26), Lizzie (17), Charley (4), and a one month old baby named Ida Shawnee. This family is listed as Shawnees but they were probably mixed bloods.

There is also a Cherokee Shawnee (age 25) and Lydia Shawnee (age 19) listed as Cherokees. See JAIFR, vol. X, #3, p. 18.

Jim Shaw and Jane Shawnee appear on on the list of Delawares admitted to the Cherokee Nation in 1867. See Prevost, p. 22. On page 12, Prevost says that John Shawnee was a Delaware who spoke seven languages, and that the family was originally French, not Shawnee.

William (Bill) Shawnee is quoted throughout James H. Howard's Shawnee! (1981), a book on Shawnee customs and ceremonials.

A son of Bill and Nellie (Beaver) Shawnee was William Shawnee, born in 1918. William Shawnee enlisted in the United States Army and retired after thirty years. After he died in January, 1979, Bert Ellis spoke in Shawnee as a part of the funeral rites. An honor guard from Ft. Sill, Lawton, Oklahoma, provided full military honors, bearing his casket, playing "Taps," and giving a gun salute.

Survivors included his wife, Marie, and children who included five sons — Curtis, Lewis, Lynn, Markus, and Keith — and three daughters who included Mrs. Billie Marie Chism and Linda Sue Shawnee, both of Oklahoma, and Mrs. Beverly Ann Pope of Kansas. Two sons preceded him in death: Richard Dwayne Shawnee who drowned in 1958, and PFC Clark Shawnee who was killed in Viet Nam. For further details and a picture of William Shawnee, which shows him to have looked as white as any of the Ohio Shawnees, see SOCC, vol. 2, p. 260, information from Dorothy Nix.

SHERLOCK – a Delaware name.

James Sherlock was one of the defenders of Ft. Jefferson, several of whom, tradition says, had Indian wives.

Along with David Owens, he was living among the Indians in 1761. I do not yet know where he came from nor where he received his education. Perhaps he was one of the family of the early Virginian, Thomas Sherlock, an Anglican priest. James Sherlock read and wrote well, especially when you consider that not many on the frontier could even sign their names.

The Indians trusted Sherlock, and at the Easton Pennsylvania peace conference in July, 1761, an Onondaga chief recommended him as interpreter, saying to the Pennsylvania Lt. Governor, "Brother, when I receive a letter, I cannot understand it...wherefore I take my child James Sherlock by the hand and present him to you, that with your leave, he may live amongst us, and serve as interpreter on all occasions."

The Lt. Governor replied that he would have to check into the qualifications of James Sherlock, who was "a young man and a stranger" to him. I'm guessing that Sherlock was a teenager at the time, and he must have been with the Iroquois at least a year to have learned their language so well. He did serve as interpreter on at least one occasion during the subsequent councils.

He was still living among the Indians during Pontiacs War. Perhaps, with the idealism of youth, he sympathized with the Indians and their cause — which was, really, to stop the loss of their lands to the English. Former captives told of James Sherlock among the Indians..."that Sherlock was a bad man and went around painted...that after Du Coigne's visit there, two deserters had run off, but that Sherlock remained and that the chief would not give him up..."

Such reports cause Sir William Johnson to stipulate in Article Fourteen of the ensuing treaty that the Indians "deliver up the deserter Sherlock."

He does not appear to have been punished after the peace; I find his name listed that following spring as a trader for the firm of Baynton, Wharton, and Morgan. Then, for fifteen years, I find no trace of him. Maybe he returned east to live in the cities. Maybe he was with Baptist Ducoign in Arkansas. But he may just have been living quietly amongst the Delawares, keeping his name out of the records.

At any event, when next I find his name, he is one of George Rogers Clark's men. He accompanied Clark to what would become Louisville. He went on with the army to Kaskakia as interpreter to the friendly Indians, especially Baptist Ducoign's band. He accompanied Ducoign to Ft. Jefferson and was in the battle there.

In 1781, he was with Baptist Ducoigne and Capt. John Dodge enroute to an audience with Thomas Jefferson in Virginia, but just as they arrived, the British attacked and Jefferson fled. While Sherlock helped to save some of the public documents, the British arrived and captured his horse. The small party escaped and came back to Louisville by way of Ft. Pitt.

In 1782, Clark sent Sherlock down the Ohio river to help Robert George make peace with the Chickasaws.

He served as interpreter in the council on October 24th, 1982, during which the American Revolution was explained to them in the following words, translated by Sherlock, "...the English and the Americans were even as one family, but the English grew proud and thought themselves our superiors, that we should be deprived of our liberties and rights, and like servile slaves support them with our labor, but our spirits would not permit us to condescend to such impositions—in opposition to their tyrannical proceedings we took arms in defense of ourselves..."

While Sherlock was with the Chickasaws, George Rogers Clark took an army to destory the Shawnee towns. The warriors were all gone, but Clark's forces killed some of the women and old men, burnt the towns and the crops, and brought seven squaws back as hostages along with their children.

The hostages were taken to the Danville area, and held a long time. A Danville/Louisville merchant, Bartholomew Tardiveau, wrote Clark in the spring of 1783 that, "One of the Indian squaws, your prisoner, councils that of she was permitted to return to her people in the company of Mr. Sherlock, the interpreter, she can easily bring her nation, and in all probability several others, to terms of peace. She offers to leave her child as a pledge of her faith and if she does not succeed, promises to come back and surrender herself a prisoner for life..."

Tardiveau related that "the squaw has great sway among the Shawnees," and suggested that at least an exchange of prisoners might be worked out should her plan be followed. He reminded Clark that peace would be good for Louisville's business community.

Perhaps they had trouble getting Sherlock to go along with the plan. But eventually he agreed — for $100.00. When Sherlock and the squaw arrived at the

Shawnee towns with the letter of peace, however, they were both thrown into confinement. Sherlock told them that, if they didn't believe him, they might at least believe the squaw; but the Indians said that she had associated with white people for so long, they were afraid that she had become as corrupt as they were. The Indians said that they would take the letter to Alexander McKee, an Indian whom they trusted. If the letter did not read right, they said that Sherlock and the squaw would be put to death.

At this time, the squaw's brother came into camp and happened to look through a crack in the door and see Sherlock and his sister. He immediately released his sister, and convinced the other Indians to take Sherlock along with them to see Alexander McKee.

At McKee's trading post, the Indians agreed to stop all hostilities and also to the terms of the exchange of prisoners as laid out in the letter. Sherlock left the council on May 29th, 1783, with a letter from McKee to Major George Walls, then commander at Louisville. But shortly after he left, some Kentuckians raided a Shawnee hunting party and stole some horses from them, and a Shawnee was killed in the skirmish. Angered at this turn of events, a war party set out to cut Sherlock off before he could cross the Ohio River, but they were too late.

However, this put a kink into the peace negotiations, and Sherlock's services were extended on the promises of future reimbursement. On September 12th, 1783, Major Walls instructed Sherlock to go to the Shawnees and return by October 30th with as many prisoners as possible. But the negotiations dragged on.

Finally, on March 2nd, 1783, the Indians sent letters of peace to Louisville in Sherlock's handwriting. Still, no prisoners were released.

On April 10th, Major Walls wrote Sherlock, "...The Governor, from my recommendation of you, has not been forgetful of you. For God's sake, do not do my recommendation discredit. Your own fortune in great measure depends on the results of your present conduct. Your detention during the winter, I expect, will be rather advantageous than detrimental; especially, as I have hopes that it paves the way for your bringing in the prisoners without fail. And you have just reason, not only to expect but in a great measure be assured of receiving to yourself a valuable consideration for every prisoner you bring in — from the parents, guardians, or friends of them respectively. Exclusive of the views I have from Gov't in your favor — in that, exert yourself on this occasion, and there is next to a certainty of your being a man of consequence ever hereafter..."

This "man of consequence" stuff may not have appealed to James Sherlock. His entire lifestyle seems to have been one of unattachment. He was not enthused with Louisville's social life. During Louisville's first Christmas celebration, it was James Sherlock whom Clark selected (or perhaps he volunteered) to stand guard over the ammunition stores on Corn Island while the rest of the garrison joined in the festivities. James Sherlock was literate, yet he made no land claims in Kentucky despite his abundant opportunities to do so.

The Jefferson County Court records show that he was involved in small suits from time to time, but not once is his name connected with theft, nor assault, nor scandal, nor drunken behavior. Set against the records of the average citizen, he seems remarkably soft-spoken and clean-cut.

Anyway, the peace was made. The terms agreed by both sides were that Kentuckians were to stay south of the Ohio River except for trading parties. The language of the treaties suggests that Sherlock gave his personal word that there was to be no hunting and no settlement of whites upon Indian land as it was then defined. But it was the struggle for land, more than anything else, that made a lasting peace impossible.

In May of 1785, he again attended a council at the Shawnee town. Captain Johnny said that, since the last treaty they had "found the white people settling in many parts of the country...We see your intention. You are drawing close to us and so near our bedsides that we can almost hear the noise of your axes falling our trees and settling the country..."

Sherlock brought several prisoners home. One of them was John Moffitt, who later, with his brother George, made his home in Guernsey County, Ohio. Sherlock was not rewarded for the prisoners he was able to free, but was instead sued by several people for debt. Finally, he was sued by John Rogers in August of 1785, the last of his military certificate was garnished, and Sherlock was broke.

The United States commissioners were in Louisville to re-negotiate the treaty with the Indians at the time. The commissioners wanted to push the Indian boundary north and allow settlement of southern Ohio.

One of the commissioners, Richard Butler, noted in his journal in September, 1785, "One Sherlock and Dolman having offered some information to the commissioners some days ago and were directed to take their time and consider matters fully, were preparing to go to the Shawnee towns with the Indians and again proposed giving in the information which they thought affected the United States. The Commission ordered Mr. Campbell, the secretary, to qualify them and take their depositions..."

The depositions were to the effect that the Shawnees and Delawares were for peace, but that there was a banditti of some Cherokee and Mingo warriors living on Paint Creek causing mischief, and that these warriors were beyond the control of the tribes. After giving this information to the commissioners, Sherlock apparently went back to reside among the Delawares.

The next notice I can find of James Sherlock (as Shirelock) is in Hay's Journal in March, 1790. He was working for a Mr. Leith, for whom Sherlock arrested and brought in a thief named Montroille. Sherlock delivered Montroille to Mr. Leith, who agreed to let him work the damages off. Then Hays noted that Sherlock and George Girty went back to their wintering camps.

Quaife identifies the Mr. Leith as a Detroit trader, but there was also John Leith, an adopted Delaware who married another adopted Delaware, and after the Treaty of Greenville, they lived among the Monravians for a while, then settled in Guernsey County, Ohio. On the first tax lists of that county, a John Leith, a George Moffitt and a James Sharock (sometimes Sharlock, Sharrok, Sharrick, etc.) appear. This was certainly the George Moffitt who had been a captive, but was the James Sharock actually James Sherlock?

James Sharock's sons appear in the early Ohio records, including John, Timothy, Everitt, and Benjamin Sharrock. According to the History of Wyandot County, Ohio, it was Ben Sharrok who killed "the notoriously bad" Seneca, Nickels, after he and his brother, Everard Sharrok had been threatened. An Elizabeth Sharlock married John Collins in Belmont County on January 9, 1809.

Were these people descendants of James Sherlock and his Delaware wife? Was the Delaware chief, James Swannuck, the son of James Sherlock? The name was sometimes given as Swarnock, and we know that the Delawares would have trouble pronouncing the "R" sound.

I wonder.

For references and additional notes, see Sherlock.

SHIELDS – a Shawnee/Miami/Peoria name.

John Tipton married Jeanette Shields, his cousin, the daughter of John and Nancy Shields. His father-in-law went on the Lewis and Clark Expedition. Was his mother-in-law a Shawnee or Miami? Was his wife a cousin to John Tipton or his previous wife? And was she a Shawnee? See Yater, p. 8.

Mary Shields, formerly Mary Dageny, was a Wea Indian who was allotted land. See American State Papers, Indian Affairs, vol. 2, p. 168.

SHILLING – a Shawnee name.

Jacob and/or Palsor (Baltzer, Beltser, Palser, Peltser. etc.) Shilling was among the men serving in George Owens Company at Ft. Jefferson. The family appears to have had a long association with the Owens family.

Balser Shilling was an indentured servant of the Eckerlins. The Eckerlins, pious folk, had some differences with their church, the ephratians, sometimes called the Dunkard Church.

The Eckerlin brothers robbed the Church of a treasure in silver and precious gems, and they moved to the wilderness — land that is now a part of southwestern Pennsylvania. Here, they helped to establish one of the first white settlements in the area.

One of their sisters, Rebecca Ann Eckerlin, married Adam Doane of "The Terrible Doanes," who later robbed and murdered throughout the area of the Upper Ohio and Monongahela Rivers.

Another sister, Mary Eckerlin, married in 1736 to Thomas Newton, who left her a widow when he drowned in the Susquehanna River near present Harrisburg, Pennsylvania. She then married, in 1737, to Indian trader Simon Girty, Sr., and they became parents of several children, including Simon Girty jr., George Girty, and James Girty. These three were captured and adopted by Indians when young, and later all became Indian traders and infamous on the frontier during the Revolution. They were not necessarily by the same father, as Mary Eckerlin was known to play around when her husband was away. In fact, Simon Girty sr. was killed by one of her lovers, John Turner, whom she later married.

Anyway, Beltzer Shilling was the ten-year-old indentured servant of the Eckerlin brothers at the time their settlement was attacked in 1756. The boy was captured, along with two of the younger members of the religious order. Shilling managed to escape after a time, and he was found on the trail by John Owens who took him back to his trading post. There was no love lost between Owens and the Eckerlins. Owens referred to them in his trading journal as "the goddamn holy brothers." For a more detailed account of this story, see especially historian Glenn Lough's *Now and Long Ago*, p. 51-64 and also the account in the *Pennsylvania Magazine of Biography & History*, July, 1944, p. 306-308.

Shilling probably engaged in the Indian trade. He served with his neighbor Peter Hildabrand in the militia in the defense of Wheeling early in the Revolution, and he was probably in some of the companies for which we have no muster, such as David Owens Company enlisted at Ft. Jackson. In what is now Washington County, Pennsylvania, Shilling established a plantation near John Owens, Andrew Linn, Peter Hildebrand, and others who sold out about the same time to move to Kentucky.

In March of 1778, Shilling was charged with "disaffection to the commonwealth," but was acquitted by a jury of his neighbors. In the spring of 1779, he had a suit pending in the Yohogania County Court when he gave his power-of-attorney to George McCormick (father of John McCormick), and Shilling moved to Kentucky.

Before going to Ft. Jefferson, Shilling claimed 400 acres of Kentucky "lying near Clark's Station known by the name of Round Spring" where he had made an improvement in May, 1779. The pay abstract of Capt. George Owens shows that Shilling was among those who left Ft. Jefferson in September, 1780, went to the Arkansas Post and then on to the Natchez area, along with the Iller family, Daniel Grafton, and others. In Spanish Natchez, he established a plantation adjacent to Daniel Grafton's. The names of both of these men, along with those of other Ft. Jefferson defenders, are associated in several suits in the Old Natchez court records.

His name appears frequently in McBee's Natchez Records. In 1787, his trading boat was salvaged by the Tunica Indians who threatened to chop it into firewood unless he paid a ransom for it.

Shilling's plantation flourish by all accounts, and it is a family tradition that he and his heirs engaged in the breeding of fine horses.

According to his deposition in Carter's Territorial Papers of the United States, vol. 5, p. 338, Shilling was sixty years old in 1804, "...came to Natchez in 1782 and was there when the town was laid out..."

His will is dated January 12, 1805, and it was probated April 13, 1808 in Adams County, Mississippi. It mentions wife Mary, who was given the plantation; sons John, Abraham, Jacob, and Matthew; daughters Lorain, Barbara, Elizabeth Ann, and Mary. A codicil to the will was made March 31, 1808, perhaps when Shilling was dying. It provides a guardian for daughter Mary, who was perhaps still a minor. It was witnessed by Daniel Grafton.

Some of his family seems to have been left behind in Ohio. There is a tradition among some of these Ohio Shillings that they have Indian blood. A Shilling was among the Lewistown Senecas and Shawnees who signed the treaty of 1817.

SHOREY – a Cherokee name.

William Shorey was captured by Oconostota and his warriors in 1760, but Attakullaculla (Little Carpenter) obtained his release. Shorey served as an interpreter and traded among the Cherokees. He married a Cherokee woman. Their daughter, Anna Shorey, married John McDonald, who along with Alexander Cameron, became an assistant to John Stuart in supervising southern colonial Indian affairs.

SILAS – a Seneca name.

Among the Shawnees and Senecas who were paid for the improvements on their property in Ohio that they were forced to leave behind was Joseph Silas. See Watson, vol. 5, pt. 3, p. 11. The Quapaw Agency's 1877 Seneca Census listed the household of Nancy Silas which consisted of one one man, one woman, and one female child.

SILVERHEELS – a Seneca/Shawnee name.

Silverheels (Aroas) was a Seneca warrior closely associated with the Half King (Tanacharisson) at Ft. Necessity was later at Braddock's Defeat with Monacatoocha, Old Belt, and about five or six other reds loyal to the English. After Pontiac's War, Silverheels worked for trader George Morgan and was his runner whenever their was a message to be sent.

Historian Seineke detailed many of his trips across the country and says that this Silverheels was a stepson of the Old Belt, a major Seneca chief who lived on the Upper Ohio and who was another of Tanacharisson's old companions. Some of the Old Belt's daughters were identified as "sisters of Silver Heels" in the *Dictionary of Canadian Biography* but I wonder if these women were not by Old Belt's last wife, who might have been Shawnee. One of Silverheel's sisters had a son by an English officer named Francis and may have started the Francis surname among the Shawnee.

Silver Heels accompanied George Morgan down the Ohio River in 1770. Above the falls of the Ohio (now Louisville), on April 5, 1770, they disembarked, and Morgan noted:

"This afternoon put in at the little creek above the falls where I left my boat and proceeded with Silver Heels by land to view the falls and determine the best method to pass them..."

At Kaskakia in May of 1770, George Morgan wrote in his journal:

"Last night...about 2 o'clock was called to and informed by the guard that Silver Heels was kill'd by Montour & an old French Mohawk who had run off...Thus expired without even a knife to defend himself a most faithful & brave friend and ally to the English...I have paid all the respect I could to the memory of this brave man by as decent an internment as possible here in the Churchyard. At which Lt. Chapman & all the English soldiers and inhabitants attended and showed the most evident sensibility of the loss..."

Morgan began to use another runner named Silverheels, a Shawnee, to act in the same capacity as the old Silverheels, as a messenger across the Ohio country. Historian Gregory Schaaf, who has had the best look at George Morgan's papers, says that the young Silverheels was the son of the older man who was stabbed in the Illinois country, which indicates that the older man had a Shawnee wife.

Silverheels attended the council at Ft. Pitt in 1775 along with Cornstalk, Wryneck, Nimwha, and Blue Jacket. After the death of Cornstalk (if not before), Silverheels aligned himself with the British (or rather, against the colonists). See Journal of the Illinois Historical Society, vol. 69, p. 189; Seineke, pp. 11, 13, 14, 17, 18, 81, 82, 159, 184, 185, 453; Dictionary of Canadian Biography, vol. III, p. 320.

Former Indian agent John Johnston thought that "Silverheels was a Munsey and might have lived among the Shawnees." Johnston said that he did not know the original Silverheels, but knew his son who kept the name. The younger Silverheels became involved in an altercation with one of his own sons and both were mortally wounded. See Draper 11YY32.

Draper interviewed Moses Silverheels in Kansas in 1868, and they discussed She-men-e-to, Cornstalk, Brighthorn, Spybuck, John Coldwater (who had married Silverheel's sister), and others. Draper's impression of Moses Silverheels was that he was "Not much educated, but very intelligent." See Draper 23S165.

Moses Silverheels, as the head of a family, was allotted land in Kansas in the 1850's. His wife, Betsey (Bartlett) Silverheels was given an adjoining allotment.

Among the Shawnees who settled on the lands of the Cherokee nation by 1869 were John, George, and Eliza Silverheels and their families. See JAIFR, vol. IV, #2, pp. 100-111.

Moses Silverheels died June 11, 1871, and his wife, Betsy, died in 1885. Their children included John, who married several times; Mary, who married William Chouteau; Charles, who died in Kansas fighting for the North in the Civil War; Eliza, who married David Likens Bluejacket; and another daughter who married John Captain in Kansas.

Eliza Silverheels married David Likens Bluejacket in 1861. They went to Indian Territory with the Shawnees where they ran a large farm. Their annual picnics held on their property drew large crowds. Their children included Robert (b. 1862); Katherine (b. 1864); Rosella (b. 1866); Sally M. (b. 1870), Cinderella (b. 1873), married Cyrus Bunt Mills; Mary (b. 1877), married James Franks, then 2nd Edward Babcock; Julia (b. 1880); Bessie May (b. 1883); Elizabeth (b. 1888), married Thomas Cope; and Charles (b. 1891). See SOCC, pp. 256, 585.

The Shawnee Nancy Silverhale (likely Silverheels) married A. J. Smith, a white man, in the Cherokee nation on August 2, 1885.

Among the Shawnees listed on the 1900 Census were John Silverheels, a Shawnee, born 1871, and Rachel Silverheels, a white woman, born 1858 in Texas, listed as a widow. Her father had been born in Pennsylvania, her mother in Ohio. Her Shawnee son, George Silverheels, had been born in 1879, and his father had been born in Kansas. Rachel's brother, George A. Barnes, lived in the household. See Prevost, pp. 74-75.

SIMMONS, SIMONS, or SIMONDS – a Delaware name.

Ben and Jim Simonds, both Delaware hunters and both very large men, were trapping in Snake Country in what is now Montana in 1858. Jim Simonds (Delaware Jim) was in the employ of Major John Owen for many years and accompanied him on his trading trips. See Forty Years on the Frontier by Granville Stuart, ed. by Paul C. Phillips, The Arthur C. Clarke Company, Glendale California, 1957, p. 126-127.

In 1860, Neconhecond was still the chief of the Wolf Clan of Delawares, an assistant to principle chief John Connor, who was head of the Turtle Clan. Neconhecond's councilors were Big Nichols (Big Nigger), John Sarcoxie, Jim Simond, Big Raccoon, and George Washington. See Weslager, p. 408.

Among the Delawares living in the Cooweescoowee District and appearing on the 1880 Cherokee census was Neg-uat-she Simons, a woman of 115 years of age. She was living with Jackson Simon (age 36), his wife (27), and an Alice Simon (3).

Another Delaware named Alice Simons (19) appears on the census and was apparently living with the Simon Secondine's family. See JAIFR, vol. X, #3, pp. 18-19.

SIMPSON – a Shawnee name.

John, Thomas, and Joseph Simpson were Indian traders who lived near John Owens in the Monongahela area. Some of their descendants share an Indian blood tradition.

Hannah Simpson was living among the Naragassett Indians in the 1760's.

On January 12th, 1776, in western Virginia, an Indian named Simpson was tried by a General Court Martial for shooting and wounding a sergeant in the leg. He was sentenced to receive 39 lashes and be drummed out of the camps. See Dandridge's *Historic Shepherdstown*, p. 123.

SIZEMORE – An Indian blood tradition in the Kentucky Sizemore family according to Kelly in The History of Clay County, Kentucky.

According to the deposition of Capt. Dixon Bailey Reed of Pensacola, Florida, the Sizemore's were Creeks. He said that his grandmother's sister married a Sizemore, and that he knew Alex and William Sizemore, Creeks, who lived in Little River, Alabama. His Creek grandmother, Peggy Bailey, was at Ft. Mims in 1813, but was out of the fort picking blackberries when the massacre occurred. See *Cherokee By Blood*, vol. I, p. 363-364.

Some of the descendants of these Sizemores also settled with other Creeks in the Florida counties of Baldwin and Monroe. See "West Florida's Forgotten People," by Lucius F. Ellsworth and Jane E. Dysart which appeared in the FHQ, vol. 59, #4, 1981, pp. 426-429.

SKY, SKYE, SKYLER – a Seneca/Shawnee/Peoria name.

The Sky was long a "risen up" name among the Senecas. Tanacharisson was the Half King, and his name meant "this side of the sky." Monacatoocha or Scaroady was the vice-regent who succeeded Tanacharisson as "the head Seneca warrior" and Half King, and his name meant "ye sky," according to Indian trader James Kenny. More than among any other tribe, there were frequent references to the sky in Seneca names, such as Hold Back the Sky, and Set the Skies on Fire.

The Seneca, Jim Sky, lived among the mixed Shawnees, Senecas, and Wyandots at Sandusky, Ohio. Lang says that Jim Sky was the executioner for the tribal council, and he recounts several such executions, including the killing of several "witches" with a pipe tomahawk. See Lang, p. 205.

On the Quapaw Agency's 1877 Seneca Census are listed the households of Nora Skyler and the Widow Skyler who was living with a male child.

On the 1900 Peoria census is listed Frank Sky, 27, a mixed-blood Peoria, his wife Anna Daugherty Sky, 19, an Eastern Shawnee, and Emmett Sky, their one-year-old son.

Nancy Sky is mentioned in Shawnee!, a book on Shawnee customs and ceremonials. See Howard, p. 183.

SLOCUM – a Delaware/Miami name.

Frances Slocum was captured by Delawares on November 2, 1778, in the Wyoming Valley of the Susquehanna River near present day Wilkes-Barre, Pennsylvania. She was adopted by them, and her first husband was a Delaware brave.

Years later, she nursed a badly-wounded Miami brave, Shepocanah, back to health, and took him for her second husband. She lived at the Miami town near Ft. Wayne for many years, then she, her husband, and her relatives settled near a big spring on the Mississinewa River, in what is now Miami County, some eight miles south of Peru, Indiana.

Frances Slocum was called Maconaqua, or Little Bear Woman. In Indiana legend, she is sometimes referred to as the White Rose of the Miamis. Her village became known Deaf Man's Town after Shepocanah became deaf in his later years.

In September, 1837, Frances Slocum's brothers Issac, Joseph, and their sister, Mary, came from Pennsylvania to Peru, Indiana to see her. She became reunited with her white relatives, but she told them that she had been happy in her Indian life, and she had no desire to return to Pennsylvania.

George Winter, whose art was to become famous, came to Deaf Man's Village in 1839 and made portraits of her and her family.

But when the Miami tribe was forced to move to a reservation west of the Mississippi in 1846, Frances did not want to go. She wanted to live on in Deaf Man's village until death, and then to be buried beside her husband. Her white friends and Slocum relatives petitioned the government, and by special agreement, she and her family were allowed to remain. She died on March 9, 1847, and was buried beside the grave of Shepocanah.

With the Deaf Man (She-pay-con-na), Francis Slocum had four children. One of her daughters married Peter Bundy (Wah-pop—pe-tah), who signed the treaty of 1854 and was then still living in Miami County, Indiana. Another married Tah-quac-yaw, a half-breed Potawatomi, better known as Capt. Bruriette (Brouillett, etc.), who was drowned in the Wabash river but left children.

See Draper 1YY117-118; and see Arville I. Funk's

article which appeared in his Hoosier Scrapbook column, October 11, 1976. A copy can be found in the Indiana Collections at the New Albany, Indiana Library.

SLOVER – a Miami name.

Among the captives delivered up to General Henry Bouquet in 1764 were Elizabeth Slover and her daughter, Elizabeth, that she had among the Indians. See Hanna, II, p. 388.

John Slover was captured at the age of eight and adopted by Miami Indians. He lived with them six years, and then became an Indian trader among the Shawnees for six more years. In 1773, he met some of his white relatives at Pittsburgh who persuaded him to return home with them. He re-adapted to live among the whites, and returned to the Ohio country as the guide of Col. William Crawford's expedition. He was captured again by Shawnees, and historian Parker B. Brown says that "clearly some squaws remembered and liked him. He recognized many chiefs and at council spoke their tongue fluently and defended himself ably." See Brown, p. 332.

John Slover's deposition concerning the burning of Col. Crawford was misworded when published, edited by Brackenridge, so as to vilify Simon Girty, but the original is still in existence and has been recently published. John Slover came to Kentucky, settled down, and had several children. He lived for a while near Dr. John Knight (a few miles from Taylorsville) but settled in Henderson, moved to Vincennes, Indiana, then back to Logan County, Kentucky, where he joined the South Union Shakers. He died there in 1833, leaving several children including John, jr., Issac, James, Preston, Eunice, and Jane.

John Slover also signed the bond when Elizabeth Slover married Charles Morgan in early Jefferson County, Kentucky. Who was she? She may have been from a previous marriage or she may have been the young Elizabeth Slover who was given up with her mother to General Henry Bouquet in 1764.

One of John Slover's sons, Issac Slover, married Peggy Lowder and went to Indiana where his wife died about 1816, apparently in childbirth. Her death seems to have coincided with the birthdates of twins. Issac took the older children to Arkansas and the twins joined them later.

This Issac Slover trapped beaver in the Rocky Mountains, and became famous in the west as a hunter, scout and mountain man. He associated with Kit Carson, Jim Bridger, and other famous men known to have married Native American women. In California, he married Barbara Aragon, apparently of Spanish descent. He died there at an advanced age, killed by a bear, and was buried at the foot of Slover Mountain near San Bernardino. See the Slover Family File at the Filson Club, Louisville, Kentucky.

SMITH – a Wyandot/Shawnee name.

I intend to cover the Wyandot/Smith families in greater detail in an upcoming volume of Indian Blood.

James Smith had spent many years among the Indians and was probably well acquainted with the Kentucky region. He had led an expedition through Cumberland Gap in 1766 and explored southern and western Kentucky. When Kentucky was settled, he became a resident of Bourbon County and represented his county in the state legislature for several years. His exploits are recorded in the autobiographical *Remarkable Occurrences in the Life of Col. James Smith* (Philadelphia, 1834); *Captivity with the Indians* (Cincinnati, 1870); and *Treatise on the Mode of Indian Warfare* (Paris, Ky, 1812). His narrative of his Indian captivity is given in abridged form in John A McClung, Sketches of Western Adventure (Maysville, 1832), and it is given in full in Charles A. McKnight's *Our Western Border* (Philadelphia, 1876).

Edmund Smith was one of the forty-four members of George Owens Company during the siege of Ft. Jefferson.

Edmund was the nephew of Capt. Henry Smith and the son of James Smith and his wife, nee Magdalene Woods. She was the daughter of Michael Woods who was killed when his house was attacked during Pontiac's War. Magdalene was captured, adopted, and lived for many years among them and, tradition says, was "greatly honored and beloved" among the Indians.

Harry Smith, better known by his stage name of Jay Silverheels or Tonto, was a son of Capt. A. G. E. Smith, a Mohawk, said to have been the most decorated Canadian Indian soldier in World War I. Some of Harry Smith's brothers were steel construction workers who worked on many of the large buildings in New York City. Another brother was secretary of the Six Nations Council.

Harry Smith started out as a successful young athlete, a lacrosse player, and went on to hockey, football, and track. He was Eastern States Golden Glove boxing champion in 1937 and Niagara District Middleweight wrestling champion in 1937 and 1938.

In Hollywood, he played some bit parts, and then got his big break in the film, "Broken Arrow." He first accepted the part of Tonto, the Lone Ranger's "faithful friend," in 1946. See Gridley, p. 131.

SMOCK – Two sons of Jacob Smock — John Smock, a lad of fourteen, and Peter Smock, a boy of twelve — were taken by Indians in Shelby County (Ky). They were adopted by Winnemac, a Potawatomi chief, and were not returned until the treaty of Greenville, reportedly ransomed by an Indian trader for a keg of rum. Draper 16S179, 201; family tradition quoted by Akers, The Low Dutch Company..., p. 41.

SNAKE – a Shawnee name.

The Snake is listed among the Indians dealt with by the Ohio Company Traders. Snake was a "risen up" or re-occuring name among the Shawnee, and there seems to have always been one prominent warrior or chief among them who carried the name.

Thomas Ridout met the Great Snake in 1788. While hiding from (the young) Blackfish, he encountered George Ash and asked him for help. Ash took him "to the cabin of the Great Snake who received me with kindness and assured me of his protection. He was an elderly man, robust, and rather corpulent. His wife a pretty, well-looking woman, nearly his age, walked very stately with a handsome staff with a gold head to it. He ordered a bear's skin and blanket for me alongside his own bed, and til my departure, three days after, he treated me with the greatest kindness." See Ridout, pp. 27-28. His children included John Snake and Thomas Snake, and one of them may have taken on their father's Shawnee name when he died.

Charles Bluejacket told Draper that She-men-e-to (or the Big Snake, Major Snake, the Great Snake, etc.) was supposed to have died, and he was laid out. His people came to view the body when he unexpectedly came to and lived some time after. He died about 1838 at the house of his nephew, Cornstalk (Stout Body), whose father, Cornstalk, had married She-men-e-to's sister. See Draper 23S167.

The Snake, a Delaware, was supposed to have been among the reds who were killed with Tecumseh at the Battle of the Thames.

Listed on the Muster Roll of Shawnee Indians of the Hog Creek and Wapakoneeta bands was the Blacksnake family which included one male and one female between 25 and 55, one male between 10 and 25, and one boy and one girl under 10. See Roy, p. 43.

Listed among the Munsey Delawares in 1859 were Wesley, Catherine, and Christian Snake. See JAIFR, vol. VI, #1, p. 58.

SOLOMON – a Seneca/Wyandot name.

Ezekiel Solomon was an early trader and Solomon's Town was an early Mingo community. James Smith saw Mohawk Solomon there with Pluggy, and he became friendly with Solomon, a good-humored man who taught Smith hunting and tracking skills. See Drimmer, pp. 33-35.

Listed on the 1843 Muster Roll of Wyandots from Sandusky, Ohio were:

1. John Solomon's family, consisting of one male between 25 and 55, one female over 55, and three females between 10 and 25.
2. Robert Solomon's family, consisting of one male between 25 and 55, one female between 10 and 25, and one male under 10.

Margaret Greyeyes Solomon, a daughter of John Grey Eyes, was one of the first students of Rev. Finley's mission school in Ohio and became an active member of the church. She went west to Kansas but returned to Ohio and after her husband, John Solomon, died, she lived alone in the vicinity of Upper Sandusky. Mother Solomon, she was then known, August 17, 1891. See Howe, vol. II, p. 900-902.

Among the students of the Methodist Mission School in Kansas were Mary Solomon, age 8 in 1850; Albert Solomon, age 11 in 1851; John Solomon 1st, age 17 in 1851; and John Solomon 2nd, age 6 in 1860. See *Methodist Missions*, p 188.

Among the Wyandot guardian cases reviewed by the Commissioner of Indian Affairs in 1871 was the case of John Solomon, a Wyandot then living in Wyandotte County, Ohio. Solomon was guardian for his daughter, Mary, who married into the Bigtree family and for Hiram Young. Mary was then deceased and Hiram lived in the Indian Territory. See JAIFR, vol. VIII, #2, p. 20.

SOVERIGNS or SEVERNS – a Shawnee name.

Joseph Soverigns was a son of Gower Soverigns (Severns, Sufferins, etc.) who was, with her children, taken captive during the French and Indian War. Joseph was among those adopted and he grew up Shawnee, married, and had a house and a family at the Shawnee towns.

John Severns, brother of Joseph, came back to live among the whites with Benjamin Linn, and both of these men served as scouts (both rode gray horses) on the 1782 expedition against the Shawnee towns. George Rogers Clark had John Severns stand on a stump and keep the Indians talking while he had other men circle around to pick them off from behind.

John Severns later claimed much land and he settled in Nelson County, Kentucky near Bardstown. Like Benjamin Linn, he was occasionally a Baptist preacher. He later moved to Indiana near Vincennes where he operated a ferry on White River. Occasionally, he was recruited for work as a scout and interpreter by Col. John Gibson.

It was Joseph Soverigns who is mentioned in the 1785 Journal of Richard Butler as "Suffren, a white Shawnee." Joseph Soverigns served as an Indian messenger and interpreter. Ebenezer Denny takes note of him in his journal as a "Mr. Sufferins," whose family was among the Shawnees.

On August 3rd, 1789, John Hardin marched from Clarksville (Indiana) with a volunteer Kentucky militia bent on seeking vengeance against the Indians. They fell upon a peaceful band of Shawnee hunters who had "kindled their fires and turned out their horses to feed with their bells open." Hardin's company heard the bells, and discovered the Indians, and killed "three men, a boy, three squaws, and a child and took two children prisoner." One of the men killed was Joseph Soverigns.

Hannah Soverigns, sister to John and Joseph, met Benjamin Linn among the Shawnees. She returned to the whites to marry him, and the couple had several children.

SPARKS – a Shawnee name.

Tecumseh's father captured and adopted Richard Sparks in the 1760's when Sparks was about 4 years old and Sparks lived some time in an extended family (or at least the clan) that eventually included Tecumseh. As a young adult, possibly in the 1770's, Sparks (or Shawtunte) was exchanged and turned over to some Kentuckians. He lived on the edge of both cultures for a while, as a red white man and as a white red man, a hunter and a trader, but he eventually sided with the whites and was a scout for General Anthony Wayne and probably served with the scout companies of Chieska, James Suggett, John Lewis, Anthony Shane, and others for which we have not yet found muster lists.

Shawtunte may have married several times, and he may have left a mixed-blood family in Ohio to whom he later returned. But his last wife was Ruth Sevier, an adopted Cherokee and the daughter of General William Sevier. Ellet says that Sparks died around 1815 and that Ruth Sevier Sparks died in Maysville, Kentucky, in 1824. Shawtunte's story, as it appears in Mrs. Ellet's Pioneer Woman of the East, doubtlessly has its omissions, but the basic traditions appear to be true. To be published in 1856, Mrs. Ellet's stories had to be fit into the Victorian strait-jacket morality of her time and place.

Allan Eckert refuses to believe Spark's story, but there were other "white Indians" who led parallel lives, including George Ash, Nathaniel Carter, Abram Pope, David Owens, James Sherlock, Joseph Soverigns, Joshua Rennick, Peter Harper, and many, many others apparently not recognized by Eckert either. Nobody knows everything.

The statement of Richard Sparks concerning his life among the Shawnees and the revenge of the Mingo, Logan, appears in Draper 14J34-37.

The will of Richard Sparks was filed in Claiborne County, Mississippi, dated March 6, 1814, probated Oct. 9, 1815. Sparks gave to his daughter, Catherine McClure, land on the east fork of the Miami in Ohio; to his daughters Polly Hall, Elizabeth Besegrade, and Eleanor Sparks, land in Tennessee; to daughter Charity Hall, land in Pennsylvania; to Capt. George W. Sevier, his gold-headed cane; to Thomas D. and Stephen Carson, all his military apparel; to Stephen Carson, his rifle, "it being my support in youth and my cane in old age"; and he mentions Edward Sparks Wooldridge, son of the late Col. William Woolridge.

Information on Sparks is to be found elsewhere in the Draper manuscripts, and Draper's notes cite Elizabeth Ellet's Pioneer Women of the East, 156-157; Claiborne's History of Mississippi, note 221; Schoolcraft's Indian Traits, vol. IV, p. 625, and the other references, including Spark's statement to Congress, appear on Draper's Index Resume, 249.

SPELMAN, SPILLMAN, SPELLMAN – a Powhatan/ Shawnee name.

Henry Spelman was one of the boys sent to live with the Powhatan Indians in order to learn their language. He later served as an interpreter and like some of the other boys, "went native."

Peter Spelman (Ooligasha, Owiligascho) married the daughter of Paxinosa, a Shawnee chief whom man historians identify as Pucksinwah, the father of Tecumseh. Spelman served as interpreter for his father-in-law at councils in 1757. See C. A. Weslager, *The Nanticoke Indians*.

In January, 1757, "Peter Spelman, a German, named in the Shawnee language, Ooligasha, who has has lived seven years past amongst the Indians was sent express by Ruddehega, King of the Shawnees living on the West Branch of the Susquehanna...." Spelman reported news from four of their nation who recently returned from a hunt on the Wabash.

In May, 1757, "Owiligaska, alias Peter Spelman, a German living among the Shawnees arrived here and brought a string of wampum to Sir William [Johnson] from his father-in-law, Paxinoa [Paxinosa], Chief of the Shawnees, acquainting Sir William of losing his gun, hatchet, and hoes which he had giving him by his canoe upsetting in the Susquehanna and hoped Sir William would make up for the loss...." See SWJ, vol. 2, p. 675; vol. 9, pp. 591, 779.

SPICER – a Mingo name.

"Peter Spicer here was captured and some others, and what of the others I know not. Peter Spicer lived and remained with them and to a certainty that Peter Spicer was along...and took an active hand in the murder of George Tush's family. Other prisoners returning at sundry times all agree in stating that Spicer was along with Indian parties on their expeditions against the whites and was often see riding a fine horse...." Some years after the Treaty of Greenville, Spicer came back to try to inherit the land where he had been captured. George Tush laid in ambush for him and wanted to kill him. Spicer returned to Ohio and died about 1815 or 1816. See Lobdell, Recollections of

Lewis Bonnett, pp. 16-17.

William Spicer's family, on Muddy Creek in what is now Greene County, Pennsylvania, was attacked in 1774 by Logan and his war party of twelve Mingo braves. William, jr., age nine, and Betsy, age eleven, were carried back to the Indian towns and later adopted. Tradition says that William became a renegade and fought against the whites. See Lough, pp. 284-285, 290.

The treaty of 1817, held at the Miami Rapids, gave 640 acres to William Spicer "who was captured by Indians and has ever since lived among them and has married a Seneca woman."

"William Spicer married a Seneca woman and moved here as heir to his land on the east bank of the Sandusky River." A sister, Betsy, who also lived among the Indians, married a man by the name of Bowen. See Draper Mss 6NN78.

"After William Spicer died, his funeral was preached by a Mr. Montgomery. George Herron, a half-Mohawk, interpreted the service to the Indians, sentence by sentence. One of Spicer's boys, Small Cloud Spicer, was a fine-looking fellow, a half-blood. He married Crow's daughter by his first wife. Little Town Spicer had three or four wives. Both of these Spicer boys went west with the Senecas." See Lang.

As we have seen with the Armstrong, Zane, Dawson, and other families, some of them stayed on the reservation, some moved off. Some moved farther west, and some moved back east.

William Spicer's son, Warmic Spicer, married Nancy Spencer, a deaf and mute Indian woman. They had eight children including Morris Spicer who later became a railroad worker in West Virginia. When Morris Spicer was very young, his father was robbed and murdered, and Morris was raised by Henry and Rhoda Duckworth in Doddridge County, West Virginia. Morris Spicer later operated a farm near Greenwood in that county. He married Mary Bertha Woodburn, and was a member of the Methodist Church. See Lough, Now and Long Ago, pp. 637-638.

On the Quapaw Agency's 1877 Seneca Census are listed the households of:

1. Joseph Spicer, consisting of one man, one woman, one boy and two girls.
2. John Spicer, consisting of one man, one woman, and one boy.
3. Armstrong Spicer, consisting of one man, two women, and three girls.
4. Daniel Spicer, consisting of one man, one woman, one boy, and three girls.
5. William Spicer, consisting of one man, one woman and three girls.

Listed on the 1881 Seneca Census were William Spicer, 30, and his wife, Ida, 32. Their children included Cynthia, 10, Fannie, 7, Lucy, 4, Jacob, 3, and Caroline, an infant. Also listed were Daniel Spicer, 40, Susan, 40, Sarah, 16, Effie, 11, Daniel, 7, Minnie, 7, and Polly, 4.

Listed on the 1894 Seneca Rolls of the Quapaw Agency was another Daniel Spicer, age 54, and his family which included Kate, 19, Polly, 14, David, 17, Carley, 9, and Ida, age not given.

SPLITLOG– a Cayuga/Seneca/Wyandot name.

Spilt Log (or Split the Logs, Between the Logs, etc) was a Wyandot subchief who followed the leadership of Tecumseh and Roundhead during the War of 1812. With the assistance of a few British troops, he led his Wyandot and Shawnee warriors against the an invading United States Army at Grand River in late October, 1814. Split Log's forces threw the invaders back, the retreat led by General Duncan McArthur, great-grandfather of General Douglas McArthur. See

R. David Edmunds, *The Shawnee Prophet*, p. 149.

On the 1843 Muster Roll of Wyandots from Sandusky, Ohio, were:

1. Charles Split the Logs family, which included one male between 25 and 55 and one boy under 10.
2. Thomas Splitthelog's household, consisting of one male over 55 and one male 10 to 25.

According to Spencer (p. 186-187): "...Another interpreter connected with Shawnee Mission was Matthias Splitlog. He was a Cayuga-Seneca by descent, having been born in Canada in 1816. He married Eliza Carloe [or Charlow, Charlieu], a Wyandot, and came west with the Wyandot nation. He made his home in the Seneca country when the Wyandots moved to the Indian Territory. Here he erected a fine church building. He died there in 1896."

SPYBUCK – a Shawnee name.

Among the Spybuck descendants who have entered the main population are to be found such alternative spellings of Spibuck, Spibbuck, Sprybuck, Shybuck, etc.

Chieska (also known as Capt. Tom or Capt. Chieska) was the father of Spybuck, and probably his mother was Polly Butler, a daughter of General Richard Butler and a sister of Cornstalk. Chieska (or Capt. Chieska as he was usually called) aligned himself with Blackhoof and he served as a scout with Anthony Shane on the side of the United States in the War of 1812. Chieska was with Capt. William Wells in the shootout with the Potawatomi warriors when Wells was fatally wounded. Those who knew Chieska praised him to Draper. And they spoke highly of his agile son, Spybuck (Saucothcaw).

Noted for his plain dress and easy manner, Spybuck was often a companion of Simon Kenton during that scout's last few years. Spybuck went west and, like James Swannock, Little Beaver, and many others, he became a free hunter.

Spybuck was the tracker in James Kirker's band of scalp-hunters who attacked and nearly wiped out Cochise's band of Apachees. When Kirker's party arrived in Chihuahua with the plunder, "Governor Trias refused to pay the scalp money, and many Mexicans were claiming the recovered mules and horses as their property. This vexed Spybuck so deeply, he stripped himself of his buckskins and walked naked except for his loin cloth and a feather in his hair. He drank a bottle of brandy, stuck a knife and tomahawk in his belt, and headed for the governor's mansion...

"The Shawnee broke through a guard at the governor's door, grabbed Trias by the throat and threatened to kill him if he were not paid immediately for his scalps. He was paid and, returning to the bull ring, he gathered up his share of mules and horses and announced that he would not stay and do business with people who would not keep their word. He then headed for Bent's Fort..."

See Dawson's *William Henry Harrison*, pp. 416-419; Draper Mss. 17S75; 17S270-272; 11YY37; 3YY103; William Cochran McGaw's "James Kirker," appearing in vol. 5 of *The Mountain Men*, ed. by Leroy R. Hafen, p. 138-140.

Spybuck "acted more like a white man than an Indian," people said, and his family was white enough that most people took them for whites. A Shawnee told Draper (in 1YY) that "Spybuck married the half-breed daughter of Col. Barbee of Kentucky...a fine-looking woman..." [See BARBEE.]

The list of monies paid to Shawnees for the improvements made (and left behind) on their Ohio property shows that Spybuck must have been relatively wealthy, at least by the white standard of the time. He was given $370 — by comparison, much more than such other prominent Shawnees as John Perry ($235), Joseph Barnett ($158), Peter Cornstalk ($162), Martin Hardin ($57), and Bill Parks ($213).

Listed on the 1832 Muster Roll of Shawnee Indians of the Hog Creek and Wapakonetta bands was the Spybuck family which included one male and one female between 25 and 55, two males and one female between 10 and 25, and four children under 10, three of them girls. See Roy, p. 40.

Among the Shawnees who went to the Florida War with Chief John Perry and Capt. Joseph Parks and served against the Seminoles in 1837 were John Spybuck and Young Spybuck, probably Spybuck's two oldest sons after George Spybuck, who had married a Wyandot and was still in Ohio at the time.

George Spybuck came to Kansas with the Wyandots from Sandusky, Ohio in 1843. The family of George Spybuck, a son of Spybuck, is listed on the muster roll as consisting of one male 25 to 55, one female 10 to 25, one male under 10 and one female under 10.

The Wyandot family of George Spybuck included George, Mary, Margaret, Virginia, and James, all of whom were allotted land in Kansas.

Among the Wyandot guardian cases reviewed by the Commissioner of Indian Affairs in 1871 was the case of George Spybuck who had died in Sandusky, Ohio in November, 1870, having moved back to Ohio in the fall of 1857. He had been the guardian for his brother, John Spybuck, and for his niece, Mary Williams [see WILLIAMS]. See JAIFR, vol. VIII, #2, p. 20.

Among the Shawnees allotted land in Johnson County, Kansas in the 1850's were Peggy Spybuck and her family and Pharisse Spybuck. See KHC, vol. 15, p. 179.

Among the Shawnee Spybucks then living by

permission on the Cherokee Reserve in 1869 were George, French, Nancy, John, and Eliza Spybuck. See JAIFR, vol. IV, #. 2, p. 108.

Among the Shawnees living in the Cooweescoowee District and appearing on the 1880 Cherokee census were Jack Spybuck (age 25), Henry (28), Mary (20), Becky (4), Frank (2), William (2 months) and Peter Spybuck (17). Also appearing as Shawnees on the census and most likely in the same family are listed George Shybuck (26), Nancy Shybuck (40), and Jane Shybuck (10). See JAIFR, vol. X, #3, p. 18-20.

The Spybuck name continues among the Shawnees today. George, Henry, and Ernest Spybuck (the Shawnee artist) are quoted throughout James H. Howard's Shawnee! (1981), an excellent book on Shawnee customs.

SQUIRREL – a Shawnee name.

The Squirrel (Anequpi) was one of the Shawnee warriors of Mackachack Town when it was invaded and burnt by Benjamin Logan's army in 1786.

Later, the Squirrel later seems to have been associated with Blackhoof and his band. He may have been among the Harrison's Shawnee scouts in the War of 1812, along with Anthony Shane, Capt. Chieska, Blackfeather, John Perry, and others. Matthew Elliot found four of these Shawnee scouts in the mob of prisoners taken at Ft. Meigs. He gave them to Tecumseh, who talked "companionly" to them, telling them that they had nothing to fear. He freed them, sending them back to Blackhoof's people "with a talk." See Gilbert, p. 298.

Listed on the Muster Roll of Shawnee Indians of the Hog Creek and Wapakonetta bands was the family of James Squirrel which included two males and a female between 25 and 55, and one male between 10 and 25. See Roy, p. 41.

Among the Shawnees who settled on the lands of the Cherokee nation by 1869 were Daniel Squirrel and his family. See JAIFR, vol. IV, #2, pp. 100-111.

Among the Squirrel family living among the Shawnees, Delawares, and Cherokees were William (age 30), Lizzie (1), Rosie (30), and Mary Squirrel (14), listed as Cherokees. Also there were Daniel (30), Anna (20), Lizzie (10), Amanda (3), and Filmore Squirrel (40), listed as Shawnees. See JAIFR, vol. X, #3, p. 20.

Betsy, Rufus, and Mary Squirrel are mentioned in Shawnee!, an excellent book on Shawnee customs and ceremonials. See Howard, pp. 111, 302, 317.

STAND – a Shawnee/Peroia name.

A white woman married Kishenosity (Kishshinosttisthee, Keissinauethat, Kishenosithe, etc.), whose name translated as the Hard Man. His name appeared on the petition transcribed and carried by Peter Chartier and George Meranda to the Pennsylvania authorities, demanding that no more liquor be brought to the Shawnee towns. Later, the Hard Man led the other leading Shawnee chiefs at a council with Bouquet in 1764 when 36 whites were delivered up, most of them unwillingly. Many Pennsylvania Indian traders extended credit to the Kishenosity whose name appears variously on their ledgers in its Shawnee form and translated as the Hard Man, the Hard Fellow, and Stiff Dick.

This concept of the man with the perpetual erection need not refer to Kishenosity himself, but like other Shawnee concepts such as Tecumseh and White Day, it appears to be a recurring name and possibly alludes to the hero of some legend, now forgotten. He was living on Deer Creek in 1773, and an account of him can be read in the journal of the Rev. David Jones, who said that Kishenosity's wife was a white woman. Colonial Indian agent George Morgan said that Kishenosity, the Hard Man, was Kawkawatchety's son (see Schaaf, p. 136).

Wasegoboah was another translation of the same concept, and a Shawnee warrior going by became known by early historians as Stands Firm. Wasegoboah married Tecumpease, Tecumseh's sister, and although after a time they separated and she remarried, he continued to be Tecumseh's friend and associate.

Stand Firm was with Tecumseh's forces in the War of 1812 and was one of those who fell by his side at the Battle of the Thames. Many believe that Stand Firm's body was misidentified as Tecumseh. After the battle, apparently some Kentuckians stripped the skin from Stand Firm's thighs to make souvenir razor straps.

Among the Shawnees who settled on the lands of the Cherokee nation by 1869 was Julia Stand. See JAIFR, vol. IV, #2, pp. 100-111.

On the 1876 Shawnee Payroll is listed the family of Thomas Stand, consisting of a man, a woman, and one child. Thomas Stand seems to have married at least three times. In 1880 his current wife was Na-co-quah Parks and they were the guardians of Dela Thomas. In 1898, Thomas Stand was the guardian for Solomon Daugherty.

Some members of the Shawnee family with the surname Stand intermarried with the Peorias. On the 1900 roll is listed Nancy Smith Stand, 41, as head of a family, with children Matilda. 13. Leander, 8, Raymond, 5, and Wilson Stand, a year-old infant.

The last-named child may be the Wilson Stand who fought in World War I and whose name appears on the monument dedicated to those Peorias who served in the United States Armed Forces and are buried in the Peoria Cemetery.

On the 1930 census are listed the Eastern Shawnees Dorothy Marie Stand, age 5, and Loretta Stand, age 3.

A picture of Nancy Stand, on whose allotment the town of Peoria was established, appears on page 92 of Valley and Lembcke's excellent book on the Peoria Nation.

STANLEY – a Delaware/Peoria/Modoc name.

According to the early histories of Madison county, Indiana, Chief William Anderson's village stood where Anderson, Indiana is now. The chief lived in a two story double cabin. One of his daughters, Oneahye or Dancing Feather, married Charles Stanley, an early Madison County settler. See Forkner, p. 22.

The Stanley name became associated with the Peorias. On the 1900 Peoria Census is listed: Charles Stanley, age 40, a Peoria, along with his wife, Etta, listed as a half-breed Modoc, age 33, daughters Ida S., 16, Ramona, 12, and sons Sampson Arthur Stanley, 10, Ardlus (?), 3, and an infant whose name is not given.

STANDINGSTONE, or STONE – an Onieda/ Wyandot name.

A Mingo named the Stone is mentioned in several early accounts, including Butler's journal. The name Onieda is supposed to mean, in Iroquois dialects, the Standing Stone.

"Connected with this company was the Standing Stone. He was a Mingo, and a great drunkard, and when drunk not vicious at all. He would sing and laugh like a manaic; yet when sober, he was a man of some standing and a great hunter." See Finney, p. 519.

Among the Wyandots listed on the 1843 Muster Roll of those from Sandusky, Ohio, were:

1. John Standingstone's family, consisting of a man and a woman, both between 25 and 55, two females between 10 and 25, and four males under 10.
2. J. P. Standingtone's family, consisting of one

male and one female 10 to 25, and two males and one female under 10.

3. Thomas Standingstone's household, consisting of one male and one female between 10 and 25, and two males and one female under 10.

Mary Standingstone was listed on the Quapaw Agency's 1877 Seneca Census. Listed in 1894 were John Standingstone, 39, Fanny Standingstone, 37, and Thorn Standingstone, 20.

STEEL, STEELE – a Seneca/Wyandot/Shawnee name.

In 1756, "Steel's son" was among the Indians who dealt with Indian trader John Owens. Steel (Custaloga's nephew) signed at least one of the treaties made during the French and Indian wars. When the Delawares surrendered to General Henry Bouquet in November, 1764, they were forced to give up six members of their tribe as hostages until they delivered up all whites and blacks among them (whom Bouquet mistakenly believed were being held against their will). At least five of the six given up then were all whites living red: Mondeaticker (William Davis), Noondias (Andrew Trump), Killackchcker (Simon Girty), Katepakomin (John Compass), and Possquetonckmy (Steel). See SWJ Papers, vol. 11, p. 459.

Cuthbert Steel is on the prisoner list, having been captured in Virginia in June, 1780. See McHenry, p. 24.

John Steel (Seneca Steel) was a Seneca who later lived among the Sandusky, Ohio Wyandots. According to Lang, he was involved in the fraternal political squabble among his native tribe in the fall of 1828. Steel was indicted for murdering a chief in 1829, but was released. See Lang, p. 205-206.

When the Wyandot Henry C. Greyeyes died in 1857, his heir was Mary Steel, his sister.

Among the Shawnee guardianships reviewed by the Commissioner of Indian Affairs in 1871 was the case of George Steele, guardian for two half-sisters of his wife, Sarah and Mary Collier. See JAIFR, vol. VIII, #2, p. 20.

Among the Shawnees who settled on the lands of the Cherokee nation by 1869 were John and Mary Steele. See JAIFR, vol. IV, #2, pp. 100-111. Mary Steele's maiden name was probably Mary McClain or McLane.

STEVENS, STEPHENS – a Delaware/Shawnee name.

Among the Shawnees and Delawares dealt with by the Ohio Company traders as early as 1756 were Frank Stephens and John Stevens. Francis (Frank) Stevens was a trader at Allegheny in 1734, and Frankstown was named for him. See Hanna, II, p. 341.

When Rev. David Jones visited Newcomerstown at the mouth of Captina Creek in 1772, he preached to the Delawares, using David Owens as his interpreter. "Mr. Owens was well acquainted with them and let them know what sort of man I was. They all seemed to show respect to me, even afterwards when some were drunk. They were not rude to me, but would take hold of my hand and say, `you be minsta.' We remained here over the Sabbeth and in the evening I instructed when Indians came over. The man of most sense and consideration in this place is called Frank Stephens...."

In somewhat broken English, Frank Stephens told Jones that he "looked on God as the giver of all things. If he killed a deer, he thought that God gave him that good luck." See Jones, p. 245.

STINSON – a Shawnee/Potawatomi name.

Mrs. Julia Ann Stinson "of Tecumseh," born 1834, widow of Thomas Nesbit Stinson, was a grandchild of Henry (or Jimmy) Rogers, a white man who had been captured and adopted when small. He grew up Shawnee and married a daughter of Blackfish. He became a wealthy man in Kentucky (or Ohio?) and Missouri. "Mrs. Rogers came on to Kansas, bringing with her twenty slaves." Later, Mrs. Stinson said, Thomas Johnson borrowed $400 from her grandmother Rogers, and built the Shawnee school. Her parents, Mackinaw and Polly (Rogers) Boshman, were married about 1824 as their oldest child, Annie (Mrs. N. T. Shaler), was at least eight years older than Mrs. Stinson. See Caldwell, Methodist Missions Among the Indians in Kansas, KHC, pp. 170-171.

STUART – a Cherokee name.

Capt. John Stuart was the major southern colonial Indian agent, the equivalent to what Sir William Johnson was in the north. His wife was Susanna Emory, a quarter-blood granddaughter of the Scotch Indian trader Ludovic Grant.

This John Stuart was called Bushyhead by the Cherokees, due to his bushy blond hair. He became the original Anglo-Saxon ancestor of the Bushyhead family among the Cherokees. See "Aunt Eliza of Tahlequah," by Carolyn Thomas Foreman, Chronicles of Oklahoma, vol. 9, p. 43 & on.

Charles Stuart, his wife, his four-year-old son, William, and his six-year-old daughter Mary were captured by a party of Shawnees, Delawares, and Mingoes on October 29th, 1755. See "The Captivity of Charles Stuart," MVHR, vol. XIII, #1, p. 59.

STUDIBAKER – Elizabeth Studibaker was among the whites delivered up to Bouquet in 1764. On the march home, she escaped and went back to her Indian family. See Gilbert, p. 81.

SUGS, SUGGS, SUGGETT– a Shawnee name.

Another mystery. What is the source of the

Shawnee blood tradition in some branches of the Suggett family?

James Suggett was the chaplin and major of spies in Col. Richard M. Johnson's regiment. McAfee's journal shows that they went to Wapakonetta in June, 1813, and enlisted thirteen Shawnees as scouts and spies, including Anthony Shane.

I looked in some Suggett family files. Someone wrote that James Suggett was the name Col. Richard Johnson's grandfather on his mother's side, that the James Suggest that he commissioned as regimental chaplin must have been a relation on his mother's side. This surprised me, and I am not certain that I understand it yet.

There's more. Later, at the Battle of the Thames, Col. Richard Johnson moved forward on his horse toward an Indian who was next to a tree. He shot the Indian, but was himself wounded in the arm, at which point he turned and retired from the battle. Some of his regiment put forth the notion that he had killed Tecumseh. At first, Col. Johnson was modest about the possibility, but afterwards, with so many people whooping it up, he did the politically expedient thing and said that, yes, he had killed Tecumseh.

On that reputation, he was elected Vice President of the United States. He might even have been the President — had he not done the politically inexpedient thing and taken a mulatto slave for his wife. Her name was Julia. We know very little else about her. She was literate, as she often wrote her husband when they were apart. We think of her as part white and part black. Could she have been part red? One biographer says that she was from Richard Johnson's mother's side, the Suggetts — one of their people.

Richard Johnson did not respond to the amalgamation criticism. He said nothing. It was obvious that he loved his wife more than ambition. Out of the public limelight, Johnson lived like he wanted to live. Their daughters grew up happy and married white men. Johnson established an academy dedicated to the education of Indians — the Kentucky Choctaw Academy. Anthony Shane's Shawnee son, Charles Chein, was educated there, and so was Joseph Napoleon Bourassa, later a chief of the Potawatomis.

And what of the Reverend James Suggett? He appears to have been cast out of the Great Crossing Church that he had helped to establish. A Rev. James Suggett then became connected with the Shawnee mission, and Suggett became a Shawnee surname. In Kansas, a James Suggest was one of the trustees of the Shawnee Mission School along with Charles Bluejacket, Samuel Cornatzer, Moses Silverheels, and Eli Blackhoof. A William Suggett married Martha A. Wheeler in 1857, the marriage recorded by the Shawnee Mission Steward. A William J. Suggett, relation unknown, married Maria Rogers, the widow of Chief Lewis Rogers, another minister for the Shawnees and a descendant of Blackfish. This marriage may have taken place in Ohio, as their daughter, Caroline Suggett, was listed as being born there in 1830. Not all the records make sense, of course. We always hope they will in time.

The children of Samuel and Caroline (Suggett) Cornatzer included Lycurgus L. (Hige), Ninya E., Adelia A., Samuel L. (born 1868, supposed to have gone to Colorado as a young man), and Cyrus C.

Lycurgus Cornatzer, son of Samuel and Caroline (Suggett) Cornatzer, was born in 1857. He married Effie Stone, daughter of Thomas and America Stone, and their children included Adelia (b. 1896), Tessie (b. 1897), Felix, Vesta, Clarence, Juanita (Anita), Onas L. (b. 1899), and Effie. Lycurgus Cornatzer operated a dairy farm in Vinita, Indian Territory. He died of typhoid fever in 1909. See SOCC, vol. I, pp. 308; information from Patricia M. Chambers. For the family of Cyrus C. Cornatzer, see CORNATZER.

SULLIVAN, SULLOVAN – a Shawnee/Delaware name.

Dennis Sullivan was a Pennsylvania Indian trader as early as 1747. He was in a council with the Half King (Tanacharisson) and such other traders as Jacob Pyatt and John Owens at Logstown in 1751. See Hanna, II, p. 341.

Daniel Sullivan was a scout and interpreter. He was captured by Delawares in 1761, adopted by them and lived as an Indian for nine years. He sought out his relatives in Virginia in 1772 and lived with them for some time, but said that "the present war coming on between Britain and America and having no way but my gun to maintain myself, I removed back to my Delaware relations and determined to live with them until I could do better...."

But Daniel Sullivan made a mistake, and he visited Detroit as a neutral. Pluggy's Son discovered him among the Indians and complained "...on account on my having in the fall of 1776 killed his brother-in-law near the Kenkawa. John Montour seconded this information and as a proof referred to the wound I had received in my left arm at the time..." He was put in irons by the British, but his Delaware relations plotted to free him.

"I think the Delawares have always and still are well-disposed for peace, unless the late unfortunate affair at Beaver Creek and the other murders committed at Ft. Pitt have sour'd their minds..." Deposition of Daniel Sullivan, sworn to John Campbell. Letter of Daniel Sullivan to Col. John Cannon, Ft. Pitt, March 20, 1778. Draper Mss. 13CC121.

Daniel Sullivan and his brother, James, were two of the first settlers around what would become

Louisville, Kentucky. Daniel was one of the roughest men in the area by all accounts, but there was strong competition in that regard — men such as Peter Smith and Moses McCan. At the March, 1782, term of the Jefferson County Court, it was recorded that James Carr had bitten a piece of Daniel Sullivan's ear off in a fight. See Johnston's *Memorial History of Louisville*, vol. 2, p. 4.

Also in 1782, Sullivan served as a guide on Logan's expedition against Piqua. One of the Shawnee prisoners taken was an Indian woman whom had befriended Sullivan during his life among the Indians. The Kentuckians offered to release her, but she insisted on returning to Kentucky with the Indian prisoners. Sullivan gave her his horse to ride. See Draper Mss. 8J149; 9J195-196; 6S158; 9CC42-44; 11CC54-66; 12CC137.

In May, 1784, Daniel Sullivan had a suit in Jefferson County Common Court against Vincennes Indian trade Moses Henry.

Daniel's brother, James, founded Sullivan's Station on the south fork of Beargrass Creek. Daniel later founded another Sullivan's Station on the Patoka River in Indiana territory. It was reported in 1788, that two friendly Indians were killed by hostiles at his station. Le Gris was with the party who killed them.

Like David Owens, he had friends among the Indians — but also enemies who had long-held grudges against him. He was killed by Indians near Vincennes in 1790. See Draper Mss. 13CC121: "Dan Sullivan went to the O'Post.

Was the stoutest man I ever saw...was shot all to pieces in an Indian fray..." The old Vincennes Court wrote to his brother James relative to him dying intestate. An inventory of Daniel Sullivan's estate showed him holding 41 land deeds and 15 notes.

His offspring included Daniel Sullivan jr., who was prominent in local affairs in Kentucky and southern

Indiana and was at Tippecanoe with his cousin, George Rogers Clark Sullivan, in the War of 1812. In 1808, Daniel Sullivan jr. was said to have married his cousin, Susan Sullivan, a daughter of James Sullivan of Jefferson County. Daniel Sullivan jr. died in 1830 and left five orphan daughters.

SUMMERS – a Shawnee name.

Among the Shawnees who settled on the lands of the Cherokee nation by 1869 were Susan, Alonzo D., Mary, George, and Rhoda Summers. See JAIFR, vol. IV, #2, pp. 100-111.

SURPHUS, SURPHLIT – a Shawnee name.

According to Doleman's report from the Shawnee towns, Robert Surphus was a renegade who lived among the Shawnees in 1785. See Draper 14S216. One historian says that Robert Surphlit was Alexander McKee's cousin. See Butterfield p. 108. Simon Surphlet also appears in the records.

SWATZEL – a Shawnee name.

Rev. Gideon Seymour performed the marriage ceremony of John Swatzel to Catherine Donaldson on July 5th, 1858, in Shawnee, Kansas. See Shonkwiler, p. 15. Among the Shawnees who settled on the lands of the Cherokee nation by 1869 were John, Katherine, and Charles Swatzel. These people were probably related to Chief Joseph Parks. See JAIFR, vol. IV, #2, pp. 100-111.

SWANNUCK, SWANOCK, SWARNUCK, SHAWANOCK – a Delaware name.

James Sherlock and his Delaware wife may have been the parents of James Swanock. The names of both men were variously spelled in the Indian traders ledgers. James Sherlock appears as Shireluck, Sharlock, and Shawlock. Anyone whose native language was Shawnee or Delaware would have had trouble pronouncing the English "r" and would substitute the "l" or "W" sound.

Referring to James Swanock, trader William M. Boggs referred to the Delaware scout as James Swarnock and trader Alexander Barclay used James Sharnock. In his excellent study of the man, Harvey L. Carter listed all the variations but decided to use Swanock for the purpose of his sketch, but I will use Swannuck, which is what the name became.

James Swannuck was born in Indiana territory and he appears to have been the adopted son of Chief William Anderson, who listed him as a son and requested a special annuity for him. Swannuck was probably one of William Connors band of thirty Delaware scouts at the Battle of the Thames in 1813. He belonged to the Wolf clan and was later recognized as a war chief.

Those Delawares under James Swannuck's leadership reverted to their old style of living as wide-ranging free hunters, traversing the west in search of beaver furs, which were then high in demand. Often their hunting parties included Shawnees. As Carter points out, these hunters "seem to have been generally accepted by the white trappers and to have associated with them on a basis of virtual equality. They appear to have mastered the technology of the whites as it applied to hunting, trapping, and warfare, while retaining all of the basic Indian lore on these subjects."

Carter presents several documented stories about James Swannuck and his Delawares and their clashes with the Pawnees, Cheyennes, and other tribes. The core of his hunting band consisted of Swannock, Big Nigger (Nichols), Little Beaver, and Jim Dickie, but at various times it must have included some other famous names as well.

Once, his hunting party of six Delawares were joined by a band of seventeen white trappers on an expedition into Blackfoot country. There, they were surrounded by a band of about fifty hostile Blackfeet. Swannuck singled out the leader and threatened to immediately kill him if he did not call off the attack. The chief obeyed, and Swannuck's party rode out of the trap. The Blackfeet then tried to entice the Delawares and white men to visit their camp, but Swannuck saw it as another trap and refused. Only one man of the party, called Nez Perce Jack, was willing to leave the company of the Delawares. He rode over to the Blackfeet and was immediately killed by them. The others followed James Swannuck.

There was trouble when the Delawares moved into what the Plains tribes considered their own territory. In 1829, three Delawares including Puchies (the Big Cat), another of Chief William Anderson's sons, were killed by the Pawnees. In retaliation, James Swannuck raised a war party and burnt the Pawnee village. With government intervention, a peace was made between these tribes in 1833. Then in 1841, Swannuck was hunting with his party up the Republican River. They engaged a band of Sioux, including Touch-the-clouds with his iron shirt. The Delawares fired at the armor, their bullets glanced harmlessly off, and the rest of the Sioux closed in before they could reload and killed eight of them including Swannuck.

Ruby Cranor says that Swannuck was about sixty-five years old at the time, but that he had been married in his youth and his children included (1) Bill Swannuck who married a Jackson (they had two sons and a daughter); (2) John Swannuck who married Parkee-now and had a son named Jonas who ran a livery stable in Dewey, Oklahoma; (3) Wa-le-numb, a captain in the Seminole War, later killed by the Sioux in 1844, married Co-te-pe-lay-qua on the White River in Indiana and they had three children including George Swannuck whose children included Lilly, Mary (m. Frank Lucas), and Henry Swannuck; (4) Too-loo-qua Swannuck, (5) Shanghai Swannuck, (6) Sally Swannuck, and (7) James Swannuck jr.

Too-loo-qua married Charles Elkhair, one of the traditionalists of the tribe and a leader in the Big House Ceremony. Their children married into the Young, Falleaf, Bullette, Brown, Snooks, Conklin, Matthews, Wadsworth, Strickland, Lynch, Barnes, Lankford, Sumpter, and Kerr families.

Sally Swannuck had three children by a Mr. Wilson, then married William Day by whom she had James and Lillie Ann Day. She later married Jesse Miller and had two more children. Her son James Day married Katy Whiteturkey and had a large family. This family married into the Miller, Newcomb, Shailer, Emory. Blair, Brannon, Metzner, Willey, Marling, Labadie, and Lawyer families.

James Swannuck jr. was the captain of the Delaware scouts who accompanied James C. Fremont to California. He too trapped all over the west, and he and his father are often difficult to separate. Most of the stories appear to involve this younger man rather than his father. Louis and Francis Swannuck, sons of James Swannuck, jr., joined the Union Army during the Civil War and were killed. His other children included Dora, Katy, and James M. Swannuck.

Among the Delawares residing in the Cooweescoowee District and listed on the 1880 Cherokee census were George Swannock (43), Quas-chis-pit (probably his wife, 36), and children Sallie (18), Mary (15), and Henry Swannock (13). Also there was J. M. Swannock, age 27, living with Martha Swannock, age 80. Also, John Swannock (40), Jane (21), Josie (13), Willie (6 months), Widow Swannock (80), Lilie (15), Lucy (9), Emma (7) and Henry Swannock (47). All are listed as Delawares except Henry who is listed as a Cherokee. JAIFR, vol. X, #3, p. 22.

TANNER – an Ottawa/Chippewa/Delaware name.

Nine-year-old John Tanner was captured in Kentucky in 1789 by Shawnees and Ottawas. Adopted by the Ottawas, he grew up living the free life of a hunter and warrior. He married twice to Indian women, and raised two families. In 1817, he came back to Kentucky and reunited with his brothers and sisters. He had left his children behind, so he returned north. Later he came back again to Kentucky, this time with his children.

Still later, he was employed by the American Fur Company and was an interpreter at Mackinac. He dictated a narrative of his life to Dr. Edwin James, and it was subsequently published. His third marriage was to a white woman, but she divorced him, taking their child. The end of his life is a mystery connected with the death of James Schoolcraft, brother of the Indian agent. Did he kill Schoolcraft? Did someone else kill them both? Did Tanner run off and start a new life? Was there a woman involved? See Drimmer, pp. 142-182.

Among those granted trading licenses to deal with the Indians in Michigan in 1832 and 1833 was Therese Tanner, allotted by Henry R. Schoolcraft, Indian agent. See JAIFR, vol. I, #4, p. 36.

Among the Delawares on the 1880 Census of the Cooweescoowee District of the Cherokee Nation were Nelson Tanner, 46, listed as an adopted white man, living with Rachel Tanner, 40, and children Charles, 19, Linly, 11, Louisa, 11, and Jan Tanner, 5. See JAIFR, vol. 10, #3, p. 23.

TATE – a Creek name.

Some of the members of the Tate family who were mixed-blood Creeks settled in West Florida along with the Weatherford, Sizemore and Colbert descendants of Baldwin and Monroe counties. See "West Florida's Forgotten People," by Lucius F. Ellsworth and Jane E. Dysart which appeared in the FHQ, vol. 59, #4, 1981, pp. 426-429

TAYLOR – a Delaware/Shawnee name.

From *The Western Intelligencer*, Detroit, Aug. 2nd, 1813: "...in the year 1790, and probably in the month of May, a boy about nine years of age was taken prisoner by the Indians. The place where he was captured was as near as can be ascertained, upon the banks of the Ohio in Kentucky, a short distance below the mouth of the Great Miami.

"For many years he has been living in the country upon Red River which flows into Lake Winnapee, and a few days since he arrived at this place, on his way to seek his friends and relatives. He speaks no English, and it has been thought advisable that he should remain here where he will be fed and clothed at the public expense until the opening of the council, which is to be held with the Indians on the tenth of September next at St. Marys in Ohio...

"His memory is very retentive, and he related with great precision...the circumstances of his capture. He states that his name is John Taylor, and he thinks that his father's name was John...that he had one brother older and one brother younger than himself and five sisters...that his father went to the cornfield...he was left home with a younger brother...captured when he went out to gather walnuts...He states that a party followed the Shawnees who captured him and that, in the ensuing action, the Shawnee chief Black Fish was killed...."

TECUMSEH – a Shawnee name.

Tecumseh was one of those charismatic leaders

that comes along once in a great while. Bil Gilbert, who has written the best biography of the man, made a passing comparison of Tecumseh and Robert E. Lee, a fair analogy. Both Tecumseh and Lee were great men, great leaders, but they were not infallible and they simply could not overcome the tremendous odds against them. True, the Prophet made a mess of things at Tippecanoe, and Tecumseh might have gotten a better deal for his people were it not for that. But make no mistake, the Shawnees who aligned themselves with Tecumseh had enlisted in a lost cause.

I am not going to present Tecumseh's life here, but if you have not read his biography yet, I refer you to Bil Gilbert's excellent book or the brilliant historical narrative of Allan W. Eckert, both of which will probably be in print for the next twenty years or so, and should be. We are concerned here only with the genealogy of his family.

Was Tecumseh part-white? The accepted historical fact, the predominant opinion of historians through time, is that Opessa (Odessa, Opeththa, etc), chief of the Shawnees, had a son named Lawpareawha (Lawmarickey, Lawmawekea, etc.), who had a son Paxinosa (Pucksinwah, Puckshinewa, etc), who fathered Tecumseh (Tecumtha, Tecomtuk, etc.).

This is the genealogy endorsed by the most renown expert on Tecumseh in the history of the world, Allen W. Eckert (...*Tecumseh*, notes #1 and #20). On the maternal side, accounts vary. Most historians simply say that Tecumseh's mother was the Shawnee woman Methoastaske, Turtle Mother.

Because of Draper's and Shane's interviews with Anthony Shane and others, the genealogy was revised to allow the possibility that Tecumseh was half-Creek, his mother being a Creek adopted by the Shawnees who lived in the south near the Creek villages. Another theory goes that his mother was a Cherokee captured and adopted by the Creeks who in turn was captured and adopted by the Shawnees. Allen Eckert wrote in *The Frontiersman* that Tecumseh's mother was Shawnee and then in ...*Tecumseh,* Eckert said that new evidence had been discovered since the publication of *The Frontiersman* that made him revise his opinion, and that now he had the "undisputed" truth, and that Tecumseh's mother was Cherokee. If some diary or document was discovered somewhere, he does not mention it, and the only evidence he cites is the old evidence in Draper's manuscripts. And if those are the only cards he holds, then the game is still on.

There are yet some minority opinions that must be heard. Andrew Ice and his wife, both former captives and familiar with the Shawnees, claimed that Mrs. Ice had previously been married to a Shawnee and had a child by him who came back to the whites with her. He returned to the Shawnees while still a young boy and grew up to become the great chief, Tecumseh. This claim cannot be ruled out altogether. See BAYLES.

In the 1820s, Tecumseh's brother, the Prophet, was interviewed and asked about his personal genealogy. He told his tradition that his paternal grandfather was a Creek. That the father of Puckeshinwa (Paxinosa) went with the Creek delegation to Charlestown, South Carolina in 1770 and there met and became enamored with the beautiful white girl, the daughter of a governor or planter. With her father's blessing, he married her and became a planter himself, a slave owner and a sporting man. The couple had a son and two daughters. The son rebelled against the plantation life, and he visited his relatives among the Creeks. He met and married Methoastaske, who was among the Shawnees then living with the Creeks. The Shawnees gave him the name Puckeshinwa. When her people determined to go north and join the other Shawnees, Puckeshinwa went with them. See McKenney and Hall, pp. 75-78.

Could this be true? Count Zinzendorf visited the remarkable chief of the Wyoming Shawnee, Kawkowatchety, in 1745; and in 1754, Zinzendorf returned to find that Paxinosa had taken his place as king or head chief. He recorded in his diary that Paxinosa took his entire family to a baptism performed by the missionaries. Later, he noted that some of the Shawnees had gone south to raid Catawbas in the Carolinas.

Were there whites among the Shawnees at the time? Sure, there were. There were white children who had been captured and adopted by them. Kawkowatchety's son, the Hard Man, had a white wife. Peter Spellman lived with them, married to one of Paxinosa's daughters. Trader Thomas McKee was married to a Shawnee woman, and when some men were overheard plotting to rob Mckee, he was "inform'd by a white woman who had been taken prisoner by the Indians in their Carolina wars." See Zimmerman, p. 261.

The Prophet's story could be true. And how old was Paxinosa? When he replaced Kawkowatchety, he must have been an elder, and although not necessary the oldest man in the village, he was probably among the oldest of some fifty or sixty braves. Twenty years later, could this old chief have fought in the Battle of Pt. Pleasant?

Maybe. It also seems possible that the old Paxinosa was dead by the time of Bouquet's peace in 1765 and that the name was risen up, bestowed upon a nephew who was a budding warrior or village chief. Perhaps that's why the Shawnee peace negotiations were handled and signed by the Hard Man first, then Red Hawk, Benivissica, Cornstalk, and Nimwha. If Paxinosa was a leading chief, his name should have been on the treaty.

Dunmore's War was Cornstalk's war, reluctantly,

and the peace that followed was Cornstalk's peace. Where was Paxinosa? He fought and died at Pt. Pleasant. But was this the ancient chief, Paxinosa, the head war chief of all the Shawnee Nation? I doubt it. But the name could have been "risen up," in which case a younger Paxinosa could have been Tecumseh's father and the Shawnee who consorted with Mary Bayles.

The tradition of Mary Bayles and the tradition of the Prophet could both be based on truth.

The old traditional Shawnees would shake their heads and say that we were looking at this cockeyed, because they depended primarily on matrilineal descent as a mode of genealogical reckoning. Son, nephew, grandson, adopted son were roughly synonymous among the old Shawnee. It was not until there was a large number of adopted whites among them that the matrilineal system became secondary. When these old Shawnees were asked about who was son of whom, they always responded with the way they looked at relationships, and in the translation, the truth was lost.

I find the Prophet's account of his own genealogy highly creditable. Some historians and ethnologists say that no adopted Creek could ever be a Shawnee chief, let alone the war chief of the entire tribe. They are wrong. The Algonquin tribes gave adopted children the equal rights of the natural children. Many similar examples could be cited, but one only need look at Little Turtle, the Mohican/Mingo who became chief of the Miamis. Tecumseh's father could have been part-white and part-Creek. His mother could have been an adopted white or Creek or Cherokee. The historic Shawnees were more cosmopolitian than ethnologists would have you believe.

Whatever his nativity, Tecumseh grew up to be "light-complexioned, more of an olive-tan than red shade, whites thought....In easy circumstances, he had a pleasant, warm smile. Some thought the eyes were the most striking facial feature. They were hazel in color, deep-set, and a bit hooded by his brows, giving him a habitual — from what whites saw — intense, brooding expression." See Gilbert, p. 25.

Among Tecumseh's children was Nay-thah-way-nah who died in 1840. His wife's name was So-com-se, and she died in 1867. Their six children and their families were:

1. Way-lahsk-se, a daughter, married George Wildcat Alford. She died in 1869, but he lived until 1887. Their children included: Nancy Hood (Ah-la-maw-pa-ma); Thomas Wildcat Alford (Ga-nwah-pea-se-ka); David W. Alford (Pay-me-tah-pea-se-kah) who died Sept. 28, 1900, leaving one child; and Nellie Hood (Nah-wah-taw-pea-se).
2. May-thahsk-se, twin sister of Way-lahsk-se, was killed accidentally by a horse in 1827.
3. Nah-swah-pa-ma, the third daughter, who married Nocks-kah-way. Their children included daughter Nay-cah-twah who died March 4, 1892, leaving three children: Webster Tyner, Lucy Ellis, and William Ellis.
4. Pa-se-quah-mea-se, the fourth daughter, married Kyan-thaw-tah, one of the Shawnee Washington family. Among their children was Thomas Washington (Wayl-way-wa-se-ka) who died June 22, 1906, leaving several children.

   After Kyan-thaw-tah died in 1850, Pa-se-quah-mea-se married Na-he-pam-tha and among their children included at least one child, Ala-lay-maw-ppea, who died in 1890 at the age of 35. Na-he-pam-tha died in 1860.
5. Wal-kos-ka-ka, the fifth child, adopted the name Jim Fry. He married Pah-ke-pea-se who died September 23, 1880. The children of Jim

Fry by his first wife included Sam Fry who died Aug. 12, 1879, and James Fry who died January 6, 1875.

Jim Fry and his first wife apparently separated and he married Cha-ney-qua who died in 1866 or 1867 outliving Jim Fry who died in 1865. Their children included at least one son, Joe Longhorn (Fry), who died November 2, 1896, and left several children.

6. Wah-pah-meap-to (gives off light as he walks) was the last son of Nay-thah-way-nah. He was known among the whites as Big Jim. He married Ma-tho-tay-se who died in 1876. Among their children were Little Jim (To-tom-mo) who lived to be at least 52, and Lopa (Lah-lah-wah-pea-se) who died February 20, 1909. Lopa's husband, Charley Bobb, and one daughter survived her. After Ma-tho-tay-se's death, Big Jim married Lah-wep-pea who died in August, 1891. Big Jim himself died in Mexico on September 30, 1900. See Galbreath.

The more traditional relicts of Tecumseh seem to have intermarried with a number of tribes as well as with some blacks and whites. It should be pointed out that, according to Anthony Shane and his Shawnee wife, Tecumseh was a ladies man and had a succession of different wives. Shane said that one of his wives was half-white, the daughter of a white trader.

Tecumseh had a daughter by a Cherokee woman who later lived on the Arkansas River (see Draper 11YY46). One of his ex-wives was also a Potawatomi according to the tradition in the tribe, his descendants among them taking Tecumseh as a surname. A Potawatomi descendant of this connection, Mrs. Tecumseh, and Ralph Tecumseh, a Kickapoo, are discussed in Shawnee!, a book on Shawnee customs and ceremonials. See Howard, pp. 220-221, 274.

TENNERY, TANNERY, etc. – a Wyandot/Shawnee name.

There is a Shawnee tradition among some branches of the Tennery (Tannery) family. Listed on the 1843 Wyandot muster roll was the family of J. L. Tennery, consisting of one male and one female between 25 and 55, one male and four females between 10 and 25, and four children under 10, three of them girls.

THOMAS – a Delaware/Shawnee name,

John Thomas, a white boy, was captured by a war party and later adopted by Delawares (his capture is recounted in Wither's Border Wars). John Thomas later lived in the Ft. Wayne region. He married an Indian named Catherine and had at least one daughter named Charlotte. He was associated with William Henry Killbuck and served as interpreter. John Thomas later "reverted to heathen and became a drunk," the missionaries said. See Moravian Mission on White River, Indiana Historical Collections, p. 23.

Joseph Thomas was a Delaware scout with Calvin Everett and Capt. Fall Leaf in the 1850's. Among the Shawnees residing in the Cooweescoowee District and listed on the 1880 Cherokee census were William Thomas (age 25), his wife Nancy (23), and their daughter Betsy (1). The Delawares listed were Mr. and Mrs. David Thomas. See JAIFR, vol. X, #3, p. 24.

TIBLOW, TIBLOE – a Shawnee name.

Paul Taber and his sons, Cyrus and Samuel, were Indian traders at Ft. Wayne in Indiana as early as 1818. The Delawares and Shawnees would have had trouble pronouncing the "R" sound on the end of the name.

Henry Tiblow was a Shawnee who was educated

at the Ft. Leavenworth Shawnee Indian School and afterwards was employed by the government as an interpreter to the Shawnees and Delawares. KHC, p. 186.

In 1837. Henry Tiblow was appointed interpreter for the Fort Leavenworth Agency, for Shawnees, Delawares, and others. He was connected with the Agency in the same capacity for the next few decades. In 1851, the new Indian agent noted that "Mr. Tableau, the interpreter, is an intelligent and educated Indian." In 1854, he accompanied John Ketchem and James Connor, Delawares, on a mission to Washington with the intention to "visit their friends in Indiana on their return home." He shortly thereafter signed a treaty. See Barry, pp. 1197, 1212.

He was also connected to the Shawnee Mission Church and was active in church affairs. In the Steward's Book of the church are listed some vital statistics including the 1846 marriage of Henry Tibelau to Polly Marnall (possibly Marshall); the 1846 marriage of Zion Tibelaw to Sarah Berryman; the 1848 marriage of James Daugherty to Sarah B. Tibleu; and the and the baptism of Virginia Ann Tibleau.

Among the Shawnees who settled on the lands of the Cherokee nation by 1869 were Nancy, Caroliae, Zion, Mary, William, Eliza, Hester, Obediah, Mary, and Martha Tiblow. See JAIFR, vol. IV, #2, pp. 100-111.

Among the Shawnees residing in the Cooweescoowee District and listed on the 1880 Cherokee census were Simon (age 50), Mary (40), Overleer (36), and Bean Tiblow (5). See JAIFR, vol. X, #3, p. 24.

TIMBERLAKE – a Cherokee name.

Henry Timberlake was a British soldier who spent five months among the Cherokees in 1762. His memoirs of his stay are a valuable historical source. He married a Cherokee and his son, Richard

Timberlake, was born among the Nation. Richard's son, Levi Timberlake married a great granddaughter of Nancy Ward, the "beloved woman" of the Cherokees. Their son, Allison Timberlake, married Margaret Lavinia Rogers, paternal aunt of Will Rogers. See Alderman, pp. 25-26.

Among the Cherokees residing in the Cooweescoowee District and listed on the 1880 census were M. L. (age 45), Jennie W. (21), Kate (19), Bob (17), Ruth (20), and Willie Timberlake (11). See JAIFR, vol. X, #3, p. 25.

TIPTON – a Miami/Peroia name.

John Tipton married Jeanette Shields, his cousin, the daughter of John and Nancy Shields. His father-in-law went on the Lewis and Clark Expedition. Was his mother-in-law a Shawnee or Miami? Was his wife a cousin to John Tipton or his previous wife? And was she a Shawnee? See Yater, p. 8.

TODD – a Shawnee name.

Several members of the Todd family lived on the frontier and had contact with the Delawares and Shawnees. Among them was Samuel Briggs Todd, born in Lexington, Kentucky in 1793. When eighteen years old, he enlisted in Captain Hart's company in the War of 1812. He was wounded and taken prisoner at the River Raisin.

"The Indian women dressed his wounds with great tenderness, and an old chief wanted the young Kentucky soldier to marry his daughter...His account of his captivity among the Indians, written for his family, was loaned to a relation and was unfortunately lost..." See Visscher, p. 11.

In the fall of 1825, a seven-year-old boy named Matthew Brayton disappeared from the home of his parents in Crawford township, Wyandot County, Ohio.

"The Indian villages were examined, but the Wyandots not only expressed ignorance of the boy's movements, but joined in the search with great zeal. It was learned from them, however, that a party of Canadian Indians had passed north on the day of the boy's disappearance, but they did not know whether the boy was with them or not...

"Years passed by and the stories of the boy's disappearance became one of the unsolved mysteries of the past...Thirty-four years after the boy's disappearance, the Brayton family learned through a weekly newspaper of an Indian captive, then in Cleveland, who did not know his own name, but in youth had been stolen by Canadian Indians from some place in northwestern Ohio, had been taken to Michigan, and after thirty-four years of captivity had returned to Ohio to find his parents...

"The meeting at the family home was extremely touching, but the season of rejoicing was of short duration, for it soon transpired that it was not the long lost son and brother returned, but the child of other parents, and no tidings of Matthew Brayton ever reached his family...

"It was conclusively proven that the 'captive' was William Todd, and he was restored to his parents in Michigan. At the outbreak of the rebellion he enlisted in the cavalry service and died in Nashville, Tennessee." *See Wyandot County History*, (Ohio), p. 902-903.

Among the Shawnees who settled on the lands of the Cherokee nation by 1869 was James Todd and his family of three. See JAIFR, vol. IV, #2, pp. 100-111.

TOMAHAWK, TAMEHAWK – a Shawnee name.

Kikipelethey was an articulate, Shawnee war chief who spoke for the Moluntha's Shawnees beginning about 1784. Was he white or part-white? It could be that he was Nathaniel Carpenter, Abram Pope, or one of the many others who "went native." Henry Harvey, in his history of the Shawnees, gives the translation of his name as "Tomahawk."

Listed on the 1880 Eastern Shawnee roll are listed Jacob and Susie Tomahawk, the children of John Tomahawk, who were then wards of John Jackson and Elizabeth his wife.

Listed on the 1888 Eastern Shawnee roll is Susan (Susanna or Annie, variously) Tomahawk, mother, 17, her daughter, Alemathinque Tomahawk, 3, her daughter Jennie Chisholm, 3, and Silas Chisholm, 12, relationship not given. Of course, the last two may have been her step-children.

This family associated with the Peorias. Listed on the 1914 Peoria Roll are Susanna Tomahawk and her children and grandchildren who included Henry Chisholm, Rosa Shakkah, Anna Shakkah, and Minnie Chisholm who is identified as a daughter of a previously deceased daughter of Susanna Tomahawk.

TOOLEY, TULLEY, TULLIS, etc. – a Shawnee name.

Charles Tuley married into the Floyd family. He was killed in Jefferson County, Kentucky but not before he had a large family to carry on the Floyd Indian blood tradition. One son, Charles Tuley, jr., moved across the river into Indian country and established a trading post near present Charlestown. This became known as Tulleytown, and was one of busiest trading centers of an early day. In the early 1800s, Thomas Killbuck, among others, complained of being mistreated there.

A Shawnee tradition concerns the Rev. Aaron Tullis of early Ohio. He, along with Rev. William Barbee, Rev. Joseph Coe, Rev. Robert Marshall, among others, closely associated with the Shawnees in the early 1800s in Ohio, and while there are Indian blood traditions in these families. The Barbee and Tulli names became associated with nearly-white Shawnee families, both in Ohio and Kansas. There is probably more information on this family around than I have yet seen.

TUCKER – an Ottawa/Shawnee name.

William Tucker was born in New Jersey, but his parents moved to the frontier when he was a youth, and in 1754 he and his brother were captured were captured and adopted. William Tucker became a trader and was an Ottawa and Chippewa interpreter at Detroit in 1778, Seineke, p. 285. Captive Daniel Sullivan stayed with Tucker while he was in Detroit and spoke highly of him. Many of his descendants still live in Michigan. See Thwaites, Rev. on the Upper Ohio, p. 203n.

Charles Tucker was among the Shawnees who went to the Florida War with Capt. Joseph Parks in 1837. See Draper's interview with him, and also see Staab.

Shawnee Charles Tucker was — with Charles Tooley, Charles Fish, George Daughtery, and Jackson Rogers — a councilor to principal chiefs Paschal Fish and William Rogers in 1860. See Caldwell, p. 105.

Living among the Shawnees on the Cherokee Reserve in 1869 were many members of the Tucker family. They included Charles, Mary, Joshua, Maria, John M., Charles jr., Samuel, Dudley, Ella, Julia, Ida Mary, and Dudley Haynes Tucker. See JAIFR, vol. IV, #2, p. 109. Charles Tucker signed the settlement agreement with the Cherokees as "assistant principal chief of the Shawnee Nation."

Charles Tucker was the guardian of Hiram Johnson. See JAIFR, vol. VIII, #2, p. 28.

Among the Shawnees residing in the Cooweescoowee District and listed on the 1880 Cherokee census were Charles Tucker, a Shawnee man, 45, apparently living with his wife Harriet, listed as a white woman, age 29. See JAIFR, vol. X, #3, p. 26.

A Shawnee named Elizabeth Tucker is mentioned in *Shawnee!*, a book on tribal customs and ceremonials. See Howard, p. 261.

TURKEYFOOT – an Ottawa/Potawatomi/Shawnee name.

Little Turtle, who led the united reds to victory in the earlier battles including St. Clair's Defeat, realized that Anthony Wayne's forces were too powerful, and he urged reconciliation with the whites. Blue Jacket and Turkeyfoot disagreed, and Blue Jacket became the war chief and led the red forces at Fallen Timbers.

Turkeyfoot, the Ottawa war chief, had fought long against the whites in the Ohio Valley alongside the Shawnees and Delawares and perhaps the Potawatomis as well. At Fallen Timbers, Turkeyfoot's Ottawas charged with their hatchet raised, and Anthony Wayne's Legionaires charged back at them with fixed bayonets. Seeing his warriors fall back, Turkeyfoot "stood on an outcrop and tried to rally them, shouting that if they were brave, the Great Spirit would favor their cause. An American sharpshooter felled Turkey Foot who sang his death song and died at the base of the rock." The Ottawa broke and ran. See Gilbert, p. 181.

Afterwards the Indians etched a turkey-foot symbol into the rock. And groups of Indians would often come and pay homage to the bravery of their fallen warrior, Turkey Foot.

It is possible that Turkeyfoot, the Ottawa, had a Potawatomi or Shawnee wife. The next Turkey Foot was a fierce Potawatomi who lived on the Tippecanoe River and long associated with the Shawnees. He remained openly hostile to the United States long after the Treaty of Greenville. He continued to raid across southern Illinois, against Osages as well as against far-flung outposts of the United States. In 1802, he was leading a party of mounted Potawatomi along the Mississippi near Edwardsville where they discovered two white men clearing land to establish farms upon Potawatomi territory. Both white men were killed.

The settlers of Kaskakia petitioned the government to do something about Turkey Foot, denouncing him in particular as responsible for the raids in southern Illinois.

The United States, through William Henry Harrison, demanded that the Potawatomis turn over Turkey Foot and the warriors responsible for the deaths of the two white men, but because of the observable inequities of the United States in applying justice to Native Americans, the Potawatomis refused to deliver them up. Turkey Foot remained free. See Edmunds, p. 155.

The message of the Shawnee Prophet convinced Turkey Foot and his band to align themselves with Tecumseh. It was perhaps during this time that Turkey Foot married a Shawnee woman and thus the Turkeyfoot surname arose and was carried on as a surname among the Shawnee rather than among the Ottawa or Potawatomi.

Chief Gomaux (Massenogamaux or Gomo) of the Illinois Potawatomi, told the whites at a council at Peoria on 17 August, 1811, that they had slain Turkeyfoot due to white demands. But Turkeyfoot seems to have reappeared among the Shawnee. There is a tradition that, like Tecumseh, Turkeyfoot lived on until slain in battle at the Thames, but I suspect it was only the name that was "risen up."

A warrior named Turkeyfoot lived among the Shawnees and Wyandots in Ohio after the war. Lang wrote of Turkeyfoot as being an irreconcilable living among the Shawnees, "capable of entertaining and practicing the most diabolical ideas."

In Kansas in 1849, the Shawnee Jacob Turkeyfoot married the Shawnee/Potawatomi Louisa Bushman (Beauchemie), a descendant of Blackfish. Jacob Turkeyfoot then became an active Shawnee/Christian and took some part in the activities of the mission church. See Stewards Book.

Among the Shawnees living on the Cherokee Reserve in 1871 was James Turkeyfoot. See JAIFR, vol. IV, #2, p. 109.

On the 1882 Eastern Shawnee Census appear Mary Turkeyfoot Punch, 35, and her children Milton Turkeyfoot, 7, Mamie Turkeyfoot, 5, and Mary Punch, 1.

TUTAW, TUTAL, TUPEL, etc.– a Shawnee name.

The extensive will of Thomas Jones, "late of Vincennes, Indiana, now of Pittsburgh, Pennsylvania," mentions many nieces and nephews, brothers and sisters, including John O'Brien residing at the mouth of the Wabash, and Kennedy O'Brien of Kerry County, Ireland. But he also mentions Mary, "an Indian woman who formerly lived with me in Vincennes, daughter of an Indian chief called Tupel (?), and her two children born in Vincennes and named Nancy and Charlotte."

The will was probated in Pittsburgh, Allegheny County, Pa., Jan. 27, 1824. It was recorded in Crawford County, Indiana, May 19, 1835. I have not seen the original and present it here as abstracted in *The Hoosier Journal of Ancestry*, vol. III, p. 16. The question mark after the name of the chief, Tupel, was placed there by the person abstracting the will, and it may have been difficult to read.

It seems to me that this chief could have been the Shawnee, Tutal, whose name appears variously as Tutall, Totall, and Tu-taw. Tutal was "a noted scout and mail carrier during the campaigns of Wayne and Harrison...a half-breed Frenchman..."

In the days when he rode express between Cincinnati and Wayne's outposts, the enemy narrowly missed capturing him several times. Once, he engaged in a hand-to-hand knife fight and, although he succeeded in wounding his adversary, his own left hand was stuck by a knife, severing the tendons of three fingers. "When the wound healed, the fingers remained, ever afterward, as stiff as sticks. When intoxicated, he was quarrelsome — always ready for a fight. The pugilists of his time feared the stiff fingers more than they did the clenched fist."

After the wars were over, he made his home on Peter Hammel's farm for a number years, helping him with the farmwork. The latter portion of his life was spent hunting, fishing, and working at gardening, at which he excelled. He died at age seventy-eight, and was buried in the old Duchoquet cemetery. See C. W. Williamson, History of Western Ohio And Auglaize County, pp. 315-316.

TYNER – a Cherokee/Shawnee name. Many of the descendants of Tecumseh share the name.

Dempsey Tyner, born in 1755, married a Cherokee woman named Obedience. He fought in the Revolutionary War and lived until October 13, 1842. He was buried in Tyner's Station cemetery near Chattanooga, Tennessee. By his Cherokee wife, he had twelve children. One son, Lewis B. Tyner, moved to Missouri in 1851.

Lewis Tyner, jr. moved with his brother, Jesse, to Logan County, Arkansas. A son of Lewis Tyner, jr., named Lewis Babe Tyner, was born August 25, 1865, and he died October 18, 1937. Lewis Babe Tyner married Martha Elizabeth Tyner in 1887, and they were the parents of twelve children including Robert Lee Tyner, born 1888 at Gore, Indian Territory.. Tyner was already a common name among the Cherokees. See SOCC, vol.

II, p. 294.

Listed on the 1880 census of the Cooweescoowee District of the Cherokee Nation were:

A. V. Tyner, adopted white, age 29, roll #2978
Carter Tyner, cherokee, 24, #2998
Clinton Tyner, #3020, age and roll # not given.
Edward Tyner, cherokee, age 4/12, #2976
Emma Tyner, cherokee, 9, #2980
F. M. Tyner, cherokee, 3, #2981
Fannie Tyner, cherokee, 11, #2979
Frasier Tyner, cherokee, 2, #3023
George Tyner, cherokee, 30, #2974
James F. Tyner, cherokee, age not given, #2953
Jane Tyner, an adopted shawnee, 22, #2999
John H. Tyner, cherokee, 8, #2931
Kate Tyner, an adopted shawnee, 22, #3002
Leonard Tyner, cherokee, 11/12, #2982
Mary Tyner, cherokee, 21, #2975
Mary A. Tyner, cherokee, 27, #2930
May Tyner, cherokee, 17, #3021
Mollie Tyner, cherokee, 17, #3025
Nancy Tyner, an adopted black or mixed, 21, #2915
Prince Tyner, an adopted black or mixed, 19, #2913
Reuben Tyner, cherokee, 80, #2929
Reuben (Big) Tyner, cherokee, 37, #2977
S. C. Tyner, cherokee, 42, #2954
S. T. Tyner, cherokee, 36, #3001
Sarah Tyner, cherokee, 12, #2955
T. J. Tyner, cherokee, 2, #3000
William Tyner, adopted white, #2945

Not always, but in general those who appeared consecutively on the roll were living together, and often the head of the family was listed first.

According to Galbreath, the Tyner family intermarried with Tecumseh's Shawnee family and Webster Tyner was a great-grandson of Tecumseh. See Galbreath.

Louis Tyner was an employee of the Absentee Shawnee Boarding School in 1894. See JAIFR, vol. VIII, #4, p. 28.

Howard interviewed Arron, Alfred, Bill, and Webb Tyner and they gave him information concerning their Shawnee traditions. See Howard, pp. 231, 302-305.

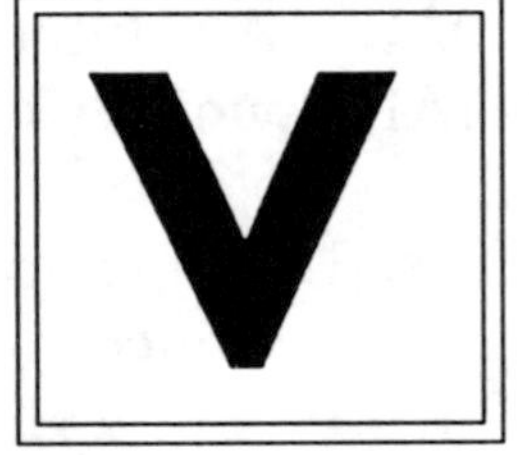

VAN METER – a Wyandot/Seneca name.

"Capt. John Van Meter, son of Henry, an early settler west of the mountains, was born about 1738. In 1771, he owned 300 acres at the site of the present town of Waynesburg, Greene County, Pa. Early in the Revolution, he commanded a company of rangers from Westmoreland. During the Indian wars, his home was raided, his wife and daughter being killed, and one son (John) carried captive. The son never returned to civilization but in habits and feeling became partially an Indian..." See Thwaites, Frontier Defense, p. 22-23.

In a treaty with the Senecas, a provision was made for the Van Meter family as follows: "To John Van Meter, who was taken prisoner by Wyandots, and who has ever since lived amongst them, and has married a Seneca woman, and to his wife and three brothers, Senecas, who now reside on Honey Creek, one thousand acres of land..." See Lang, p. 199.

"John Van Meter was a white man...taken prisoner when small...lived and died with the Indians. He was a heavy-built man, strong...good-natured, kind-hearted...a good hunter..." He lived on Honey Creek, in Seneca County, Ohio, with his second wife, Susan Brandt, a Mohawk woman, "a sister to the Brants from New York." He left a son by his first wife who became a class-leader in the Wyandot church in Kansas. See Finney, pp. 519-520.

Listed among the Wyandots on the 1843 Muster Roll of those from Sandusky, Ohio, was John Van Meter's household, which included one male between 25 and 55 and one female between 10 and 25.

Among the Wyandots and Shawnees in Kansas in 1855 was Thomas Van Meter, age 24. See KHQ, vol.. XVI, p. 754.

WAGGONER – a Shawnee name.

Frederick Waggoner, previously of Reading Town, Pennsylvania, was among the whites delivered up to Bouquet after Pontiac's War. Some other members of the family were apparently captured during the conflict. See SWJ, p. 783.

In 1792, Tecumseh led a war party of Shawnees on a raid against an isolated station established by John Waggoner. Two of Waggoner's daughters and a son were taken back to the Shawnee towns and adopted. The boy, Peter Waggoner, lived with the Shawnee as one of them for more than ten years, eventually taking an Indian wife by whom he had several children. Later he was discovered by friends of his father and forcibly taken back to western Virginia.

He was kept under guard until he eventually became reconciled to living amongst the whites again, "but he was ever melancholy, frequently lamenting that he had left his savage family." See Gilbert, pp. 161-162; Withers, pp 408-410; Finney, p. 184.

Did some of his children and grandchildren among the Shawnees take the Waggoner (or Wagoner) name? I think so. There is an Indian blood tradition among the descendants of the Waggoner/Wagner families who appeared in the Miami Valley near Piqua and Troy, Ohio. These families, and the many Ohio families with whom they intermarried, have spread their Indian blood traditions throughout the country. On the 1810 Miami County, Ohio, tax list appear William Barbee, Barnabas Blue, Issac Clark, Joseph Coe, John Flinn, James Frazee, John Gerard, John Mann, James Marshall, George Moffitt, Alexander Tilford, Arron Tullis, John Waggoner, William Wells, George Williams, William Wilson, and others who have red connections in their families. I hope to detail some of these relationships in future volumes of Indian Blood.

WALKER – a Wyandot name.

Many members of the Walker family were captured in the early frontier conflicts, including John and William Walker, adopted by the Wyandots.

"The John Walker Reservation is a tract of 640 acres in Seneca Township, just west of the Van Meter grant, which was bestowed upon the Wyandot woman, Catherine Walker, and her sons John and William." See Lang, p. 199-200.

William Walker was an interpreter at the Ft. Wayne Agency in 1814.

On the 1855 Wyandot Census were listed:

William Walker, 55, with Hanna Walker, 55; Martha R. Walker, 29; Harriet P. Walker (now Mrs. Mullen).

Matthew R. Walker, 45, and his family which included Lydia B., 38, Adaline, 14, Sarah L., 12, Thomas G., 10, Malcolm, 8, Percy L., 6, Clarence P., 4, and Lillian, 1.

Joel Walker, 41, and his family which included Mary, 34, Maria, 8, Justion, 6, Ida C., 4, and Everett, 2.

Isaiah Walker, 29, and his family which included Mary, 25, Emma, 1, and Alice, an infant.

Among the Shawnees who settled on the lands of the Cherokee nation by 1869 were Thomas, Sarah, Mary, James, and Peter Walker. See JAIFR, vol.. IV, #2, pp. 100-111.

Among the guardianships reviewed by the Commissioner of Indian Affairs in 1871 was the case of the Wyandot, William Walker, a Wyandot who was absent at the time of the hearing, having gone to Larue, Hardin County, Ohio.

Also heard was the case of Isaiah Walker, guardian for Eliza Young, Issac Peacock, and George Whitewing.

Also heard was the case of Joel Walker, who was then dead. His widow was Mary A. Walker and Isaiah Walker was the administrator of his estate. His wards were Abraham Williams, Zachariah Longhouse, Boyd and Daniel Peacock, Thomas Van Meter, John Warpole, and the half-brothers Smith Bigsinew and Smith Nichols (also known as Bigsinew).

Other wards of Joel Walker included William M. Blacksheep (then in New Mexico), Rebecca Hooper (also known as Rebecca Van Meter), Thomas Hill, George and James Whitewing, Thomas Manoncue, George Coon, Mary and Sarah Williams, Sarah Hicks, and Mary Coonhawk (daughter of Sarah Hicks). Among those who testified were Isaiah Walker, William Johnson, John Sarrahass, Jacob Whitecrow, and Matthew Mudeater. See JAIFR, vol.. VIII, #2, p. 17-18.

WALLS – a name associated with Indian blood traditions.

It is a common thing for family traditions of Indian blood to lead back to Indian traders and Indian captives — and sometimes to military men, especially to the commanding officers of frontier outposts. Such men as Col. George Slaughter, Col. Thomas Barbee, Gen. George Rogers Clark, and Col. John Gibson probably had their chances at some attractive Indian women.

It is possible that, just as Col. Benjamin Logan adopted the part-Shawnee son of Joshua Rennick, and Capt. John Hardin adopted Humingbird, said to have been a beautiful girl — so too, other officers may have taken white-looking Indian orphans as their wards and raised them as their own.

There is an Indian blood tradition leading back to Maj. George Walls, who took command of Ft. Nelson from George Rogers Clark, who then had gone to Virginia to petition the Virginia Assembly for funds.

Clinkenbeard, discussing the 1782 expedition to the Shawnee towns, told the Rev. Shane, "When I saw Major George Walls, he had the king's squaw behind, riding into camp. Had been out and caught her, not caught in the towns. Most splendid looking squaw I ever saw...She came in right back of the tent where we lay. She was left at the towns. 'Twas said some of the men turned back and took her." See Draper 11CC66.

All I have seen on Major George Wall's family is that he is supposed to have married a daughter of Col. George Slaughter, another officer in the George Rogers Clark's forces at one time. One of Walls' daughters married the Christopher Miller who had been adopted by the Shawnees. See MILLER.

Another daughter, Elizabeth Walls, married Robert Clark, born 1780, the son of Robert Clark and Agnes Elizabeth Gay Clark. The children of Robert jr. and Elizabeth Walls Clark included Lucinda, John, and Robert. Robert Clark III, born 1819 in Bourbon County, Kentucky, married Sarah Ruth Ward, the daughter of James and Martha Wright Ward. And their children included Martha (m. R. P. Barnett), John Clark, and William H. Clark.

There's probably more on this family concerning their Indian blood connections. If you know it, drop me a line and let me know too.

WARD – a Shawnee/Cherokee name.

John Ward was captured by Indians in 1758, adopted by Shawnees with whom he took a wife. His Shawnee name was White Wolf by which he is mentioned in some early journals and on at least one treaty. He, his wife, and his several children were in camp in 1793 when it was attacked by Simon Kenton and a party of white men that included John Ward's brother, Capt. James Ward. Tecumseh led a counter-fire and afterwards a retreat. John Ward was said to have been killed. See History of Mason County, p. 440-441. See Draper 9BB63.

"James B. Ward, half Indian and half Irish. was born in South Carolina in 1794. In the early nineteenth century he lived in western Georgia working as an Indian trader and cattle driver. During the War of 1812, the American government hired him as a spy. He married Elizabeth English, an orphaned full-blooded Lower Creek who had been adopted at about age five by another white trader, John English. Protected by other Indians before removal, the Wards lived in Dale County, Alabama, where they farmed and raised a family of at least seven children." The later history of this family, most of whom settled in the Florida counties of Walton and Holmes, exemplifies the reluctance of people to openly admit their Indian ancestry. For the well-documented study of these and others, see *West Florida's Forgotten People*, by Lucius F. Ellsworth and Jane E. Dysart which appeared in the Florida Historical Quarterly, vol.. 59, #4, 1981, pp. 426-429.

With the help of the Iroquois, the Delawares drove the Cherokees south of the Ohio River toward the Smokey Mountains and the area which became known as the "traditional" home of the Cherokees. The major town of the Cherokees became Chota, and it was there, in the 1730s, that the legendary Nancy Ward was born. Her mother was Tame Doe, a brother of Little Carpenter and a niece of Old Hop, the longtime principal chief of the Cherokees. The war chief, Dragging Canoe, was a son of Little Carpenter and hence her cousin. According to most sources, including her great-grandson Jack Hildabrand, the father of Nancy Ward was a Delaware chief.

There are plenty of interesting stories about Nancy Ward — too many to recount here. She held the position of "Ghisau" or "beloved woman" among the Cherokees. She was called Nan-ye-hi or Tsistuna-giske (the wild rose), and she is often referred to as "the wild rose of the Cherokees."

She married the noted warrior Kingfisher, whom she sometimes accompanied in battle. By Kingfisher, she had two children, Catherine and Little Fellow (later Chief Fivekiller). During the 1750s, she married the white Indian trader Bryant Ward whose last name she then adopted. By Bryant Ward, she had Elizabeth (Betsy) Ward. Betsy Ward married Indian agent and later Revolutionary War General Joseph Martin.

John (Jack) Ward, a white son of Bryant Ward by a previous marriage, married half-Cherokee Catherine (Katy) McDaniel and their children included James, George, Samuel, Charles, Bryant, Betsy, Susie, and Nancy Lucy Ward.

Catherine, daughter of Kingfisher and Nancy Ward, married at least three times, once to Indian trader Ellis Harlan by whom she had a daughter, Elizabeth (Betsy) Harlan, who married Peter Hildabrand.

Nannie Martin, daughter of Joseph Martin and Betsy Ward, married Michael Hildabrand.

WARNER – a Seneca name.

A white man named Benjamin Franklin Warner grew tired of white civilization and sought refuge with the Indians. He married the Mohican woman named Konkepot and joined the Senecas in Ohio. When the couple were on their way west, Konkepot died at the mouth of the Missouri leaving a small child for Warner to raise by himself. Lang says, "Warner was the man-of-all-work, liberal, sober, industrious, and always agreeable." See Lang.

Among those Shawnees, Senecas, and Wyandots allotted money for improvements made on their Ohio property was Benjamin F. Warner, allotted $81. Warner was also given $150 for building a cabin and $20 for riding express from St. Louis to the Seneca sub-agency with dispatches from the Superintendent of Indian Affairs. See Watson, vol. V., pt. 3, p. 10, 11, 27, 34.

On William Clark's list of expenses of the Indian Agency in concluding the Treaty of Castor Hill with the Kickapoo Nation in October, 1832, is a payment to Benjamin Warner for services, including taking out eleven horses to the Kickapoos and building a log cabin for the Senecas. At the Treaty with the Shawnee and Seneca in December, 1832, he served as a guide and an express rider. See Watson, vol.. V., pt. 2, p. 31; pt. 3, p. 11, 27; pt. 9, p. 3.

WARPOLE, WALPOLE, REDPOLE, PAINTED POLE – a Shawnee/Wyandot name.

The Warpole (Routondy) was one of Richard Butler's guides in 1786 to the Indian towns where he met with Tarhe and Captain Pipe. See Draper 14S195-214. The family was connected to that of White Wing, Round Head, and the Zanes.

Among the Wyandot families appearing on the 1843 Muster Roll were:

1. Warpole's family, consisting of one male over 55, one female over 55, one female 10 to 25, and one male child under 10.
2. Henry Warpole's family, consisting of one male and one female between 10 and 25 and one female under 10.

In some documents, the name appeared sometimes as Walpole.

On the 1855 Wyandot Census were John Warpole, 30, and his family which included Catherine, 26, Mary, 7, James, 5, and David, 7 months. Allotted land next door was the family of Catherine W. Warpole, 35, and her family which included Francis Whitewing Warpole, 15, Sarah Whitewing Warpole, 13, Mary Whitewing Warpole, 6, and Henry Warpole, 5 months.

WASHINGTON – a Delaware/Shawnee name.

Queshawsey, "a Delaware who lived among the Shawnees," took on the name George Washington whom he once met when a youth. The name appears to have stuck among his descendants up to the present day.

In 1782, it was Queshawsey who was detailed to guard Dr. John Knight, the captured surgeon of Col. William Crawford's expedition. Dr. Knight persuaded Queshawsay to untie his hands, vowing not to escape. As soon as Queshawsay turned his back, however, Knight clubbed his trusting companion with a piece of firewood so hard that Queshawsey "ran howling into the woods," and Knight took his rifle and escaped.

Historian Parker B. Brown, writing of the incident in 1982, says, "As for the Shawnees at Wapatomica, they were philosophical and amused when they learned that Knight had escaped. They enjoyed a good story, and the guard gave them one when he strode into the town alone with a head wound. He related how he had freed Knight's hands and why, but then said he had been hit with his rifle. He in return stabbed the prisoner in the back and stomach, but the man was so 'great, big, tall, strong,' that he got away. [John] Slover, an adoptee turned army guide and now a captive himself, overheard the tall tale and objected, saying that the doctor was a 'weak, little man,' whereupon the audience roared with laughter..."

Queshawsey seems to have been but a mere youth at the time, and he must have learned by his experience, later gaining a reputation for stealth as well as honesty. He appears to have been in several scraps in later years, yet he survived. Lewis Wetzel shot Washington, but the wounded man managed to get away on his horse and went to General Harmar.

In 1789, a white officer wrote that, "This George Washington is a trusty confidential Indian and was wounded by some vagabond whites from the neighborhood of Wheeling. He is well known to Governor St. Clair, and I believe there is not a better Indian to be found. The villain who wounded him I am informed is one Lewis Whitzell. I am in hopes to be able to apprehend him and deliver him to Judge Parsons to be dealt with; but would much rather have it in my power to order such vagabonds hanged up immediately without trial."

Lewis Wetzel was arrested in 1789, but escaped jail. He was arrested again, but inasmuch as George Washington recovered and there were no other witnesses against him, he was released. See Outpost on the Wabash, p. 208-209.

Brown says of George Washington, "Then at Zanesville, Ohio, in 1802, he became drunk and threatened a settler. When he left the place of drinking, he was followed by the friends of the settler and never heard of again." See "The Fate of Crawford Volunteers," by Parker B. Brown, Western Pennsylvania Historical Magazine, vol.. 65, October, 1982, p. 330.

Sounds like they killed him. But more probably, he was just beaten up or chased out of town.

John Lee came to Indiana and in 1805 was charged with assault and battery in Clark County, Indiana, for attacking "the Shawnee" George Washington in Clarksville.

In his Seneca County, Ohio, recollections, Lang says that he lived on, that the Shawnee "George Washington, who served as a scout during the Revolution, reached a ripe old age in 1822. During that year his squaw — Martha Washington — was condemned to death for witchcraft. The executioners entered her cabin, saw the old scout looking on at his doomed wife pounding hominy, and then without ceremony, Shane stepped forward, struck her with the tomahawk, and called upon Jim Sky to cut her neck." See Lang, p. 207.

The Washington name continued among both the Shawnee and the Delaware. It is probable that it was one of the Delaware or Shawnee Washington family who served in the Seminole War with John Perry and Capt. Joseph Parks.

A George Washington was one of Capt. James Swannock's band of Delaware and Shawnee scouts in the 1840's. In 1886 — more than thirty years after they served with Fremont — George Washington was still trying to collect the money due him and the others of the Swannock's band.

George Washington was — along with Big Nichols, John Sarcoxie, Jim Simond, and Big Raccoon — a councilor to old Neconhecond, Delaware chief of the Wolf Clan in 1860. See Weslager, p. 408.

Charles Washington is listed among the Delaware and Shawnee scouts in Capt. Fall Leaf's band in 1860 along with George and Fred Falleaf and John and George Swannock. See Chalfant, p. 247.

Among the students named Washington at the Delaware Baptist Mission School in Kansas in 1858 were William, age 12; Francis, 8; Charlie, 8; and John Washington, 5. Among the students at the school in 1867 were Albert and Edson Washington, both age 9; Ryland, 7, and Cyrus Washington, 5.

WEATHERFORD – a Creek name.

William Weatherford was the leader of the Red Sticks, the splinter Creek group that aligned themselves with Tecumseh during the War of 1812. He was almost white, only 1/8 Creek. The Weatherford family was divided during the Red Stick war, two sisters and a brother on one side and a sister and a brother on the other. See Draper 4YY5.

"Col. Lewis was with the friendly Creeks when Weatherford surrendered to Jackson. He said Jackson had offered five hundred dollars for Weatherford, dead or alive. The friendly Creeks knew he was near them and all wanted the reward.

"The morning before he surrendered, Bill killed a deer and very early the next morning he threw it across his pony and mounted behind it and rode into Jackson's camp in that way, The friendly Creeks saw him but supposed it was one of their own men taking a deer to Jackson. They not being near enough to recognize him. He rode up to Jackson's tent, threw off the deer, and told Jackson who he was that he wanted peace for his women and children. He could not fight him any longer. That there he was, do as he pleased with him..." See Draper 4YY6-7.

Some of the Weatherford descendants settled with other Creeks in the Florida counties of Baldwin and Monroe, around what became known as the Poarch community northwest of Atmore, Florida. See *West Florida's Forgotten People,* by Lucius F. Ellsworth and Jane E. Dysart which appeared in the FHQ, volume 59, #4, 1981, pp. 426-429

WELLS – a Miami/Delaware/Shawnee name.

William Wells (or Apekonit, the Wild Carrot, or Carrot Top, supposedly named for his red hair) was born in the vicinity of Jacob's Creek, Pennsylvania in 1770, the son of Samuel Wells, Sr., and Elizabeth Wells. He had four brothers and a sister, he being the youngest child. In 1775, his eldest brothers, Samuel Wells, jr, and Hayden Wells, explored the region of Beargrass Creek, present Louisville, Kentucky.

Four years later, the entire family moved there, coming down the Ohio on flatboats with the families of William Pope, William Oldham, and others. William Wells' mother died early, and in 1781, his father Samuel Wells was ambushed by Indians. William Wells was taken into the home of William Pope, who ran a school out of his home. While out hunting or playing with some other boys, he was captured and taken to the Miami Towns, eventually being adopted into the family of an Eel River warrior named Gaviahatte, the Porcupine.

William Wells adopted Indian ways, and was an agile warrior. At Harmar's Defeat, he said he was scalping the dead and wounded until his arms fatigued. Later, he changed sides and became captain of a band of scouts in the interest of the United States.

Wells commanded sixty scouts, but the core of his detachment included William Polke, Robert McClellan, Nicholas Miller, Christopher Miller, Paschal Hickman, Dodson Thorp, William Ramsey, Tabor Washburn, Joseph Young, William May, David Thomson, William England, Thomas Stratton, Fielding Pilcher, David Reed, Benjamin Davis, George Casterson, Chatin Dogged, James Elliot, and Charles Evans. See Hutton, p. 194. Most of these scouts had either previously lived with the Indians or were the sons of Indian traders and familiar enough with their ways that they could pass for red.

Wells also served as an interpreter, guide, and Indian agent. Heckewelder was with him on a hunt when Wells' mortally wounded a large bear. Dying, the bear cried out loudly, making what the Rev. Heckewelder thought were pitiful sounds. Wells went up to the bear "and with seemingly great earnestness, addressed him in the Wabash language, now and then giving him a slight stroke on the nose with his ram-rod. I him, when he had done, what had he been saying to the bear? `I have,' said he, `up-braided him for acting the part of a coward; I told him that he knew the fortune of war, that one or the other of us must have fallen; that it was his fate to be conquered; and that he ought to die like a man, like a hero...that if the case had been reversed, and I had fallen into the power of my enemy, I would not have disgraced my nation as he did, but would have died with firmness and courage, as becomes a true warrior." See Heckewelder, p. 256.

As became a true warrior, William Wells was killed by Peesotum in a blazing shootout between his own scouts and a band of Winnemac's Potawatomis.

A tract of 640 acres was reserved for William Wells' half-breed daughter, Rebecca Hackley, on the present site of Muncie, Indiana. T. S. Smith noted that the half-breed children of William Wells "were at a mature age taken to Kentucky and educated. The females possessed fine accomplishments; they married to gentlemen of respectability..." T. S. Smith, p. 9.

William Wells first wife was Anahquah, a sister of Little Turtle, the great Miami chief. Their children included Ann (Ahpezzahquah), who married Dr. William Turner; Rebecca (Pemesahquah), who married Captain James Hackley; Mary (Ahmahquauzahquah), who married Judge James Wolcott; William Wayne Wells; and Samuel G. Wells.

The children of Judge James Wolcott and Mary Wells Wolcott included Mary Ann Wolcott who married Smith Gilbert, Henry C. Wolcott, Frederick A. Wolcott, and James M. Wolcott. The children of Smith and Mary Gilbert included Frederick, E., Albert W., and Smith W. Gilbert.

After the death of his first wife, William Wells married Little Turtle's daughter, Sweet Breeze (Wahmangopath). Their children included Juliana (who is supposed to have died in infancy) and Jane Turner Wells who married John H. Griggs.

The third wife of William Wells was a daughter of Colonel Frederick Geiger. Among their children was Yelberton Wells, a West Point cadet.

Ann Wells Turner, daughter of William Wells and the widow of the former Indian agent Dr. William Turner, was educated at the Catholic seminary (Nazareth) in Bardstown, Kentucky. See Indiana Historical Collections: Fort Wayne, p. 31; Tipton Papers, 1824, p. 398.

Among the Shawnees who settled on the lands of the Cherokee nation by 1869 were Julia, Ellen, and John R. Wells. See JAIFR, vol.. IV, #2, pp. 100-111.

Among the Delawares, Shawnees, Cherokees, and adopted whites and blacks living in the Cooweescoowee District of the Cherokee Nation as they appeared on the 1880 census were Randolph (age 35), July (27), Wash (19), Jonah (7), and Fred Wells (2), all listed as Shawnees. See JAIFR, vol.. X, #3, p. 31.

Among the guardianship cases reviewed by Ely S. Parker, the Commissioner of Indian Affairs, in 1871 was the case of G. W. M. Welles, a Shawnee who had been guardian for his brother and sister. It was said that he robbed the safe of the Shawnees and left the country and his whereabouts at the time of the hearings was unknown. Jonathan Gore, lawyer for the Shawnee Nation, was assigned to track him down. See JAIFR, vol. VIII, #2, p. 28.

WEST – a Shawnee name.

In 1779, Major Arnet De Peyster wrote Alexander McKee to use his influence with the Munsey Delawares to bring in "a woman named Peggy West," taken a year before twelve miles east of Ft. Pitt "near the Widow Miers." The Delawares also captured two of her daughters at the same time. The three women were divided up between different bands. One daughter was taken to Detroit and was then living with De Peyster's wife. The other daughter, Nancy West, was living with a Delaware whose name, her sister thought, was Noughboughballen. See MHC, vol. 10, p. 371.

The Shawnee Mission Steward's book records the marriage of Sarah J. West to Winchester Massy in 1856.

Among the Shawnees who settled on the lands

of the Cherokee nation by 1869 were James, Hester, Margaret, John, and Anna West. See JAIFR, vol.. IV, #2, pp. 100-111.

WETZEL, WHEETZELL, WEITZEL, etc. – a Shawnee name.

Capt. John Wetzel was born in Switzerland. He migrated to American, settling in Rockingham County where were born his well-known sons, Martin, Lewis, Jacob, George, and John. About 1769, he moved to Wheeling Creek. He was a ranger and a scout, and often he commanded a company during Dunmore's War and later during the Revolution. He was later killed by Indians while trapping near the mouth of Captina Creek. See Thwaites, *Frontier Defense*, p. 296; Draper 2E8-10, 24S46; 8NN25.

In 1777, his sons Lewis and Jacob were captured but escaped before reaching the Indian towns. In April, 1778, his son Martin was captured and adopted by Shawnees. Martin Wetzel was adopted by Cornstalk's widow and was with them two years and four months. See Draper 1S269.

WHEELER – a Shawnee name.

Samuel Wheeler, a white man who served in the Civil War, married Mary Ann Fish, a part-Shawnee, of Chief Fish's family.

The children of Samuel and Mary Ann Wheeler included Tolbert Wheeler who married Mary Jane Mills, the daughter of Abraham and Eliza (Dodge) Mills; Julia Ann Wheeler who married James Madison Fletcher Gamble, of Indiana, son of William and Elizabeth (Plunket) Gamble, also of Indiana.

The children of James and Julia Ann (Wheeler) Gamble included Verdie Gamble (b. 1883), Burnie Gamble (b. 1885); Dudley Gamble (b. 1888), and Maudie Gamble (b. 1890).

One of Tolbert Wheelers's daughters was Jennie Olga Wheeler who married Oscar Morgan on November 18, 1921. A son of the Tolbert and Mary Jane Wheeler was named Aldon Everett Wheeler, born in 1902. See SOCC, vol. I, p. 663.

Martha A. Wheeler married William Suggett at the Shawnee Mission in 1857.

Among the Shawnees who settled on the lands of the Cherokee nation by 1869 were Betsy, Joseph, Henry, Mary, Samuel, Polly, Mary Ann, Julia, Sarah, Louisa, Mary Jane, and Talbert Wheeler. See JAIFR, vol.. IV, #2, pp. 100-111.

Among the Delawares, Shawnees, Cherokees, and adopted whites and blacks living in the Cooweescoowee District of the Cherokee Nation as they appeared on the 1880 census were Jack (age 40), Mary (30), Robert (14), Anna (13), John (6), Cataline Wheeler (3), all listed as Delawares. Apparently living with them was Jacob Wheeler (19) and his Cherokee wife Amanda (16). See JAIFR, vol.. X, #3, p. 31.

WHITAKER – a Wyandot name.

James Whitaker was captured by Wyandots when a young man (1774), taken back to their village in what is now northern Ohio, made to run the gauntlet, and adopted into the tribe.

Whitaker married Elizabeth Foulks (Folke, Foulke, etc.), another adopted Wyandot, and later became an Indian trader, running a store at Upper Sandusky. Their children included Nancy who married William Wilson, Issac who moved to Indiana, James who moved to Michigan, Mary who married George Shannon, another Mary who married James A. Scranton, Elizabeth, Charlotte, and George.

Homer Everett, author of the History of Sandusky County, Ohio, interviewed Mrs. Rachel Scranton, one of James Whitaker's daughters. Draper interviewed

Maj. James Whitaker of Shelbyville, Kentucky, who was this man's cousin.

WHITE, CROW, KNISELY, NICELY – a Delaware/ Wyandot name.

Crow was a German boy and was stolen by Wyandots in Pennsylvania when quite young. He squalled like a crow as he was being carried away, it was said, hence the name. His genetic father, Jacob Knisely, found him years later, but Crow was then so attached to his Wyandot relatives that he would not return to live among the whites. See Lang, pp. 126, 216.

Crow's first wife was a Wyandot and after she died he married a half-breed daughter of William Spicer, another white who had been adopted by the Wyandots. Jacob Knisely Whitecrow, a son of Crow by his second wife, visited the old reservation in Seneca County in 1852 after leaving two of his sons in school in Dayton, Ohio. Lang says that Crow died of cholera, and that his son, Jacob Whitecrow, became rich and "adopted the name of his grandfather Knisely," or at least the first name.

Among those Shawnees, Senecas, and Wyandots allotted money for improvements made on their Ohio property was a Jacob Nicely, allotted $950. Among the attending the Ft. Leavenworth Shawnee Indian School in 1851 was Jacob Whitecrow, a Wyandot. Jacob Whitecrow served as interpreter in 1869. Among the guardianship cases reviewed by the Commissioner of Indian Affairs in 1871 was the case of Jacob Whitecrow who had been the guardian for John Bigarms. Bigarms was a half-brother to Jacob Whitecrow's wife and also to Eliza Stone (Lucinda Standingstone). People said that John Bigarms went to California in 1849 and had not been heard of in nineteen years. See JAIFR, vol. VIII, #2, p. 18-19.

On the 1881 Wyandot and Seneca rolls, the family

of Jacob Whitecrow, age 43, included his wife Melinda, 36, sons Alfred, 15, and Jacob, 2, and daughters Susan, 5, and Lona, 1.

Joseph Whitecrow died by December, 14, 1894, when his heirs were named in the Wyandot Nation. Besides his wife, Polly, mentioned as heirs were his daughter Mary Jane Vandal "who now resides in Greenwood," deceased son Robert Whitecrow, and Charles Whitecrow "of Mix County, South Dakota." Joseph Bomberry and James C. Jones were administrators of the estate.

WHITEDAY – a Shawnee name.

This Shawnee name was, like the name Tecumseh, a recurring name among the Shawnee and probably represents some concept, the exact meaning of which has been lost over time. It may have been simply, "the day the valley was covered with snow and the whole world seemed white," or it may have been the name of some hero in a Shawnee legend, lost back there in the long night of history unwept.

The first Shawnee chief named Whiteday of whom we have record resided on what became Whiteday Creek in Maryland. His Shawnee name was Oppekhorsa (Oppekiska, Oppewiska, etc.). Many runaway servants found refuge with him on White Day Creek and were adopted by his band of Shawnees. See Glenn Lough's *Awhile Ago Times*, vol.. 3, #8.

A warrior named White Day was among the Shawnees paid for property that they were forced to leave behind in Ohio in 1833. He was paid $55. See Watson, vol.. V., pt. 3, p. 16.

Among the Shawnees allotted individual tracts of land in 1855 was Henry Whiteday (Wa-pa-cuna).

Among the Shawnees who moved into the Cherokee Reserve and are listed as living there in 1869, were William Whiteday, Lot Coffman Whiteday, Henry

Whiteday, George Whiteday, and others of the family. See JAIFR, vol.. IV, number 2, p. 109-110.

WHITE EYES – a Delaware name.

According to Weslager, the original White Eyes had "eyes a lighter color than the eyes of most Indians," and was "a resolute yet thoughtful man who acted with sound judgment."

He was a warrior during Pontiac's War, became a councilor and a village chief, and then chief of the entire Turtle division, with Capt. Pipe as chief of the Wolf division, and John Killbuck, jr. as head of the Turkey division and hence, chief of the Delawares. Leading chief or not, it was White Eyes who kept the Delawares out of Dunmore's War, which must have been difficult, as that unjust war against the Shawnees was an example of how the land grabbers were to promote war all across the continent.

In 1778, White Eyes, Captain Pipe, and John Killbuck, jr. attended a council with General Lachlan McIntosh of the American Army. White Eyes, commissioned a lieutenant-colonel, was engaged to guide the army through the Ohio territory to Detroit, which was then held by the British. White Eyes came to the council with the proposition that the Delaware Nation would become the fourteenth state in the American Union. The language of the ensuing agreement alludes to such a state, but it contained the disclaimer that nothing was conclusive nor binding without the approval of Congress. It is the closest an Indian tribe ever came to setting up an equal state of the United States. The idea might have taken a better hold had White Eyes lived. Lewis Wetzel and another man murdered him on the expedition. His death was covered up, and officially he was supposed to have died of smallpox.

Captain White Eyes was killed by a white man in Columbia, Ohio..there was Joe White Eyes and George

White Eyes. See Draper Mss. 11YY39.

In May, 1795, George White Eyes, "uncle to the one educated at Princeton," was at Ft. Defiance in 1795. See Knoft.

"White Eyes, Delaware chief, was one of the great Indian statesmen. He envisioned the time when his tribe should become civilized, live in peaceable trade relations with their white neighbors, and pursue agriculture. He went to Philadelphia to confer with Governor Hamilton in 1762. The treaty at Ft. Pitt, 1778, was largely his work. While attempting to carry out the provisions of the treaty, White Eyes died..." Thwaites and Kellogg, Frontier Advance..., 20-21; Hanna, II, 241; Williams, note 88, p. 155.

WHITEFEATHER – a Shawnee/Delaware name.

Among the Shawnees and Delawares who signed the ratification of the treaty in 1819 was White Feather (Nawabasheka or Wabasheka).

Among the Shawnees allotted individual tracts of land in 1855 were Susan, Nancy, and Jacob Whitefeather. Jacob was listed as the head of a family.

Among the Shawnees who settled on the lands of the Cherokee nation by 1869 were Ira and Sally Whitefeather. See JAIFR, vol.. IV, #2, pp. 100-111.

Among the Delawares, Shawnees, Cherokees, and adopted whites and blacks living in the Cooweescoowee District of the Cherokee Nation as they appeared on the 1880 census were Sallie A. White Feather (age 26) and her daughter Jane (3), both listed as Shawnees; and Old Widow White Feather (age 50) with Frank (25), Charlie (15), Nancy (7), and Al-me-now White Feather (5), listed as Delawares. Also appearing to live with the last named White Feather family was We-che-la-quah, a Delaware. See JAIFR, vol.. X, #3, p. 31.

WHITE MINGO – a Mingo name.

The original White Mingo was John Cook, a leader of mixed Iroquois and Delaware during Pontiac's War. He was reported to have been in company with Indian Corneilius, John Campbell, Jones and others when he was killed by Frederick Stump and John Ironcutter in 1768.

Either the report was wrong or another took his name. Two white men in hunting shirts tried to kill him near Ft. Pitt in 1775. After checking to make sure his family was safe, he went to George Croghan's and issued the complaint. The colonial Indian Agents investigated the matter, taking along Simon Girty and John Montour, both of whom were to go over to the British during the Revolution. The White Mingo was on the list of possible Tory agents in 1777. See Seineke, p. 197. For his speeches, see Thwaites and Kellogg, *Rev. on the Upper Ohio*, pp. 27-28, 40, 77. Schaaf's recent and excellent book on the colonial Indian Agent George Morgan shows that the White Mingo was active in red/white political affairs throughout most of the 1770s.

WHITE TURKEY – a Delaware name.

In the spring of 1811, a Delaware named White Turkey stole some property from a white settler living near Madison, Indiana. The Delawares recovered the stolen property for the settler, but they refused to turn over White Turkey, saying that whites who murdered Indians were never brought to justice. However, they promised to punish him in their own way, and it was said that he was put to death. See Thompson, p. 211.

I doubt that the Delawares would do this, and it appears that they did not, as White Turkey signed the ratification of the treaty in 1819 as one of the Delaware Nation.

Among the Delawares living in the Cooweescoowee District of the Cherokee Nation as they appeared on the 1880 census were the Widow Mrs. White Turkey (age 46), Dutch (22), Sam (20), Liender (21), Robert (19), Katie (18), Albert (12), Willis (10) and Lelie White Turkey (8), all listed as Delawares. See JAIFR, vol. X, #3, p. 31.

These people are all identified in a remarkable book entitled *White Turkey: A Delaware and His Descendants*by Verna Lerdall and Lucille Whiteturkey. It is one of the best family histories to be found, and it should serve as an example of the kind of thing that can be done on any family, given hard work and dedication.

Simon Whiteturkey (Opao Cheekaunum) was one of the roving hunters of the Smokey Hill River region. In the 1850s he was one of the leading councilors of his tribe.

In 1863, Simon Whiteturkey led his band of hunters in an encounter with the Cheyennes (Old Gray Beard's warriors). The detailed account of this confrontation is included in the book, as well as many other interesting stories. Whiteturkey, who "spoke pretty good English and always sported an eagle feather dangling from his hat," later faced down William Quantrill, the renegade who shot up Kansas before going to Kentucky where he would be captured.

Simon White Turkey married a daughter of Anderson Sarcoxie. The children of Simon White Turkey included To-an-tox-qua Whiteturkey, Dutch Whiteturkey (m. 1st Nellie Falleaf, 2nd Lizzie Thompson), Robert Whiteturkey (m. Josephine Sykes), Katie Whiteturkey (m. James Day), Albert Whiteturkey (m. 1st Elizabeth Mefford, 2nd Julia Johnson), George Willis Whiteturkey (m. Katherine Wheeler), and Lillie Whiteturkey (m. James Fugate).

The children of Dutch and Nellie (Falleaf) Whiteturkey included Dennis (m. 1st Pearl Alma Thaxton, 2nd Bessie Morley), Charles, and Artie (m. Frank Coleman). The children of Robert and Josephine

(Sykes) Whiteturkey included Frank, Rosa E. (m. Clinton E. Sadler), Nona (m. Porter Miller). The children of James and Katie (Whiteturkey) Day included Clarence, Erick, Harrison, Ida, Willie, Dolly, Nora, Lloyd Day. For the additional genealogy of this family, see the Whiteturkey book.

WILLIAMS – a Wyandot/Shawnee name.

Issac Williams was one of several brothers who distinguished themselves on the frontier. He was a trader at the Indian towns in 1775, and is mentioned in Richard Butler's journal.

In 1790, Issac Williams traded at Sandusky where a traveler spoke of him as "a stout, boney, muscular, and fearless man. One one of those days which I spend waiting until we were ready to embark for Detroit, a Wyandot Indian, in his own language which I did not understand, uttered some expression offensive to Williams. This produced great irritation on both sides, and a bitter quarrel ensued. Williams took down, from the shelf of the store in which the incident occurred, two scalping knives. Laid them on the counter. Gave the Wyandot the choice of them. And challenged him to combat with these weapons. But the character of Williams for strength and courage was so well known to his adversary that he would not venture on the contest, and soon afterwards retired." See Van Der Beets, pp. 294-295.

Issac Williams was an interpreter during the war and land was allotted to the half-breed Issac Williams for his services in the War of 1812 and was given to his children by the treaty of 1817. His children and grandchildren intermarried with the mixed-blood members of other tribes, especially the Shawnees, Senecas, and Delawares.

Among the Wyandots allotted land in Kansas in 1855 were Issac and Susan Williams, both listed as ninety years old. A plat of land was given to Charlotte Williams, 70, and another to David Williams, 30. Plat #179 was allotted to Joseph Williams, 38, his wife, Mary, 40, and daughter Margaret, 6. Plat #175 went to John Williams, 38, with Margaret, 36, Sarah, 15, and Mary Jane, 5.

Among the guardianship cases reviewed by the Commissioner of Indian Affairs in 1871 was the case of Issac Williams, a Wyandot, guardian for Thomas H. Williams, Thomas Hill, or Nicholas Williams. Nicholas Williams's mother was a Wyandot who married a Delaware. The boy was denied some of the money that would otherwise have been due him if she had married within the Wyandot Nation, but he continued to be raised by Issac Williams. See JAIFR, vol.. VIII, #2, p. 21.

Among the Hog Creek branch of Shawnees was George Williams (Pamothaway), said to be a "solid, upright, honest man." See Harvey, p. 245, 252.

A Williams was among Capt. Fall Leaf's small band of Delaware scouts in 1860, and Sam Williams was listed among Capt. Fall Leaf's select band of Delaware and Shawnee scouts in 1874.

"When Lewis Henry Morgan visited the Delaware reservation in 1859, he conversed with Charles Journeycake's elderly mother, who was born Sally Williams, and who died in Oklahoma on February 6, 1873, at the approximate age of seventy-six." Weslager, p. 391.

Among the Delaware students at Baptist Mission School in Kansas in 1867 was Julia A. Williams, age 7.

Among the Delawares living on the Anadarko Reservation in 1876 was the family of Jack Williams. Weslager, p. 519.

Among the Shawnees who settled on the lands of the Cherokee nation by 1869 were Richard, Margaret, Charles, Eliza, Alonzo, Millissa, Prisella, Mary, Fanny, George, and Samuel Williams. See JAIFR, vol.. IV, #2, pp. 100-111.

Mary Williams is among the Shawnees quoted by James H. Howard in his book on Shawnee customs and ceremonies. See Howard, pp. 174, 186-188, 218.

WILSON – a Shawnee/Delaware name.

James Wilson was a Pennsylvania Indian trader.

William Wilson, whose mother was a Shawnee, assisted John Gibson during Dunmore's War, trying to keep the peace. He was an interpreter, Indian trader, and an express rider with Joseph Nicholson. In 1776, he was George Morgan's ambassador at a council with Cornstalk, White Eyes, John Montour and the Wyandot Half King. See Schaaf, pp. 34, 36-45, 87, 113-114, 127, 184. Schaaf says that William Wilson was a Shawnee half-breed, and that this was the same William Wilson who protested against the treatment of the Indians, and there are other accounts (Thwaites and Kellogg, Rev. on the Upper Ohio, p. 202) that identify Wilson as the man who testified against Samuel Brady for the wanton slaughter of peaceful Indians. Wilson was called a traitor who had furnished aid and comfort to the Indians during a time of war. Nothing happened to Brady, of course. Thwaites says that Wilson went to Cincinnati, then to Greeneville where he died in 1796.

"A John Wilson who left Indiana Co. was married to a squaw." See Draper 6NN202.

Robert Wilson also lived among the Ohio Delawares and Shawnees.

On May 4, 1795, Andrews noted in his journal at Ft. Defiance, "Mr. Robert Wilson came in this day; he mentions that the British at Fort Miamis attempted to stop his goods, but being well protected by Buckingehalas and a large party of Delawares...he passed with little difficulty. Mr. Wilson was taken prisoner in 1782 and has been with the Indians ever since. He appears to be a decent, well behaved man..."

See Knoft.

"Capt. Wilson belonged to Killbuck's outfit. Small in size but a fine warrior. Killed by whites by mistake." Draper 3S63, 3S129.

Billy Wilson, a Delaware, was killed in 1842 by refugee Cherokees. See Hoig, p 50-51.

In 1860, John, Ice, and Buffalo Wilson were among the traditionalists of the tribe. See Weslager, pp. 408, 443-444.

A Wilson was one of the six Delaware scouts under Capt. Fall Leaf on the Kiowa and Commanche Campaign of 1860. See KHQ, vol.. 23, p. 395.

Among the Delawares in Capt. Fall Leaf's band of scouts in 1874 were Ice and George Wilson. See Chalfant, p. 247.

Carney (alias Henry Wilson), To-hun-doox-wha (alias Young Wilson), Wa-le-que-na-xing (alias Robert Wilson), Wa-la-le-mah (alias Eliza Wilson), E-yar-tup (alias Tain Wilson), John, James, James M. C., Joshua, Edward, Clara, and George Wilson appear on the Delaware rolls appearing in the JAIFR, vol.. IV, #1, 1985, pp. 31-52.

Weslager says that in 1944, one of the older people struggling to maintain Delaware traditions was Reuben Wilson (Week-peh-kee-xeeug, or he who is like receding water). Weslager, p. 14.

WOLF – a Shawnee/Delaware name.

Among the children of the Shawnee chief, Cornstalk, were sons Cornstalk jr., Peter Cornstalk, Black Wolf, and John Wolf. John Wolf was the father of Henry Clay. Several members of the family had white connections.

Black Wolf (Bieseka) was the leader of many raids during times of war, and he was greatly feared in Pennsylvania, Virginia, and Kentucky. Returned captives spoke well of him. James Moore, captured by

Shawnees, screamed with all his might until Black Wolf "laid his hand on the top of my head and bade me hush. There were only three Indians in the company. Their leader, Black Wolf, a middle-aged man, of the most stern countenance I ever beheld, about six feet high, having a long black beard, was the one who caught hold of me."

I am have not yet seen a description of the Shawnee subchief, Black Beard, but perhaps he also had a beard. Or were Black Beard and Black Wolf the same man? Black Beard was a name associated with the Shawnees who dealt with the Ohio Company traders as early as 1756, and he may have been the man one trader referred to as "the Pirate." A Black Beard was listed as one of the subchiefs at the siege of Boonesboro along with Captain Will, Blackfish, and Blackhoof. Where was Black Beard when Boonesboro was being attacked? A speech of "Blackbeard" is in Michigan Pioneer and Historical Collections, and in Draper 11CC34, it says, "Blackbeard was near the mounds when he camped on Mayslick near Copper Creek. He was known as the oldest Indian anywhere." Additional research will probably reveal the answers. If someone who reads this already knows the answers, please send them to me.

Anyway, this Black Wolf who captured James Moore made a name for himself as his description was passed about, and his war party was spotted in several raids on the frontiers of Pennsylvania, Virginia, and Kentucky. He was seen with the warriors who killed Col. William Christian and it was Black Wolf who captured young John Crawford. Crawford was with Linn's party, making tomahawk claims some forty miles into Ohio Territory on Hocking Creek. Besides Crawford, this party included the brothers, Peter and William Johnson, and Andrew and William Linn. Interviews with the John Crawford and members of the

Linn family are preserved in Draper's manuscripts.

According to Crawford's own account, "This Black Wolf had a select party of warriors, some Shawnees, some Cherokees. The different nations were intermixed and...they selected them from the whole..." A white man who was with Black Wolf's band nicked Peter Johnson as he ran, and Black Wolf shot William Linn in the left arm, but all escaped except John Crawford.

Black Wolf took him to the Indian towns, Crawford said, "where Simon Girty came and talked with me. Said he didn't think the Indians would kill me. I was but a boy. He inquired of me if I was any relation to Col. Crawford. When the council assembled, they set me right in the midst of them. The council sat for two hours in perfect silence. At length, Blue Jacket rose and made a speech. Girty interpreted and Wilson the trader wrote it down. Blue Jacket said they were going to make the Ohio the line; and after this, to burn every prisoner they caught on this side of the river. That they had been driven farther and farther back. They would all die before they would give another inch of their land." See Draper 12CC156-163, 37J32-38.

Like Little Turtle, Blue Jacket, and many others, Black Wolf staunchly opposed the United States until after the Treaty of Greenville, whereupon he became active in working toward peace, although not agreeing with the policies in force.

Black Wolf married "the half-breed daughter of Jackson." His wife perished in an accident when her clothes accidentally caught on fire. Draper's notes say that Black Wolf himself died a few years before the Shawnees moved west in 1832. But if that is true, then the name Black Wolf was risen up. See Indian agent John Johnston's letter to Draper in 11YY37c.

Johnston wrote that Black Wolf was a peace chief and had saved his life more than once, one time by riding 30 miles through the night to warn him of a war party that was coming to murder him. John Wolf was also devoted to Johnston, and I suspect that it was John Wolf that he meant.

Draper 11YY25 contains two letters, one by John Wolf to John Johnston, and the other Johnston to Draper. The letters tell a story, and the gist of the story is this:

John Wolf (Lawathtucker) signed the 1831 Shawnee Treaty. Black Wolf was given only $6 for his Ohio property, which probably means he claimed no land but was residing with relatives. John Wolf was given $297 for his property in Ohio, and Nancy Wolf was given $121 for hers. See Watson, pt. #, pp. 14-16.

John Wolf, a reservation Shawnee, worked for the Indian Agency in Ohio, and Johnston found him to be a good, reliable worker. Unfortunately, some of the other Shawnees were always chiding Wolf for being Johnston's slave, and one day this made Wolf angry enough that he decided to quit and head west.

He approached Johnston to tell him this, but he was so uptight with emotion that he could hardly speak. Johnston calmed him down, got the words out of him, and was supportive and understanding. Johnston got a map and laid it out upon the grass. He then explained to Wolf the boundaries of the reservation and the direction he must travel to go where he wanted to go.

Some fourteen years later, Johnston was back at his farm in Piqua, Ohio where he received a letter from John Wolf, then at the Kansas reservation. The letter said, "I am yet alive, but I am getting old," and spoke of Johnston's kindness to him. John Wolf then goes on to say, "Now I have some sorrowful news," and he tells Johnston of the death of John Perry the previous fall, and of the death of Henry Clay two weeks ago, and of the death of councilor Blackbody just four days after that.

I found these letters rather touching. The deaths around him may have made John Wolf a bit conscious of his own mortality and made him want to thank Johnston for his kindness before it was too late. John Wolf opens his letter saying "I am old, but still alive..." See Draper 11YY25-38.

Among the Shawnees who settled on the lands of the Cherokee nation by 1869 was the family of Billy Wolf. See JAIFR, vol.. IV, #2, pp. 100-111.

WRIGHT – a common name among most tribes.

Jemmy Wright was among the Indians at Conestoga in January, 1755. See PA, p. 242.

A William Write and a John McCotter were supposed to have been captured and killed by Wapthamy while trading at the Lower Shawnee Town during Pontiac's War. But many of those reported killed later turned up among the Indians. The John Cotter delivered up to Bouquet in 1764 may have been John McCotter, and it is possible Write survived also as both Cotter and Wright became surnames long associated with the Wyandots. See Hanna, II, p. 380.

Elizabth Wright is listed in the accounts of the Ft. Wayne Agency in 1813 along with Francois Duchoquet and John Shaw. See Thornbrough, p. 183. Among the Wyandots on the treaty of 1817 was Tawaumanoeay or E. Wright.

George Wright and his son, David Wright, were connected with the Wyandots attached to the Ft. Wayne Agency in Indiana and to the Piqua Agency in Ohio. Both George and David Wright were among the Wyandots allotted land in 1855 in Kansas. See KHC, vol. 15, p. 161, 169. George Wright died and his estate went to his last wife, Martha, a white woman.

On the 1880 Wyandot roll appears James Wright, 48, living with Martha Wright (an adopted Wyandot and probably James Wright's step-mother), 77, Molly

(James Wright's wife, a white woman), and children named William, 24, George and Martha Jane, 21, Grant, 19, Charles, 17, Henry, 13, and Hattie Wright, 6. See the Quapaw Agency Records.

Among the Delawares, Shawnees, Cherokees, and adopted whites and blacks living in the Cooweescoowee District of the Cherokee Nation as they appeared on the 1880 census were Nancy Wright, a Shawnee, age 35, and her infant twin daughters Sarah M. and G. B. Wright. The Widow Wright, age 30, was living with Wiskepake, age 19, both Delawares. See JAIFR, vol. X, #3, p. 36.

YOKEHAM – a Delaware/Stockbridge name.

George Yokeham was captured by Indians in 1764. Among the whites delivered up to Bouquet in 1764 was Margaret Yokeham. Among the Stockbridge (Mohican) and Munsee Delawares in 1856 were Clarissa and Juliett Yoccum, single women, and John Yoccum, who was the head of a family. See JAIFR, vol.. XI, #2, pp. 19, 23, 24.

YOUNG – a common name among most tribes.

The Delawares captured and adopted Stephen Young when young and he became a chief warrior among them. He came to Gen. Anthony Wayne seeking terms of peace in 1794.

Stephen Young came personally to Ft. Defiance to deliver up prisoners, but he went back to live among his adopted people, at least for a time. See Knoft, p. 67.

John Young was allotted a sum of money for providing provisions for the Indians attending treaties in 1832, and among the signers of the 1831 Treaty with the Seneca was "Totala Chief or John Young." Listed as signing the 1832 Treaty with the Seneca and Shawnee were John Young (To-ta-la) and William Young. See Watson, vol. V., pt. 2, pp. 9, 67; pt. 3, p. 43.

According to the Wyandot Treaty of 1832, individuals were to be paid for the improvements they had made on their Ohio property that they were forced to leave behind. David Young was given $203 for his property in Ohio, and Jacob Young was given $251 for his. See Watson, vol.. V., pt. 3, p. 19.

Among the Wyandots from Sandusky, Ohio, appearing on the 1843 Wyandot Muster Roll were:

1. David Young's family, consisting of one male and one female between the ages of 25 and 55,

one female between the ages of 10 and 25, and two boys under 10.

2. Jacob Young's household, which included two women between 25 and 55, two women between 10 and 25, and a boy under 10.

Among the Wyandots allotted land in 1855 were Margaret Young, 34, and her children Elizabeth, 12, and Martha B., 6. Catherine Young, 21, was given her own section. Jacob Young, 45, is listed with his family which included Eliza, 16, Hiram S., 8, Peter, 6, and Adam, 4.

Among the Delawares, Shawnees, Cherokees, and adopted whites and blacks living in the Cooweescoowee District of the Cherokee Nation as they appeared on the 1880 census were Old Mrs. Young, 71, with John Young, sr., 36, Eley T. Young, 19, and apparently her son Edmund Young, 1. See JAIFR, vol.. X, #3, p. 37.

ZANE – a Wyandot/Delaware name.

This was the famous family of Zanesfield and Zanesville, Ohio, and of Zane Grey, the famous author of western fiction. The Indian blood in the family goes back to the 1600's and William Zane. However, most people with the tradition in Ohio, Indiana, and Kentucky also descend from the part-Wyandot wife of Issac Zane.

Issac Zane was born in 1753. At the age of nine, he was captured and adopted by Wyandots. He lived with them for seventeen years, and later became a guide, trader, and interpreter. For his services, he was given 1800 acres of land on Mad River in what is now Logan County, Ohio. He married Myeera (a walk in the water), a half-breed daughter of Chief Tarhe, the Wyandot Half King. One of Zane's daughters married John McCullooch, and other children and grandchildren married into the Robitaille, Armstrong, McColloch, Reed, Rankin, Dawson, Gardner, Charlow, and other Wyandot families. Issac had a son named Ebenezer as well as an older brother of the same name who came to Ohio. A large number of the Wyandots listed on the 1843 Wyandot Census returned to Ohio, including a large portion of the Zanes.

Issac Zane, the former captive, and his part-Wyandot wife had three sons and four daughters, including William, Ebenezer (who built the historic McCormick house), Issac, jr., Nancy, Elizabeth, Kitty, and Sally. William Zane went to Upper Sandusky and became a leading councilor for the Wyandots. Ebenezer made a name for himself by building the historic McCormick house in 1804. Issac, jr, was left a fine farm by his father's will, the fine house becoming known as "the Zane Mansion."

Nancy Zane met her future husband, William

McColluch, while on a visit to her grandfather, Tarhe, about 1797. The couple moved to Zanes' Town about 1803, when their first son, Noah Zane McCulloch, was five years old. Kitty Zane married Alexander Long, who together with the Zanes founded the town of Zanesfield in Logan County, Ohio. Sally Zane married Robert Armstrong, who had been captured when young and adopted by the Wyandots. Sally Zane married 1st, Robert Robitaille, sr., and after he died, she married James M. Reed. Sally Zane Robitaille Reed died about 1819 or 1820. See MMV, pp. 180-181.

These people and their children and grandchildren have spread the Indian blood tradition arcoss the county.

Hester (Hetty) Zane, a cousin of John M. Armstrong, married the part-Shawnee, Paschal Fish. She died in 1852. See Barry, p. 1077.

Among the Wyandot families appearing on the 1843 Muster Roll of those from Sandusky, Ohio, were:

1. Issac Zanes Sr.'s family, consisting of seven males, three of them children under 10, and seven females, two of whom were children under 10.
2. Issac Zanes Jr.'s family, consisting of one woman over 55, three males and one female 25 to 55, two females 10 to 25, and one female under 10.
3. John Zane's family, consisting of a male and a female, both between 100 and 25.
4. Noah E. Zane's family, consisting of one male 25 to 55, one female 10 to 25, and one male under 10.

Among the Wyandots and Shawnees allotted individual tracts of land in 1855 were Hannah, 73, and Issac W. Zane, 30. Susanna D. Zane, 37, is listed with children Eldridge B., 10, Mary E., 3, and Sarah R. Zane, 11 months. Isaiah Zane, 23 is with Elizabeth, 18.

Ebenezer O. Zane, 31, is with his family which included, Rebecca, 28, Hannah E., 9, Issac O., 7, Joseph C., 5, Irvin P., 3, and Lawrence G. Zane, 9 months. Plat #194 went to Noah Zane, 37, and his family which included Tabitha, 28, Ethan, 9, Amanda, 5, Alonzo, 3, and an infant. Plat #195 went to Jane S. Zane, and her family which included Alexander H., Julia C., and Elizabeth Rebecca Zane, ages not given. Given individual tracts of land were Hannah Zane, 19, Sarah Zane, 35, and Issac R. Zane, 29.

Also listed in 1855, was the family of John Zane, 43, with Theressa, 33, and children Jefferson, 12, Louisa, 10, and Margaret, 9. See KHC, vol. 15, p. 123.

Among the Delawares, Shawnees, Cherokees, and adopted whites and blacks living in the Cooweescoowee District of the Cherokee Nation as they appeared on the 1880 census were Jeff (age 41), Matilda (26), Lillie (9), and Mary Zanes (6), all Delawares. See JAIFR, vol.. X, #3, p. 37.

Among the Wyandot cases reviewed by the Commissioner of Indian Affairs in 1871 was the case of Ebenezer O. Zane, guardian for William and Eli Leslie Zane, possibly his brothers. Both William and Eli Zane attended school in Ohio for a time. William Zane traveled to Pike's Peak. See JAIFR, vol.. VIII, #2, p. 22.

ZIEGLER – a Shawnee/Delaware name.

The Indian blood stems from an early Pennsylvania/Ohio frontier connection but I do not yet know which marriage originated the tradition.

Among the Delawares, Shawnees, Cherokees, and adopted whites and blacks living in the Cooweescoowee District of the Cherokee Nation as they appeared on the 1880 census were the Delaware Henry Ziegler, age 36, and his twenty-two year old wife who is listed as a Creek.
See JAIFR, vol. X, #3, p. 37.

Among the Delawares on the 1900 Census of Indian Territory was Henry W. Ziegler, born 1859 in Kansas. His father was born in Pennsylvania, his mother in New Jersey. Members of this family were buried in the Delaware or Fall Leaf cemetery near Eudora, including Arthur, Borbac, Charles, Emma, Logan, and Sophia Ziegler. Logan Zeigler was born in 1823 and died in 1895. See Prevost, p. 44.

SOURCES

AKERS, Vincent Akers, The Low Dutch Company: A History of the Holland Dutch Settlements on the Kentucky Frontier, n. d., unpublished manuscript of Vince Akers of Bargerville, Indiana. History of the best sort, gleaned from the raw court depositions and local records and making full use of the Draper Manuscripts, copy in the author's collection.
The American Revolution in Kentucky, 1781: The Long Run Massacre (Boone's Defeat) and Floyd's Defeat, unpublished manuscript, 1982. This is the only well-documented account of the events of 1781 that I have seen, and it is magnificent. Someone needs to get buy rights to Akers' work and publish it.

ANSON, Bert Anson, *The Miami Indians*, Norman, Oklahoma, University of Oklahoma Press, 1970.

BAIRD, W. David Baird, ed., A Creek Warrior for the Confederacy: *The Autobiography of Chief C. W. Grayson.*

BARB - Kirk Bentley Barb, *A History and Genealogy of the Ruddle Family*, copy in the Jeffersonville Indiana Township Public Library.

BARRY, Louise Barry, *The Beginning of the West: Annals of the Kansas Gateway to the American West 1540-1854*, Kansas State Historical Society, Topeka, 1972.

BEATTIE, George William Beattie and Helen Pruitt Beattie, "Pioneer Linns of Kentucky, Part III," Filson Club Quarterly, vol. 46, p. 221.

BECKWITH, Hiram W. Beckwith, Illinois and Indiana Indians, Chicago, Fergus Printing Company, 1884.

BEERS, W. H. Beers, *History of Miami County, Ohio*, Chicago, 1880.

BELUE, Ted Franklin Belue, "Did Daniel Boone Kill Pompey, the Black Shawnee, at the 1778 Siege of Boonesborough?" The Filson Club Quarterly, vol. 67, #1, pp. 5-12.

BRELSFORD, Bridgie Brill Brelsford, *Indians of Montgomery County, Indiana*, published by the Montgomery County Historical Society, 1985, copy in the Jeffersonville Indiana Township Public Library.

BRIEN, Lindsay M. Brien, *Miami Valley Will Abstracts from the Counties of Miami*, Montgomery, Warren, and Preble, Ohio 1803-1850, Dayton, 1940.

BROWN, Parker B. Brown, "The Fate of Crawford Volunteers," *Western Pennsylvania Historical Quarterly*, October, 1982.

BUCHANAN, Robert C. Buchanan, "A Journal of Lt. Robert C. Buchanan During the Seminole War," Frank F. White, jr., editor, *The Florida Historical Quarterly*, vol. 29, 1950.

BURNET, Jacob Burnet, *Notes on the Early Settlement of the Northwest Territory*, Cincinnati, Ohio, 1847.

BUTTERFIELD, Consul W. Butterfield, *History of Seneca County, Ohio*, D. Campbell & Sons, Sandusky, Ohio, 1848.

CALDWELL - Martha Bell Caldwell, *Annals of the Shawnee Methodist Mission*, copy at the Filson Club, Louisville.

CARTER, Harvey L. Carter, "Kit Carson" and "Jim Swanock and the Delaware Hunters," published in vol. VII of *The Mountain Men and the Fur Trade of the Far West*, under the editorial supervision of Leroy R. Hafen, 1969.

CASE #900, Jefferson County, Kentucky, Old Circuit Court Case #900, Joseph Saunders assee, David Owens assee, Joseph Soverigns, assee vs Papers of Conrad Coleman, June 17, 1785. This court case contains promissory notes that were carried from Indian town to Indian town and it identifies some of the people who were there. The first note, dated at Detroit, 26 Nov. 1783, was a drought of

Issac Williams assigning his note against Conrad Coleman to David Owens "of Washington County," but Washington County was crossed out, as David Owens had then moved to the falls.

The next notes, dated at the Shawnee Towns, March 4th, 1784, were from Conrad Coleman to Joseph Soverigns and then from Joseph Soverigns to David Owens. The witnesses of the notes were James Sherlock, Uriah Coulson, John Townsend, William Hickman, jr., and John Parker.

In 1785, David Owens assigned these notes to Martin Carney and John Jackson, two of his neighbors on the Indian side of the river. It is interesting to find Coulson and Townsend at the Shawnee towns at this time. This tends to collaborate a legend told by Glenn Lough and others.

Their are differing versions, but the basic story is that Townsend, a Quaker trader whom the Shawnees called "a wide hat," was always welcome in the Indian towns as long as he dressed as a Quaker, but the reds forbade any whites to come on their land in hunting shirts. Townsend and Coulson were later caught hunting on Indian land, and his sentence was to be burned at the stake. Some Shawnee women were still mourning the loss of their husbands, and the sentence was actually carried out, to make Townsend and Coulson examples. It took Townsend all night to die, and young Tecumseh was among those present who heard him screaming in pain. The story was told that Tecumseh, at this time, argued passionately against the cruelty of this practice, and Coulson was released.

CHALFANT, William Y. Chalfant, *Without Quarter: The Wichita Expedition and the Fight on Crooked Creek,* University of Oklahoma Press.

The list of scouts in Capt. Fall Leaf's band is from the W. C Brown Papers, Western Historical Collection, University of Colorado, Boulder, Colorado, "Baldwin Indian Territory Expedition, From His Own Diaries," and "Gen. Baldwin's Scout in Panhandle of Texas, Sept 6-9, 1874."

CHERRY, P. P. Cherry, *The Western Reserve and Early Ohio*, R. L. Fouse & Co., Akron, Ohio, 1921.

CHRISTOPHER, Adrienne Christopher, "Chief Joseph Parks: Chief of the Shawnees," and "The Shawnee Treaty of 1832," in *The Westport Historical Quarterly*, vol. V, #1, June, 1969.

CRANOR, Ruby Cranor, *Kik Tha We Nund: The Delaware Chief William Anderson and His Descendants*, Norman, Oklahoma, n.d.

DARLINGTON, Gist's Journals.

DAWSON, Charles C. Dawson, A Collection of Family Records & Biographical Sketches of the Dawson Family, Joel Munsell Co, Albany, New York, 1874.

DEAN, Thomas Dean, *Journal of Thomas Dean: A Voyage to Indiana in 1817*, ed. by John Candee Dean, *Indiana Historical Society Publications*, vol. 6, #2, Indianapolis, 1918.

DEMAREST, Mary A. and William H. S. Demarest, The Demarest Family, New Brunswick, New Jersey, 1938.

DERR, Mark Derr, *The Frontiersman: The Real Life and the Many Legends of Davy Crockett*, William Morrow & Co., New York, 1993.

DRAPER, the Draper Manuscripts, property of the State Historical Society of Wisconsin, Madison, Wisconsin. Significant among the interviews were those in the Kentucky Papers, several volumes of the George Rogers Clark Papers, as well as the many interviews in the Tecumseh Papers with Moses Silverheels, Charles Bluejacket and others.

DRIMMER, Frederick Drimmer, *Captured by the Indians: 15 Firsthand Accounts 1750-1870*, Dover Publications, New York, 1961.1

DOTLE, Joseph B. Doyle, *History of Jefferson County and Representative Citizens*, Stenbendle Co., Chicago, 1910.

DUNNINGAN, Alice Allison Dunningan, *The Fascinating Story of Black Kentuckians" Their Heritage and Traditions*, The Associated Publishers, Inc., Washington, D. C., copy at the Kentucky Historical Society, Frankfort, 1982.

ECKERT, Allan W. Eckert, the brilliant author of several historical narratives which many historians despise, without reason. Most historians who write books will only say maybe two or three new things, and if they get two of the three correct, the critics will say, "pretty good; only one mistake." But that's 33%. Allan W. Eckert, on the other hand, says three hundred new things in each book, and when he makes twenty-five mistakes, the critics say, "Look at all those mistakes; how awful!" But in reality, it's less than 10%. And look that all he has gotten right! Who else in America has accomplished what Eckert has? Nobody. I think he deserves the Pulitzer Prize.

Especially recommended here are: *A Sorrow in Our Heart: The Life of Tecumseh*, Bantam Books, New York, 1992; *The Frontiersman*, Boston, 1967; *The Conquerors*, Boston, 1970; *Wilderness Empire*, 1969; *The Wilderness War*, 1978; *Twilight of Empire*, 1988; *Gateway to Empire*, 1983.

EDMUNDS, R. David Edmunds, *The Potawatomis: Keepers of the Fire*, University of Oklahoma Press, Norman, Oklahoma, 1978.

– The Shawnee Prophet, University of Nebraska Press, Lincoln, 1983.

ELLET, Elizabeth Ellet, *Pioneer Women of the West*, Charles Scribner, New York, 1856.

ELLIOTT, Lawrence Elliott, *The Long Hunter: A New Life of Daniel Boone*, Reader's Digest Press, New York, 1976.

ENGLISH, William Hayden English, Conquest of the Country Northwest of the River Ohio 1778-1783 and Life of George Rogers Clark, two volumes, the Brown-Merrill Company, Indianapolis, Indiana, 1896.

FCQ, the *Filson Club Quarterly*, published by the Filson Club, Louisville.

FINNEY, Rev. James B. Finney, *Life Among the Indians*, Cincinnati, Ohio, Curts & Jennings, n. d.

FORKNER, John L. Forkner, *History of Madison County, Indiana*, Lewis Publishing Company, New York and Chicago.

FP, various documents contained in Fort Pitt and Letters from the Frontier, J. R. Weldin & Co., Pittsburgh, 1892.

FUNK, Arville I. Funk's article which appeared in his Hoosier Scrapbook column, October 11, 1976. A copy can be found in the Indiana Collections at the New Albany, Indiana Library.

GALBREATH, C. B. Galbreath's "Tecumseh and His Descendants," in the Ohio Archaeological and Historical Quarterly, Vol. 34.

GALLOWAY, William Albert Galloway, *Old Chillocothe, Xenia, Ohio*, The Buckeye Press, 1934.

GARRARD, Lewis H. Garrard, *Wah-to-yah and the Taos Trail*, ed. by Ralph P. Bieber, Arthur H. Clark Co., Glendale, California, 1938.

GILBERT, Bil Gilbert, *God Gave Us This Country: Tekamthi and the First American Civil War*, Doubleday, New York, 1990.

GILLIS, Norman and Robinson, Synopsis of the Litigation over the Estate of William Gillis, Kansas City, Missouri, 1901.

GOFF, William A. Goff, "What Happened To En-Di-Ond?" *Westport (Mo.) Historical Quarterly*, vol. 10, March, 1975, pp. 108-116.

GREENE, Richard A. Greene, The Indians of Delaware County, prepared by the Staff of the Public Library of Ft. Wayne and Allen County, Indiana, 1954.

GRIDLEY, Marion E. Gridley, *Indians of Today*, Chicago, 1960.

HALEY, James L. Haley, *The Buffalo War*, Doubleday & Co., Garden City, New York, 1976.

HARVEY, Henry Harvey, *History of the Shawnee Indians from 1681 to 1854*, E. Morgan & Sons, Cincinnati, 1855.

HLCO, *History of Logan County, Ohio*, O. L. Baskin & Company, Chicago, 1880.

HOIG, Stan Hoig, Jesse Chisholm: Ambassador of the Plains, University Press of Colorado, Niwot, 1991.

HORN, W. F. Horn, The Horn Papers, in three volumes, published for a committee of the Greene County Historical Society by Herald Press, Scottsdale, Pennsylvania, 1945. Not everything, but many of the things that Horn states as fact are far afield if not completely imaginary. I recommend that you read him with caution. I have only quoted him twice in this volume, and I have flagged both quotes with warning labels.

HOWARD, James H. Howard, *Shawnee! The Ceremonialism of a Native Indian Tribe and Its Cultural Background*, Ohio University Press, Athens, 1981.

HUNTER, William A. Hunter, *Forts on the Pennsylvania Frontier*, p. 402. Hunter cites the Pennsylvania Gazette of July 29, 1756.

HWC, *History of Wyandot County, Ohio*, Leggett, Conway, & Co., Chicago, 1881.

JACKSON, Donald Jackson, ed., Letters of the Lewis and Clark Expedition with Related Documents 1783-1854.

JAIFR, Journal of American Indian Family Research, Histree, Laguna Hills, California.

JAMES, James Alton James, *The Life of George Rogers Clark,* University of Chicago Press, Chicago, Illinois.

JONES, Rev. David Jones, A Journal of Two Visits Made to Some Nations of Indians on the West Side of the River Ohio in the Years 1772 and 1773, Arno Press, Inc., New York, 1971.

JORDAN, Jerry Wright Jordan, Cherokee By Blood, Heritage Books, several volumes.

KENT and DEARDORFF, the excellent article "John Adlum on the Allegheny," by Donald H. Kent and Merle H. Deardorff in the Pennsylvania Magazine of History and Biography, 1960.

KENTON, Edna Kenton, Simon Kenton: His Life and Period 1755-1836, Ayer Company Publishers, Inc., Salem, New Hampshire, n. d.

KHC, Kansas Historical Collections.

KHQ, Kansas Historical Quarterly.

KNAPP, H. S. Knapp, History of the Maumee Valley, Blade Mammoth Co., Toledo, 1872.

KNOFT, Richard C. Knoft, ed., "The Andrews Journal," in vol. 66 of the Ohio Historical Quarterly.

KYHC, Register of the Kentucky Historical Society, Frankfort, Kentucky.

LAFFERTY, Maude Ward Lafferty, The Destruction of Ruddle's and Martin's Forts in the Revolutionary War, Kentucky Historical Society, Frankfort, 1957.

LAMB and SHULTZ, E. Wendell Lamb and Lawrence W. Shultz, Indian Lore, Light and Life Press, Winona Lake, Indiana, 1964.

LANG, W. Lang, ed., The History of Seneca County, Ohio, 1880.

LECKEY, Howard L. Leckey, The Tenmile Country and Its Pioneer Families, Greene County, Pennsylvania Historical Society, Waynesburg, Pennsylvania.

LEMAY, J. A. Lemay, "The Tall Tales of a Colonial Frontiersman," in Western Pennsylvania Historical Quarterly, January, 1981.

LERDALL & WHITETURKEY, Verna Lerdall and Lucille Whiteturkey, Whiteturkey: A Delaware and His Descendants, Oklahoma City, Oklahoma, 1978.

LEWIS, Clifford M. Lewis, S.J., "A Frontier Store in Western Virginia," in West Virginia Historical Quarterly, vol. 32, pp. 238-241.

LOBDELL, Jared C. Lobdell, ed., Recollections of Lewis Bonnett, jr. and the Bonnett and Wetzel Familes, Heritage Books, Bowie, Maryland, 1991.
– Indian Warfare in Western Pennsylvania and North West Virginia at the Time of the American Revolution, Heritage Books, Bowie, Maryland, 1992.

LOCKWOOD, James Lockwood, "Early Times and Events in Wisconsin, 1816," Wisconsin Historical Society Collections, vol. 2.

LONG, Fern Long, "Revised Indian History/Re: Paschal Fish Sr," article from the Eudora Enterprise, June 22, 1978, continued July 6, 1978, Kansas.

LOUGH, Glen Lough, Now and Long Ago: A History of the Marion County Area, Marion County, West Virginia, Historical Society, 1969. Also, the Awhile Ago Times, a periodical published by Glenn Lough.

MAHON, John K. Mahon, "Missouri Volunteers at the Battle of Okeechobee: Christmas Day 1837," in The Florida Historical Quarterly, vol. 70, October, 1991.

MARYE, William B. Marye, "Notes on the Primitive History of Western Maryland," Maryland Historical Quarterly, vol. 38, 1903, pp. 161-166.

MASTIN, Bettye Lee Mastin, Lexngton, 1779: Pioneer Kentucky, Lexington-Fayette County Historic Commission, Cincinnati, 1979.

McMURTRIE, H. McMurtrie, Sketches of Louisville, S. Penn, jr, Louisville, 1819, copy at the Louisville Free Public Library.

MATTHIESSEN, Peter Matthiessen, Indian Country, Viking Press, New York, 1984.

MESERVE, John Bartlett Meserve, "Chief Peasant Porter," appearing in Chronicles of Oklahoma, vol. 9, pp. 318-334. – "Chief Thomas Mitchell Buffington and Chief William Charles Rogers," appearing in Chronicles of Oklahoma, vol. 17, pp. 135-138.

MMV, Memoirs of the Miami Valley, edited by John C. Hover, et al, in three volumes, Robert O. Law Company, Chicago, 1919.

MORE, John H. More, "A Captive of the Shawnees 1779-1784" in West Virginia History Magazine, vol. 23, pp. 287-296.

MORGAN, George Morgan's Journal, in The Journal of the Illinois Historical Society, vol. 69.

MORGAN, Kelly Morgan, The History of Clay County, Kentucky.

MULKERN, Lois Mulkern, "Half King, Seneca Diplomat of the Ohio Valley," Western Pennyslvania Historical Magazine, vol. 37, #2, pp. 65-82.

MURCHISON, A. H. Murchison, "Intermarried-Whites in the Cherokee Nation Between the Years 1865-1887," in vol. 6 of Chronicles of Oklahoma.

MVHR, Mississippi Valley Historical Review.

NETTERVILLE, J. J. Netterville, The Centennial History of Madison County, Indiana, vol. I, Anderson, Indiana, 1925.

OAHQ, Ohio State Archaeological and Historical Quarterly, Columbus, Ohio.

ORR, Captain Robert Orr's Account of the Lochry Expedition, Draper Mss. 6NN163-185.

OWENS, see English, vol. 2, p. 675; Pennsylvania Colonial Records, vol. 6, p. 589; vol. IX, p. 222-223; Jones; David Owens' was Clark's interpreter in 1781, Draper 60J78; George Owens was the interpreter for the commissioners at the falls in September, 1785, Draper 1M122; George Rogers Clark's notice of his George Owens' death is in 26CC29; Hanna, II, p. Magee, p. 29; The Thruston Papers K-1-28; Two Hundred Years in Cumberland County, published by the Hamilton Library and Historical Association of Cumberland County, Carlisle, 1951, pp. 43-44; Weslager, p. 256; Sir William Johnson Papers, vol. 4, pp. 452, 586, 620, 646, 723; vol. 10, p. 533; vol. 11, pp. 224-225, 241, 451, 585, 597-598, 617; William A. Hunter, Forts on the Pennsylvania Frontier, p. 402. Hunter cites the Pennsylvania Gazette of July 29, 1756; Hulbert, The Old Glade Road, p. 100; Loudon, Indian Wars, II, p. 100; Revolutionary War Pensions, depositions of David Carter and James Ballard; Parkman's Pontiac, p. 482; .

PORTER, Kenneth W. Porter, "The Seminole in Mexico," Hispanic American Historical Review, vol. 31, February, 1951, pp. 1-35.
– "John Caesar: Seminole Partisan," The Journal of Negro History, vol. 31, #2, April, 1946, pp. 190-207.
– "Seminole Flight from Fort Marion," Florida Historical Quarterly, vol. 22, January, 1944.

PREVOST, Toni Jolley Prevost, The Delaware and Shawnee Admitted to Cherokee Citizenship and the Related Wyandotte & Monravian Delaware, Heritage Books, Inc., Bowie, Maryland, 1992. Let me say that anyone doing research on the their Delaware, Shawnee, and Wyandot ancestry needs this book as a companion volume to the works of Eckert, Gilbert, and my own. Prevost did a great job, and there are many, many, families mentioned in this work not mentioned in mine.

PUTNAM, The Memoirs of Rufus Putnam, Rowena Buell, ed., Houghton, Mifflin, and Co., Boston, 1903.

QUAPAW, Quapaw Agency Records, National Archives, Ft. Worth, Texas, division, on microfilm.

RAVE, Herman Rave, Country Jottings, an undated newspaper column in the Indian file of the Indiana Room, New Albany Public Library, New Albany, Indiana.

RIDOUT, Thomas Ridout, "An Account of My Capture by the Shawnee Indians," reprinted in the Western Pennsylvania Historical Magazine, Vol. 12, 1929.

ROUNTREE, Helen C. Rountree, Pocahontas's People: The Powhatan Indians of Virginia Through Four Centuries, University Of Oklahoma Press, Norman, 1990.

ROY, Jerry C. Roy, "A Shawnee Muster Roll: 334 Shawnees of the Wapakonetta and Hog Creek, Ohio Bands Emigrating to Kansas in 1832," appearing in the Johnson County Genealogist, vol. VII, #2, pp. 38-43, Shawnee Mission, Kansas, 1979.

SANDERLIN, Eva Sanderlin, "Warriors and Chiefs: The Seminole Scouts," in Wild West, vol. 1, #4, December, 1988.

SCHAAF, Gregory Schaaf, Wampum Belts & Peace Trees: George Morgan, Native Americans and Revolutionary Diplomacy, Fulcrum Publishing, Golden, Colorado, 1990.

SHACKFORD, James Atkins Shackford, David Crockett: The Man and the Legend.

SHERLOCK, notes for James Sherlock; New York Colonial Documents, vol. VII, p. 632; Pennsylvania Colonial Records, vol. 8, pp. 630-654. Sherlock traded for the firm of Baynton, Wharton, and Morgan; Sir William Johnson Papers, vol. 2, p. 812; vol. 4, pp. 492-498; vol. 5, p. 247; George Rogers Clark Papers, James, ed, vol. 2, pp. 286-287; Thruston Papers, D-2-295, deposition of James Sherlock, taken at Ft. Pitt, Aug 20, 1781. They made their way back to the falls by way of Ft. Pitt; Calendar of Virginia State Papers, vol. III, pp. 356-357, 529-530, 574; Quaife, Ft. Wayne in 1790, Hays Journal, p. 18, 49; Neville Craig, The Olden Time, vol. 2, pp. 490, 511; Draper 12CC97-110, 14S201. The Indian messengers Daniel Elliot and James Rinken (Ranken) said that they had been furnished two horses on October 11, 1785, by "Messrs. Sherlock and Dollman."

See Draper 1W37: The United States Commissioners at Ft. McIntosh were Richard Butler, George Rogers Clark, and Arthur Lee. Joseph Nicholson, an adopted Seneca who had been one of David Owens' rangers during Dunmore's War, served as interpreter. Arthur Lee wrote Col. Josiah Harmar from Ft. McIntosh on January 22nd, 1785, concerning the suspected character of James Sherlock; George Owens was the interpreter later when Clark, Butler, and Samuel Parsons browbeat Kikipelathey and Moluntha into the treaty. Moluntha was given a copy of this treaty and one account has him waving it as Hugh McGary rode up to kill him. For the different accounts of these negotiations, see "Journal of Richard Butler," in Neville Craig's The Olden Time, The Military Journal of Ebenezer Denny, Richard Henry Lee's Life of Arthur Lee, and The Journal of Griffith Evans, 1784-1785, in Pennsylvania Magazine of Biography and History, vol. 65, pp. 202-233; Jefferson County, Kentucky, Old Circuit Court Case #900, Joseph Saunders assee, David Owens assee, Joseph Soverigns, assee vs Papers of Conrad Coleman, June 17, 1785; Michigan Pioneer and Historical Collections, vol. 20, pp. 122-127, 152-155; vol. 25, pp. 691-693

SIPES, C. Hale Sipe, The Indian Chiefs of Pennsylvania, Ziegler Printing Co., Butler, Pennsylvania.

SKARSTEN, M. O. Skarsten, George Drouillard: Hunter and Interpreter for Lewis and Clark and Fur Trader 1807-1810, Arthur H. Clark Co., Glendale, California, 1964.

D. L. SMITH, Dwight L. Smith, An Unsuccessful Negotiation for Removal of the Wyandot Indians from Ohio, 1834, appearing in the OAHQ, vol. 58, p. 305.

HARRY SMITH, Harry Smith, Fifty Years in Slavery in the United States, West Michigan Printing Co., Grand Rapids, Michigan, 1891.

SPECK, Gordon Speck, Breeds and Half-breeds, Clarkson N. Potter, Inc., New York.

SPENCER, Joeb Spencer, "The Shawnee Indians," Transactions of the Kansas State Historical Historical Society, vol. 10, 382-402.

STAAB, Rodney Staab, at this time assistant curator of the Shawnee Mission Historical Museum. If there is anyone more expert on the Shawnees and Delawares of Kansas, I do not know of them. Mr. Staab is the author of numerous articles relating to the early history of Kansas, and has given timely assistance when called upon. I wish I knew everything he knows. Of use here was:

– "Bluejacket Led Shawnees through Traumatic Period Here," Journal Herald, June 11, 1986, p. 11; Shawnee, Kansas.

– "A History of Shawnee's Fabled Mountain Man," Journal Herald, September 23, 1992, p. 8D; Shawnee, Kansas.

– "Shawnees Were Pitted Against Seminoles in 'Unnatural War'" Journal Herald, February 17, 1988, p. 6; Shawnee, Kansas.

– "Paramilitary and Entrepreneurial Activities of the Kansas Delawares, 1830-1860," unpublished, compiled by Rodney Staab.

– Fall Leaf: Delaware Scout, unpublished text of a speech given by Rodney Staab before the Eudora Historical Society, April 24, 1986.

– A List of Delawares furnished to me by Rodney Staab, "Statement of Delaware Indians, residents on the Indian Reserves of Texas, who claim to be fully identified with the Delaware Indians of Missouri," Brazos

Indian Agency, 1857, from National Archives Microcopy 234, roll #274, frame 290.

STEPHENS, John H. Stephens, History of Miami County, Peru, Indiana, 1896.

SUTTEN, History of Shelby County, Ohio, R, Sutten & Co., Philadelphia, Pennsylvania, 1883.

SWJ, Sir William Johnson Papers, the Post-War Period.

TANNER, Helen Hornback Tanner, "The Glaize in 1792," Ethnohistory, vol. 25, #1, Winter, 1978, pp. 15-39.

TEAS, Thomas Scattergood Teas, Journal of a Tour to Fort Wayne and the Adjacent Country in the Year 1821.

THOM, James Alexander Thom, Panther in the Sky, Ballantine Books, New York, 1989.

THOMPSON, Charles W. Thompson, Sons of the Wilderness, Indiana Historical Publications, vol. 12.

THYCC, D. W. Thompson, chairman ed. committee, Two Hundred Years in Cumberland County, Hamilton Library and Historical Association, Carlisle, Pa., 1951.

TIPTON, The John Tipton Papers, three volumes, published in the Indiana Historical Collections, vol. 24-26, Indianapolis, 1942.

THOM, James Alexander Thom, Panther in the Sky, Ballantine Books, New York, 1989. This is historical fiction, and Thom does certain scenes exceptionally well. On some segments of Tecumseh's life, Thom's versions are as plausible as any.

THORNBROUGH, Gayle Thornbrough, ed., Letter Book of the Indian Agency at Fort Wayne 1809-1815, Indiana Historical Society, Indianapolis, 1961.

TOOKER, Elizabeth Tooker, Wyandot, in Handbook of North American Indians, William C. Sturtevant, general editor, Smithsonian Institution, Washington, 1978.

TRIPLETT, Colonel Frank Triplett, Pioneer Heroes and Heroines of America, N. D. Thompson & Company, New York and St Louis, 1883.

VALLEY and LEMBCKE, Dorris Valley and Mary M. Lembcke, The Peorias: A History of the Peoria Indian Tribe of Oklahoma.

VISSCHER, "The Todd Family," Kittochtinny Magazine (1905), from the manuscript papers of Mrs. Emily Todd Helm, compiled by Nina M. Visscher, June, 1939.

WALLACE, Anthony F. C. Wallace, King of the Delawares: Teedyuscung 1700-1763, University of Pennsylvania Press, Philadelphia, 1949.

WATSON, Larry S. Watson, Senate Documents (13 parts), Laguna Hills, California, 1987.

WESLAGER, C. A. Weslager, The Delaware Indians: A History, Rutgers University Press, New Brunswick, New Jersey, 1972.

WHIPPLE, Mary McDougall Gordon, ed., Through Indian Country to California: John P. Sherburne's Diary of the Whipple Expedition 1853-1854, Standford University Press, Standford, California, 1988.

WICKLIFFE, Charles A. Wickliffe, to the editor of the Bardstown Gazette, Nov. 25, 1859, appearing in "Tecumseh and the Battle of the Thames," Register of the Kentucky Historical Society, vol. 60 (1962), 45-49.

WILLIAMS, Edward G. Williams, "The Journal of Richard Butler, 1775," Western Pennsylvania Historical Magazine, October, 1963, January, 1964, and April, 1964.

WILLIAMS AND FARRELLY, Joyce G. Williams and Jill E. Farrelly, Diplomacy on the Indiana-Ohio Frontier 1783-1791, Indiana University Bicentennial Committee, Bloomington, Indiana, 1976.

WILLIAMSON, C. W. Williamson, History of Western Ohio and Auglaize County, W. M. Linn & Sons, Columbus, 1905.

WILSON, Paul C. Wilson, A Forgotten Mission to the Indians: William Smalley's Adventures Among the Delaware Indians of Ohio in 1792, Galvenston, Texas, 1965.

WINGER, Otho Winger, The Frances Slocum Trail, 1961.

WINKELMAN, Jerry Winkelman, "Chief Graham Rogers Played Important Role in Local History," from the Journal Herald, February 3, 1988, p. 5; Shawnee, Kansas.

WOLFE, William G. Wolfe, Stories of Guernsey County, Ohio: History of an Average Ohio County, published by the author, Cambridge, Ohio, 1943.

WPHM, Western Pennsylvania Historical Magazine.

WRIGHT, J. Leith Wright, jr., Creeks and Seminoles: The Destruction and Regeneration of the Muscogulge People, University of Nebraska Press.

YATER, George H. Yater and Carolyn S. Denton, Nine Young Men from Kentucky, Lewis and Clark Heritage Foundation, Inc., May, 1992.

YOUNG, Chester Raymond Young, ed., Westward Into Kentucky: The Narrative of Daniel Trabue, University of Kentucky Press, Lexington, 1981.

ZIMMERMAN, Albright Gravenor Zimmerman, The Indian Trade of Colonial Pennsylvania, University Microfilms, Ann Arbor, Michigan, 1966. Zimmerman quotes the Shippen Papers in regards to Thomas McKee speaking to the white woman from the Carolinas who had been adopted by the Shawnees.

ZINZENDORF, Count Zinzendorf, "Count Zinzendorf in the Wyoming Valley," Proceedings and Collections of the Wyoming Historical and Genealogical Society, vol. VIII.